The Mirror up to Nature

✒ ✒ THE TECHNIQUE OF SHAKESPEARE'S TRAGEDIES

BY VIRGIL K. WHITAKER

The author, an eminent Renaissance scholar, is Sadie Dernham Patek Professor of
Humanities in English at Stanford University. He is also Associate Provost and Dean
of the Graduate Division. His works include
*Shakespeare's Use of Learning: An Inquiry
into the Growth of His Mind & Art*, first
published by the Huntington Library in
1953.

THE HUNTINGTON LIBRARY
SAN MARINO, CALIFORNIA · 1965

COPYRIGHT 1965
HENRY E. HUNTINGTON LIBRARY AND ART GALLERY
LIBRARY OF CONGRESS CATALOG CARD NUMBER 65-15370

Printed in the United States of America
by Anderson, Ritchie & Simon
Designed by Ward Ritchie

*Suit the action to the word,
the word to the action; with this special observance, that you
o'erstep not the modesty of nature. For anything so overdone is
from the purpose of playing, whose end, both at the first and now,
was and is, to hold, as 'twere, the mirror up to nature; to show
virtue her own feature, scorn her own image, and the very age
and body of the time his form and pressure. Now this overdone,
or come tardy off, though it make the unskillful laugh, cannot
but make the judicious grieve; the censure of the which one must,
in your allowance, o'erweigh a whole theatre of others. O, there
be players that I have seen play, and heard others praise, and that
highly, not to speak it profanely, that, neither having the accent
of Christians nor the gait of Christian, pagan, nor man, have so
strutted and bellowed that I have thought some of Nature's journeymen had made men and not made them well, they imitated
humanity so abominably.*

—Hamlet III.ii.19-39

❦ PREFACE

THIS STUDY of Shakespeare's tragedies has been slow in seeing the light of day, and the protracted agony of its birth has no doubt left scars. A first draft was written in 1955-1956 during a sabbatical year. Then a variety of pressing interests led to its being put aside until the summers of 1962 and 1963, when it was substantially rewritten. During all these periods I found leisure for work, and the help and stimulus which are as necessary as leisure, at the Henry E. Huntington Library. During 1955-1956 I held a Library fellowship, for which I am profoundly grateful.

With the passing of years many ideas that I once flattered myself were original have appeared in essays and books. This is inevitable when many students of Shakespeare are pursuing similar lines of inquiry and building upon the same facts and theories. I trust, however, that the fundamental thesis can still bear inquiry. It is, quite simply, that Shakespeare was at one with his dramatic contemporaries. Even in his greatest plays their habits of workmanship appear, and we will understand him better if we first recognize the implications of this fact and then ask why, and in what ways, he differed from his fellows and surpassed them. I believe, as do many of my colleagues, that Shakespeare was a profoundly thoughtful man, familiar with the standard learning of his day; but I have discovered, as I have lectured throughout the country on viewpoints I was developing, that this view of Shakespeare and especially the attempt to interpret his works in traditional Christian terms still need to be argued to an extent I would not have anticipated. I am also convinced that Shakespeare believed ideas have consequences and that he felt obliged, more than any of his contemporaries, to square his plays with his moral and philosophic assumptions. How he did so becomes one approach to a study of his technique as a writer of tragedies.

All quotations of Shakespeare are from the New Cambridge Edition, *The Complete Plays and Poems of William Shakespeare*, edited by William Allan Neilson and Charles Jarvis Hill (Boston, 1942).

Editions of other plays are to be found in the List of Tragedies and Chronicle Histories, modern editions, if used, being inserted in square brackets. In this list and in citations of titles in the text, where the Elizabethan form is the basis of theories being argued, every attempt has been made to preserve the exact title page of the first publication. In the text, *u*'s and *v*'s, *i*'s and *j*'s have been normalized and contractions have been expanded. Dates given in parentheses without comment are those of first performance, usually conjectural and subject to a wide margin of error. Dates preceded by "pub." are those of first publication. This ordinarily followed so long after composition and first performance as to be almost useless in establishing chronology and lines of development.

For reasons indicated above, I have inserted references only to modern scholars of whose influence or parallel studies I am especially aware. I have too often, in rereading some book, encountered what must have been the source of an idea that I had attributed to some other scholar or even fancied to be my own. To document a lifetime's reading would be impossible. I am conscious of many debts —most of all, to my two great teachers, Professors William Dinsmore Briggs and Hardin Craig. It is no accident, I think, that the names of two of their students, Professors J. V. Cunningham and Madeleine Doran, recur frequently in the notes. The names of my own doctoral candidates, I am well aware, should appear more often than they do. But I also owe my profound thanks to the numerous audiences, public and private, willing and captive, who have listened to me expound my views and then reacted to them.

I am grateful to the Trustees and to the Friends of the Huntington Library for aid in the publication of this book. My thanks are due also to four ladies who have helped me unstintingly: Miss Gwen Staniforth and Mrs. Carol B. Pearson, who typed the manuscript and helped with research; Mrs. Nancy C. English and Mrs. Anne Kimber of the Huntington staff, who have spared no editorial labors and done without complaint much of the checking that I should have done. It has been a pleasure to work with them, but a real joy to let them work!

V. K. W.

Stanford, California
April 1964

❧ CONTENTS

ix

THE MIRROR UP TO NATURE

Chapter One *&* THE GAIT OF CHRISTIAN,
PAGAN: SHAKESPEARE'S TRAGIC MILIEU

THAT SHAKESPEARE's best tragedies are among the supreme achievements of the human mind no one doubts. Their position in the literature of Western civilization is well understood. But their position in their own age is less understood—often, in fact, misunderstood. For we tend to regard them as the pinnacles of Elizabethan dramatic achievement, and this notion implies that other dramas of the age, or at least other tragedies, are built of the same stone, even though it is less carefully chiseled and occupies no such dizzy eminence. But, as a matter of fact, Shakespeare's mature tragedies differ from their fellows, except for two or three others, not only in quality but also in kind. Their unique quality is, in fact, partly a result of their unique kind. Shakespeare progressed beyond his fellow playwrights not only because he was a more careful craftsman than most of them but also because he apparently attempted, in accordance with contemporary critical theory, to build his tragedies in terms of the best learning of his day as he understood it. To establish these generalizations and to inquire how Shakespeare came to write the tragedies that he did will be the object of this book.

This investigation of Shakespeare, like all attempts to get behind the texts of his plays, will be subject to serious limitations. The chief of these is that, for all practical purposes, we know nothing about Shakespeare the creative artist except what can be demonstrated from the text of the plays or inferred from them. Jonson had elaborately developed theories which he felt compelled to proclaim to the world and to exemplify in his plays, sometimes at considerable cost to their effectiveness. Shakespeare, too, undoubtedly had views about his work, but he has left us almost no record of them. The allusions in his plays are explicit enough to show that he had theories, but too brief to give more than tantalizing hints of what they were. The only proof that can be offered for a conjectural reconstruction of Shakespeare's tragic theories and techniques is, therefore, that the views

3

assumed are consistent with the critical remarks in his text and ex-plain the plays as they stand.

Modern scholarship has abundantly demonstrated that Shake-speare was a thoughtful man. He was aware of the political issues and of the philosophic currents of his day, and he was disposed to use these ideas in building the structure of his plays. Though not a scholar, he possessed a sound grammar-school education that enabled him to deal with Latin texts, not only by construing the sentences but also by detecting the rhetorical formulas by which the texts had often been constructed and in terms of which they were usually analyzed critically. It seems unlikely that a man with this intellectual bias and this rhetorical training would remain indifferent to critical theories about his trade, particularly when the most important critical document, Sidney's *Defence of Poesie* (or *An Apologie for Poetrie*), was among the masterpieces of contemporary prose.

The method of this study will therefore be circular. It will begin by making the intrinsically probable assumption that Shakespeare was alive to the implications not only of contemporary dramatic practice but also of critical theory about drama and that he reflected seriously and carefully about the problems posed. It will first examine the achievements of Elizabethan tragedy to the end of Shakespeare's productive career about 1613, and it will then move on to consider contemporary critical theory in England—in England only, because assuming that Shakespeare also knew Continental criticism would seriously strain the hypothesis and there seems no need to do so. We will find, incidentally, that Elizabethan practice and critical theory are in much closer harmony than has sometimes been supposed. After a survey of Shakespeare's early tragedies, the fourth chapter will test the hypothesis by examining the technique of his maturity in the light both of theatrical practice and of contemporary critical theory. It will argue that he differs from his fellow dramatists not only because he had more of the unfathomable gift called genius but also because, as a serious thinker, he used contemporary theology and metaphysics to develop the full implications of the best tragic theory of his day. It is possible, of course, that genius involves a capacity for hard thinking as well as a transcendent capacity for taking trouble.

Concentrating upon Shakespeare's use of contemporary thought

4

involves neglecting a very large part of his learning and of his technique. His grammar-school training was centered upon the rhetorical arts, from figures of speech to the structuring of discourse, and he undoubtedly participated in the rich poetic development of his age; in dramatic poetry, at least, he carried that development to its highest achievements. The following discussion will focus its attention elsewhere as a matter of methodological convenience rather than of critical astigmatism. One cannot cover all, or even any considerable part, of Shakespeare's rich dramaturgy in a single book. Much of the most fruitful modern criticism of Shakespeare has been concerned with his use of poetry for dramatic ends. In attempting to explore another aspect of Shakespeare's art, one may surely be pardoned for not trying to do again what others have been able to do better.

Our first task, in terms of the limited goals just described, will be to attempt a brief survey of Elizabethan dramatic practice and critical theory. The practice will be examined first not only because it is more important for our purpose but also because scholars have sometimes assumed that drama went one way and critical theory another. I had so assumed at least, though, as sometimes in other matters, I may have mistaken my own ignorance for an accepted view. At any rate, it may be interesting to look at dramatic practice first so that, in surveying critical theory, we can see to what extent it conformed with and perhaps even influenced the popular drama.

Once again a disclaimer is in order. I have made no attempt to do original research in the chronology of Elizabethan drama or its records. In these matters I have relied upon the findings of other scholars, most notably E. K. Chambers and Alfred Harbage.[1] I have been interested, rather, in surveying the range and the achievements of other dramatists to see how they illuminate Shakespeare's work —often by contrast. My purposes will be adequately served even though I accept an erroneous dating for some plays or even miss several plays—granted, of course, that I do not miss a play crucial to the generalizations that I shall need to make. Unless I am mistaken, no one has attempted to break down the surviving Elizabethan trage-

---

[1]Chambers, *William Shakespeare: A Study of Facts and Problems* (Oxford, 1930), I, 270-528 passim, and *The Elizabethan Stage* (Oxford, 1923), Vols. III, IV passim; Harbage, *Annals of English Drama 975-1700* (Philadelphia, 1940), pp. 36-84.

	Tragic Interludes	Tragical Histories	Narratives Ending in Death but Loosely Constructed			Tragic Romances
			Historical Tragedies: Roman	Historical Tragedies: English	Historical Tragedies: Other	
1560–64	R. B., *Apius and Virginia*					Preston, *Cam*
1565–69	Pikeryng, *Horestes*					
1570–74						
1575–79						
1580–84						
1585–89		Peele, *David and Bethsabe* *Warres of Cyrus*	Marlowe, *Dido* Lodge, *Wounds of Civill War*			
1590–94		*Selimus* Marlowe, *Edward II, Massacre at Paris* B. J., *Guy Earl of Warwick*		*Locrine* *True Tragedie of Richard the Third*	Peele, *Alphonsus Emperour of Germany*	Kyd, *Solyman Perseda*
1595–99		Munday & Chettle, *Death of Robert Earle of Huntington*				Shakespeare, *Romeo and Juliet* T. W., *Thorny-Abbey* (?)
1600–04						Day, *Lusts Dominion* Shakespeare, *Troilus and Cressida*
1605–09		Brewer, *Love-sick King*	Marston, *Sophonisba* Heywood, *Rape of Lucrece*		Barnes, *Divils Charter*	Mason, *The Turke*
1610–13		Daborne, *A Christian Turn'd Turke*	Jonson, *Catiline* Chapman, *Caesar and Pompey* (?)	Fletcher, *Bonduca*	Webster, *The White Divel* Chapman, *Chabot* (?)	Marston, *Insa* *Countesse* *The Second Maiden's Tragedy* Beaumont & Fletcher, *Cupids Rev*

A question mark indicates such uncertainty of dating that it is questionable whether the play belongs in the ta

...nified "Casibus" ...gedies	Inns of Court and Academic Plays	Closet Drama	Domestic Tragedy	Revenge Tragedy	Quasi-Aristotelian Tragedy (Tragedy of Moral Choice)
	Norton & Sackville, Gorboduc				
	Gascoigne, Jocasta Wilmot, Gismond of Salerne	Cheke, Freewyl			
	Goldingham, Herodes (L)	Golding, Abrahams Sacrifice			
	Legge, Richardus Tertius (L)				
	Eedes, Caesar Interfectus (L) Gager, Meleager (L) Solymannidae (L) Gager, Dido (L), Oedipus (L)				
...ve, 1 & 2 ...burlaine, ...of Malta	Hughes, Misfortunes of Arthur			Kyd, Spanish Tragedie	
...speare, ...ard III	Alabaster, Roxana (L) Gager, Ulysses Redux (L)	Wilmot, Tancred and Gismund Salterne, Tomumbeius(L) Daniel, Cleopatra	Arden of Feversham Yarington, Two Lamentable Tragedies	Shakespeare, Titus Andronicus	Marlowe, Faustus
...speare, ...ard II	Caesars Revenge	Greville, Mustapha Brandon, Tragicomoedi of the Vertuous Octavia	Warning for Faire Women	Marston, Antonios Revenge	Shakespeare, Julius Caesar
...n, Sejanus ...Fall ...nan, ...ssy D'Ambois	Gwinne, Nero (L) Verney, Antipoe	Greville, Alaham Percy, Cupids Sacrifice Alexander, Darius, Croesus Cary, Mariam Daniel, Philotas	Heywood, A Woman Kilde with Kindnesse	Shakespeare, Hamlet Chettle, Hoffman	Shakespeare, Othello
...speare, ...non of Athens ...nan, ...2 Charles ...ke of Byron	Sansbury, Philomela (L), Periander Claudius Tiberius Nero	Alexander, Alexandraean Tragedie, Julius Caesar	A Yorkshire Tragedy	Tourneur, Revengers Tragaedie, Atheist's Tragedie	Shakespeare, King Lear, Macbeth, Antony and Cleopatra, Coriolanus
		Stephens, Cinthias Revenge		Chapman, Revenge of Bussy Fletcher, Valentinian (?)	Beaumont & Fletcher, The Maides Tragedy

dies into categories as a means of definition or to examine the range of Shakespeare's tragedies with relation to the work of his contemporaries. For the assignment of plays to dramatic genres I alone am responsible. In particular, though usually I accept the dating in Harbage's *Annals of English Drama*, I have not hesitated to depart from his classifications.

The task of isolating Elizabethan tragedies and inferring from them the notion of tragedy that obtained among practicing dramatists is easier than one might think. The number of extant tragedies is relatively small, and they are surprisingly well identified. Any attempt to classify dramas and to subject them to a rough critical analysis must be based, of course, upon plays that are extant in whole or at least in substantial part. It must also exclude mere translations, although it may and should include adaptations like Gascoigne's *Jocasta* made for actual dramatic performance, since the latter are part of a living theater and the process of adaptation reflects contemporary practice. It must take into account, finally, the rapid evolution of dramatic genres.

In short, the following theorizing is based wholly upon extant plays that are, to some extent, original compositions, and it tries to take into account dramatic evolution.

The accompanying table of extant Elizabethan tragedies to 1613, arranged in chronological order according to the rough classification that I have worked out, lists just under one hundred tragedies. It includes two plays that are really tragic moralities (R. B.'s *Apius and Virginia* and John Pikeryng's *Horestes*) and all plays based upon English history that were clearly regarded as tragedies by contemporaries (for example, Shakespeare's *Richard III*). It also includes academic and closet dramas. They constitute a third of the total.

To contrast other genres, there are about thirty chronicle-history plays. If the remaining extant plays be lumped together as comedies, that category will obviously be unsatisfactory in that it covers comic interludes, dramatized mythology, and tragicomedy, as well as the commonly recognized comic types; but it will include a little under two hundred fifty plays, somewhat less than a fifth of them academic.

In other words, Elizabethan drama is predominantly comedy. In this, as in many other respects, it resembled Roman drama, which was well known, in contrast to Greek drama, which was almost un-

known. Several factors have probably tended to obscure this pre-
ponderance of comedy. First of all, Shakespeare is unrepresentative
in that the tragedies and histories together constitute over half his
plays—twenty as against seventeen in terms of the customary table
of contents. Qualitatively they outweigh the comedies even more
decisively. Furthermore, the effective recovery of Aristotle's *Poetics*
has given critics an instrument for the analysis of tragedy far superior
to the traditional comic theory. The exact opposite was true of the
Elizabethans, as we shall see, who inherited a detailed theory of
comedy but not of tragedy and whose normal point of departure in
thinking about dramatic problems was comedy, despite the more
exalted rank that they conceded to tragedy. Tragedy, moreover, is
perhaps easier to deal with intellectually than comedy, simply because it must grapple in some fashion with the problems of suffering
and evil that it inevitably raises. The poet's tragic view becomes an
important part of the critic's business. At any rate, we have Shakespeare's tragedies, and we have A. C. Bradley's *Shakespearean Tragedy*, which, despite weaknesses, is a critical monument. We have
Shakespeare's comedies; but they are lesser in themselves, and, though
interesting and provocative studies of them exist, no Bradley has
written a definitive work about them. Finally, for its full effect
comedy is more dependent than tragedy upon stage presentation
—upon pantomime and expression, upon pace, upon the physical
presence of actors to keep incongruous situations before us. And
few Elizabethan comedies except Shakespeare's and Jonson's are still
performed. But perhaps I am wrong in thinking that many students
habitually assume that Elizabethan drama as a whole is at its best
in tragedy.

If I may interject a personal, and largely irrelevant, impression,
I am convinced, after reading through the corpus of extant plays in
roughly their order of composition,[2] that Elizabethan comedy—at
least to the end of Shakespeare's career—represents a far more considerable artistic achievement than Elizabethan tragedy. As a writer
of tragedy Shakespeare stands beside Aeschylus, Sophocles, and
Euripides; but he does not stand above them. No Elizabethan comic

---

[2]To be precise, I have read through extant plays in English. For academic plays in
Latin I have relied to a considerable extent upon summaries and discussions in
Frederick S. Boas, *University Drama in the Tudor Age* (Oxford, 1914).

writer duplicates the achievement of Aristophanes, although Jonson's object was similar, his accomplishment was very great, and his satire was, on the whole, more wisely directed. But both in range and in quality Elizabethan comedy is enormously superior to Roman comedy and apparently to Greek new comedy. If one reads too many of Shakespeare's contemporaries, one becomes tired of credulous and patient wives, grasping fathers, scheming gallants, and hard-hearted whores, just as one becomes weary of the virtuous slave girls, young men in love, and clever slaves of Roman comedy. But after the abler Elizabethan comedies the best of Plautus and Terence seem pale and thin and contrived. The English plays have more gusto, much more action, better characterization, and better dramatic techniques. They also have a far greater range of subject matter and of mood.

To extend these parenthetical remarks about comedy, Shakespeare's comedies are almost as untypical of the age as we shall find his tragedies to be. In retelling stories from popular romances, whether English or Continental, and in handling potentially tragic situations from these romances in a way that anticipated Jacobean tragicomedy, they had analogues; and in exposing the hollowness of contemporary poses and intellectual fads, plays like *Love's Labour's Lost* and *As You Like It* shared the satiric aim of most Elizabethan comedy, though not its method. But romance narratives were a small proportion of contemporary comedies, which were predominantly concerned with the loves and intrigues of middle-class life. In contrast, plays like *The Comedy of Errors* or *The Merry Wives of Windsor* are a minor part of Shakespeare's output, both quantitatively and qualitatively; but they are closer to the norm of Elizabethan comedy. A thoroughgoing study of the evolution of Elizabethan comic techniques is long overdue.

The remainder of this chapter will attempt, however, to survey extant tragedies written before the end of Shakespeare's productive career and, in particular, to divide them into rough categories for the purpose of understanding the Elizabethan notion of tragedy and comparing Shakespeare's dramatic practice with that of his contemporaries. Elizabethan tragedy, whatever its ultimate worth, is relatively easy to study not only because one is dealing, for most purposes, with less than seventy plays written for the popular theater but also because Elizabethan playwrights and their publishers apparently had an adequate notion of dramatic genres and labeled plays carefully. This should not surprise us, of course, because successful dramatists do not ordinarily indulge in parody that is meaningless to their audience. Polonius (*Hamlet* II.ii.415 ff.) begins his catalog of types by listing the three standard categories of tragedy, comedy, and history that any playgoer would be familiar with. The fun consists in his then evolving hybrid types, some of which do indeed appear in contemporary titles but the more involved of which exceeded the ingenuity even of Elizabethan playwrights. Polonius' attention to dramatic genres needs stressing, however, because the editors of the 1623 Folio, for good reason, departed from accepted categories. Apparently they wished to preserve intact Shakespeare's treatment of English medieval history. *Richard III* and *Richard II* were therefore included among the "histories," though the quartos had called them tragedies, and the original designation "The Tragedy of" survives even in the Folio text of *Richard III*. Conversely, since the "histories" had become exclusively English, a place was found for *Troilus and Cressida* and *Timon of Athens* among the tragedies, though neither play is clearly tragic.[3] The quarto, in fact, had been entitled *The Historie of Troylus and Cresseida*, and the Folio itself has only *The Life of Tymon of Athens*.[4] This sacrifice of precision in terminology to other considerations is, however, unique to the Shakespeare folios, and the point deserves stressing. Elizabethan titles are almost invariably a sound guide to dramatic genres.

We cannot know, of course, who was responsible for a given title or at what stage in the progress from author's manuscript to printed book it appeared. But if the titles reflect some uniformity of practice,

[3] The weight of critical tradition denies to *Troilus and Cressida* the status of a tragedy. Cf., e.g., A. C. Bradley, *Shakespearean Tragedy: Lectures on Hamlet, Othello, King Lear, Macbeth* (London, 1905), p. 7; William Witherle Lawrence, *Shakespeare's Problem Comedies* (New York, 1931), pp. 122-173; and Oscar James Campbell, *Comicall Satyre and Shakespeare's "Troilus and Cressida"* (San Marino, Calif., 1938), especially pp. 185-191.

[4] It is worth noting that all plays classified by the Folio as tragedies, including *Cymbeline*, have "The Tragedy(ie) of .." as head title, except for *Troilus and Cressida* and *Timon*. The former has "The Tragedie of Troylus and Cressida" as head and running titles on pp. 79-80, the leaf salvaged from the original printing. Thereafter its running title is "Troylus and Cressida." "Timon of Athens" appears consistently as the running title.

they will indicate a consensus about drama, and, the farther from the authors the titles originated, the more widely must notions about dramatic categories have been disseminated. For our purpose it is not crucial who devised the title. It is also questionable how much reliance can be placed upon the dramatic categories implied by titles. I should perhaps explain, therefore, that, as a precaution against taking titles too seriously, I first listed the plays I thought to be tragedies in terms of the Elizabethan concepts of tragedy that I had inferred from my reading over the years; I then compared my classification with the complete titles in early editions. The agreement astonished me. The more I have worked on the titles, the more I have been imprssed by the accuracy with which they describe the plays, granted Elizabethan critical notions and terminology.

A few definitions are, however, necessary before we can consider what Elizabethans understood by the terms that they used for dramatic categories. "History" is the most slippery term. As part of the title of a play it has only the meaning of the popular cognate derived via French—"story." We encounter, for example, *The Most Excellent Historie of the Merchant of Venice* (pub. 1600) or *The Tragicall Historie of Hamlet Prince of Denmarke* (pub. 1603), though the Folio has *The Tragedie of Hamlet, Prince of Denmarke*. Such titles should remind us that the Elizabethan playwright was concerned, from first to last, with telling a good story—that most Elizabethan drama is narrative in origin and in purpose. But "history" tells us nothing about dramatic genre; the adjectives carry this meaning.

Three plays, however, are simply called "histories" without adjectival qualifications: Shakespeare's *The History of Henrie the Fourth* (pub. 1598), John Marston's *The History of Antonio and Mellida* (pub. 1602), and Shakespeare's *The Historie of Troylus and Cresseida* (pub. 1609). The last two look like deliberate attempts to avoid categorizing difficult plays, and the same conjecture will be made of *The Life of Tymon of Athens* in the Shakespeare First Folio.

But *1 Henry IV* is clearly a chronicle history. As such, it is unique in its title. All other chronicle histories were published under a variety of formulas obviously meant to indicate that the play was "true" history in the narrower modern, though not Elizabethan, sense of the term. So we find Robert Greene's *The Scottish Historie of James the fourth, slaine at Flodden. Entermixed with a pleasant*

Comedie (pub. 1598) or Drayton's *The first part Of the true and honorable historie, of the life of Sir John Old-castle, the good Lord Cobham* (pub. 1600), where the adjectives are an obvious dig at Shakespeare's Sir John Falstaff (once Oldcastle), or *The Famous History of the Life of King Henry the Eight* (1623 Folio). The commonest formulas, however, are variations of the two to be found spliced in *The True Chronicle Historie of the whole life and death of Thomas Lord Cromwell* (pub. 1602) or simply an indication of the historical subject matter as in George Peele's *The Battell of Alcazar . . . With the death of Captaine Stukeley* (pub. 1594) or in *The Raigne of King Edward the third* (pub. 1596). Two plays that were deliberately planned to seem chronicle histories also use the standard formulas. *The First Part of Jeronimo. With the Warres of Portugall, and the life and death of Don Andræa* (pub. 1605) will be noticed later. *No-Body, and Some-Body. With the true Chronicle Historie of Elydure, who was fortunately three severall times crowned King of England* (pub. 1606) parodies title as well as substance.

I have tried, therefore, to avoid ambiguity by invariably using the term "chronicle history" to denote the dramatic genre. The term "history play," though frequently used, would not only be false to most Elizabethan usage but might mislead the modern reader, who sometimes forgets that Renaissance theory required all tragedies to be historic and that the use of history as such cannot be the basis of a dramatic genre.

The term "comedy" might be used, in medieval fashion, to designate any play with a happy ending—that is, an outcome other than death. But comedies were less carefully labeled than either chronicle histories or tragedies, although a large majority of published plays in that category are described in the title as "comedy" or "comical" or "humorous" (again with the Elizabethan meaning, not ours) or, toward the end of the period, as "tragicomedy." The title of *The Widdowes Teares. A Comedie* by George Chapman (pub. 1612) is obviously intended to lure the reader by its paradox. It is a brilliant handling of the Widow of Ephesus story that one would give a great deal to see performed. In most plays not specifically labeled, the subject matter is obviously comic.

Since what follows is intended to clarify the Elizabethan notion of tragedy, no definition will be attempted here. Tragedies, as befitted the highest dramatic genre, were labeled with great care, either with some derivative of "tragedie" or, in three plays, with the term "revenge," which clearly implied bloodshed and death.[5] Only four claimants, in fact, were published without a clear identification, and three of these present no problem. The First Folio "Catalogue" lists "The Life and death of Julius Caesar," but the head and running titles are "The Tragedie of Julius Caesar." The quartos of *King Lear* retain the title of the old chronicle history *King Leir*, but the Folio head and running titles are "The Tragedie of King Lear." Jonson's *Catiline his Conspiracy* (pub. 1611) was not formally called a tragedy until the folio of 1616. Thomas Heywood's *A Woman Kilde with Kindnesse* (pub. 1607) apparently presented difficulties in categorizing. Its main plot belongs to the well-recognized genre of domestic tragedy that appears in the table, but the important subplot is tragicomedy because of its happy ending. This may have led to difficulties in labeling. It must be noted, however, that John Marston's *The Insatiate Countesse. A Tragedie* (pub. 1613) has, despite its label, two comic subplots of a lover who must protect his beloved's reputation after injuring himself trying to climb into her window and of clever wives who outwit their philandering husbands. Although Elizabethan tragedies normally contain a good deal of comedy, these fully developed comic subplots in the two plays are apparently unique.

Granted that Elizabethans were careful to label tragedies as such, the important problem is what they meant by the term. Two ways of approaching a definition suggest themselves, and both will be used: contrast and descriptive analysis. An especially illuminating contrast is possible in plays dealing with English or Scottish history. *King Lear* or *Macbeth*, though based on what passed for history, are simply tragedies in that historical material has been radically re-shaped to produce an action dictated by ethical or metaphysical views and sophisticated in structure. But *Richard III* or *Richard II* undoubtedly are concerned with history as such, and Heminges and Condell had sound reasons, though not of dramatic structure, for including them among the histories. It is therefore illuminating to compare these and other like plays with chronicle histories, so labeled,

[5]John Marston, *Antonios Revenge* (pub. 1602); Beaumont and Fletcher, *Cupids Revenge* (pub. 1615); and John Stephens, *Cinthias Revenge* (pub. 1613).

that have a similar concern with presenting history almost for its own sake. We learn primarily the limits beyond which Elizabethans were unwilling to go in calling a play a tragedy, but this negative definition can then be supplemented by the positive results of critical description of extant tragedies.

All that distinguished many of the tragedies presenting British history from similar chronicle-history plays is the fact that the death of the hero results in some fashion from the earlier action of the play, and a loose sequence of cause and effect becomes a principle of tragic structure. How loose the sequence might be is illustrated by the contrast between *The True Chronicle History of King Leir* (pub. 1605) and *The Lamentable Tragedie of Locrine* (ca. 1591, pub. 1595). *King Leir*, though fantastic in content, has more unity of a kind than *Locrine*; but, despite confused structure, the latter play does lead to the deaths of Locrine and Sabren, his daughter. If a play is merely a narrative of events, however, it is not called a tragedy no matter how well organized, or how many people die. Compare, for example, *The True Tragedie of Richard the third* (ca. 1591) with *The True Chronicle Historie of the whole life and death of Thomas Lord Cromwell* (ca. 1601) or *The Famous History of Sir Thomas Wyat* (ca. 1604) by Dekker and Webster. *The True Tragedie* is less unified than Shakespeare's more familiar play in that it devotes several scenes to Jane Shore; politically it is more sophisticated in that it shows a better understanding of the factional quarrels of which Richard made capital, and this element complicates the action somewhat. But it is definitely a tragedy of the rise and fall of Richard, and his rise leads, despite irrelevant episodes, to his fall and death. *Thomas Lord Cromwell* covers the hero's mature life, but the real difference is that its earlier episodes, such as his exposing of the usurer Bagot or even his relations with Friskiball, have no relationship to his fall. The action of *Sir Thomas Wyat* extends only from the coronation of Mary Tudor to the execution of Wyat along with Lady Jane Grey and Guildford Dudley, but Wyat's part in getting the council to accept Mary as queen is not related to his revolt after her marriage to Philip. The two episodes are merely parts of the history of his life, even though they might easily have been given a tragic unity. Similarly, we find Shakespeare's *The Tragedy of King Richard the third* (Q_1) and *The Tragedie of King Richard the second* (Q_1), but *The first*

15

[*Second* and *third*] *Part of Henry the Sixt* (F₁) and *The life and death of King John* (F₁). (The First Folio keeps "The Tragedy of Richard the Third" as a head title, as we have already noted, but normalizes the running titles of *Richard III* and both head and running titles of *Richard II* to "The Life and Death of.")

There seems to be no difference in style or in intellectual content between the tragedies and chronicle histories as such. Comic scenes are written in a style appropriate to comedy, serious historical scenes with tragic elevation of diction. Profundity of thought varies with dramatists but not between tragedies and chronicle histories—at least in Shakespeare, who alone has written enough plays of both types to permit a contrast. Apparently, great historical events, traditionally the property of tragedy, were inevitably treated with tragic elevation of style and amplitude of political or ethical commentary. A comparison of *Richard III* and *1 Henry IV* will illustrate the generalizations just made. Or *The Troublesome Raigne of John King of England* (pub. 1591) and *Sir John Old-castle* will serve as examples outside the Shakespeare corpus.

Tragedy, in short, was obviously a recognized dramatic genre; the chronicle history was only a way of classifying plays too historical and too serious to be comedies, even though well constructed and happy in outcome, or too loosely narrative to be tragedies, even though serious in theme and studded with corpses.

So far as one can see, Shakespeare was, except for Marlowe in one play, the only dramatist who worked seriously at solving the structural problem presented by the dramatic treatment of English history; in fact, he wrote more plays based upon such material than any other dramatist (apparently even if lost plays be included). He tried a loose narrative structure in *Henry VI*. This he varied in *King John* by using the Bastard to give thematic unity to the play. In *Richard III* and *Richard II* he tried variants of the *de casibus* tragedy; in *1* and *2 Henry IV* he paired plots from history and comedy exactly as he contrasted plots of romance and intrigue in such comedies as *The Merchant of Venice* and *Much Ado about Nothing*; and in *Henry V* he used the chorus to admit defeat in his attempt to impose dramatic form upon history. From then on he boldly reshaped history into pure tragedy, except for his final collaborative effort in *Henry VIII*.

16

Another negative witness to a clear Elizabethan concept of tragedy exists in the doubtful titles of two plays that have already been mentioned. Shakespeare's *Troilus and Cressida* is called a "tragedie" by the Folio, and there is good reason to believe that the editors of the Folio originally intended to place it among the tragedies after *Romeo and Juliet* in the place now occupied by *Timon*.[6] But, though Hector dies toward the end, the seduction of an all-too-willing flirt by a lusty young gallant and his lecherous uncle is material for comedy; nor is the stuff of tragedy to be found in a war governed by long-winded debates, however philosophic, and consisting of petty bickerings conducted to an obligato of foul-mouthed comments. Both issues of the quarto call the play "The Historie of Troylus and Cresseida," and such, if anything, it is. It is a dramatized story from medieval romance, and Hector's challenge to prove his lady "wiser, fairer, truer" (I.iii.275), which can be paralleled in contemporary prose romances of chivalry, is an appropriate part. Only the "wiser" among the lady's attributes is more typical of Shakespeare's comic heroines than of romance. *Timon of Athens* is also doubtful for other reasons than its being used to fill up space intended for *Troilus*. It is tragic only in that it ends with the death of Timon; but his death is not an outcome of the action, most of which lacks tragic dignity, and the play is really a moral *exemplum* from history. The Folio calls it "The Life of Tymon of Athens," despite its place among the tragedies. If I may conjecture, it seems likely that the Folio editors, having restricted the "histories" to medieval English history, were compelled to place *Troilus* and *Timon* elsewhere. Both plays were (for them) historical in content, often serious and philosophical in tone, and dignified by death, although not as an outcome of the main action. Consequently, the plays were classified as tragedies. If this conjecture is sound, the consequences are important, for it seriously invalidates the generalization made below that extant plays tend to convert material from other than English history into tragedy.

Granted that tragedy had to present some sequence of events which, despite irrelevant or loosely related episodes, led to death, the next problem is to describe the form or forms actually assumed by Elizabethan tragedies. The best approach will perhaps be to attempt

[6]See Walter W. Greg, *The Shakespeare First Folio: Its Bibliographical and Textual History* (Oxford, 1955), pp. 445-448.

an analysis of extant tragedies composed from the accession of Queen Elizabeth until the end of Shakespeare's productive career. The plays designated as tragedies seem to fall into a number of fairly well-defined categories, and these categories, in turn, have somewhat different principles of structure. The following discussion is reflected in the categories in the accompanying table, to which reference has already been made. It attempts very roughly to relate the extant tragedies to some principle of dramatic structure that seems to operate in them. Since the aim is to facilitate critical understanding of Shakespeare and to assess his unique achievements rather than to trace lines of historical development, the categories are arranged in what is taken to be an ascending order of clarity and sophistication in dramatic structure, from the rambling "tragical histories" to the carefully organized revenge plays or the intellectually sophisticated and well-planned tragedies which very closely approximate the tragic ideal described by Aristotle in his *Poetics*. This amounts to asserting that the development of a tragic form was a major problem facing Elizabethan playwrights. Plays which might possibly fall into several categories are therefore assigned to that assumed to be of highest rank. Shakespeare's *Macbeth*, for example, presents the fall of a great and proud man to destruction. But to categorize it with other plays in the *de casibus* tradition of the fall of princes,[7] though a sound procedure in terms of dramatic history as the inevitable comparison with *Richard III* shows, would be to miss most of what makes it great, as comparison with *Richard III* also demonstrates. *King Lear*, too, shows this fall of a prince. But, even though in magnitude of action it goes far beyond what Aristotle deemed possible, it conforms in other fundamental respects to his standards and, if it is to receive critical justice, must be judged by them. It is therefore listed, like *Macbeth*, in the last and highest category of "quasi-Aristotelian" tragedies. (The term will be explained when the plays in this category are discussed.)

There seems little doubt that the episodic and narrative structure of most Elizabethan tragedies derives from medieval drama. But, in setting up a category of plays which one regards as predominantly in the medieval tradition, one runs immediately into a scholarly con-

[7]See Madeleine Doran, *Endeavors of Art: A Study of Form in Elizabethan Drama* (Madison, 1954), pp. 124-126.

troversy of long standing—the relative influence of Seneca and the medieval stage upon Elizabethan drama. Like most intellectual problems, this one requires a few distinctions.

There can be no question whatever of the enormous influence exerted by Seneca's plays upon Elizabethan tragedies and histories. Nashe's charge that "*Seneca*, let blood line by line and page by page, at length must needes die to our Stage" (1589)[8] is inaccurate in its prophecy but sound in its statement of fact. In this respect Seneca enjoyed the advantages accruing to him as a dramatist fond of sensationalism whether in epigram or in situation, as a philosopher given to sententious moralizing, and as a major Latin writer. But the Bible, Virgil, and Ovid were similarly rifled, at least for lines, and occasionally even for situations. Elizabethan criticism inculcated the theory of imitation, and Elizabethan grammar-school practice taught the technique of assimilating gems of speech. As a source of epigrams or plot elements Seneca simply enjoyed the advantage of being *the* Latin tragic dramatist and of dealing in usable situations as well as in quotable sentiments. Furthermore, if blood was to be borrowed, no potential donor was his equal.

But Elizabethan drama drew upon Seneca for more than lines and situations. It also took over dramatic techniques: the villain's soliloquy, though this could be paralleled in medieval plays; the ghost bent on revenge or dramatic exposition; stichomythia; the moralizing chorus; and so on. For example, *Locrine* presents Ate, goddess of strife, as a prologue to each act, assisted by the dumb show, which became characteristic of early Senecan plays. The ghosts of two British kings, Albanact and Corineus, appear to their slayers. Ghosts and other imitations of Seneca's techniques are ubiquitous in the serious plays of Shakespeare's time, though devices like stichomythia and the chorus became less common.

But another influence was more important than such dramatic devices, which can actually be paralleled outside Seneca and would many of them doubtless have occurred to playwrights independently. This was the spirit that informed the plays in the sense that it dictated their choice and treatment of material and their dramatic structure. Seneca's plays, by and large, follow the Greek practice

---

[8]Quoted in Chambers, *The Elizabethan Stage*, IV, 235.

of concentrating upon the climax of an action much of which is revealed in exposition. We see Phaedra driven by her passion to contemplate suicide, propose incest, and accuse falsely; we only hear how her fierce love grew, to what extent Hippolytus had devoted himself to a life of chastity, and why Theseus could wish Hippolytus to death. We hear enigmatically of Pelops' curse and the sins of Thyestes; we see the wrath of Atreus and the fatal banquet. In each play our attention is riveted upon passion's fatal overthrow of reason and the immediate consequences to which it leads. The play is a Stoic *exemplum* of passion at its height.

Elizabethan drama, on the other hand, inherited something of its point of view, as it derived its episodic technique and some of its methods of staging, from the great medieval mysteries that had attempted to present the whole divine plan itself from creation through redemption to last judgment. The earlier and better moralities, too, had seen human life as a struggle between forces of good and evil operating throughout the life of man. The habit of giving a full account of man's life, as part of a larger plan, persisted even when dramatists were not conscious of the metaphysical basis of their techniques. A fresh infusion of medieval thought came from *A Mirror for Magistrates* and similar narratives in the *de casibus* tradition.

The medieval mind was at once less and more philosophical than Seneca's. It was less concerned with the cause of a particular action by man the individual, more concerned with the lot of man the human being and with the meaning of his life as a part of a much larger whole ordered by God's providence. This life it tended to see as a progress from birth to death to judgment—a progress in which none can be sure of happiness and in which pride goeth before a fall. Refusing to deny with Seneca's Stoicism the worth of human emotions and the right of man to happiness, it saw as profoundly tragic man's brief tenure of earthly greatness and his probable overthrow, in this world, by the forces opposed to him, whether Fortune or his fellow men. This conviction of tragedy was enhanced by man's unique position as a creature of God for whom all else had been created.

Death, too, had a new meaning, since it was no longer a release from woe but a closing of accounts to await the audit of the last judgment. The dreadful finality of death consisted not in its ending man's existence but in its determining his existence through all eternity. Up to the instant of death salvation was possible even to the vilest sinner, and man's fate was not settled until that instant. The manner of death was therefore profoundly important. In *Hamlet*, for example, Shakespeare ignores the physical agony of the hero's death and concentrates our attention upon its moral accompaniments —upon Hamlet's exchanging forgiveness with Laertes, vindicating his good name, and attending, as a good and dutiful king, to the future of the kingdom now indubitably his. This is equally true of Shakespeare's other tragedies, and only in *Measure for Measure* among his comedies do we find, as Claudio faces death, a portrayal of all too human fears and torments like our own. The same concern with manner of death motivates details of tragic action. Hamlet is unwilling to kill Claudius at prayer lest he go to heaven; Frankfort, in *A Woman Kilde with Kindnesse*, refuses to slay Wendoll and Mistress Frankfort in adultery lest they go to hell.

Death was therefore the only possible end to a drama that seriously considered man's lot, and the medieval and Elizabethan equation of tragedy with death was something more than an ignorant oversimplification of traditional literary theory. The mistake had a sound basis in a view of life and death. In their concentration upon human woe in this life, Elizabethan tragedies are thoroughly of the Renaissance in taking a secular point of view. Though he mentions the future life, Macbeth is concerned with "all our yesterdays," and Shakespeare is at pains to show that those yesterdays, not human life itself, have been the "tale told by an idiot . . . signifying nothing." The struggle and death of Everyman, in contrast, are as nothing beside his eternal happiness, and the play is not tragic in tone. But Christianity itself had never denied or minimized human agony; that agony itself, like human life, gained dignity as part of the divine plan of redemption and potentially a means thereto. Elizabethan dramatic tragedies, like those narrated in *A Mirror for Magistrates*, though centered in this world, are therefore played against the background of eternity, and sometimes that background emerges into the foreground of explicit statement. The death of Hamlet, like that of Everyman, leads to "flights of angels." The blinding of Oedipus is an ultimate acknowledgment and symbol that the tragic outcome of human blindness is irrevocable. The blinding of Gloucester in *King Lear* is, as we shall see, one purgatorial experience among many, and his confession "I stumbled when I saw" implies the converse experience written into the action of the play. Before the final accounting of death, he, like Lear his master, will prove to have gained "in this world knowledge of Thy truth" and even—so the play leads us to infer—"in the world to come life everlasting."

Elizabethan tragic narratives, moreover, were concerned with the life and death of an individual primarily because the progress of his life and the manner of his death might serve as an *exemplum* to his fellow men. Their emphasis that events really happened—that the tragedy is "true"—is intended to guarantee the value of their witness to moral truth. In this respect they had roots in medieval Christianity that determined both the point of view and the dramatic form that resulted. Their concern is with revealing the pattern of human life and indicating the still larger background design, not with dissecting a particular human emotion. Seneca's devices and even Seneca's structure, where it seems to occur in them, are at best but super-imposed upon something that is fundamentally different. To those who wrote and produced tragic plays in this tradition, dramatic structure undoubtedly seemed much less important than the revela-tion of human experience; it existed, in any real sense, only if the playwright was an artistic genius.

Two of the plays listed are, in fact, primarily interludes that have been based upon tragic stories and have a tragic outcome. The con-fusion of genres and the moral *exemplum* intended are alike indicated by the full titles: *A New Tragicall Comedie of Apius and Virginia, Wherein is lively expressed a rare example of the vertue of Chastitie, by Virginias constancy, in wishing rather to be slaine at her owne Fathers handes, then to be deflowred of the wicked Judge Apius* (ca. 1564) by R. B.; *A Newe Enterlude of Vice Conteyninge, the Historye of Horestes with the cruell revengement of his Fathers death, upon his one naturtll Mother* (ca. 1567) by John Pikeryng. Both plays introduce a Vice, who clowns in the traditional fashion. Conscience tries to restrain Apius. Comfort prevents Virginius from killing himself, and other allegorical figures appear. Horestes debates with Nature the propriety of killing his mother, Revenge laments that Horestes' becoming a king leaves him the beggar, and Horestes

22

concludes the play by discussing with Commons, Truth, and Duty the ideal kingdom. In their preservation of comic elements and their use of allegory these plays are, however, an invaluable guide to the transmission of earlier methods and attitudes of mind to Elizabethan tragedy.

A considerable number of Elizabethan tragedies—a large majority, in fact, of those written for the popular stage—have in common that they narrate the crucial part of a great man's life and present his death as the outcome of that life, though several characters and their deaths may be presented in the same play. These I have classified as "narratives ending in death." They, in turn, admit of several subclassifications.

On the very border line of tragedy is a group of plays with titles which are themselves significant in that they seem to reflect careful attention to dramatic categories. Several of the plays involved come very close to being chronicle history, all of them are very loose in structure, and all of them lay chief claim to historical interest and subordinate "tragedy" or "tragical," often as if it were an afterthought. I say "claim" because they have, in fact, no more historical background than other tragedies. Four of them are, in fact, pure romance except for the use of historical names. These nine plays I have listed in a separate category of "tragical histories." This category, however, is not necessarily exclusive. None of these plays is as well organized as many of those listed in the various other categories under "narratives ending in death," and to this extent they are a genuine category on the border line between genres. But they are almost indistinguishable in structure from several plays labeled simply as tragedies. They also exemplify, like the other narrative tragedies, the use of various kinds of historical material and of pure romance masquerading as history.

The title of George Peele's *The Love of King David and Fair Bethsabe. With the Tragedie of Absalon* (pub. 1599) exactly describes the play, which covers the highlights of David's mature life and falls hopelessly into the two parts mentioned. The formula continues in *The Warres of Cyrus King of Persia, against Antiochus King of Assyria, with the Tragicall ende of Panthæa* (pub. 1594), which is largely romance, and in a play that almost, but not quite, achieves tragic unity and certainly achieves tragic power, Marlowe's

The troublesome raigne and lamentable death of Edward the second, King of England: with the tragicall fall of proud Mortimer (pub. 1594). "Death" is an obvious substitute for "tragedy" in the title of Marlowe's *The Massacre at Paris: With the Death of the Duke of Guise.* But Henslowe calls the play "the tragedey of the guyes" (1593).[9]

The First part of the Tragicall raigne of Selimus, sometime Emperour of the Turkes, and grandfather to him that now raigneth . . . (pub. 1594) is like Marlowe's *Tamburlaine* in that Selimus causes endless suffering to others but flourishes in wickedness himself. It is, however, much less successful than Marlowe's play in focusing the action upon Selimus or giving it unity of tone.

Two plays are based upon the materials of traditional English romance. *The Tragical History, Admirable Atchievments and various events of Guy Earl of Warwick. A Tragedy* was not published until 1661 but apparently dates from the early 1590's, though a *Life and Death of Guy of Warwicke* by Day and Dekker is listed in the Stationers' Register under 1620. Of all the plays listed it surely has least right to be called a tragedy, though Athelstane, the king, and Guy's long-neglected wife, Phyllis, provide a kind of unifying frame for the action, which ends with Guy's death and burial. *The Death of Robert, Earle of Huntington. Otherwise Called Robin Hood of merrie Sherwodde: with the lamentable Tragedie of chaste Matilda . . .* (pub. 1601) by Anthony Munday and Henry Chettle emphasizes the death of Robin Hood and Matilda and in passing disposes of at least four other persons, but it is primarily about King John.

Anthony Brewer's *The Love-sick King, An English Tragical History: with The Life and Death of Cartesmunda, the fair Nun of Winchester* (pub. 1655) also strains the category of tragedy, though in a totally different way from *Guy of Warwick*. It has a relatively unified action (plus a minor comic subplot) in which Canutus, king of Denmark, defeats and kills the English king, Ethelred, and his followers but falls in love with Cartesmunda. The English rally and defeat Canutus, who is, however, allowed to live and return to Denmark. But Cartesmunda has already been killed by a Danish

[9]Fol. 8, l. 43, in *Henslowe's Diary*, ed. Walter W. Greg (London, 1904), I, 15.

soldier, and, by Elizabethan standards, the claim to tragedy must rest upon her death. Last in point of time is Robert Daborne's *A Christian turn'd Turke: or, The Tragicall Lives and Deaths of the two Famous Pyrates, Ward and Dansiker* (pub. 1612). Though a tale of criminal adventure seasoned with the edifying spectacle of a Turk who reprimands the pirate Ward for deserting his Christian faith, it has some basis in contemporary piracy.

The classification of other narrative tragedies as history or romance is an attempt to clarify a state of affairs that we have already noted in discussing the tragical histories. All these tragedies claim a historical basis, and theory required that they be based upon history. In many, moreover, the focus is very clearly upon the tragic aspects of lives that were indeed historical or were so regarded by most Elizabethans. In such plays as Marston's *Sophonisba* (pub. 1606), Heywood's *The Rape of Lucrece* (pub. 1608), or Jonson's *Catiline* (pub. 1611) one suspects, in fact, that the poet felt constrained to write tragedy but was actually more interested in history. Marston seems to be more concerned with the progress of war than with Sophonisba's feelings, Heywood begins with the revolt against Tarquin, and Cicero dominates too much of Jonson's play. For this failure of design there may have been a good reason.

The evidence suggests that Elizabethan playwrights tended to restrict the category of chronicle histories to plays dealing with British history and, in some fashion and to some extent, assimilated plays dealing with other nationalities to what they regarded as tragedy.[10] For one thing, the playwright would feel much freer to reshape relatively unfamiliar material to give it tragic structure, just as Shakespeare could take much greater liberties with remote "historical" accounts of Lear and Macbeth than with Richard II. The anonymous *The First Part of Jeronimo. With the Warres of Portugall, and the life and death of Don Andrea* makes an obvious claim to being a non-English chronicle history, in that pseudo-Spanish history is treated in chronicle-play fashion and the title adopts a "life and death" formula, avoiding the word "tragedy." But the anonymous playwright faced an unusual problem in that he was trying to provide background for, and to capitalize upon the popularity of, *The*

[10]If my earlier conjecture is sound, *Troilus and Cressida* and *Timon of Athens* would be obvious exceptions.

25

Spanish Tragedie. Peele's *Battell of Alcazar*, though Portuguese history, includes "the death of Captaine Stukeley," who was himself the subject of another English history play. *A Larum for London* (ca. 1599), based upon Gascoigne's account of the sack of Antwerp by the Spaniards, sees the episode through English eyes, even though the application indicated by the title is not developed in the play.

To return to the narrative tragedies, a high proportion of them actually have some genuine historical basis. Of those based upon Roman material, only Marlowe's *The Tragedie of Dido Queene of Carthage* (ca. 1587-1593, pub. 1594) does not have its main source in Roman history or in writers who drew upon Roman history; and Marlowe, like other Renaissance writers, probably regarded Virgil's narrative as having historical authority. Writers of academic and closet tragedy drew upon Greek history and upon Greek and Roman mythology, but the popular dramatists working in narrative tragedy for the public theaters did not do so. Even if we glance at other kinds of popular tragedy, the same generalization still holds, though Shakespeare provides two exceptions. His *Titus Andronicus*, among plays having a Roman setting, lacks a genuine historical basis. *Troilus and Cressida*, if we include it among his tragedies, derives from Greece via the Middle Ages. Like the *Aeneid*, the Trojan War had the status of history.

The number of narrative tragedies based upon English history is small, as we might expect, because the dramatist who was not interested in tighter and more sophisticated types of tragic structure had available the relatively easier and more flexible history play itself. *Locrine* and *The True Tragedie of Richard the third* have been alluded to briefly; Fletcher's *Bonduca* will be mentioned later. All other tragedies from English history are to be found in other more specialized classifications. Those in the category of domestic tragedy, though historical in that they were based upon actual occurrences, involved a special use of recent events for homiletic purposes. Of plays based upon the historical past, Marlowe's *Edward II*, though placed among the "tragical histories," might arguably have been listed among the unified *de casibus* plays or even among those called "quasi-Aristotelian," so great are its positive achievements in spite of weaknesses. The other tragedies from English history—*Richard III, Richard II, King Lear, Macbeth*—are all by Shakespeare, and

26

this fact reflects the concern with dramatic structure which is so important among the various factors that make his plays outstanding in their age. Attention has already been called to his experiments in giving dramatic unity to English history.

A considerable number of other plays, however, were also based upon material regarded as historical. Among the plays classified as tragical histories, Peele's *David and Bethsabe* draws upon the Old Testament; *Selimus* upon the Mohammedan world; Marlowe's *The Massacre at Paris* upon recent events in France. Barnes's *The Divils Charter* (ca. 1607) and Webster's *The White Divel* (pub. 1612), among later and somewhat better constructed narrative tragedies, draw upon Italian history; Chapman's *Chabot Admirall of France* (ca. 1613, pub. 1639) is from French history. In fact, if we note the more tightly constructed *Bussy D'Ambois* (1604) and two-part *Charles Duke of Byron* (1608), Chapman emerges as something of a specialist in French history.

A number of these narrative tragedies, however, are in fact simply romances in tragic guise. But the "in fact" is important, for the writer is invariably careful to maintain the pretense that they involve historical personages in a historical setting. Preston's *Cambises King of Percia* (ca. 1560) is too notorious to require comment. Kyd's *Solyman and Perseda* (ca. 1590), like the earlier and looser *Warres of Cyrus*, uses materials characteristic of the romances of chivalry and centers about the trials of faithful lovers separated by war and fate. But appearances are maintained, since Cyrus figures in the one and Solyman, Sultan of Turkey, in the other, which also includes two sieges of Rhodes. Shakespeare may himself have regarded *Romeo and Juliet* (ca. 1595) as derived ultimately from a historical event, though his interest was centered in telling a romantic story and perhaps in working on the problem of presenting Romeo as morally responsible for the tragedy. Incidentally, the quarto title, *An Excellent conceited Tragedie of Romeo and Juliet* (pub. 1597), shows, in the Elizabethan "conceited," real critical discrimination as to both the origin and the poetic development of the material. As drama, of course, the play rises far above any other in the group, not only in imaginative power but also in dramatic unity. *Thorny-Abbey, or The London-Maid* (ca. 1595, pub. 1662) by T. W. belongs to the same level of storytelling as *The Death of Robert, Earle of Hunting-*

ton. Lusts Dominion; or, The Lascivious Queen. A Tragedie[11] (ca. 1600, pub. 1657) involves a Queen of Spain infatuated with a Moor, Eleazar, who wishes to destroy the Spanish aristocracy from motives of vengeance and very nearly succeeds. It resembles *The Spanish Tragedie* in its setting and in its theme of vengeance, but in its erotic sensationalism it reflects the shift in taste just beginning about 1600.[12] Barnes's *The Divils Charter: A Tragædie Conteining the Life and Death of Pope Alexander the sixt* (ca. 1607) may be compared with Mason's *The Turke. A Worthie Tragedie* (ca. 1607) to illustrate the thin line between history becoming romance and mere romance. The former is based upon the doings of Pope Alexander the Sixth and his children, but Alexander discovers the extraordinary (and largely unhistorical) wickedness of his children from devils, to whom he has sold his soul and who have led him to misunderstand the length of his diabolical contract. All this imposes a considerable strain upon the historical elements. In *The Turke* Mason tells how the villain Borgias, guardian of his niece Julia, Duchess of Florence, schemes to marry her after disposing of his wife, Timoclea, with the aid of Mulleasses, a Turk, who has been promised their daughter Amada as his reward. But Mulleasses has his own plans to become duke himself. He kills Borgias, is himself killed by a lord, and the Duke of Venice gets Julia. The resemblance to history is obviously remote, but the pretense is gallantly maintained. *The Second Maiden's Tragedy* (1611) presents plot situations characteristic of comedy—separated lovers, the jealous husband who tests his wife's fidelity, the maid with a lover; but it works these situations out to a tragic conclusion and adds necrophilia for good measure. Unlike the other plays mentioned, it makes no pretense to a historical setting, although it occurs in court circles.

A second characteristic of these plays need be mentioned only briefly, since it follows logically both from the use of historical or quasi-historical material and from the motives that led to a choice of such subjects. The dramatis personae are almost invariably of exalted rank—the kind of people who make history and whose suf-

[11]The title page continues: "Written by Christopher Marloe, Gent." But this attribution has been rejected in favor of Day, Dekker, and Haughton. See Chambers, *The Elizabethan Stage*, III, 427.

[12]Cf. Alfred Harbage, *Shakespeare and the Rival Traditions* (New York, 1952), pp. 186-221, 347.

ferings, like their lives, are greater and more intense than those of ordinary mortals. By decorum their speech is exalted in style, adorned with the colors of rhetoric, and almost invariably in verse. It has been said that Shakespeare never lets the English monarchy down. The intentions of other Elizabethan dramatists were equally good, however limited their powers, and their respect extended to all kings in all ages.

To turn from subject matter to structure, it must be obvious that what these plays present is not a tragic action but simply a tragic story, and that their only principle of structure lies in their presenting a framework of episodes constituting a narrative unit and having some relationship of cause and effect that eventuates in death. Within this framework various subordinate narratives or episodes may be added, sometimes with little or no relation to the main theme. Often the framework has little logical unity but is based upon covering a traditional unit of history or tying up all threads in a romantic story. I am aware that my words are less than precise, but I have used some care to achieve a vagueness of statement appropriate to the indefiniteness of the form.

Adherence to a segment of history traditionally presented as a unit is shown best by the tragedies based upon Roman material. Lodge's *The Wounds of Civill War* (ca. 1588, pub. 1594) presents "the true Tragedies of Marius and Scilla." The two tragedies are part of a civil war that provides the real principle of structure for the play. The same thing is equally true of plays toward the end of our period, two of which we have already commented upon. One does not expect unity of Heywood, and his *The Rape of Lucrece* (ca. 1607) includes everything from the time when Tarquin, the father, seizes the crown until the Tarquins, father and son, are killed, the latter by Brutus in single combat. We also get Horatius at the bridge and "severall Songes in their apt places, by Valerius, the merrie Lord amongst the Roman Peeres." Poor Lucrece is not only raped but also slighted. Jonson is a far better dramatist, but the Elizabethan in him could indulge the scholar's devotion to the full account. His *Catiline his Conspiracy* (1611) is just what the title implies. It narrates the formation and betrayal of the conspiracy, Cicero's countermeasures, and Catiline's defeat and death. There is no attempt to give it a tragic action centering in Catiline. Chapman's *Caesar and*

Pompey: A Roman Tragedy, declaring their Warres (ca. 1613, pub. 1631) is extremely crabbed and confused, but it narrates events from the rivalry between Caesar and Pompey in Rome to the murder of Pompey (at Lesbos!) and the suicide of Cato. Once again, the unifying principle is the history of a civil war.

Other plays could be used to illustrate the same kind of thing in a structure for which the dramatist must be held responsible. Fletcher's *Bonduca* (ca. 1613, pub. 1647), having established Caratach as an *exemplum* of virtue and chivalry and developed a touching relationship between him and his young nephew Hengo, in effect subordinates the heroic death of Bonduca and her daughters to the pathetic end of Hengo and Caratach's surrender with honor. Here the principle at work is that all characters must be disposed of and all sources of interest carried to conclusion.

In tragic romances a full narration of circumstances is equally demanded. Once a pair of lovers are separated or someone begins a career of adventure or crime, the play goes on until deaths make it impossible for the lovers to be reunited or the dramatist to find other human beings of whom to make corpses. Some suitable person must be left alive, of course, to take over the kingdom, but otherwise all those involved must be disposed of. The principle as stated is sound enough, though crude, provided that the dramatist strictly controls his imagination by reference to his plot line and avoids distracting details. Such control Elizabethan playwrights were simply unwilling to exercise, and, having wandered into a bypath, they had to explore its full length.

This is fundamentally the method used by Webster in *The White Divel*. The rambling structure is well implied by the title: *The White Divel; or, The Tragedy of Paolo Giordano Ursini, Duke of Brachiano, With the Life and Death of Vittoria Corombona the famous Venetian Curtizan*. But the title might have continued: "and of her brothers, with the punishment of Count Lodovico." We are so impressed by Vittoria's magnificence in death that we forget the forty lines more devoted to Flamineo's final speech and death and to the arrival of Giovanni, son to Ursini by his wife Isabella, who comes as ranking survivor to tidy up and to arrest Lodovico. Vittoria gives the play its life and greatness, but she does not give it unity.

Since the tragic story is the important thing rather than a tragic action, it is not surprising that one finds no clear concept of a tragic protagonist—sometimes no real tragic hero. Of the narrative tragedies, the following have a tragic hero of some sort (or a pair of heroes): *Locrine, The True Tragedie of Richard the third, Selimus, Lusts Dominion*, Peele's *David and Bethsabe* and *Alphonsus Emperour of Germany*, Kyd's *Solyman and Perseda*, Marlowe's *Edward II*, Marston's *Sophonisba* and *The Insatiate Countesse*, Mason's *The Turke*, Webster's *The White Divel*, and Chapman's *Tragedie of Chabot*.

Richard III, Selimus, Alphonsus, and Mason's Borgias are villain heroes. They initiate a series of crimes and, except for Borgias, thoroughly dominate the play. In that sense they are protagonists, although in each play, and especially in *Alphonsus*, there is a good deal of irrelevant action. By way of contrast, Marston's insatiate Countess Isabella and Webster's Vittoria are not true villain heroines because they have no clearly dominant role. Isabella, who completely manipulates the action surrounding her, is lost in two comic subplots, and Vittoria is to a considerable extent a passive part of a crowded action. To return to the plays with true villain heroes, *Selimus* also provides us with a clearly defined conflict between protagonist and antagonist in the struggle between Selimus and Acomat for the throne. Peele achieves much more effective drama, however, as Alexander, bent upon revenging the murder of his father, serves as tool of Alphonsus throughout the play and finally emerges as antagonist destroying Alphonsus, the real murderer, only at the end of the play. In each play, however, the antagonist emerges late from a confused welter of action. Mason, on the other hand, so clumsily handles his *The Turke* that we are in some doubt who is protagonist and who antagonist as between Borgias and the Turk. In *Lusts Dominion* such uncertainty is complete as between the Queen of Spain and Eleazar.

As compared to the dominant villains, the relatively virtuous heroes have less claim to the role of protagonist. Peele's David is the center of the story but not always of the action. Erastus and Perseda, the joint heroes of Kyd's play, qualify better. But, in a considerable section of the play, which has fundamental resemblances to contemporary romances of chivalry, the pair are involved in a series of romantic adventures, and only Perseda emerges as a genuine

31

force in her own tragedy toward the end of the play. A similar ob-
servation can be made of *Locrine*. The exigencies of historical legend
restrict Locrine to the central part of the play. We must first trace
the division of the kingdom and the invasion of Britain by Humber.
Locrine does not appear at all in Act II. Not until Act IV does he encounter Estrild, the cause of his tragic death when his wronged wife
and her friends revolt. At the end we must follow his daughter
Sabren to her drowning in the river to which she gave her name
(the Severn).

Sophonisba has already been mentioned as victim of Marston's
historical interest. She is perhaps the clearest illustration of an almost
inevitable conflict between historical narrative and the dramatic
organization necessary to produce a genuine protagonist. Sophonisba
is central to the play, and all the activity bears directly or indirectly
upon her fate. Toward the end, in her resistance to Syphax, she develops genuine tragic stature, even if the action is melodramatic. The
play has a kind of unity altogether absent from *Locrine*. But during
much of the play Marston's eye is upon the war rather than upon
Sophonisba, and she is merely the pawn of contending forces. He
fails, especially, to develop the magnificent tragic possibilities in
Sophonisba's having to choose between her husband, Massinissa, and
her country, Carthage. For a real development of this choice we
could have spared the military activity and even the flight from
Syphax through a vault. Chapman's play *Chabot* illustrates an even
greater failure to keep the hero central to the action. Chabot is rather
a figure about whom action revolves than himself a major participant
in events. He does contribute to his troubles by tearing up a petition
bearing the King's approval and by refusing to abate his righteous
pride before the King. Otherwise his most positive contribution to
the drama is to die of a broken heart after he has been restored to
favor.

The remaining narrative tragedies either divide the main action
among a number of approximately equal characters or fail to maintain a single point of view as between two main characters. The
former weakness can be illustrated by Munday and Chettle's *The
Death of Robert, Earle of Huntington* (1598) or Daborne's *A Christian turn'd Turke* (1610).

The failure of several of these plays to maintain a consistent point of view as between two main characters deserves more extended comment. In *Othello*, for example, we have no difficulty whatever in seeing that Othello is the hero and Iago is the villain, and this point of view—that of Othello—is maintained throughout the play. Conversely, Shakespeare's Richard III is a villain, and Buckingham finally emerges on the side of right; but we are still in no doubt that Richard is protagonist and Buckingham an antagonist (if the term may be applied to one of several opponents), since the play is presented from Richard's point of view and the action emerges from him. In Marlowe's *Edward II*, on the other hand, Mortimer, though on my reading a villain throughout,[13] usurps the foreground during much of the play. In Jonson's *Catiline* we are not sure where we stand, with Catiline or with Cicero, and the play has a double focus largely resulting, I think, from Jonson's failure to discipline his sources. The same tyranny of source material can be illustrated in Marlowe's *Dido Queene of Carthage*. The action is so involved in divine jealousy and intrigue as well as in Virgil's narrative, and both Aeneas and Dido aro so controlled by the gods, that the play does not focus upon Dido until her final attempts to retain Aeneas and her suicide. But one can hardly blame upon sources the shifting of viewpoint between Sulla and Marius in Lodge's *The Wounds of Civill War* or, in a much later play not affected by historical sources at all, between Bonduca and Caratach, who are at times in moral opposition in Fletcher's *Bonduca* (ca. 1613, pub. 1647). As we shall see when we come to discuss Shakespeare's *Julius Caesar*, a similar ambiguity of viewpoint is characteristic of all extant plays on Julius Caesar and is important to our reading of Shakespeare's play.

I have been assuming that a true protagonist must be an actor in the sense that he helps to shape the outcome of the play. Granted a tragic outcome, this view means that he must have considerable share in producing his own downfall and death, whether or not he is morally responsible for the outcome. It also implies that the dramatist must have some theory of the relationship between the individual and the forces that determine his fate. Historically tragedy has inevitably confronted the dramatist with the problem of evil. But, so

---

[13]The late W. D. Briggs, whose edition of *Edward II* is still of importance, objected strenuously to this interpretation when I first ventured it. For him Mortimer illustrated a shift in character all too common in Elizabethan drama.

33

long as the dramatist concentrates upon retelling an exciting bit of history, he can also concentrate upon action and moralizing to the exclusion of metaphysics. He feels responsible for revealing what has happened and labeling it correctly, not for pondering why it has happened.

Whatever the reason, this is in fact what Elizabethan narrative tragedy did. It is almost completely innocent of metaphysical speculation into the nature of things or of restatement and application of the traditional philosophy which it often reflects. Of outright didacticism and of moral precepts it has plenty. In this, as in many other things, Seneca's example was reinforced by the whole bent of Elizabethan education, and Elizabethan tragedy is nothing if not sententious. Political wisdom and political maxims especially abound, particularly in the Roman plays and in others with a genuinely historical context. *Locrine*, for example, involves the division of a kingdom and the relations between Locrine and his powerful father-in-law. These problems are discussed in political terms. Heywood's *Rape of Lucrece*, developing the figure of Brutus, has much to say about tyrants and their ways and the woes of their subjects. Webster's *Appius and Virginia* (ca. 1609, pub. 1654) presents another *exemplum* of the ways of tyrants driven by lust. But only Shakespeare's *Troilus and Cressida* and Shakespeare's great tragedies attempt to explain in fundamental terms why such dreadful things occur and why human beings behave as they do; these plays alone reach the level of interpretation achieved by many Greek tragedies (Shakespeare's acceptance of a moral system prevents, quite logically, the probing speculation of Greek tragedy). In going behind moralizing or even moral commentary to expound the principles of morality grounded in natural law and in presenting a psychology of human sin, *Troilus* is, I think, unique. Its criticism of life is cynical, but the fundamental principles of good and evil are clearly stated by Ulysses and Hector. Its metaphysical depth is surely that characteristic of tragedy, though its long-winded didacticism is fatal to effective drama and its prurient cynicism is fatal to tragic effect.

What, then, was this narrative tragedy? It was not a mere retelling of history. Neither was it simply a tragic hero struggling to work out his destiny. It was not a serious reflection upon the meaning of human life. It had none of the simple clarity of a plot with a beginning, a middle, and an end. It was a crowded and often confused narrative of a nexus of events, which somehow led to the final destruction of the major participants. It was, or pretended to be, historical in background, and it was often governed by tradition in the range of material presented, as well as in the handling of episodes. It portrayed characters of exalted rank engaged in violent and often frenzied action that led ultimately to death, and its effect depended as much upon the crowded violence of their lives as upon the "tragedy" of their deaths. Its heroes might be good, bad, or indifferent —one, or two, or even more. Their role might be active or passive. But there was always an exciting story to be told, with a sad ending, and it was the story that mattered.

There are among plays predominantly in the medieval tradition which narrate the fall of the great a few that display a much tighter structure than the preceding; and this unity results from a more careful attention to principles of organization logically implicit in the concept of Fortune's wheel, or the notion that pride goeth before a fall, or similar elements of the *de casibus* tradition. Shakespeare's *Richard III* (ca. 1593, pub. 1597) and *Timon of Athens* (ca. 1607, pub. 1623), Jonson's *Sejanus His Fall* (1605), Chapman's *Bussy D'Ambois* (1604) and his two-part *The Conspiracie, And Tragedie of Charles Duke of Byron* (1608) all illustrate a plot unified about one hero, whose rise and fall are narrated. In all of these except Chapman's *Byron* actions of the hero during his rise to power set in motion forces that contribute to his downfall. In Jonson's *Sejanus* (in my opinion one of the greatest English tragedies) the action is enriched by the irony of Sejanus' mounting security as the forces aligned against him muster for his destruction. Chapman's two-part *Byron* has a clear turning point in the Duke's failure to profit morally from King Henry's lecture and forgiveness at the end of "The Conspiracie," but the episodes of that first part hardly contribute to the "Tragedie"; there is no logical reason why La Fin should become an informer, and Henry would have justified Byron's security by forgiving once again had Byron confessed.

Marlowe's *Jew of Malta* (ca. 1589, pub. 1633) complicates the formula by providing a fall and recovery of sorts before the final catastrophe, and Shakespeare's *Richard II* (ca. 1595) replaces the standard metaphor of Fortune's wheel with a balanced rise and fall:

Now is this golden crown like a deep well
That owes two buckets, filling one another,
The emptier ever dancing in the air,
The other down, unseen, and full of water.
That bucket down and full of tears am I,
Drinking my griefs, whilst you mount up on high.

(IV.i.184-189)

The play is constructed in terms of this simile, and it involves a double contrast. Bolingbroke rises as Richard falls, but conversely Richard's hold upon our sympathy rises as Bolingbroke alienates us. Except for the doubtful inclusion of the Aumerle conspiracy, *Richard II* probably has the most skillful structure to be found in these plays.

Marlowe's *Tamburlaine* (2 parts, ca. 1587, 1588) is so great a departure from the norm that its inclusion in this category demands explanation. Apparently it confused contemporaries. The Stationers' Register enters: "The twooe commicall discourses of TOMBERLEIN the Cithian shepparde."[14] But the first edition is entitled: *Tamburlaine the Great. Who, from a Scythian Shephearde, by his rare and woonderfull Conquests, became a most puissant and mightye Monarque. And (for his tyranny, and terrour in Warre) was tearmed, The Scourge of God. Devided into two Tragicall Discourses.* . . . Both parts of *Tamburlaine* are obviously unified both in action and in theme, whether or not they constitute a single dramatic whole (I do not think that they do).[15] They present a single hero who vanquishes one enemy after another and finally defies heaven itself before he dies, not by an enemy's hand but by sickness. Marlowe's prologue says, in effect, to make what we can of this record (unless we assume that it merely anticipates the epilogue's conventional plea for applause):

View but his picture in this tragic glass,
And then applaud his fortunes as you please.[16]

---

[14]Aug. 14, 1590. *A Transcript of the Registers of the Company of Stationers of London, 1554-1640 A.D.*, ed. Edward Arber, II (London, 1875), 262b.

[15]For the contrary view see Roy W. Battenhouse, *Marlowe's Tamburlaine: A Study in Renaissance Moral Philosophy* (Nashville, 1941), pp. 252-258.

[16]Quotations are from *Tamburlaine the Great: In Two Parts*, ed. U. M. Ellis-Fermor (London, 1930).

The two plays obviously depend both for their point and for their structure upon the tradition with which we are dealing. Tamburlaine's pride and his actions both have tragic magnitude, and his pride, at least, ought to lead to his fall. But it does not do so, and the repeated testing of this principle by his successes is what makes those successes incremental and not merely iterative. Even death by sickness is, in a sense, a logical tragic fall in that it proves Tamburlaine, who has defied heaven, a mere man like other men:

> Shall sickness prove me now to be a man,
> That have been term'd the terror of the world?
>
> (V.iii.44-45)

Tamburlaine is therefore a *de casibus* tragedy at least in the sense that it depends upon the tradition for its form and its meaning. This categorizing is, I realize, on the principle of the famous Latin etymology *lucus a non lucendo*. But I hope that my category is sounder than the etymology; at least, it is supported by the title page.[17]

Granted that these plays are far more carefully constructed than others of the same general type, it becomes doubly significant that even they exemplify no concept of a tragic hero except that he must be of such exalted rank that his fall (or failure to fall) can have meaning. He may be, like the Jew of Malta, Richard III, or Sejanus, a thoroughly evil person with no redeeming quality except his "virtu." He may be, like Bussy D'Ambois or Byron, a potentially good man who falls into evil. In neither hero, however, is either the potential goodness or the betrayal of it developed dramatically; both men are potentially, but only potentially, Aristotelian tragic heroes.[18] Richard II is fundamentally a weak man who falls, in part, because of his inadequacy to his rank. Shakespeare's *Timon* would probably fall into this category if we conceded it to be a tragedy. But Timon himself is completely ambiguous. He is presented as a virtuous man, betrayed by his false friends, an example of magnificence and liberality; yet he violates Elizabethan standards of prudence as well as our own and falls from wealth to poverty as a result.

It is also significant that only four dramatists are represented in this category, and they are all among the greatest of the age. Structure

[17]For a similar view see Willard Farnham, *The Medieval Heritage of Elizabethan Tragedy* (Berkeley, 1936), pp. 368-373.

[18]Cf. Ennis Rees, *The Tragedies of George Chapman: Renaissance Ethics in Action* (Cambridge, Mass., 1954), pp. 31-32, 96, etc.

of any kind did not come easily to an Elizabethan playwright, and only the ablest achieved it. Even rarer than unity of action is the power to give that action intellectual meaning or to relate it to a moral norm, and in this respect, too, these plays are far superior to the preceding. Jonson presents his action straightforwardly and without moral ambiguity. Chapman seems to me unable to integrate into his plays the philosophy with which he struggles manfully. But *Tamburlaine* has far more frequent ethical signposts than most readers notice, and they are far more skillfully written into, and in a sense concealed in, the play than the obvious moral tags in most tragedies of the time. Marlowe may not explain—may not even wish to explain—how such a figure as Tamburlaine can be reconciled with Christian principles, except perhaps as a divinely appointed scourge raised by God to punish the sins of others; but he does make very clear just how Tamburlaine violates sound morality, wishing at last to plant his bloody banners in the firmament where Faustus correctly saw Christ's blood streaming. Shakespeare's skill in writing into *Richard III* a providential reunion of England and into *Richard II* accepted Tudor concepts of sovereignty will be discussed later. In structure and intelligence these plays stand apart. *Tamburlaine* was epoch-making in its day. *Richard III, Richard II,* and *Sejanus* are obviously tragedy of a high order—not Aristotelian tragedy, it is true, but nonetheless tragedy. They still provide far more interest for the reader—or, if one is lucky, the spectator—than most tragedies of the period.

I remarked that the plays already discussed seemed to me predominantly "medieval" in spirit, even though frequently Senecan in details of technique. In another group of plays the imitation of Senecan drama is, on the whole, more careful, and both his meaning and his dramaturgy are better understood. But the habits of thought that produced medieval drama still appear, and influences derived from the narrative tragedies are at work. It is no accident that these predominantly Senecan plays are all learned in origin and intended either for a learned stage or apparently merely for the edification of writer and reader. Daniel's *Philotas* (1604) is the only exception, and Daniel intimates that it was entrusted to the public stage only because he needed money.[19]

[19]Chambers, *The Elizabethan Stage*, III, 275-276.

The plays produced by the Inns of Court were surely the most influential of these Senecan tragedies in their day, and they are undoubtedly the best known to modern students. They were *Gorboduc* (1562), written by Thomas Norton and Thomas Sackville for the Gentlemen of the Inner Temple to produce before the queen at Whitehall; *Jocasta: A Tragedie written in Greke by Euripides, translated and digested into Acts by George Gascoygne, and Francis Kenwelmershe of Grayes Inne, and there by them presented* (1566);[20] *Gismond of Salerne* (ca. 1566), written by Robert Wilmot and four other Gentlemen of the Inner Temple and performed before Queen Elizabeth, later revised by Wilmot as *The Tragedie of Tancred and Gismund* (1591) in a version that belongs among closet dramas; and *The Misfortunes of Arthur* (1587), by Thomas Hughes, a belated example included among *Certaine Devises and shewes presented to her Majestie by the Gentlemen of Grayes-Inne at her Highnesse Court in Greenewich.*

These plays illustrate even more clearly than the Oxford and Cambridge plays in Latin the influence of native tradition and habits of thought even upon men of learning imitating Seneca for a learned audience. The three completely original plays are thoroughly Senecan in dramatic trappings, except that *Gorboduc* and *The Misfortunes of Arthur* (as well as *Jocasta*) add dumb shows. The dumb show, as a matter of fact, became itself a staple feature of the English Senecan play. In addition to the usual chorus and messenger, *Gismond of Salerne* presents Cupid as prologue and gives a scene to Megaera come from hell; *The Misfortunes of Arthur* opens with a prologue by the ghost of Gorlois demanding revenge and closes as he admits himself satisfied and prophesies the golden reign of Queen Elizabeth. These plays are also Senecan in that they have a unified dramatic action such as few of the plays already discussed possess —none, in fact, if we exclude *Richard III* and *Sejanus*. But that action shows in its narrative sweep the medieval and English habit of mind. *Gorboduc* is like an English history play in that it narrates Gorboduc's fatal decision to divide the kingdom and the ensuing civil war

[20]Farnham (*The Medieval Heritage of Elizabethan Tragedy*, pp. 356-357) stresses that Lodovico Dolce's Italian version of the *Phoenissae* "is a forced adaptation of Euripides to the Gothic taste in tragedy by use of Seneca. The English translation from the Italian goes ever farther in compelling Euripides to take on Gothic color."

even beyond his death. And the chorus, like the protatic characters, is concerned to drive home the lessons taught by that history.[21] In his first act of *The Misfortunes of Arthur* Hughes develops the guilty perplexity of Guenevora in a fashion that might open a thoroughly Senecan study of human passion, but by the end of the act he has turned his attention to preparations for war. From then on he is primarily concerned with tracing the alignments of forces and the fortunes of war. Only in the fifth act do Arthur's laments return to Senecan themes, and even they (to anticipate a later discussion) acquire a medieval accent. *Gismond of Salerne* is simply a romantic love story with a sensationally unhappy ending, and the story is what really matters; but the choruses are Senecan in their emphasis upon Fortune and morality, granted that the morality must reflect Christianity or at least the Elizabethan version thereof.

These plays also differ from Seneca in that they shift the moral emphasis from private to political conduct. In this shift they reflect, of course, the thoroughly practical bias that Elizabethan adapters, following the example of Cicero, gave to classical ethics and learning in general. Hughes's first chorus in *The Misfortunes of Arthur* sees the private sin of rulers as leading to wars and discord:

> In *Brytain* warres and discord will not stent:
> Till *Uther's* line and offspring quite be spent.
>
> (ll. 23-24)[22]

The second chorus points out that the happiness of royal power is an illusion; yet,

> How many millions to their losse you lead:
> With love and lure of Kingdomes blysse untryed?
>
> (ll. 27-28)

The third chorus is a characteristic meditation upon the cares of royalty as compared with the happiness of a quiet life. But it opens with a stanza on the evils of civil war that resembles the Homilies and Shakespeare in its use of the standard commonplaces, although not in eloquence of statement. The passages allotted to the chorus in the kommos of the fifth act contain commonplaces of the sort associated

[21]Farnham also stresses the native elements in *Gorboduc* (ibid., pp. 352-356).

[22]Quotations are from *Early English Classical Tragedies*, ed. John W. Cunliffe (Oxford, 1912).

with *de casibus* narratives, and the epilogue develops the same theme. Its references to Fortune and the Fates can be paralleled in Seneca, but the reference to pride and the general tenor are medieval and Christian.

I have itemized the choruses in *The Misfortunes of Arthur* to show how Senecan tragedy and even Senecan themes were accommodated to the intellectual heritage of the Middle Ages and to political concerns of Tudor England. In *Gorboduc*, of course, no such accommodation was needed. The play was simply a political *exemplum* drawn from pseudohistory; and its didactic passages merely draw the obvious lessons that kings should rule, that inexperienced rulers are prey to flatterers, that desire for power leads to tyranny and further civil strife.

In general, both tendencies mentioned continued and became more marked in the academic plays. The narrative tendencies observed in *Gorboduc* and *The Misfortunes of Arthur* are present in many of them. Legge's *Richardus Tertius* (1579) represented a heroic attempt to reduce English history to Senecan form.[23] It consists of three "actions" each equivalent to a Senecan play, although the middle one is short. The third action has a prologue by Furor and an omnipresent "Nuntius" but no chorus. It extends, however, from the murder of the Princes to the death of Richard and is further extended by an un-Senecan epilogue, which foretells the birth of Queen Elizabeth as the final happy outcome of the events presented. The *Caesar Interfectus* of Richard Eedes (1582), if we may judge by the extant epilogue, was also a history play adapted in part to Senecan form. Gager's *Ulysses Redux* (1592) simply converts to dramatic form Homer's story of Ulysses' return. The English plays *The Tragedie of Cæsar and Pompey Or Cæsars Revenge* (ca. 1595, pub. 1606), *The Tragedie of Claudius Tiberius Nero* (1607), and John Sansbury's *Periander* (1608) are, in fact, well-nigh indistinguishable from contemporary narrative tragedies for the popular stage. In *Cæsar and Pompey Or Cæsars Revenge*, "Privately acted by the Studentes of Trinity Colledge in Oxford," perhaps about 1595, Discord serves as a prologue, there is a chorus between acts, and Caesar's ghost effects a reconciliation between Octavius and Antony as well as appearing

---

[23]See Boas, *University Drama in the Tudor Age*, pp. 115-116.

to Brutus. But it covers, or tries to cover, events from Caesar's refusal to kill Brutus at the battle of Pharsalia to the death of Brutus, including Caesar's love for Cleopatra and the death of Pompey (but Antony makes no funeral speech!). By contrast, Alexander's closet drama *Julius Caesar* extends only from the episode of the kingship (of which we only hear a discussion) to the killing of Calpurnia after that of Caesar, although Juno as prologue relates the action to her long-standing hatred of the Trojans and the chorus prophesies the future.

Claudius Tiberius Nero, of which we know only that its "Father was an Academian,"[24] is simply a chronicle history of the reign of Tiberius from his becoming emperor until Caligula murders him. Its only pretense to unity lies in some emphasis upon the conflict between Tiberius and Germanicus and his family, and its only Senecan characteristic is the appearance of Germanicus' ghost demanding revenge. Sansbury's *Periander*, the performance of which on February 13, 1608, concluded elaborate Christmas festivities at St. John's College, Oxford, is also merely a dramatized narrative. It is based upon the story in Herodotus and Diogenes Laertius of Periander, tyrant of Corinth, who killed his wife, destroyed his two sons and daughter, and then managed to have himself killed and buried so as to conceal the place of his burial.[25] The writer is not quite equal to making clear the elaborate stratagem of the burial. The prologue and choruses become discussions of the play as drama among the Master of the Revels, his boy, Detraction, and Resolution, the last two serving as chorus. The Latin *Philomela* presented earlier during the same festivities has a similar ingenious perversion of the chorus in that Sea and Land (Mare and Terra) debate which should bear the onus of such crimes.

The academic tragedies therefore approach the narrative form characteristic of the popular stage. It is also obvious that a majority

---

[24]Epistle dedicatory, signed by Francis Burton (*The Tragedy of Tiberius 1607*, Malone Society Reprints [London, 1914]). The epistle also commends the playwright's knowledge of Tacitus, and the "Ad Lectores" is significant:

> I use no Sceane suppos'd as many doe,
> But make the Truth my Sceane, and Actors too.

[25]See *The Christmas Prince*, Malone Soc. Reprints (London, 1922), pp. xvi-xviii. For the attribution of *Periander* to John Sansbury see Alfred Harbage, "The Authorship of *The Christmas Prince*," *Modern Language Notes*, L (1935), 501-505.

of the subjects have been chosen because of their political implications. Even *Periander* becomes an *exemplum* of the ways of tyrants and the evils of tyranny as it affects the lives and characters of ruler and ruled alike.

The academic tragedies have, on the whole, slight dramatic value. As differentiated from the Inns of Court plays, they apparently had little influence upon the development of English tragedy. The influence operated, in fact, in the other direction, and therein lies their value to students of Elizabethan tragedy. They demonstrate how strong and how pervasive were the influences that operated in the popular narrative tragedy. They also suggest that these influences came not only from dramatic tradition but also from habits of mind common to educated Elizabethans.[26] One suspects, in fact, that Elizabethans emphasized in Seneca himself what interested them and made something else out of his plays than we do.

The closet dramas, in contrast, remain tight in structure and are more varied in theme. Greville's tragedies are more broadly philosophical than most; Wilmot's slightly revised *Tancred and Gismund* (1591), Daniel's *Cleopatra* (1593), and Elizabeth, Lady Cary's *Mariam, The Faire Queene of Jewry* (ca. 1604, pub. 1613) dramatize the private tragedies of those who love. Daniel's *Cleopatra* is without the political context so important for Shakespeare. Daniel's *Philotas* (1604), on the other hand, is so thoroughly political in viewpoint that he was apparently called before the Privy Council to account for supposed resemblances to "my L. of Essex troubles."[27] "The Monarchicke Tragedies" (pub. 1607)—*Croesus, Darius, The Alexandrœan Tragedy, Julius Caesar*—of Sir William Alexander, Earl of Stirling, are appropriately named.

If I may recapitulate, the two types of tragedies so far discussed —the narrative and the Senecan—both had their roots in traditional dramatic techniques and in traditional ways of seeing human life. Both types involved, to some extent, a dramatic structure and a philosophy of man. The narrative tragedy inherited the episodic struc-

---

[26]The importance of such habits of mind in controlling the way in which Elizabethans viewed and interpreted models and authorities is a major theme of Madeleine Doran's excellent study *Endeavors of Art*, to which references recur throughout this work. See, especially, the introductory statement (pp. 3-23).

[27]Chambers, *The Elizabethan Stage*, III, 276.

ture of medieval drama and the habit of seeing the overall pattern of a great man's life as part of a still larger pattern of events that derived from God's providence and imposed itself upon the dramatist. The dramaturgy was appropriate to, and in large part grew out of, the metaphysics, even though, as we have noted, the metaphysics was seldom explicit in the plays and the pattern of individual life might be almost if not quite lost in the larger context rather than clearly related to it. This is simply to say that dramatists were often, if not prevailingly, clumsy.

Seneca's tragedies, on the other hand, presented structured plays, at least by medieval standards, and they largely concentrated upon a particular failure to master a hostile Fate in the only way available to man—by subjecting human emotions to human reason conforming to the law of nature. Having no philosophy that demanded that each event be related to the larger order lest, if unexplained, it challenge the existence of that order, Seneca could concentrate upon the particular human experience. Because tragedy must present the deviation and not the norm, Seneca concentrated upon case studies of emotional pathology in which reason gave way before passion. An ethic that denied human emotions a rightful place in the scheme of things therefore produced paradoxically a preoccupation with extreme emotional states and an extraordinarily passionate and violent tragedy. A Senecan hero (or heroine) was necessarily the obverse of the Stoic sage. I am oversimplifying, of course, and overlooking other forces inherent in Seneca's life and environment.

We have seen, however, that the narrative tragedies took over many of Seneca's dramatic devices or at least assimilated them to similar elements in the native dramatic tradition, though the borrowing grew less obvious. Conversely, imitations of Seneca had much in common with narrative tragedies at first and grew to have more. Seneca's philosophy—his concentration upon human emotions at their peak—presented no problem to Elizabethans, since they largely shared his fundamental psychology and found a better explanation for human depravity in man's fallen nature as a child of Adam. But they did want to see how such emotions reached their peak—or preferably several peaks or a sustained mountain range—and what the valley beyond was like, granted that the hero would himself fall and perish in the descent. So they tended to incorporate Seneca's philosophy and moralizing as purple passages in a larger context. They also tended to see and present that context as one of political affairs, necessarily complex.

Senecan tragedies, therefore, even though produced by learned writers for a learned audience, inevitably took on a more episodic structure than their prototypes, and this multiplication of episodes reflected a concern with narrating a pattern of events rather than studying emotional pathology. But Seneca's plays themselves are certainly not without narrative interest, granted their restricted compass. Even educated Elizabethans may well have been unable to understand Seneca's concentration of action, as they were certainly incapable of appreciating it. Their plays never approximated Seneca's restriction of action, even in the earlier and closer imitations. As time passed, the distinction between narrative and Senecan tragedy, never clearly defined, very nearly disappeared even in the academic play.

This process of dramatic evolution resulted not only in the assimilation just discussed but also in three dramatic types that are predominantly Elizabethan. Once again the word "predominantly" needs to be stressed; but, if the ingredients are old, the end product is substantially different from what had preceded, though the medieval element bulks larger in domestic tragedy, the Senecan in revenge tragedy. In talking about domestic tragedy, revenge tragedy, and quasi-Aristotelian tragedy, I am to some extent defying logic. The first two types rest on plot material, the third on organization. But the categories will be convenient, I hope, even if not altogether sound; furthermore, the domestic tragedies involved a kind of structural principle, in that the material was manipulated in terms of religious concepts to exemplify and inculcate moral principles, and the term "revenge tragedy" has traditionally been restricted to plays reflecting the structural formula invented by Kyd. Partly for this reason, the species set up do not actually overlap.

Both domestic and revenge tragedies are the subject of excellent books, by Henry H. Adams and Fredson Bowers respectively,[28] although Bowers is interested in the entire problem of revenge as a theme in serious tragedies.

[28]Adams, *English Domestic or, Homiletic Tragedy 1575 to 1642* (New York, 1943); Bowers, *Elizabethan Revenge Tragedy 1587-1642* (Princeton, 1940).

The domestic tragedies are simply narratives of a sequence of crime and punishment in the lives of people of middle-class status. They differ, therefore, from other Elizabethan narrative tragedies in the relatively humble rank of the participants and in being set in homes rather than in courts or palaces. But they are thoroughly in accord with normal tragic practice in that all but Heywood's *A Woman Kilde with Kindnesse* (1603, pub. 1607) are based, in part at least, upon actual crimes. The Calverley murder, basic to *A Yorkshire Tragedy* (ca. 1606), also became the basis for *The Miseries of Inforst Mariage* (1607) by George Wilkins, who concentrated upon an earlier part of the account and substituted a happy ending. *Arden of Feversham* (ca. 1591) presents a crime that did attain the status of "history," for it derives from Holinshed's account of a murder committed in 1551/2.

It is also significant that the crimes treated by the various dramatists, including the murder of Arden, were used by preachers and pamphleteers as moral *exempla*, for without exception the domestic tragedies present their material as examples of God's providence in the prevention or revelation of crime and carefully underline the chain of sin or the course of repentance that operates in the guilty. The dramatist is concerned not only with extracting the maximum sensationalism from the crimes that he narrates but also, and very emphatically, with relating his action to that order of grace in which the Christian achieved, or failed to achieve, salvation. If the unsuccessful attempts to murder Arden add suspense to the play, they also illustrate God's providence at work giving Arden time to repent. But Arden fails to heed the call of grace operating through Reede, who begs him to restore his land, for charity if not for justice; it is doubtless providential that his murdered body soon lies unburied in the very land that Reede had begged him to return. As the epilogue says:

> But this above the rest is to be noted:
> Arden lay murthred in that plot of ground
> Which he by force and violence held from Rede.[29]

His wife Alice repents before his bleeding corpse, and we are permitted to hope that her execution, as well as that of her lover's sister Susan, will be accepted by God as an act of penance and that they

[29]*The Shakespeare Apocrypha*, ed. C. F. Tucker Brooke (Oxford, 1908).

46

both will find salvation; her lover Mosbie and Arden's servant Michael die impenitent, and we have little doubt that eternal punishment awaits them.[30] Both Yarington's *Two Lamentable Tragedies* (ca. 1594, pub. 1601) and *A Warning for Faire Women* (pub. 1599) go further and add an apparatus of symbolic characters to reinforce the homily of the text. In short, these plays achieve a nice fusion of sensational drama and pious edification. To what extent the latter was purpose or merely pretext we do not need to determine.

Heywood's *A Woman Kilde with Kindnesse* merits further notice because it furnishes an extraordinary example of a plot affected by theological considerations—that is, of an action conducted with reference to the orders of nature and of grace somewhat as is *King Lear*. It is only in this connection, I think, that domestic tragedy significantly illuminates Shakespeare's practice. Even in the first shock of discovering his wife in adultery with Wendoll, Frankfort hesitates to kill her because to die in an act of sin would damn her for all eternity, and his conduct combines due attention to the just punishment of an erring wife in this world with the salvation of her immortal soul. She must be forced, in fact, to meditate upon her sins so that she may repent; and, when she seeks her husband's forgiveness, just as contemporary teaching enjoined that the penitent sinner should do as part of an amendment of life and a proof thereof, he is bound in Christian charity to reconsider his decision never to see her again. Clearly her death to this world leads to life in the world to come.[31] Heywood, like other Elizabethan playwrights, sees no impiety in attributing to Frankfort something of the providential care associated with the Almighty and in appropriating to himself the functions of the Last Judgment. Both his title and his subplot also suggest that, while sincere in his teaching, he was not insensitive to other and more theatrical considerations.

Revenge occurs frequently as a motive in Elizabethan tragedy. Marlowe's Barabas in *The Jew of Malta* betrays Malta to the Turks because the Christians have seized his wealth. In *Locrine* the ghost of Albanact pursues Humber, crying "Revenge! revenge for blood!" (III.vi.40) and later "*Vindicta, vindicta*" (l.54).[32] In *Alphonsus Em-*

[30]Cf. Adams, *English Domestic or, Homiletic Tragedy*, pp. 104-107.
[31]Ibid., pp. 146-154.
[32]*The Shakespeare Apocrypha*, ed. Brooke.

perour of Germany (ca. 1594, pub. 1654) Alexander becomes the tool of Alphonsus in a series of crimes because he thinks that he is avenging his murdered father, formerly secretary to Alphonsus. Learning that Alphonsus was the true criminal, he murders his master without compunction. Here a character motivated by desire for revenge takes an important part in the action. Were he the protagonist rather than a tool in the play, the unifying principle of which is Alphonsus' Machiavellian ambition, we should have a true revenge tragedy.

The revenge tragedy, as distinguished from tragedies involving revenge, has for its theme the execution of blood revenge by a hero who is faced with almost insuperable difficulties. In practice, the plays in this category all exemplify variations of a formula developed by Thomas Kyd. The earliest extant example and the great exemplar is, of course, *The Spanish Tragedie* (ca. 1587). But no source of the play is known, and Bowers has argued convincingly that the plot of *The Spanish Tragedie* is best explained if we assume that Kyd first wrote the old *Hamlet* of which we have so many traces and then used roughly the same formula in working up *The Spanish Tragedie*.[33] If we reconstruct the old Hamlet play from surviving dramatic versions and the source in Belleforest, it becomes clear that its episodes grow out of the source and are necessary to the action, whereas variants of the same episodes in *The Spanish Tragedie* are poorly motivated or awkwardly worked into the texture of the play. John Ratliff, covering the same ground in greater detail, has unearthed further evidence that elements common to both plays, but not present in the parallel passage in Belleforest, have grown out of hints in other contexts in Belleforest's version.[34] I am convinced, therefore, that Kyd first developed his formula in the old *Hamlet*, working directly from Belleforest and providing necessary departures from its version by levying upon various sources such as Italian stories of intrigue and especially upon Seneca (for example, a ghost to reveal the crime so that it might be doubtful to the revenger and secret from all others but the culprit).

Be that as it may, Kyd established a dramatic formula for the revenge tragedy that gives it a characteristic structure as well as a

[33]*Elizabethan Revenge Tragedy*, pp. 85-97.

[34]"The Kydian Revenge Play," unpublished Stanford University dissertation, 1955.

theme. The formula is roughly as follows. A crime against a close relative is revealed to the hero under circumstances so dubious that he cannot proceed with assurance. He must therefore delay while he acquires further proof. At the same time circumstances are such that he cannot secure justice by legal means, and he is in the only situation in which private revenge, at least according to some Elizabethan theorists, was justified. But, even while waiting for proof, he lashes himself for inaction and is, in general, emotionally close to the breaking point. Finally proof comes, and he is free to act; but he next confronts the culprit under such circumstances that he is prevented from action. He finally achieves revenge, at the cost of his own life, during some kind of celebration or public ceremony, so that the catastrophe develops amid rejoicing. Lust is the main or an important motive in the crime which is to be revenged. This formula operates in detail in the first four of the extant revenge tragedies: Kyd's *The Spanish Tragedie* (ca. 1587), Shakespeare's *Titus Andronicus* (ca. 1594), Marston's *Antonios Revenge* (ca. 1599), and Shakespeare's *Hamlet* (ca. 1601). Purely from the standpoint of plotting, *Hamlet* is obviously the best of these plays. It has strengths peculiarly its own, such as its use of a double uncertainty, so that Claudius must probe Hamlet's antic disposition while Hamlet tests his guilt, and its subplot that parallels and illuminates the main action. It also handles staple situations more effectively than other revenge plays. The play within the play is a plausible means of unmasking a guilty criminal and doubtless was such in the old play; its use for wholesale murder in *The Spanish Tragedie*, to say the least, strains dramatic credibility. Unwillingness to send Claudius to heaven provides a sound reason for delaying revenge, once guilt was known; Marston, in *Antonios Revenge*, was reduced to letting Antonio decide that Piero must suffer longer. Similar comparisons could be multiplied.

The remaining revenge tragedies—Chettle's *Hoffman* (ca. 1603), Tourneur's *The Revengers Tragædie* (ca. 1606) and *The Atheist's Tragedie* (ca. 1609), Chapman's *The Revenge of Bussy D'Ambois* (ca. 1610), and Fletcher's *Valentinian* (ca. 1610-1614)—involve attempts, probably deliberate, to vary the formula in one way or another. Chapman in effect reversed the basic postulate by providing in *The Revenge of Bussy D'Ambois* a revenger, Clermont, who refused altogether to take revenge as such but insisted upon fair and open combat with Montsurry. Even after he had been compelled to trap Montsurry, who would not accept a challenge, he forced the latter to fight instead of proceeding to execution upon a coward as any other revenger would have done. The code of revenge became in this play the code of the duel.

Too often students of Shakespeare have forgotten the simple fact that *Hamlet* is one of the revenge tragedies. Its intellectual subtlety places it far above the other plays, but they raise the same basic ethical problems even though their heroes do not discourse so philosophically or so poetically. Its superiority in thought and poetry only parallels its superiority in many elements of plot construction; it differs from the other plays in quality but not in kind. It is therefore a mistake to treat it critically as parallel to the other tragedies of Shakespeare's maturity. If I may anticipate, it is above all a mistake to regard Hamlet as dramatically akin to Othello or Macbeth or to seek in him for the clearly formulated tragic error of the other great protagonists. A tragic error was not included in the conventional formula of revenge tragedy. It had, in fact, no place in Elizabethan tragedy as a whole.

There are, however, a few tragedies, mostly Shakespeare's, in which one finds a tragic protagonist who is great and potentially good but who falls to destruction because of some moral weakness. These plays, furthermore, are organized in terms of a clearly defined action hinging upon a tragic error of the protagonist which is carefully motivated and fully worked out. They are, however, in the Elizabethan tradition of narrative tragedy; not only can they explore the awful consequences of the hero's error, as classical tragedy had often done, though with less amplitude, but they can also deal at length with what led up to the tragic error.

These tragedies I have called Aristotelian because they embody the kind of tragic action and of tragic hero that Aristotle postulated in his *Poetics* as ideal. The prefix "quasi" recognizes that Aristotle cannot possibly have exercised any direct influence upon these plays. At least, it would strain possibility almost into impossibility to assume that Marlowe and Shakespeare might have known and understood the *Poetics*.

But the fact remains that Marlowe's *Dr. Faustus* (ca. 1588) and all Shakespeare's great tragedies from *Julius Caesar* to *Coriolanus*, except *Hamlet*, present us with a carefully unified plot (except for the clowning in *Faustus*) in which a hero who is great and initially good falls into sin and brings destruction upon himself as well as others. In Shakespeare's plays, at least, an Aristotelian plot with a genuine beginning, middle, and end results from an action involving a fall of one of "those in the enjoyment of great reputation and prosperity" which "is brought upon him not by vice and depravity but by some error of judgement [*hamartia*]."[35] Two other plays to some extent belong in the same category, although they deviate from the norm. Marlowe's *Edward II* (ca. 1592) seems to me an Aristotelian tragedy with respect to Edward himself, but Mortimer, on my reading the antagonist, himself undergoes an obvious *de casibus* tragedy of the rise and fall of an ambitious man. The play is like other tragical histories in being extremely episodic (as becomes painfully evident in a mediocre performance), in scattering its attention, and in carrying the chronicle to a historical, though not a tragic, conclusion in Edward III's triumphant accession to the throne and in the punishment of the guilty. Marlowe's entire final scene devoted to this material is, of course, like the brief tidying up by the ranking survivor which is characteristic of many Elizabethan tragedies, including Shakespeare's. But it far exceeds them in dramatic importance and in its effect of shifting the focus of the play. It may have seemed to Marlowe—as indeed it is—an integral part of the entire historical narrative in that it included "the tragicall fall of proud Mortimer." The very greatness of the play makes it perhaps the most illuminating example of the prevalent failure to distinguish between historical narrative and tragic structure that was noted earlier.

Beaumont and Fletcher's *The Maides Tragedy* (ca. 1610, pub. 1619), because it is of a piece in its unity of action as well as its shallowness of thought, belongs in this category as *Edward II* does not, but it deviates from the norm in two respects. Evadne has fallen from goodness before the play opens, and the choice from which her tragedy directly results is presented as reversing her first sin. But the morality of her choice is thoroughly ambiguous. She goes through the motions of repenting her sin in yielding to the King, it is true, but

[35]*Aristotle on the Art of Poetry*, ed. Ingram Bywater (Oxford, 1909), 1453a 8-10 (p. 35).

her amendment of life takes the form of murder, a sin. The play is therefore ethically irresponsible and uses the conventional views on repentance merely for sensational effect.[36] But Evadne's "repentance" leads to the tragic outcome of the play.

These tragedies are, however, *quasi*-Aristotelian not only in that they do not actually derive from the teaching of the *Poetics*. They also represent a narrower and more elaborately developed set of concepts than those to be found in Aristotle. As heirs of the Christian intellectual tradition, Elizabethan dramatists inherited a habit of precise moral analysis. All men, as children of Adam, are dreadfully liable to sin, and this is true of the greatest and most virtuous as well as of those who seem weaker. The pride of those sure of their virtue may be, in fact, a most dangerous weakness, as in *Othello*. Aristotle's tragic error becomes a moral error—that is, an act of sin. This particularization of the concept of tragic error may perhaps be compared to the intellectual development by which the Aristotelian *hamartia*, or "error" (compare the cognate verb *hamartano*, "miss the mark" or "fail of one's purpose"), became the New Testament *hamartia*, or "sin." The tragic hero's error now consists in an act of will, to which the reason consents, and in the overt deed which results from the act of will. Furthermore, the Aristotelian dictum that character reveals itself in choice gains a new urgency. Insofar as a moral issue was involved, each act of will might confirm a disposition to virtue or sin, or it might initiate the development of a new habit—might be, in specific terms, the first link in the dreadful chain of sin. Each act of moral choice was therefore potentially crucial; and, by converse, every fallen human being might in theory trace his destruction to an initial false step, even though it were only the rejection of the first promptings of grace in the unregenerate. In fact, of course, it would be well-nigh impossible to isolate the crucial moral act among the thousands of venial sins committed by the ordinary human being. But the tragic poet could so simplify his action as to trace cause and effect with dreadful clarity and thereby to provide a powerful moral *exemplum*.

The centering of the dramatic action upon a crucial moral choice and the act resulting from the interior movement of will often pro-

[36]Cf. Dolora G. Cunningham, "The Doctrine of Repentance as a Formal Principle in Some Elizabethan Plays," unpublished Stanford University dissertation, 1954.

duced a genuine reversal or peripety in the Aristotelian sense which became the climax of the play. Dramatically this might be the movement of will, as in *Othello*, the crucial act resulting from it, as in *Julius Caesar*, or even a second resulting act which began the conversion of the individual sin into a habit, as in *Macbeth* (where internal and external action are nicely related, in that the attempt to murder Banquo and Fleance fails of complete success and makes Macbeth's plight worse not only as man but also as king). By contrast, *Richard III*, for example, in which the hero's fortunes rise and fall, has no clear-cut episode that can be singled out as a peripety. But the effectiveness of the reversal depends upon the skill of the dramatist as well as the intellectual scheme. In Marlowe's *Dr. Faustus* the movement of will occurs during the key soliloquy immediately after the prologue, and it is followed almost immediately by the pact with Lucifer. These initiate the action. Thereafter Faustus is repeatedly prompted to repentance, but no fundamental reversal occurs during the play. As a result, *Faustus* may be said to have a beginning and end, but no middle, and this fact militates seriously against its dramatic effectiveness. It was published as *The Tragicall History of D. Faustus* (1604), and the organization of much of the play in terms of a series of episodes, serious or comic, is like the structure of plays categorized as tragical histories. In *King Lear*, on the other hand, the major reversal is the new moral insight that comes to Lear even as he loses his wits during the storm. In *The Maides Tragedy*, too, the reversal involves a new moral insight in that Evadne comes to see, at the point of her brother's sword, the error of her ways. But, as we have noted, the moral insight leads to an immoral act, and the play, though incredibly brilliant as dramatic sensationalism, fails as tragedy simply because it is false to the moral premises from which its pattern of action is derived.

Whatever the exact form of the reversal, the three playwrights —only Shakespeare with complete effectiveness—produced it by shaping their plots in terms of the concepts outlined above. They must reveal the predisposition to error characteristic of the hero as a son of Adam; the forces, external and internal, supernatural and natural, leading to a false moral choice; the deed which results from the choice; and the outcomes both of choice and of deed. The choice would lead to a habit of sin unless it were sooner or later corrected by a valid repentance. "My heart is harden'd, I cannot repent," cries Faustus in despair (II.ii.18).[37] The deed, in tragedy, must produce disaster. Since these plays also inherited the medieval preoccupation with human life as a part of God's larger plan, the effect of the action upon the soul of the individual as finally determined by his state at death must be assessed, even though the dramatist was on very shaky ground theologically since he could not know God's secret purposes even though he might presume to know the secrets of his creature's heart. The effect of the action upon the larger social order in this world must also be indicated, and, in general, the wreckage must be tidied up. The point of the play as a moral *exemplum* must also be made perfectly clear—these are, after all, Elizabethan plays despite their superior excellence. We are all familiar with the final pronouncements usually assigned to the ranking survivor or survivors in Shakespeare's tragedies. But Marlowe's final Chorus warns us to regard Faustus' "hellish fall" and not to meddle with unlawful things. The new Edward III metes out punishment to Mortimer and his mother, Isobel, for their treachery and protests his own "grief and innocency." Lysippus, in concluding *The Maides Tragedy*, must make sure that the murder of the wicked king may not seem an acceptable precedent:

> May this a fair example be to me,
> To rule with temper: for on lustful Kings
> Unlookt for sudden deaths from heaven are sent!
> But curst is he that is their instrument.[38]

To one interested in the history of critical theory, these dramas present a striking paradox. As I remarked above, there is no evidence that either Elizabethan dramatists or Elizabethan critics really understood Aristotle's newly recovered *Poetics*. I have never seen evidence that Italians or English fully grasped Aristotle's concept of the tragic *hamartia* or even of the tragic hero. Yet, if we leave out of account incidentals like Aristotle's generalizations about length of action or his treatment of Greek staging and concentrate upon his notion of a tragic action and a tragic hero or his statements about the

[37] *The Tragical History of Doctor Faustus*, ed. Frederick S. Boas, 2nd ed. (London, 1949).

[38] *The Works of Francis Beaumont and John Fletcher*, ed. A. R. Waller, Vol. I (Cambridge, Eng., 1905).

intellectual substance of tragedy (that is, if we extract the philosophic heart of Aristotle's concept), Marlowe's *Faustus* and even *Edward II* can be discussed in Aristotelian terms, and Shakespeare's mature tragedies are easier to analyze in these terms than Greek tragedy. Or, to be specific, if we omit song and spectacle and concentrate upon Aristotle's other four parts of tragedy—plot, character, diction, and thought—*Macbeth* is a neater example of his principles than his own favorite, Sophocles' *Oedipus Rex*. I take this fact—if it is a fact—to mean simply that two profound thinkers worked out a theory of tragedy in terms of very similar assumptions about the nature of man. If Shakespeare did not know Aristotle's *Poetics*, he did inherit a theology and ethics that derived in important respects from Aristotle. The next chapter will examine the critical tradition for a further explanation of Shakespeare's development of Aristotelian tragedy without Aristotle's guidance.

Chapter Two ☙ THE PURPOSE OF PLAYING:
THE ELIZABETHAN VIEW OF TRAGEDY

THIS SURVEY of Elizabethan critical theories, like the preceding survey of extant tragedies, must begin with statistics. Most of us inevitably think of published material in terms reflecting the staggering output of modern presses. It therefore takes a continuous effort to keep in the forefront of our consciousness the slight foundations upon which generalizations about literature of the sixteenth century rest. And Elizabethan writers themselves mislead us. William Webbe, for example, begins "A Preface to the Noble Poets of England" introducing *A Discourse of English Poetrie* (1586): "Among the innumerable sortes of Englyshe Bookes, and infinite fardles of printed pamphlets, wherewith thys Countrey is pestered, all shoppes stuffed, and every study furnished: the greatest part I thinke, in any one kinde, are such as are either meere Poeticall, or which tende in some respecte (as either in matter or forme) to Poetry."[1] But a check of the chronological listing of titles in the *Short-Title Catalogue* reveals that in 1586, the year of Webbe's *Discourse*, 159 items are listed as published in England, of which five are editions of the Bible and fifteen official documents (two French). In contrast, twelve titles might be classified as prose literature, fourteen as poetic. The comparable figures for 1585 are 198 titles, of which seven represent prose literature, seven plays and pageants, and ten poetry, half in Latin. Many of the books are very slight in bulk. Some of them, however, are still important to students. In 1585 came editions of *The Paradise of Daintie Devises*, Lyly's *Euphues*, Preston's *Cambises*, Wilson's *The Arte of Rhetorique*, and the poems of Surrey. In 1586 appeared Bright's *A Treatise of Melancholy*, Angell Day's *The English Secretorie*, Lyly's *Euphues and his England*, Spenser's *The Shepheardes' Calender*, Warner's *Albions England*, and translations

---

[1]In *Elizabethan Critical Essays*, ed. G. Gregory Smith (Oxford, 1904), I, 226-227.

of La Primaudaye's *French Academy* (in part) and of *Lazarillo de Tormes*. In addition, of course, a good many ballads were printed and circulated each year, and Webbe may be thinking of these, too. I do not vouch for the absolute accuracy of my statistics. I have not crosschecked elaborately, since exactness is not necessary to my purpose. But it is obvious, I hope, that there is a great deal more reading matter, quantitatively speaking, on the magazine rack in any corner drugstore than appeared in England during 1585 or 1586 (or any year, probably, until after 1600). There is several times as much if we include a rack or two of pocket books. England was pestered with "innumerable" or "infinite" pamphlets only by contrast to medieval standards before the invention of printing. This fact itself is important, of course, to a discussion of Shakespeare. It would be rash to assume, in the absence of specific evidence, that a modern novelist had read even outstanding works of fiction by his contemporaries, so great is the output of novels. It is highly probable, however, that a man of Shakespeare's intellect and reading habits would have read any book bearing on his special interests. He would have had ample time to do so.

Literary criticism, in any age, amounts to a small part of the total literary output, and the proportion was very much smaller in Shakespeare's day than in ours, since the whole modern apparatus for evaluating new books was unknown. The reader needed no guide in his choice, for no choice was forced upon him. Generalizations about critical theories will inevitably rest, therefore, upon a few writers, and in the following discussion the same names will recur monotonously. The small number of writers is not a serious limitation, however; for with a few significant exceptions those who do exist merely repeat with slight variations the same formulas and the same ideas. Nowhere, in fact, is the Elizabethan habit of thinking in commonplaces more apparent than in literary criticism, which is very largely an elaboration of a few traditional formularies. The best approach to a study of theories about the drama will probably be to consider these commonplaces and notice their reappearance in significant writers. We shall begin with accepted notions about poetry as a whole, including drama, and then proceed to those about drama in particular. Many of these notions will be thoroughly familiar, but I hope that we may acquire a new perspective toward them.

The most important nexus of ideas about poetry, including drama, is that reflected in Sidney's definition: "Poesie therefore is an arte of imitation, for so Aristotle termeth it in his word *Mimesis*, that is to say, a representing, counterfetting, or figuring foorth: to speake metaphorically, a speaking picture: with this end, to teach and delight."[2] This definition is, as everyone knows, a combination of sources. The concept that poetry is imitation came ultimately from Plato. The comparison of poetry to a picture, which was a Renaissance commonplace, apparently derives in this form from Plutarch;[3] but it had the authority of Horace's *ut pictura poesis*.[4] The notion that all poetry should simultaneously teach and delight represents the typical Renaissance oversimplification of Horace. The power of habit to overcome scholarship is perfectly illustrated by Webbe, who first says that poetry should "mingle delight with profitt" and then, for authority, blandly translates correctly the passage in Horace: "All Poets desire either by their works to profitt or delight men, or els to joyne both profitable and pleasant lessons together for the instruction of life."[5]

In the same context one regularly finds, as one does in Sidney and Webbe, the notion that poetry should move to virtuous action. The addition of "moving" as an end of poetry has been traced to the rhetorical tradition, but actually it would inevitably occur to anyone who tried to explain how poetry should mingle delight and profit in terms of Renaissance psychology. Richard Willes puts the problem succinctly in the Epistle to William Cecil prefixed to a volume of Latin poems published in 1573: Since youth, he argues, is especially attached to the lusts of the flesh, will glory have any chance

---

[2] *An Apologie for Poetrie*, in *Elizabethan Critical Essays*, I, 158.

[3] Cf. *Elizabethan Critical Essays*, I, 386-387. Plutarch says: "We shall steady the young man still more if, at his first entrance into poetry, we give a general description of the poetic art as an imitative art and faculty analogous to painting. And let him not merely be acquainted with the oft-repeated saying that 'poetry is articulate painting, and painting is inarticulate poetry', but let us teach him in addition that when we see a lizard or an ape or the face of Thersites in a picture, we are pleased with it and admire it, not as a beautiful thing, but as a likeness" ("How the Young Man Should Study Poetry," 17-18, in *Plutarch's Moralia*, tr. Frank Cole Babbitt [London, 1927], I, 91, 93).

[4] *Ars Poetica*, l. 361.

[5] *A Discourse of English Poetrie*, in *Elizabethan Critical Essays*, I, 250.

unless the seductive delights of literature nourish the minds of the young?[6] The Puritan attack upon poetry, and especially upon plays, lent a new urgency to the poet's assertion that his blandishments made his teaching produce positive results in action, but this view of poetry was at one with the practical bias and the moral seriousness of Elizabethan England. Witness, for example, the Elizabethan grammar school, in which every other aim was firmly subordinated to that of inculcating sound morality. It is, I think, a mistake so to focus upon the Puritan attack that one overlooks the traditional basis of this view of poetry and its thorough harmony with Elizabethan habits of thought.

In some particulars, however, the critical tradition was confusing. From our point of view, the most important is that all attempts to categorize literature failed to see drama as a genre of which tragedy and comedy are species.[7] This failure was itself a serious impediment to meaningful discussion of drama as a form of imitation. But two of the more original attempts to categorize poetry also have something to show about attitudes toward tragedy.

The first of these efforts, that of Webbe in *A Discourse of English Poetrie* (1586), represents a thoroughgoing classification in terms of content or rather of mood. Webbe has no notion whatever of drama as a kind of imitation or as a literary form with an appropriate structure. Comedy includes epigrams, elegies, and "delectable ditties"; tragedy, "what soever is poetically expressed in sorrow and heavines"; a third unnamed category, everything else.[8]

In his *The Arte of English Poesie* (1589), George Puttenham attempted to classify poetry in terms of its use, and his results show a great deal about his view of the purpose of poetry and the nature of drama. Poets, he tells us, next to praising God, "chiefly studied the rebuke of vice, and to carpe at the common abuses. . . . the said aun-cient Poets used for that purpose three kinds of poems reprehensive, to wit, the *Satyre*, the *Comedie*, and the *Tragedie*." Comedy grew out

---

[6]*Poematum Liber* (London, 1573), sig. Aiii^v. Cf. Edmund Spenser, *The Shep-heardes Calender*, "October," *Minor Poems*, I, 96, ll. 19-24, in *The Works of Edmund Spenser, A Variorum Edition*, ed. Edwin Greenlaw et al. (Baltimore, 1932-49).

[7]Cf. Ascham, *The Scholemaster*, in *Elizabethan Critical Essays*, I, 23; Sidney, *An Apologie for Poetrie*, ibid., I, 159.

[8]In *Elizabethan Critical Essays*, I, 248-250.

of satire and added solace and recreation to "the good amendment of man by discipline and example." In tragedies the infamous lives of tyrants were exposed, "their wickednes reproched, their follies and extreme insolencies derived, and their miserable ends painted out in playes and pageants, to shew the mutabilitie of fortune, and the just punishment of God in revenge of a vicious and evill life."[9] Both in approximating comedy to satire and in seeing tragedy as a moral *exemplum* of the fall of the great and sinful, Puttenham is thoroughly in accord with Elizabethan practice. His categorizing is based altogether upon use, and, to that extent, it has merit and consistency. It also gives the standard explanation of how tragedy may teach. But it obviously overlooks distinctions of meter and of form, except insofar as comedy and tragedy are differentiated from satire by dramatic presentation.

One more traditional attitude is of interest because it can be traced into Shakespeare. When Hamlet tells the players that "the censure of the which one [the judicious] must, in your allowance, o'erweigh a whole theatre of others" (III.ii.29-30), he is taking the prevailing side in a critical argument of some importance. Ascham had cited classical precedent: "For, as the worthie Poetes in *Athens* and *Rome* were more carefull to satisfie the judgement of one learned than rashe in pleasing the humor of a rude multitude, even so if men in England now had the like reverend regard to learning, skill, and judgement, and durst not presume to write except they came with the like learnyng. . . ."[10] George Gascoigne was equally emphatic in speaking for himself: "For I esteeme more the prayse of one learned Reader, than I regard the curious carping of ten thousande unlettered tattlers."[11] Strangely enough, the most emphatic dissent that I know of came from an academic dramatist writing in Latin for a university audience. In his epistle "Ad Criticum" prefixed to *Ulysses Redux* (Oxford, 1592), William Gager defended his somewhat unusual procedure in dramatizing the last episode of *The Odyssey*: "In fact, I put forward this tragedy or play or chronicle history or whatever it is

[9]In *Elizabethan Critical Essays*, II, 32, 33, 35.

[10]*The Scholemaster*, in *Elizabethan Critical Essays*, I, 31.

[11]*The Posies*, in *The Complete Works of George Gascoigne*, ed. John W. Cunliffe, I (Cambridge, Eng., 1907), 7.

right and proper to call it, not for an assay of poetic art like that of the goldsmith but for the measuring scale of popular judgment, and I poured it out rather than wrote it."[12]

Drama was governed, of course, by the concepts of poetry just described. They had been developed, in fact, largely with reference to drama. Not only Aristotle's *Poetics*, which was little known, but also Horace's *Ars Poetica*, which was a major source of critical doctrine, were primarily concerned with drama. There was no doubt, therefore, that comedy and tragedy, like all poetry, should teach and delight. The problem was simply to show how drama might teach and move to virtuous action. We have already seen Puttenham's solution. Thomas Heywood merely restated the traditional view in the explanation that he gave twenty years later in *An Apology for Actors* (ca. 1608, pub. 1612): "If we present a Tragedy, we include the fatall and abortive ends of such as commit notorious murders, which is aggravated and acted with all the Art that may be, to terrifie men from the like abhorred practises."[13]

But the English Renaissance also inherited a considerable body of purely dramatic theory. This came primarily from three sources: the treatises on comedy which went under the name of Aelius Donatus and were published in the more elaborate editions of Terence; Horace and Aristotle as schematized by Italian critics; and the practice of Seneca and Terence. To these we should perhaps add the assimilation into comic theory, especially by Jonson, of a good deal of theorizing by Horace and Juvenal about the nature and ends of satire.

The meat of "Donatus," for our purposes, is contained in a few short passages. The first of these enshrined the indifference to drama as a form and the habit of equating comedy with a happy ending, tragedy with death. "Homer," says Donatus, "is the principal font of most poetic theory, and he also provided examples for these poems and gave rules as if by the law of his own poems—who is shown to have made the *Iliad* like a Tragedy, the *Odissey* as the image of a

---

[12]"Equidem ego hanc sive tragediam, sive fabulam, sive narrationem historicam, sive quicquid eam dici jus fasque est, non ad exquisitam artis poeticæ tanquam aurificis statêram, sed ad popularis judicii trutinam exigendam proposui, & effudi potiús quám scripsi."

[13]*An Apology for Actors* (London, 1612), Bk. III, sig. F3ᵛ.

comedy."[14] From this it is but a step to Webbe's classification of poems, noticed above, which in its emphasis upon contents completely obliterates the notion of drama as a mode of imitation.

Two other passages describing the subject matter proper to comedy and tragedy to some extent duplicate each other, since "Donatus" is in fact two treatises spliced end to end. Together they furnished doctrine accepted by all Elizabethans. First of all, they further reinforced, just as they had originally helped to develop, the medieval tendency to regard the outcome as the test of comedy or tragedy rather than the kind of action involved. One sentence, in particular, became a commonplace. The best-known rendering is Thomas Heywood's: "Comedies begin in trouble, and end in peace; Tragedies begin in calmes, and end in tempest."[15] This is, in general, true of Elizabethan drama, and the exception to this rule to be found in Shakespeare's tragedies constitutes, as we shall see, a major subordination on his part of dramatic theory to metaphysical principles.

A second effect was to distinguish social strata appropriate to comedy and tragedy. Tragedy was to be concerned with courts and noble personages, comedy with the life of ordinary citizens.[16] The precepts of Donatus and the practice of Terence both encouraged a comedy of London middle-class life which might also involve country gentry, the middle-aged acquiring wealth and the young spending and marrying. Most Elizabethan comedies belong in this category. The romantic comedies of Shakespeare are, of course, an exception to this tendency, and, in their derivation from contemporary romances or novellas which lead to concern with courts and noble personages, as well as in other respects, they are in the line of development to tragicomedy.

Donatus' remark, in the same context, that tragedy is often derived from historical fact is thoroughly in accord with Elizabethan practice, and it was reinforced by Italian theory based upon the notion

---

[14]"Homerus tamen, qui ferè omnis Poeticæ largissimus fons est, etiam his carminibus exempla præbuit, et velut quadam suorum operum lege præscripsit: qui Iliadem instar Tragœdiæ, Odysseam ad imaginem comoediae fecisse monstratur." "De Tragoedia ac comœdia non pauca, ex Aelio Donato," *P. Terentii Comoediae opera Des. Erasmi Roter. Castigatae* (Basel, 1534), sig. B2v.

[15]Heywood, *An Apology for Actors*, Bk. III, sig. F1v; Terence, *Comoediae*, sigs. B4v-B5.

[16]Terence, *Comoediae*, sig. B5r-v.

that deeds of tragic horror and grandeur would not be unrecorded in history if they had occurred and that a historical basis was therefore necessary to credibility. But Italian logic, like Italian critics, had little influence upon Elizabethan practice, and it is probable that the tradition which Donatus enshrined was the primary force at work.

Most important of all, however, was Donatus' emphasis upon externals of plot rather than upon the dramatic action itself. Heywood is borrowing from Donatus when he writes: "[Comedies] are distributed into foure parts, the *Prologue*, that is, the preface; the *Protasis*, that is, the proposition, which includes the first Act, and presents the Actors; the *Epitasis*, which is the businesse and body of the Comedy; the last the *Catastrophe*, and conclusion."[17] Ben Jonson applies the same structural theory to tragedy.[18] But beyond this rudimentary analysis of structure Heywood, like Donatus, does not go. Any grammarian can talk of sad or happy endings, social rank and historical material, or even the four parts of a play. He can also, be it added, lay down rules for the unities. But it takes a profoundly philosophic mind like Aristotle's to speculate about the nature of tragic action or of the tragic hero. This kind of thinking does not appear in English remarks on drama, and the failure to do this kind of thinking is reflected in the chaotic practice that we noticed in the preceding chapter. To some extent, at least, the faulty performance of Elizabethan dramatists probably reflected the faulty training, ultimately derived from Donatus, that they received in grammar school. We shall recur to this point.

In addition to "Donatus," Horace and Aristotle, in that order of importance, contributed to Elizabethan dramatic theory. From Horace came the all-important emphasis upon decorum, both of characterization and of speech. The notion that human beings of different ages, sex, and rank had characteristic manners was a fundamental part of Elizabethan ethics and psychology—and even law. It was, after all, legal for a nobleman to wear an ornate costume forbidden to the yeoman, and gradations in social rank were an omnipresent part of English institutions. Popular treatises on psychology and manners are full of passages describing the characteristic be-

---

[17] *An Apology for Actors*, Bk. III, sig. F1v; Terence, *Comoediae*, sig. B5.

[18] Cf. *Critical Essays of the Seventeenth Century*, ed. J. E. Spingarn, I (Oxford, 1908), 58.

havior of various kinds of people. Jaques' disquisition on the seven ages of man is merely a study in decorum by ages that can be paralleled widely in various manuals of the times. Horace's admonitions that various characters must be true to type therefore seemed eminently reasonable. So did his injunctions that they must talk in a way appropriate to station and background. Distinctions of this kind were a fundamental part of the rhetorical tradition, with its insistence upon levels of style and propriety in speech. It is no accident, therefore, that kings talk like kings and clowns like clowns, and it required no great skill for the dramatist to make them do so by applying principles that he had been learning since childhood.

From Aristotle came the doctrine of the unities—or rather from Aristotle's sanction. For it is well known that Aristotle required only unity of action and remarked that the tragic action was usually confined to one day. The most extreme formulation of the three unities of action, time, and place comes from Castelvetro, who was actually reasoning logically from the mistaken premise that verisimilitude was impossible unless the action presented in the play closely approximated in time and space the action on the stage. But it seems to me that historians of literary criticism have vastly exaggerated the practical importance of this doctrine for the Elizabethan period. It is perfectly obvious that Elizabethan playwrights generally ignored it, and even so neoclassical and doctrinaire a dramatist as Jonson, who does talk of the doctrine, violates it without compunction when it suits his purpose to do so. Shakespeare, too, paid his respect to the unities in writing *The Tempest*, though one can but wonder why. The great prestige of Sidney has led us, however, to overemphasize the attention given to the unities by theoretical writers as contrasted with playwrights. So far as I know, the passage in which Sidney condemns contemporary dramatists for violating the unities cannot be paralleled in scope among the few other writers on dramatic theory. They are almost entirely concerned with the principles from Donatus and Horace and with explaining how drama may teach and move to virtue.

The same thing may be said of Aristotle's catharsis of pity and fear which so preoccupied Italian critics. It simply did not concern Elizabethan writers. Once again Heywood is a good example, since he writes at the end of the period under discussion and is nothing if not conventional in thought. He argues that a description "can neither shew action, passion, motion, or any other gesture, to moove the spirits of the beholder to admiration." But "so bewitching a thing is lively and well spirited action, that it hath power to new mold the harts of the spectators and fashion them to the shape of any noble and notable attempt."[19] Obviously he is thinking of drama as moving to virtuous action; he also has in mind the ancient doctrine stressed by Minturno that poetry should lead to *admiratio,* or wonder, which had far more influence than Aristotle's notion of catharsis. But occasionally one does encounter an Aristotelian echo. The most interesting, for our purposes, are three allusions in Shakespeare which seem to prove that he was familiar with theories as to the outcome of tragedy. As Fortinbras appears at the end of *Hamlet,* Horatio asks:

> What is it ye would see?
> If aught of woe or wonder, cease your search.
>
> (V.ii.373-374)

Toward the end of *Lear,* Albany commands:

> Produce the bodies, be they alive or dead.
> The judgement of the heavens, that makes us tremble,
> Touches us not with pity.
>
> (V.iii.230-232)

Both are comments upon a tragic outcome. The first combines pity, the proper response to woe, and wonder;[20] the second, fear and pity. Horatio's reaction to the ghost completes the circle: "it harrows me with fear and wonder" (I.i.44). Milton, of course, makes the echo of Aristotle unmistakable in what may also be an echo of Shakespeare, when the Attendant Spirit is "harrow'd with grief and fear" at the sound of the Lady's voice (*Comus,* l. 564).[21]

I remarked, in speaking of decorum, that the rhetorical tradition operated powerfully in developing a sense of style appropriate to speaker and occasion. It also supplied the whole apparatus of tropes

---

[19] *An Apology for Actors,* Bk. I, sigs. B3ᵛ-B4.

[20] Cf. J. V. Cunningham, *Woe or Wonder: The Emotional Effect of Shakespearean Tragedy* (Denver, 1951), pp. 62-105.

[21] *The Works of John Milton,* ed. Frank Allen Patterson (New York, 1931-38), I, Pt. I, 106.

and schemes which playwrights used to give to their works the amplitude appropriate to tragedy in an age that still preserved the medieval notion of poetry as matter plus the colors of rhetoric—that is, artful schemes of sentence structure and figures of speech. But I do not propose to discuss these matters or the much larger and more important question of the ways in which rhetorical training guided the playwrights in organizing long speeches or perhaps even whole scenes. A careful study of these larger aspects of the application of rhetorical training in Elizabethan literature seems to me one of the major gaps in our critical apparatus.

All of these critical principles were disseminated in two ways. So far we have been noting their appearance in formal treatises or occasional remarks about dramatic theory. But in fact they operated in England before any of the critical discussions had been written. In the dedicatory epistle to *Christus Redivivus* (1540), Nicholas Grimald relates that his tutor "Johannes Aerius" approved the play and urged him to publish it and then summarizes the tutor's critical comments at some length.[22]

This approval, incidentally, is interesting as a sidelight on what was said about academic drama in the previous chapter. L. R. Merrill comments in his preface to the text and translation of the play: "The play presents a wider departure from the classical model of the drama than one would expect from a student and a devotee of the humanities. Indeed, Grimald's play rather invites comparison with the popular, or Shakespearean, variety."[23] Be that as it may, Grimald and his tutor clearly believe that drama should delight and teach and move to virtuous action; they attach great importance to decorum; they know the staple material in Donatus and accept Terence as the standard for comic writing, though they are aware of Plautus; they are familiar with the unities of place and time. They regard rhetoric as providing the specific techniques of composition to be used in solving the problems of comic decorum. In short, Grimald very nearly provides a digest of ideas about poetry and drama that have been outlined in the preceding pages. It seems a fair inference that Grimald and his tutor got most of their ideas from the traditional ap-

[22]*The Life and Poems of Nicholas Grimald*, ed. and trans. L. R. Merrill (New Haven, 1925), pp. 103-105, 109-111.
[23]Ibid., pp. 58-59.

paratus used in the teaching of Terence. The study of Terence and Seneca was, in fact, a major source of critical ideas about drama. Commentaries on Terence were far more important than Seneca even in the development of tragic theory, because no such body of critical theory had been attached to the latter. Unless I have overlooked it, there is no edition of Seneca approaching in elaborateness the great folio Terence of Joannes de Roigny, published in Paris in 1552,[24] which collected and reprinted Renaissance as well as late classical commentary, and there was no traditional apparatus for dealing with Seneca's plays comparable to that associated with Terence. All this must be qualified, of course, by the fact that if we turn from dramatic theory to the details of writing tragedies, Seneca's example was the vital and pervasive influence.

Erasmus' 1534 edition of Terence published by Froben at Basel, which may be taken as an example because it was much less elaborate and therefore more likely to be in a schoolmaster's hands, consists of a dedicatory epistle; a treatise by Erasmus on the meters of Terence; a section on "the life of Terence, and some remarks on tragedy and comedy, from Aelius Donatus"; the texts of the plays, with marginal notes on meters and problems of scansion. Each play is preceded by a "periocha," or verse summary, of the action by C. Sulpitius Apollinaris; the *Eunuch* is also prefaced by very brief character sketches of the dramatis personae. The book concludes with "Arguments" to the various plays, not identified but attributed to Melanchthon in the 1552 folio of Terence. These are arranged under "Protasis," "Epitasis," and "Catastrophe." The argument to the *Andria* contains interesting remarks on what the students should get out of the play. First of all, they should learn to converse in Latin, Terence being the best guide available. Then they should be reminded of the material in "Donatus." As they study different plays, the teacher should discuss with them the rhetorical structure of the play and its parts, the *Andria* being like an oration of the deliberative cause. Lessons about human nature and conduct should be derived from the various characters. Above all, the teacher "must cause the boys to

[24]*Comoediae, Andria, Eunuchus, Heautontimorumenos, Adelphi, Hecyra, Phormio, Ex emendatissimis ac fide dignissimis codicibus summa diligentia castigatæ, Versibus in suas dimensiones restitutis, ac variis lectionibus in margine appositis. Elenchum interpretum, qui in has Comœdias doctè simul & eruditè scripserunt, proxima subinde pagina demonstrabit.*

marvel at this author so that they may love him. . . . From these examples let the boys grow accustomed to find words and figures of Latin speech and a mode of speaking."[25]

This edition probably gives a pretty good indication of the way Elizabethans read comedy and, more to our purpose, drama of all kinds. It also suggests how plays were taught in schools. One notices, first of all, an extreme preoccupation with metrical analysis, which seems almost to have taken precedence over everything else.[26] Interpretation of the plays was thoroughly rhetorical. Plays and scenes were treated simply as examples of the various types of orations and themes taught in contemporary texts such as the *Ad Herennium* or Aphthonius' *Progymnasmata*. The verse was analyzed for examples of various figures of speech. All this included, of course, the attention to the characteristics of various kinds of people and of emotional states that was a traditional part of rhetoric. It merged easily with attention to episodes in the plays as *exempla* to illustrate various maxims of conduct. I say "maxims" because this criticism does not rise to a consideration of fundamental principles but is concerned rather with the level of teaching to be found in the *Moral Distichs* of Cato, a standard school text, or, for that matter, in Lyly's *Euphues* or Polonius' advice to Laertes. As we shall see, Shakespeare learned to write the maxims, as well as the *exempla*, into his plays.

The insertion of "sentences"—aphoristic statements that summed up a situation or dilemma or moral principle—was, in fact, a staple part of Elizabethan dramatic practice. It had, of course, the authority of Seneca's constant use of aphorism, and his plays were printed in England at least once with the "sentences" standing out in a different type face.[27] The practice, and in fact the logic just hypothecated, is summarized in George Chapman's Epistle prefixed to *The Revenge of Bussy D'Ambois* (pub. 1613): "Poor envious souls they are that cavil at truth's want in these natural fictions; material instruction, elegant and sententious excitation to virtue, and deflection from her

[25]Sigs. X1-X5.

[26]Cf. Ascham, *The Scholemaster*, in *Elizabethan Critical Essays*, I, 24.

[27]*L. & M. Annæi Senecae Tragoediæ*, ed. Thomas Farnaby (London, 1624). Earlier editions published in 1589 and in 1613 (by Farnaby) do not have this feature; but the topical index in the former was largely based on sentences, and the "Index Rerum Maxime Memorabilium" in the latter provided ready guides to many of them.

contrary, being the soul, limbs, and limits of an autentical tragedy."[28] But Jonson, once again, is an even better witness; and he implies, both in what he mentions as excellences of a tragic writer and in what he fails to mention, much of what has so far been said. Note especially the first place given to fidelity to history. Anticipating objections that *Sejanus* (pub. 1605) "is no true *Poëme* in the strict Lawes of *Time* . . . as also in the want of a proper *Chorus*," he retorts: "if in truth of Argument, dignity of Persons, gravity and height of Elocution [style], fulnesse and frequencie of Sentence, I have discharg'd the other offices of a *Tragick* writer, let not the absence of these *Formes* be imputed to me."[29] For this reliance upon "sentences" Jonson had the authority not only of Seneca but of the Latin version of the *Poetics* which he used, that of Theodore Goulston, who rendered Aristotle's *diávoia*, or "thought," one of the elements necessary to tragedy, as *sententia*.[30]

To return to the teaching of drama, there was some discussion of parts of the play and of sources of dramatic conflict, but, so far as I can see, no attention was paid to the total play as a work of art or to dramatic as opposed to rhetorical or ethical values. Dramatic structure, in particular, was lost in rhetoric and ethics. The edition of Terence discussed was probably untypical, if at all, rather in the attention that it did pay to dramatic values, however slight, than in its failure to go further. In 1540 John Palsgrave published his *Ecphrasis Anglica in comoediam Acolasti*. The *Acolastus* was a Latin comedy on the prodigal-son story published in 1529 by the Dutch humanist Willem de Volder, who called himself Fullonius or, in a Greek version, Gnaphaeus. It was acted at Trinity College, Cambridge, in 1560/1.[31] Palsgrave had the praiseworthy idea of demonstrating how

[28]*The Plays and Poems of George Chapman: The Tragedies*, ed. Thomas Marc Parrott (London, 1910), p. 77. The first clause shows unusual aesthetic grasp, which Chapman undoubtedly possessed; but he was trying to defend an unhistorical sequel to a historical play.

[29]In *Critical Essays of the Seventeenth Century*, I, 10.

[30]*Aristotelis de poetica liber, Latine conversus, et analytica methodo illustratus* (London, 1623), p. 15. Goulston glosses: "Tertio gradu stat *Sententia*: Cujus vis est, ut verbis rationes exprimere possis, rei insitas atque aptas." This translation would repay careful study as an example of the way in which Renaissance scholars adapted the classics to their own preconceptions.

[31]Frederick S. Boas, *University Drama in the Tudor Age* (Oxford, 1914), p. 19. The colophon of Palsgrave's version indicates that the play was composed by Wylliam Fullonius for performance at The Hague in 1529.

a play should be taught, so that English speech might be made uniform, schoolmasters might know how to do their job, and boys might enjoy their studies (and incidentally learn far more).[32] But the book consists in fact of a pedestrian translation, in which the sense gets lost in alternative versions of the Latin and the marginal notes concentrate upon Latin idioms, figures of speech, and adages to be remembered. The prefatory "declaration what the names used by the auctour in this Comedy, do signifye" involves something amounting to brief character sketches as well as etymologies. After the first scene comes "A briefe Introductory to have some generall knowledge of the dyvers sortes of meters Used of our auctour in this Comedye," and each scene is headed by a statement of the Latin meters used. There is, however, no discussion of the general meaning of the play, although Gnaphaeus had thoughtfully provided a Peroration explaining the moral lessons to be gained.

It is, in short, a fair inference that the study of Terence or Seneca did not carry the understanding of drama beyond the concepts already outlined. The important texts of Terence did make available Donatus and other rudimentary commentaries that reflected the critical tradition about drama. They did point out how principles of composition were used by a working dramatist. They did exemplify the organization of material into acts and scenes, something to which theorists were indifferent.[33] In these respects they enjoyed the advantage that an example always possesses in contrast to theoretical precepts, and their importance was very great. But they did not stimulate a more penetrating consideration of the nature of drama or even of dramatic structure.

Let me hasten to add that what precedes is not intended as a criticism of Elizabethan educational methods. The evidence actually indicates that the teaching of Terence was considerably broader and more meaningful than the methods characteristic of college courses in this country, which often concentrate upon interpreting the text on the purely verbal level and add only some discussion of the nature and origins of Roman comedy and of metrics. The concern with

---

[32]John Palsgrave, *Ecphrasis Anglica in comoediam Acolasti* (London, 1540), sigs. bii-biii.

[33]This problem has been elaborately investigated, of course, by Thomas W. Baldwin in *Shakspere's Five-Act Structure* (Urbana, Ill., 1947).

ethical principles characteristic of Elizabethan instruction is gone today, as is the thorough training in rhetoric. I am myself convinced that Elizabethan grammar-school teachers did a very good job, and I have no intention of complaining that they did not accomplish more than they did. I merely wish to emphasize that, except for the very great value of studying specific examples of dramatic art, formal teaching of the Latin dramatists did not carry the investigation of dramatic structure and methodology beyond the very narrow limits characteristic of the critical writing.

In summary, the Elizabethan notion of drama regarded it as at one with all poetry in being an art of imitation and in having as its final cause to delight and teach and move to virtuous action. If tragedy, it must "begin in calmes, and end in tempest," and it must deal with historical material occurring in courts and among the great. If comedy, it must "begin in trouble, and end in peace," and it must be "the imitation of life, the glasse of custome, and the image of truth," "comprehending civill and domesticke things."[34] Its events should be fictitious. Both tragedy and comedy must observe decorum in characterization and in language. Both consisted of four parts: the prologue, or preface; the protasis, or proposition (we should call it the dramatic exposition); the epitasis, or body of the play; and the catastrophe, or conclusion. As to the unities, more attention was apparently paid to unity of time than to unity of action, and many writers ignored the unities altogether.

A moment's reflection will show that the series of ideas just outlined actually raised more problems than they solved. And the problems were fundamental. Perhaps the most important aesthetically and certainly the oldest historically was the nature of poetic imitation. Ironically enough, Elizabethan writers took over Plato's notion of imitation even while crying out indignantly against the rejection of poets which was for him the logical consequence of his view. As Ascham puts it, "The whole doctrine of Comedies and Tragedies is a perfite *imitation,* or faire livelie painted picture of the life of everie degree of man. Of this *Imitation* writeth Plato at large in 3. *de Rep.,* but it doth not moch belong at this time to our purpose."[35] Plato's philosophical discussion is not to Ascham's purpose because he is in-

[34]Heywood, *An Apology for Actors,* Bk. III, sig. F1v.
[35]In *Elizabethan Critical Essays,* I, 7.

terested in the practical business of how the writer goes about imitating, not because he rejects Plato's views. "Everie degree" is the significant phrase in his definition, for, like his age, he has no concept of an art that deals in universals. Tragedy and comedy are concerned with particulars. The same medieval taste for amplitude of realistic detail, as well as the medieval view of tragedy, is indicated by Spenser's words attributed to Melpomene:

> My part it is and my professed skill
> The Stage with Tragick buskin to adorne,
> And fill the Scene with plaint and outcries shrill
> Of wretched persons, to misfortune borne:
> But none more tragick matter I can finde
> Than this, of men depriv'd of sense and minde.

> For all mans life me seemes a Tragedy,
> Full of sad sights and sore Catastrophees;
> First comming to the world with weeping eye,
> Where all his dayes like dolorous Trophees,
> Are heapt with spoyles of fortune and of feare,
> And he at least laid forth on balefull beare.[36]

Jonson, however, partly because he was a man of genuine learning, shows most clearly of all the limitations of this view of imitation. It is notorious that he weakened *Catiline* by writing whole passages of Cicero into his text, and his preface to *Sejanus* tells us why he did so: ". . . least in some nice nostrill the *Quotations* might savour affected, I doe let you know that I abhor nothing more, and have onely done it to shew my integrity in the *Story*. . . ."[37] We shall recur to the consequences of this view, but the important thing is that Jonson feels his integrity as a dramatist to consist in minute fidelity to the historical sources. The imitation is of life as it has been lived, not of life as it might or should be lived. Other historical dramatists, who adhered much less carefully to their sources, deviated in the interests of easy and effective dramaturgy rather than because they differed from Jonson in their view of poetic imitation, which is, to repeat, certainly not Aristotle's. If anything, it is Plato's.

This view of imitation shows, among other things, how uncrit-

---

[36]"The Teares of the Muses," *Minor Poems*, II, 67, ll. 151-162, in *Works*, ed. Greenlaw et al.

[37]In *Critical Essays of the Seventeenth Century*, I, 10-11.

ically Elizabethans read their classical sources. But it also provides one of several reasons why the doctrine of imitation took the pedantic form that it did. Jonson's view implies, logically, that any series of related events sufficiently historical and horrible to constitute a warning are material for tragedy. It provides no theoretical basis for plot structure or for the selection of details, except the requirement of clear narrative. In other words, it squares with what we have seen to be Elizabethan practice. But classical drama did have structure, and the only course left open, at least to scholars sensitive to the excellences even of Seneca, was to imitate dramatists who had succeeded. In the absence of principles, a poet had to proceed by rule of thumb. For Ascham, in other words, Plato was not to his purpose because he was too theoretical. "The second kind of *Imitation* is to folow for learning of tonges and sciences the best authors. . . . The third kinde of *Imitation* belongeth to the second: as, when you be determined whether ye will folow one or mo, to know perfitlie, and which way to folow, that one . . . ."[38] Ascham then illustrates how various approved writers have imitated their predecessors.

It would be easy to demonstrate that poets and playwrights alike practiced the technique recommended by Ascham. But the most explicit statements on the subject are to be found in the academic dramatists. In his preface "to the academic reader," William Gager justifies the liberties that he has taken with sources in his *Meleager* (1582, pub. 1592) by pointing out that Antiphon, Euripides, and Accius must each have varied the distribution and treatment of events, as he has done, and by arguing that he has thereby achieved more variety and more horribleness (*atrocitas*).[39] Appeal to precedent is used even to justify departure from precedent.

Accepted dramatic theory also provided no concept of a tragic hero. In fact, so long as tragedy was regarded as a moral *exemplum* from history, showing the fall of the wicked from greatness to disaster, it mattered little what kind of men fell, all sons of Adam being more or less wicked. The *exemplum* recommends itself not because the action is such as might have happened to Everyman but because

[38]In *Elizabethan Critical Essays*, I, 7-8.
[39]Cf. Boas, *University Drama in the Tudor Age*, pp. 167-168; also Matthew Gwinne, *Vertumnus sive annus recurrens Oxonii, XXIX Augusti Anno. 1605* (London, 1607), sig. A3v.

it did happen to a particular man. The failure to develop a theory of a tragic hero is a corollary of the emphasis upon historical warrant as guaranteeing the value of the teaching. Jonson's meticulous quotation of his sources for *Sejanus* and *Catiline* springs from the same view of tragedy as titles involving the formula "The True Tragedy of . . . ." In this respect the medieval moralities were a far better guide to a writer of tragedy than was accepted dramatic theory. Fortunately their influence, as we shall see, pervaded Marlowe's *Faustus* and most of Shakespeare's mature tragedies.

Other consequences of this view of tragedy are equally important. If the dramatist is presenting a moral *exemplum* drawn from history, it follows that, provided the play be reasonably unified in terms of the story that furnishes the *exemplum*, plot structure is relatively unimportant. The important problem is to get the facts before the playgoer. One should no more expect to judge an Elizabethan historical tragedy in Aristotle's terms or in terms of a modern course in playwriting than to find the morning paper's account of a murder exemplifying the principles of the short story. And this is true even of a great play like *Julius Caesar*, though, to my cost, I long overlooked that fact.

One does find in other writers on drama allusions to such structural concepts as the four parts or five acts or the unities. But once again Jonson illustrates the care with which inferences should be drawn even from such limited references. A passage in *Timber, or Discoveries* (pub. 1640-1641) begins with a reference to Aristotle's doctrine that a whole and perfect play "hath a *beginning*, a *mid'st*, and an *end*"; but it soon demonstrates that Jonson is thinking almost wholly in quantitative terms, except that the fable must be "compos'd of many parts" and "beginnes to be one as those parts grow or are wrought together." Comedy and tragedy do have fit bounds. But "every bound, for the nature of the Subject, is esteem'd the best that is largest, till it can increase no more." The action has two requirements: "First, that it exceed not the compasse of one Day; Next, that there be place left for digression and Art. For the *Episodes* and digressions in a Fable are the same that houshold stuffe and other furniture are in a house."[40]

Another important consequence of viewing tragic drama as *exem-*

[40]In *Critical Essays of the Seventeenth Century*, I, 60-62.

plum was the omnipresent emphasis upon poetic justice. Puttenham tells us that tragedies present the infamous life and fall of tyrants "to shew the mutabilitie of fortune, and the just punishment of God in revenge of a vicious and evill life."[41] George Whetstone defended his *Promos and Cassandra* (1578) by arguing: "The effects of both [parts] are good and bad: vertue intermyxt with vice, unlawfull desyres (yf it were possible) queancht with chaste denyals: al needeful actions (I thinke) for publike vewe. For by the rewarde of the good the good are encouraged in wel doinge: and with the scowrge of the lewde the lewde are feared from evill attempts."[42] Chettle's *Kind-Hartes Dreame* applies Whetstone's argument more generally to the defense of all drama: "In plaies it fares as in bookes, vice cannot be reproved, except it be discovered: neither is it in any play discovered, but there followes in the same an example of the punishment."[43] When Bacon tells us in his usual magisterial way that "because *true Historie* propoundeth the successes and issues of actions not so agreable to the merits of Vertue and Vice, therefore *Poesie* faines them more just in Retribution and more according to Revealed Providence,"[44] his words are doubly significant, because the whole passage obviously derives from Sidney, who is not guilty of any such gross oversimplification.

It is clear, I trust, that the concepts summarized are an adequate explanation of Elizabethan dramatic practice. One sometimes encounters the notion that literary critics, in their devotion to the unities, went one way and the playwrights went another. This is simply not true. They all knew the same rules from the same sources. It is no accident that Jonson, Shakespeare's greatest contemporary, so often summarized the view of his age. He was at more pains than his fellows to justify his violation of the rules that they all habitually broke, but he was at one with them in his limitations of insight, even if he rose above them in determination and ability to express the insights that he had. *Sejanus* and *Catiline* are the plays that they are precisely because Jonson, being in part a pedant, insisted upon carry-

[41]In *Elizabethan Critical Essays*, II, 35.

[42]Ibid., I, 58-59.

[43]*Shakspere Allusion-Books*, Pt. I, ed. C. M. Ingleby, New Shakspere Soc., Ser. IV, No. 1 (London, 1874), p. 65.

[44]*Advancement of Learning* (1605), in *Critical Essays of the Seventeenth Century*, I, 6.

ing the generally accepted views to their logical conclusion. He was also, of course, a great writer, as his plays show. But it is arguable —although I do not propose to undertake the argument—that he was far more typical of his age and its dramatic views than Shakespeare.

Many pages back, I suspect, the reader began objecting that I have very largely ignored the most important critic of Shakespeare's age— namely, Sir Philip Sidney. And this has indeed been true—but by design. For in fundamental respects Sidney went far beyond his contemporaries in understanding what such Continental writers as Minturno and Scaliger had to say about philosophic principles, and he seems to have been more concerned than the Continental critics to integrate his critical position into his overall metaphysical view. From my point of view, the crucial passage in *The Defence of Poesie* is that immediately preceding the actual definition quoted earlier in this discussion.

Sidney begins, in traditional fashion, by discussing the antiquity and high esteem of poets and by explaining the implications of the Latin term *vates* and the Greek "poet" or maker. Most similar discussions accompany this material with a section on poetic inspiration. It is surely no accident that this conventional point is missing in Sidney and instead one finds a thoroughgoing consideration of just how the poet creates. "There is no Arte delivered to mankinde," Sidney tells us, "that hath not the workes of Nature for his principall object, without which they could not consist, and on which they so depend, as they become Actors and Players, as it were, of what Nature will have set foorth."[45] He then proceeds to show that specialists in various learned arts look upon the works of nature (*natura naturata*) and from them infer the principles or laws of nature (*natura naturans*) which operate to produce the phenomena. These principles or "laws" then become the rules of the art. Francis Bacon later embodied the same concept in his brilliant aphorism: "Nature to be commanded must be obeyed; and that which in contemplation is as the cause is in operation as the rule."[46] The poet, however, is exempt from this subjection to phenomena, according to Sidney. "Onely the

[45]In *Elizabethan Critical Essays*, I, 155.

[46]Variants of this aphorism occur at several points in Bacon's works. The variant given translates *Novum Organum*, Bk. I, No. iii, in *The Works of Francis Bacon*, ed. James Spedding, Robert L. Ellis, and Douglas D. Heath, IV (London, 1858), 47.

Poet, disdayning to be tied to any such subjection, lifted up with the vigor of his owne invention, dooth growe in effect another nature, in making things either better then Nature bringeth forth, or, quite a newe, formes such as never were in Nature, as the *Heroes, Demigods, Cyclops, Chimeras, Furies,* and such like: so as hee goeth hand in hand with Nature, not inclosed within the narrow warrant of her guifts, but freely ranging onely within the Zodiack of his owne wit."[47]

The poet, in other words, is not bound like the moral philosopher to describe how men do behave or how they should behave to be in conformity with nature. He may become another nature in one of two ways. Either he may describe a better order than the nature which we know or he may imagine forms without any counterpart in nature, such as Cyclops. But this does not imply that the poet can lose touch completely with reality. Even in his most imaginative flights he must go "hand in hand with Nature." A Cyclops, after all, is merely a very large man with one eye instead of two, and we follow the poet's imagination because he is working with data from nature. The creation of quite new forms is, however, of less interest to Sidney than making things "better then Nature bringeth forth," and his next two paragraphs are concerned with explaining how the poet can do the latter.

That the poet can create a better man than has ever lived Sidney takes as proved by experience. The reason is simply that he is not compelled to imitate any particular man; his skill consists in apprehending a perfect exemplar or *Idea* of man and in so presenting that example that men may learn from it what they ought to be. But this merely poses another question: how is the poet able to conceive the ideal as opposed to the real? This question Sidney answers in Christian terms. Man has been made in the likeness of God and set above the other works of nature. The God who breathed into him the breath of life gave him also the power to glimpse, behind the imperfect works of Nature, which participated in his own fall, the perfection in the mind of God the creator. The difference between his vision of perfection and the fallen reality that he knows is, in fact, "no small argument to be incredulous of that first accursed fall of *Adam*: sith our erected wit maketh us know what perfection is, and yet our in-

[47]In *Elizabethan Critical Essays,* I, 156.

fected will keepeth us from reaching unto it."[48] The poet therefore rises above nature, not by departing from it but by looking beyond its present fallen condition to the perfect concept or Idea in the mind of God, the first "maker." This vision we may have, even though our fallen nature prevents us from achieving it.

It is obvious that Sidney is simply restating in Christian terms the argument by which Aristotle met Plato's attack upon poetry as imitation: it imitates not the imperfect particular but the perfect universal. In fact, he later discusses Aristotle's doctrine that poetry deals "with the universal consideration" and adds: "which reason of his (as all his) is most full of reason."[49] For Sidney, I take it, this universal is the Idea or "fore-conceite" in the mind of God, just as the skill of the poet stands in the idea which informs what he, as a creator on his level, puts on paper. The poet's inspiration therefore becomes the unusual insight that enables him to see beyond the imperfect phenomena of nature to the laws of nature, or perhaps beyond the laws of nature in its present imperfection to the laws of its prelapsarian perfection. He might look, for example, beyond the "brazen" world tilted on its axis after Adam's fall and subject to seasons and storms to the "golden" world that originally stood true and perfect. I assume that Sidney made the common identification of the classical golden age with that before the Fall and that he had in mind something very nearly like what Milton committed himself to doing in *Paradise Lost* not only for the physical but for the moral order of nature. Elizabethan poetry, like Elizabethan education, became, on this view, an attempt to repair the ruin caused by our first parents.

Sidney surely read and understood Scaliger and Minturno as few of his contemporaries did, but he was able to use their ideas creatively —and this point must be stressed—because he reinterpreted those ideas and integrated them into the theological-metaphysical system that he accepted. This seems to me his great intellectual achievement. "But these arguments," he added, "wil by fewe be understood, and by fewer granted."[50] They were understood, unless I have overlooked important evidence, by very few indeed—but Shakespeare was probably among those few.

[48]Ibid., I, 157.
[49]Ibid., I, 167.
[50]Ibid., I, 157.

Sidney's theories not only furnished him with a doctrine of poetic inspiration and of imitation in terms of universals,[51] but also enabled him to handle two other problems meaningfully. For his contemporaries, the poet differed from the historian primarily in exemplifying poetic justice at work—outcomes "more just in Retribution and more according to Revealed Providence."[52] For Sidney, as for Aristotle, to whom he alludes, the poet differs from the historian in that his example illustrates a universal principle. The philosopher, Sidney argues, is so abstract that no one can understand him:

On the other side, the Historian, wanting the precept, is so tyed, not to what shoulde bee but to what is, to the particuler truth of things and not to the general reason of things, that hys example draweth no necessary consequence, and therefore a lesse fruitfull doctrine.

Nowe doothe the peerelesse Poet performe both: for whatsoever the Philosopher sayth shoulde be doone, hee giveth a perfect picture of it in some one, by whom hee presupposeth it was doone. So as hee coupleth the generall notion with the particuler example.[53]

Sidney does not deny that poetry should inculcate sound morality. Quite the contrary! But his remarks are so qualified that he does avoid the bald advocacy of poetic justice characteristic of his contemporaries.

Well may you see Ulisses in a storme, and in other hard plights; but they are but exercises of patience and magnanimitie, to make them shine the more in the neere-following prosperitie. And of the contrarie part, if evill men come to the stage, they ever goe out (as the Tragedie Writer answered to one that misliked the shew of such persons) so manacled as they little animate folkes to followe them. But the Historian, being captived to the trueth of a foolish world, is many times a terror from well dooing, and an incouragement to unbrideled wickednes.[54]

This is still a long way from the stern truth to reality that Shakespeare showed in rejecting a happy ending for *King Lear*. But the same moral insight is at work.

Sidney's triumphant answer to the charge that poets are liars is well known. "Now, for the Poet, he nothing affirmes, and therefore

---

[51]For a parallel discussion of this subject, see Madeleine Doran, *Endeavors of Art: A Study of Form in Elizabethan Drama* (Madison, 1954), pp. 72-77.

[52]Bacon, *Advancement of Learning*, in *Critical Essays of the Seventeenth Century*, I, 6.

[53]In *Elizabethan Critical Essays*, I, 164.   [54]Ibid., I, 170.

never lyeth. For, as I take it, to lye is to affirme that to be true which is false." But we sometimes fail to notice that Sidney, in meeting the argument that it was impossible to follow history and preserve the unities, stumbled into a genuine principle that contravened the practice of his age: "And doe they not knowe that a Tragedie is tied to the lawes of Poesie, and not of Historie? not bound to follow the storie, but, having liberty, either to faine a quite newe matter, or to frame the history to the most tragicall conveniencie."[55]

Sidney's principle that the poet must couple the general notion with the particular example would obviously have important consequences if applied to drama, whether by someone following his precepts or by someone who had arrived at similar views independently. If we may judge by the attempt of Fulke Greville, Lord Brooke, in his *Treatie of Humane Learning*, to erect a new epistemology on the Calvinist premises that he accepted, he was undoubtedly capable of following Sidney's thought. That he was familiar with Sidney's views there can be no doubt, and he tells us that he attempted to shape his own closet dramas *Mustapha* (ca. 1596) and *Alaham* (ca. 1600) according not only to Sidney's precepts but also to the example provided in the *Arcadia*, where Sidney's "intent, and scope was, to turn the barren Philosophy precepts into pregnant Images of life."[56] The *Arcadia* was, in Greville's view, an *exemplum* of political philosophy from which all stations of life might learn with profit. Of his own plays Greville writes:

So that (if my creation had been equal) it would have proved as easie for me, to have followed his patern, in the practice of reall vertue, as to engage my self into this *Characteristicall* kind of Poesie: in defence whereof he hath written so much, as I shall not need to say any thing. For that this representing of vertues, vices, humours, counsells, and actions of men in feigned, and unscandalous Images, is an inabling of freeborn spirits to the greatest affaires of States: he himself hath left such an instance in the too short scene of his life, as I fear many Ages will not draw a line out of any other mans sphere to parallel with it.[57]

Why he attributed to Sidney a "*Characteristicall* kind of Poesie," if not clear from the preceding discussion, can be inferred from Sid-

[55]Ibid., I, 184, 198.

[56]*Sir Fulke Greville's Life of Sir Philip Sidney*, ed. Nowell Smith (Oxford, 1907), p. 15.

[57]Ibid., pp. 2-3.

ney's remark that "it is that fayning notable images of vertues, vices, or what els, with that delightfull teaching, which must be the right describing note to know a Poet by."[58] Greville's use of "Characteristicall" probably reflects the vogue of the "character" as naturalized in England by Joseph Hall (1608) and Sir Thomas Overbury (1614).

In discussing his own dramas, Greville explains that his purpose was not to show the miseries of man's life with the ancients or poetic justice and God's providence with the moderns but to illustrate principles of political conduct: "to trace out the high waies of ambitious Governours, and to shew in the practice, that the more audacity, advantage, and good success such Soveraignties have, the more they hasten to their owne desolation and ruine." The plays are, in fact, of universal relevance not because they show what has happened but because they illustrate what always happens, so that the reader will find in them "the state he lives in, and for every part he may perchance find a Player, and for every Line (it may be) an instance of life, beyond the Authors intention."[59]

George Chapman states in the Preface to his translation of Homer views like Sidney's, and, in fact, he goes beyond Sidney in recognizing that eliminating the standard of literal truth involves accepting a standard of poetic truth which is even more exacting: "Nor is there any such reality of wisdomes truth in all humane excellence as in Poets fictions: . . . no Artist being so strictly and inextricably confined to all the lawes of learning, wisedome, and truth as a Poet. For were not his fictions composed of the sinewes and soules of all those, how could they differ farre from, and be combined with, eternitie?"[60] But, whether because he lacked dramatic skill as he certainly lacked clarity of mind or because he had accepted in neo-Stoicism a view of life fundamentally unsuited to dramatic conflict, Chapman's plays, it seems to me, do not reflect the insight of this and similar passages in his prefaces.

But these principles could be applied to interpreting existing plays as well as to writing new ones. Just such an attempt was made by Thomas Watson, a contemporary of Sidney's who was an important

[58]In *Elizabethan Critical Essays*, I, 160.

[59]*Greville's Life of Sir Philip Sidney*, pp. 221, 224-225.

[60]In *Critical Essays of the Seventeenth Century*, I, 67-68.

figure both in the cultivation of neo-Latin poetry and in the development of the Petrarchan sonnet. It is interesting that in his *Hecatompathia* one encounters the same awareness of a conflict between the Petrarchan code and rational ethics that one finds in Sidney's *Astrophel and Stella*, although his touch is not so deft as Sidney's. He was, I take it, to some extent an intellectual as well as a poet. In 1581 he published a Latin translation of the *Antigone* of Sophocles. To quote the title, "To this are added some pageants [*pompæ*] derived from the several acts of the Tragedy, and after these as many themes filled with 'sentences'."[61] The four pageants obviously derive their inspiration from the allegorical processions of Renaissance art and poetry. The poet introduces each of them, interpreting in terms of moral principles the meaning of the action. Allegorical figures representing virtues and vices then appear to indicate briefly their part in what has happened.

Prefacing the first pageant, the poet tells us that poetry is a speaking picture imprinting virtue in the mind of man and that each fictitious character shows us the course that we ought to follow. Creon, specifically, illustrates what an unspeakable evil inheres in a stubborn spirit upon which force, reason, and threats can make no impression. "This point the following pageant will demonstrate."[62] The proces-

[61]*Sophoclis Antigone. Interprete Thoma Watsono F. V. studioso. Huic adduntur pompæ quædam, ex singulis Tragœdiæ actis derivatæ; & post eas, totidem themata sententiis refertissima; eodem Thoma Watsono Authore* (London, 1581).

[62]*Antigone*, p. 54:

> Per omne scriptorum genus sapientia
> Divina serpit: illa communis libro est
> Cuique & arti justa materies: In hac
> Versantur omnes, & suum studium locant.
> Tamèn relucet clariùs nusquàm, bona
> Quàm sub Poësi; quæ loquens dici potest
> Pictura in hominis mente virtutem imprimens.
> Quò propriùs ipsam vîderis, pulcra est magis;
> Speciem bonorum signat in mente, & viæ
> Rectæ magistra corrigit vitæ malum.
> Natum est Poëma, ut mentibus nostris ferat
> Opem, vagosque ut tollat errores: in hoc
> Conficta vitæ debitum nostræ docet
> Persona cursum; quid decet, quid non sequi.
> Velùt hìc acerba clade prostratus Creon
> Suis apertè prodit ærumnis, malum
> Quàm sit nefandum dura mens, animi & rigor
> Inflexus: in quem nulla vis, ratio, minæ
> Valent, sed animo sempèr incepto tenax
> Inhæret. Hanc rem pompa monstrabit sequens.

sion consists of Justice, with a scepter; Equity, a woman with scales; Rigor, a man with a sword; Obstinacy, a man with a cuirass; Impiety, a man with a lance; Scourge, a man with a whip; Late Repentance, a man. Each of these figures enunciates maxims appropriate to the action (as Watson interprets it) but does not comment specifically upon the play. The second pageant is more closely related to the action in that it becomes an allegory of Antigone's inner conflict. Watson, the Elizabethan, pronounces emphatically against her choice; for him she violates public law and forgets her duty to her country in thinking of her private grief.⁶³ The pageant therefore illustrates a kind of chain of sin at work, as Magnanimity, who still follows Antigone even though the latter has spurned her country, is followed by Transgression, Arrogance, Opprobrium, and Punishment. The pageant devoted to Haemon personifies, as one might expect, the ancient adage that not even Jove can be wise and in love at the same time.⁶⁴ Right reason and its attendant virtues—Piety, Obedience, Safety, and Happiness—are assigned by the poet to Ismene.

The themes that follow digest the action into moral propositions and discuss each one in a verse essay as full of sentences as Watson promised in his title. The four propositions are of some interest. First, "we learn from Creon that blind self-love is the cause of many calamities." Second, "the example of Antigone shows how evil it is not to obey the public command of a magistrate." The theme begins: "Mother Nature has devised nothing whatsoever better than fair

---

⁶³*Antigone*, pp. 57-58:
       Privata magnus rispicit dum animus mala
       Partem in sinistram ductus affectu levi,
       Violare tentat publicum jus, propriae
       Memor miseriæ, in patriam officii immemor,
       Contraque fasces incito fertur gradu,
       Facinusque mortem per malum accelerat suam.
       Atque haec sepulcrum flebile Antigones docet:
       Palamque faciet jam sequens spectaculum.
                MAGNANIMITAS, *mulier*. . . .
       Incerta dubio saepe quò vertam priùs,
       Dum patria, nexus sanguinis, princeps vocat.
       Parere simùl his haùd licet. Procedite,
       Docete quam nunc ingredi præstet viam.

⁶⁴*Antigone*, p. 60:
             Verbum est vetus,
     Sapere, ac amare vix Jovi junctìm datur.

laws." It then devotes a page and a half of verse to Elizabethan commonplaces on what happens when law fails to operate in the social order. Third, "Ismene instructs that we should not concern ourselves with what we cannot correct, portraying the pattern of quiet life." Fourth, "the death of Haemon shows that hardly anyone can be wise and in love at once." A page of commonplaces on the fury of raging love (Cupido) follows.[65]

These appendices to the *Antigone* seem to me to be of unique value in showing us an Elizabethan mind interpreting—and, from our point of view, perverting—the meaning of a great play. But they also reveal the cultivated mind of an important, though minor, poet trying to make the *Antigone* more useful to his contemporaries. He obviously believes that poetry should teach and that it should provide not only an *exemplum* but also a digest of sound moral principles. The action of the *Antigone* must be related to those reasonable laws which Watson calls Mother Nature's best gift. If Sophocles neglected to write the appropriate sentences into his text, Watson will furnish them—he will provide the general notion that should have been coupled with the particular example. Watson, to the best of his ability, is providing footnotes which clarify both the nature of Sophocles' inspiration —his insight into moral principles—and the universality of his characters. He is trying to show that Sophocles did do what Sidney says the poet alone can do. As an Elizabethan, he wishes that the Greek had been more practical and more specific, and he tries to supply the defect.

These *pompæ* and these themes are important in another respect. Watson was neither a fool nor a pedant. He was a poet whom his contemporaries imitated and, once at least, plagiarized.[66] But his mind operates in terms of commonplaces and rigid systems of ideas. He is simply incapable of seeing the moral complexity of the *Antigone* because for him right is right and wrong is wrong, and once the applicable principle is determined the issue is clear-cut. His mind is amply stored with moral sentences, and they come to him automatically as he deals with moral questions. He illustrates, in other words, the way a dramatist operating on his principles might develop

[65]*Antigone*, pp. 63-68.

[66]Abraham Fraunce published in 1587, without acknowledging his debt until 1591, an English version of Watson's Latin *Amyntas* (1585).

his material and write his plays. The action would be related to moral axioms, and these would inevitably be written into the text, just as grammar-school training and rhetorical theory prescribed. The creative mind of the artist would use principles or maxims as material for the creative process because that was the habit he had developed while learning. A playwright of Watson's caliber would operate on a level above mere sententious moralizing. The action of his play would itself be grounded upon moral principles. We have no right to assume, of course, that any practicing playwright had a mind like Watson's. But, when we find a play of the sort to which Watson's methods would lead, we do have a right to suspect that similar assumptions and similar methods—particularly since the latter were fundamentally those of the age—have been at work.

A consideration of Shakespeare the practicing dramatist belongs in the following chapters. But he has left us a few critical remarks, and they show, I believe, that somehow during his career he thought his way through to a view of poetry substantially like that which I have attributed to Sidney. Analysis of his technique later on will demonstrate that his practice was like that implied by Watson, and this is why the latter's *Antigone* seems to me so important a document. I have argued elsewhere that Shakespeare from the beginning of his career showed a philosophic bent of mind. He was, for example, more interested in a metaphysical explanation of history than in tracing political intrigues; he apparently wrote more philosophy into *Troilus and Cressida* or theology into *Measure for Measure* than the dramatic framework could support. I have also argued that, at a crucial time in his career, he was powerfully stimulated either by Richard Hooker's own summary of the concept of natural law or by the system of ideas that Hooker summarized.[67] No one, I take it, except Baconians, would doubt the range and profundity of Shakespeare's mind. If he read Sidney, he would certainly have interpreted him, at least after the late 1590's, in the light of the philosophic system that he was writing into his plays. If, by some strange accident, he did not read Sidney, he would have had little difficulty arriving at similar views as soon as he started thinking carefully about the traditional doctrines concerning drama in terms of a philosophic

[67]See *Shakespeare's Use of Learning: An Inquiry into the Growth of His Mind & Art* (San Marino, Calif., 1953), pp. 56-61, 209-214, 220-222.

system derived ultimately from Aristotle—little difficulty, that is, when thinking as a Shakespeare, not as a less gifted individual.

Three crucial passages seem to me to hint at the direction and the extent of Shakespeare's thinking. I say "hint at" because I am well aware that the implications that I propose to read into these lines have not been found there by others more qualified to interpret Shakespeare than I am. I can only hope that my way of looking, in this instance, has sharpened my insight. Shakespeare's words are, furthermore, part of a dramatic context and means to a dramatic end. They do not in themselves constitute a complete statement of a literary theory. One must inevitably draw inferences or choose among various possible meanings. The test of the interpretations proposed is whether they agree with Shakespeare's dramatic practice and illuminate it. I trust that my interpretations will not do violence to the text; I hope, in fact, that they will seem its obvious meaning. But in the last analysis they will be confirmed or falsified by the investigation of Shakespeare's technique that follows.

As one reads through Shakespeare's plays, one comes to expect certain phrases or commonplaces that apparently attracted his attention and stuck in his memory. The contrast between art and nature is one of these. At times the two words merely distinguish between what is innate and what is acquired by training. As Corin remarks, "he that hath learned no wit by nature nor art may complain of good breeding or comes of a very dull kindred" (*As You Like It* III.ii.30-32). But more often Shakespeare is impressed by the capacity of art to go beyond nature. The most elaborate treatment of this idea in his early work occurs in *Venus and Adonis*:

> Look, when a painter would surpass the life
> In limning out a well-proportioned steed,
> His art with nature's workmanship at strife,
> As if the dead the living should exceed;
>   So did this horse excel a common one
>   In shape, in courage, colour, pace, and bone.
>
> (ll. 289-294)

Here the meaning is clearly that the painter's horse is perfectly proportioned in every respect, whereas, except in the horse being described, some parts of every living horse are inevitably faulty. The superiority of art to nature consists in perfection of every detail. But

86

the advantage is not always with art, especially when human emotions are involved. When Edgar comments at sight of the mad Lear, "O thou side-piercing sight!" Lear retorts: "Nature's above art in that respect" (IV.vi.85-86).

The most elaborate discussion of the subject occurs, however, in *Timon of Athens* (1607). The poet compliments the painter on his picture in words that suggest a new insight:

> I will say of it,
> It tutors nature. Artificial strife
> Lives in these touches, livelier than life.
>
> (I.i.36-38)

Art is no longer in conflict with nature; it is another nature, superior in its grasp of nature's own principles. Timon himself gives the same idea a new twist—that art sees beyond the false appearances of life to the nature that they partly conceal:

> The painting is almost the natural man;
> For since dishonour traffics with man's nature,
> He is but outside: these pencill'd figures are
> Even such as they give out.
>
> (I.i.157-160)

Shakespeare's best efforts are lavished, however, upon the poet's masterpiece, which is an allegorical description of the fickleness of Fortune, intended specifically to teach Timon as well as to delight him. The poem is, incidentally, the kind of word painting that Spenser so often employed for his great allegorical set pieces such as the Bower of Acrasia. Fortune is enthroned on a hill. Up the slope are struggling those whom she favors; down it is sliding one whom she has spurned, unassisted by those who followed his rise. The painter is quite right in recognizing it as a common theme of "A thousand moral paintings" (I.i.90). The poet's method is obviously to give specific embodiment to an abstract principle—to couple the general notion with the particular example. The choice of examples is that characteristic of allegory—representative selection:

> The base o' th' mount
> Is rank'd with all deserts, all kind of natures,
> That labour on the bosom of this sphere
> To propagate their states.
>
> (I.i.64-67)

But among them appears Lord Timon, and with him the method of drama intrudes upon that of allegory—for the particular person appears among the representative types. With him the rule of Fortune is particularized from all operations of nature to the life of Timon of Athens. The poet's artistry is crude in its confusion of methods appropriate to two genres, but Shakespeare has made his point. The play itself is an *exemplum* not of the caprice of fortune but of a universal principle—that all sorts and conditions of men by nature seek for fortune, attaching themselves to anyone who can help them rise, rejecting anyone who may drag them down. The painter's words take on a new meaning. A thousand moral paintings show the quick blows of fortune, but the poet does well

> To show Lord Timon that mean eyes have seen
> The foot above the head.

(I.i.93-94)

The poet's allegory is somewhat confused, but it is clear that Shakespeare thinks of his art as teaching various principles from nature and applying them specifically to Timon. In *The Winter's Tale* (1610) Shakespeare reverts in specific terms to the relationship of nature and art. Perdita refuses to have streaked gilly flowers in her garden because

> There is an art which in their piedness shares
> With great creating Nature.

To which Polixenes, the voice of wisdom, replies:

> Say there be;
> Yet Nature is made better by no mean
> But Nature makes that mean; so, over that art
> Which you say adds to Nature, is an art
> That Nature makes.

(IV.iv.87-92)

Surely the general form of the statement suggests that Shakespeare had been thinking about the whole problem of art transcending nature. He had come to see that the painter of the horse had bettered nature simply by understanding and applying the principles that determined excellence in a horse; that Timon's painter had penetrated the false appearances of phenomenal nature (*natura naturata*) only because he understood the governing principles of nature (*natura naturans*); and that Timon's poet had seen beneath the tradi-

88

tional caprice of fortune to the fundamental principles of human behavior that made men pursue fortune in the way they do. The art that hybridizes flowers and seems to change their superficial nature depends upon an understanding of their fundamental nature as it determines their reproduction and growth. Just so the poet must grasp the fundamental laws of human nature if he is to better the fallen natures of men.[68] Shakespeare, too, had grasped Bacon's axiom: Nature to be commanded must be obeyed.

Shakespeare's most considerable utterance on dramatic theory is, of course, Hamlet's advice to the players. Though his point of departure is acting, he is obviously thinking of the play as a whole. We habitually distinguish between the play as poetic content and the play as acted spectacle, between reading and performance. For Shakespeare, fortunately, no such distinction existed, not only because most of his plays lived only in the theater for which they had been written but also because the whole rhetorical tradition in which he had been educated dealt with spoken discourse. For him the purpose of playing was to deliver the play in its totality, with due attention to meaning in the sense of intellectual content. Hamlet, I take it, is also thinking of tragedy, the kind of play to be performed before Claudius and the court. Characteristically, he moves from a minor point to the general principle that governs it. "Suit the action to the word, the word to the action," and "o'erstep not the modesty of nature," he argues, because in this, as in all respects, drama is an imitation of nature. Or, to quote his words:

For anything so overdone is from the purpose of playing, whose end, both at the first and now, was and is, to hold, as 'twere, the mirror up to nature; to show virtue her own feature, scorn her own image, and the very age and body of the time his form and pressure. Now this overdone, or come tardy off, though it make the unskillful laugh, cannot but make the judicious grieve; the censure of the which one must, in your allowance, o'erweigh a whole theatre of others. O, there be players that I have seen play, and heard others praise, and that highly, not to speak it profanely, that, neither having the accent of Christians nor the gait of Christian, pagan, nor man, have so strutted and bellowed that I have thought some of Nature's journeymen had made men and not made them well, they imitated humanity so abominably.

(III.ii.22-39)

[68]Madeleine Doran (*Endeavors of Art*, pp. 59-60) applies this passage from *The Winter's Tale* more narrowly to poetic composition.

In the first place, Shakespeare roundly asserts that plays should be directed toward the approval of the judicious spectator as opposed to a whole theater full of the injudicious. In so doing, he took his stand on one of the critical problems of his age. Apparently he practiced what he preached, at least in *Hamlet,* for the acting version of the First Folio is several hundred lines shorter than the apparently original text in the Second Quarto, and the Folio cuts mostly delete passages interpreting the action in philosophical and psychological terms of interest only to the "judicious."

In the second place, the end of playing is "to hold, as 'twere, the mirror up to nature." This sentence has been taken to imply a doctrine of verisimilitude, or even something approaching the "slice of life" sought by some modern writers. It means, in fact, the precise opposite, as an examination of Shakespeare's terms will show. "Mirror" denotes for him an exemplar, a perfect pattern, whether of good or of evil. So Henry V is called "the mirror of all Christian kings" (II.Pr.6); Buckingham's admirers praise him as "The mirror of all courtesy" (*Henry VIII* II.i.53). This is indeed the common Elizabethan meaning, preserved in the title of *A Mirror for Magistrates* or in Greville's line describing God himself as the fatal mirror of man's transgression, the perfect pattern by contrast with which man's imperfections are revealed.[69] "Nature" is once again ambiguous.[70] It may be *natura naturans,* the principle impelling creatures to fulfill the purpose for which they were created; or it may be, as often in Shakespeare and his period, *natura naturata* as participating in the Fall, especially fallen man. The subsequent reference to nature's journeymen seems to imply something close to *natura naturans.* If so, the sentence means that playing must provide an exemplar by relating the action to the relevant laws of nature. If not, the "mirror" held up to fallen nature must be the principles of creative nature in its perfection. The ambiguity is not fatal, since either meaning of nature yields roughly the same result; it may even be deliberate, just as Shakespeare's explanation of the relationship

[69]*Cælica,* Sonnet XCIX, in *Poems and Dramas of Fulke Greville, First Lord Brooke,* ed. Geoffrey Bullough (Edinburgh, [1939]), I, 144. The relevant stanzas are quoted below in Ch. iv.

[70]John F. Danby discusses this ambiguity but seems to have overlooked the meaning of "mirror." See *Shakespeare's Doctrine of Nature: A Study of King Lear* (London, 1949), p. 214.

between art and nature turned on the same double meaning. The end of playing is therefore not only to present an action but also to provide an exemplar or pattern—the very feature of scorn, the image of virtue, and the form and forces shaping the time. Form has, of course, the meaning implied by the traditional distinction between form and substance;[71] it is the "nature" of a thing, the pattern or exemplar operating as law but subject, in each creature, to special pressures that modify results as form actualizes itself in substance. Either meaning of nature orients the passage in the Christian metaphysical system developed by the Middle Ages, primarily out of Aristotle, and transmitted to the Renaissance. Tragedy (assuming that Shakespeare is thinking especially of that genre) must therefore relate the particular action to relevant principles derived from the accepted metaphysical scheme. This "mirroring" of the particular in the universal principle or law of nature would inevitably lead the audience, or at least the "judicious," to form a judgment of the action. In so doing, it would not only delight but also teach; and Shakespeare's view is substantially the doctrine enunciated by Sidney that the poet should couple the general notion with the particular example. As a working dramatist, Shakespeare states the concept in terms of a practical theory for implementing it.

Our survey of theory thus arrives at this outcome. We should expect Shakespeare to exemplify the ideas and assumptions about drama characteristic of his age. These do indeed control his early tragedies, and they operate even in the last that he wrote. But we should also look in him for a unique technique, appearing at least in his mature tragedies and growing out of a philosophic view of tragedy that allies him to Aristotle and to such thoughtful contemporaries as Sidney or Chapman rather than to working dramatists or even the scholar Ben Jonson. He will deal in universals, but, as his special contribution to theory and practice, he will do so by making sure that the relevant universal principles find explicit statement even as the particular action unrolls. Throughout his career his plays demonstrate a concern with dramatic craftsmanship and a fidelity to critical principles as he understood them that is matched only in Ben Jonson. These traits alone might well have made him the best

[71]Cf. Danby, ibid., pp. 214-215.

dramatist of his age. But his critical principles evolved as Jonson's never did, and that evolution from the tradition of Donatus to the insight of a Sidney explains, in very considerable part, an incredible artistic growth. *Richard III* and *Macbeth* are superficially much alike, and that resemblance is their joint heritage from general Elizabethan critical theory and dramatic practice. But in essentials *Macbeth* belongs with the *Oedipus Rex* and not with *Tamburlaine* or even *Sejanus*; it exemplifies the precepts of Sidney, and it achieves the goal toward which Watson and Greville and Chapman were groping. In doing so, it grows out of its age, or one aspect thereof; it is not of that age, however, but for all time.

But to demonstrate that in his best plays Shakespeare rises above his age is not to prove that he invariably does so—in all plays, or in all details of any play. It is, in fact, folly to assume that Shakespeare ever ceased to be the child of his heritage and a son of his age. I know, in fact, of no responsible critic or scholar today who professes such an assumption. But the habit of thinking and talking of Shakespeare as though he were as unique in all respects as he is in his highest achievement is more insidious and therefore pervasive. What I have so far written has grown, in fact, not so much out of a need to inform others (I have no doubt stated at tedious length what many readers already knew) as out of an urge to discipline my own imagination and critical response. But anyone familiar with Shakespeare's plays or with the critical problems that keep recurring in discussions of his work has missed my intention if vaguely heretical ideas like the following have not come to his mind. So long as the Aumerle-plot episode illustrates Bolingbroke's efficiency as contrasted with Richard II's weakness and is part of the story, should we expect more relevancy in a play which, despite its superior structure, grows out of a narrative tradition? May we not grant that Shakespeare, like his fellows, might try in *Julius Caesar* to incorporate both a hero from history and a hero of tragedy, and still be grateful that, unlike his fellows, he restricted his story to manageable proportions? Should we expect in *Hamlet* a tragic flaw or a tragic error or even complete unity of action and consistency of meaning? Both the revenge tragedy and the Elizabethan tradition that contributed to it were innocent of all these virtues. Even Ben Jonson insisted that "there be place left for digression," and the evidence surely implies that playgoers were more interested in the excitement of a scene, provided it had some kind of relation to the story, than in its neat articulation into the dramatic action. If Shakespeare were true to his sources, would he have felt obliged, even after *Othello, Macbeth*, and *King Lear*, to assess accurately Cleopatra's interior and moral state at the time of her death? Any discussion of Shakespeare must begin by studying him in the context of his age. This we shall proceed to do.

Chapter Three *❧* PITEOUS OVERTHROWS:

RICHARD III, TITUS ANDRONICUS, ROMEO AND JULIET, RICHARD II, JULIUS CAESAR

W^E TEND to think of Shakespeare's tragic career as beginning with *Julius Caesar* and *Hamlet, Romeo and Juliet* being a kind of early experiment. Or perhaps I am once again being guilty of at- tributing my own faults to others. For fault it was. If we accept the classification of Shakespeare's contemporaries,[1] as I think we must, then *Hamlet* marked the mid-point of his tragedies, both in number of plays and in span of years. It was preceded by *Richard III* (1592- 1593), *Titus Andronicus* (1593-1594), *Romeo and Juliet* (1594- 1595), *Richard II* (1595-1596), and *Julius Caesar* (1599). It was followed by *Othello* (1604-1605), *King Lear* (1605-1606), *Mac- beth* (1605-1606), *Antony and Cleopatra* (1607), and *Coriolanus* (1608). If we include *Troilus and Cressida* and *Cymbeline*, which the First Folio calls tragedies, and *Timon of Athens*, which it in- cludes among the tragedies though denying it the label, the propor- tion becomes somewhat different; but I have already advanced my reasons for excluding these three plays from the category.

But if, with Bradley, we take true Shakespearean tragedy as be- ginning with *Hamlet*, or perhaps *Julius Caesar*, we are right. For, as he points out, the earlier tragedies, among which he includes *Richard III* and *Richard II*, are different in kind.[2] The later plays exemplify the kind of tragedy that we associate with Shakespeare; the earlier, various other kinds of tragedy that Shakespeare could write. The earlier tragedies are, in fact, much closer to those of his contem-

[1] Cf. Francis Meres, *Palladis Tamia (1598)*, ed. Don Cameron Allen, Scholars' Facsimiles & Reprints (New York, 1938), p. 282: "so *Shakespeare* among the English is the most excellent in both kinds for the stage . . . for Tragedy his *Richard the 2. Richard the 3. Henry the 4. King John, Titus Andronicus* and his *Romeo* and *Juliet*." Meres' testimony is weakened by his inclusion of two chronicle histories, perhaps because he was limited by his comparative method to the classical categories of comedy and tragedy. But at least he supports the ascription of the quarto title pages.

[2] A. C. Bradley, *Shakespearean Tragedy: Lectures on Hamlet, Othello, King Lear, Macbeth* (London, 1905), p. 18.

.

poraries in externals of structure than the later. Kyd might almost have written *Titus Andronicus*. Marlowe provided models for *Richard III* and *Richard II*. Brooke's poem *Romeus and Juliet*—except for the play's incomparable poetry—might equally well have been dramatized by one of the university wits; in fact, some of the less successful passages in the play read as though it had been. In other words, *Titus Andronicus* is a revenge play, *Richard III* and *Richard II* are *de casibus* tragedies of the rise and fall of the great, *Romeo and Juliet* is primarily a tragic romance. Only in *Julius Caesar* does Shakespeare achieve the tragic view of man characteristic of his great plays, and in it that view is still obscured by dramatic tradition and by imperfect technique.

In important respects, however, even these early plays differ from the works of other dramatists. *Titus Andronicus* perhaps differs less than the others, though in exuberance of horror Shakespeare bettered his rivals and in character drawing he anticipated tragic achievements that were to come. The play may not be wholly Shakespeare's, however, and it seems to stand somewhat outside the main line of his dramatic development. I shall mostly leave it out of account in discussing characteristics of the early tragedies that are peculiarly Shakespearean. In the first place, all these plays represent an attempt to achieve a dramatic structure that is at once unified and complex. Much as Shakespeare learned from Marlowe, he surpassed him most decisively in just this aspect of his art. *Richard III*, like *Tamburlaine*, derives its unity from a single dominating figure; but, as we shall see, it achieves a richness of structure and meaning far beyond that of the earlier play. *Richard II* does not seem to me so powerful a play as *Edward II*, but its structure, except perhaps for the Aumerle episode, is certainly clearer and more artful.

The concern for dramatic structure was itself symptomatic of another characteristic of these plays that led ultimately to the great tragedies. Except for *Titus Andronicus*, Shakespeare attempted to unify each of them not only in terms of the fable but also in terms of an underlying theme or concept. This theme involved placing the particular action in a context of larger forces. I have already mentioned my view that throughout the history plays Shakespeare was more concerned with seeing history in terms of fundamental forces such as providence, fortune, or human character than in following political intrigue.[3] This bent of mind seems to me to have operated with especial force in these early tragedies and to have given them a philosophic dimension or philosophic depth quite uncharacteristic of other plays of the period. The contrast between Shakespeare and other dramatists will be most apparent in *Richard III*, which can be compared with two other plays on the same theme. The themes of divine retribution and of the providential reunion of England which operate throughout that play Shakespeare took from Halle, but it was his mind that seized upon these aspects of Halle's narrative and his skill that gave these larger themes dramatic expression. In *Romeo and Juliet*, on the other hand, he took over the pattern of conflict between star-crossed lovers and feuding families from Brooke, but he confused it by stressing a notion of Romeo's own moral responsibility for the tragic outcome that he also found in Brooke. The play therefore suffers from too many philosophic dimensions that cannot be comprehended from a single point of view. *Richard II* Shakespeare managed, with brilliant success, to make an *exemplum* of the nature and extent of kingly authority, not only as it binds the subject but also as it imposes duties upon a king who is morally responsible for discharging his responsibilities with wisdom and with strength. The moral responsibility of the individual became a part of the larger intellectual design.

The concern with individual responsibility for human tragedy that confused *Romeo and Juliet* but enriched *Richard II* is, in fact, a third characteristic of all the early tragedies, not excluding *Titus Andronicus*. A villain is obviously responsible morally for whatever suffering his machinations bring upon him; and the reflection of this concern in the two earliest plays is therefore to be found not in the villains who commit crimes but in the victims who suffer. Richard's victims are almost monotonous in the regularity with which they die recalling their sins. The device is obvious, but, even so, it enables them to contribute meaning and moral depth to Shakespeare's play in contrast, for example, to Marlowe's failure to make full use of Tamburlaine's victims. But even *Titus Andronicus* opens with the cruel sacrifice of Alarbus by Titus' sons, which Tamora stigmatizes as the barbarous and unchivalrous act that it is. The play is obviously

[3]*Shakespeare's Use of Learning: An Inquiry into the Growth of His Mind & Art* (San Marino, Calif., 1953), pp. 56-61.

not much concerned with ultimate moral values, but the stress given this incident is significant. In the pride in his own rectitude that blinds him to other moral values, Titus offers a real prophecy of the great tragic heroes, especially of Brutus.

In none of these four plays, however, does hero or victim recognize the moral implications of his acts as he performs them. Brutus is the first of Shakespeare's tragic heroes to feel deep concern for the consequences of his deed before he commits himself, and only in him does a conflict of soul result.[4] In other words, *Julius Caesar* is the first of Shakespeare's plays in which a deliberate moral choice is itself central to the action. Before then moral responsibility is made clear to the audience by expository agents, or in *Richard III* by those who confess their sins in the presence of death. But Brutus' concern with moral values as dramatis persona is a logical development of Shakespeare's earlier preoccupation with them as dramatic artist.

The early tragedies therefore differ fundamentally from the great series of Shakespeare's maturity. But Shakespeare found in them invaluable training in tragic structure. They also led him to reflect upon the meaning of human life and its relationship to a larger historical and moral order, and the intellectual attitudes which they reveal are those which found fuller expression in the great tragedies. They will be examined individually from this point of view.

The usurpation and reign of Richard III had been treated dramatically at least twice before Shakespeare wrote. Thomas Legge's *Richardus Tertius* was "probably first produced at St. John's College at the Bachelors' Commencement in March 1579/80."[5] It therefore stands as the first genuine attempt to treat English medieval history dramatically. Only Bale's *King Johan*, which is religious propaganda, and Sackville and Norton's *Gorboduc*, which is political *exemplum*, had preceded it. It is nominally a Senecan tragedy, and Richard's characteristic attitudes as well as many of the episodes are indeed based upon Seneca. But it covers events from the death of Edward IV to the coronation of Henry VII and includes the traditional story of the fall and penance of Jane Shore. In sweep it is thoroughly narrative rather than Senecan,[6] and Legge was compelled to distribute

[4]Cf. Bradley, *Shakespearean Tragedy*, pp. 17-18.

[5]Frederick S. Boas, *University Drama in the Tudor Age* (Oxford, 1914), p. 112.

[6]Cf. George B. Churchill, *Richard the Third up to Shakespeare*, Palaestra, Bd. 10 (Berlin, 1900), 383.

his material through three *actiones* of five acts each. The only evidence that it may somehow have influenced Shakespeare consists in parallels between its wooing of the princess Elizabeth by Richard and Shakespeare's two episodes of the wooing of Anne and of Elizabeth the queen for her daughter. For his scene Legge drew on Seneca, and it is interesting that *Titus Andronicus* quotes in Latin garbled lines from the same contexts.[7]

The anonymous *True Tragedie of Richard the third* was published in 1594, and dates as early as 1588 have been conjectured for it, 1591 being as probable as any. The surviving text is a hopeless mixture of various kinds of verse and prose and is most probably corrupt. It seems to have been used by Shakespeare.[8]

If we compare Shakespeare's play with its predecessors, we are immediately struck with its greater unity of action. All three plays cover very much the same ground, and the parallels between *Richard III* and *The True Tragedie* are such as to suggest that Shakespeare was indebted to the older play for his choice of material. But Shakespeare has pruned away irrelevancies of two sorts. He has omitted completely the desertion of Jane Shore by her friends and her penance, and he has devoted only forty-one lines after the death of Richard to crowning Richmond, making clear that George Stanley is safe, and prophesying the end of civil war. By contrast *The True Tragedie* devotes over 220 lines to these matters, to Richmond's wooing of the princess Elizabeth, and to a final prophecy of English history up to the glories of Elizabeth. But it is more indicative that Shakespeare begins his play with Richard's plot to kill Clarence. In *The True Tragedie* the ghost of Clarence joins Truth and Poetry to provide a prologue narrating antecedent events, including the murder of Clarence by Richard as merely another detail. Shakespeare clearly conceived his dramatic action as Richard's getting and losing the crown, and the play therefore begins with the first of his plots directed toward that end.

This opening also focuses our attention upon Richard's cunning

[7]Ibid., p. 394. See also Boas, *University Drama in the Tudor Age*, pp. 130-131. Cf. *Phaedra*, l. 1180, and *Titus Andronicus* II.i.135; *Phaedra*, ll. 671-672, and *Titus* IV.i.81-82.

[8]Cf. Churchill, *Richard the Third up to Shakespeare*, pp. 396-398, 403-404; *Richard III*, ed. J. Dover Wilson (Cambridge, Eng., 1954), pp. xxviii-xxxi.

and upon his control of others, so that we see the following scenes from Richard's point of view and watch his sardonic craftiness once again at work. Shakespeare's rearrangement of the first scenes is therefore the first clear evidence that, even though he may have borrowed his choice of episodes from *The True Tragedie*, he derived his concept of Richard from Marlowe. For Richard is far closer to Tamburlaine than to the Richard of the earlier plays. Legge's Richardus is Senecan in his lack of a conscience, but he is far weaker than Shakespeare's Richard.[9] The Richard of *The True Tragedie*, on the other hand, is potentially a more credible human being than Shakespeare's. Immediately after the arrest of Buckingham he has a long aside devoted to the torments of his conscience:

> The goale is got, and golden Crowne is wonne,
> And well deservest thou to weare the same,
> That ventured hast thy bodie and thy soule,
> But what bootes Richard, now the Diademe
> Or kingdome got, by murther of his friends,
> My fearefull shadow that still followes me,
> Hath sommond me before the severe judge,
> My conscience witnesse of the blood I spilt,
> Accuseth me as guiltie of the fact,
> The fact, a damned judgement craves,
> Whereas impartiall justice hath condemned.
> Meethinkes the Crowne which I before did weare,
> Inchast with Pearle and costly Diamonds,
> Is turned now into a fatall wreathe,
> Of fiery flames, and ever burning starres,
> And raging fiends hath past ther ugly shapes,
> In studient lakes, adrest to tend on me,
> If it be thus, what wilt thou do in this extremitie?
> Nay what canst thou do to purge thee of thy guilt?
> Even repent, crave mercie for thy damned fact,
> Appeale for mercy to thy righteous God,
> Ha repent, not I, crave mercy they that list.
> My God, is none of mine. Then Richard be thus resolv'd,
> To place thy soule in vallence with their blood,
> Soule for soule, and bodie for bodie, yea mary Richard,
> Thats good, Catesbie.   (ll. 1398-1422)[10]

[9]Cf. Churchill, *Richard the Third up to Shakespeare*, pp. 311, 329, 340.

[10]Quotations are from *The True Tragedy of Richard the Third 1594*, Malone Soc. Reprints (London, 1929).

99

Before the battle his page testifies:

> Where shall I finde a place to sigh my fill,
> And waile the griefe of our sore troubled King?
> For now he hath obtaind the Diademe,
> But with such great discomfort to his minde,
> That he had better lived a private man, his lookes are gastly,
> Hidious to behold, and from the privie sentire of his heart,
> There comes such deepe fetcht sighes and fearefull cries,
> That being with him in his chamber oft,
> He mooves me weepe and sigh for company,
> For if he heare one stirre he riseth up,
> And claps his hand upon his dagger straight,
> Readie to stab him, what so ere he be,
> But he must thinke this is the just revenge,
> The heavens have powred upon him for his sinnes,
> Those Peeres which he unkindly murthered,
> Doth crie for justice at the hands of God,
> And he in justice sends continuall feare,
> For to afright him both at bed and boord.
> But staie, what noyse is this, who have we here?
>
> (ll. 1769-87)

The terror of every noise that has affected the page, too, is a good dramatic stroke. Another long speech in which Richard catalogs, with overabundance of rhetoric, all those who demand revenge upon him parallels in its effect Shakespeare's ghosts, but it comes just before the battle begins.

The Richard of *The True Tragedie* is therefore a man tortured by his conscience almost to the breaking point but driving himself on by force of his proud will. After his last tirade (l. 1915), he apparently addresses himself as "Frantike man" (the text must be corrupt, or else a second speech heading for him indicates his emergence from his trance). He reminds one of Macbeth both in his analysis of his emotions and in the emotions themselves. Potentially he is a genuinely tragic character. This conception of the anonymous play Shakespeare seems to have sacrificed in favor of a villain hero derived from Marlowe but possessed of a sardonic humor beyond Marlowe's range. Perhaps he was merely continuing what he had begun in *3 Henry VI*, where Gloucester describes himself in terms much like the opening of *Richard III*:

> I, that have neither pity, love, nor fear. . . .
> Then, since the heavens have shap'd my body so,
> Let hell make crook'd my mind to answer it.
> I have no brother, I am like no brother;
> And this word "love," which greybeards call divine,
> Be resident in men like one another
> And not in me. I am myself alone.
>
> *(3 Henry VI* V.vi.68, 78-83)

This is the Richard of his opening soliloquy who is "determined to prove a villain" and who is "subtle, false, and treacherous" (I.i.30, 37). Throughout the first part of the play others and Richard himself describe him as a villain. Anne calls him "thou dreadful minister of hell" (I.ii.46), and Richard comments on his wooing:

> And I no friends to back my suit withal
> But the plain devil and dissembling looks.
>
> *(Richard III* I.ii.236-237)

Margaret repeatedly calls him a devil or the equivalent (cf. I.iii.118, 144), and he gleefully pleads guilty:

> And thus I clothe my naked villainy
> With odd old ends stol'n forth of holy writ,
> And seem a saint when most I play the devil.
>
> (I.iii.336-338)

Shakespeare, in short, conceived Richard in terms of the Machiavel villain as a man so completely dedicated to his own evil ends that no faculty of his soul opposed his perverted will. Even in his final terror he talks of his self-love in words that stigmatize it as inordinate (V.iii.183-187). He is also a thorough opportunist, improvising from crime to crime. For his variant of the famous *sententia* from Seneca's *Agamemnon* is not, like Macbeth's, a tortured confession but a gleeful boast:

> Murder her brothers and then marry her!
> Uncertain way of gain! But I am in
> So far in blood that sin will pluck on sin!
> Tear-falling pity dwells not in this eye.
>
> (IV.ii.63-66)

But when Richmond appears, Richard becomes a different kind of man altogether—so much so that one suspects Shakespeare of sacrificing the integrity of his villain hero to establish both the rectitude of his destined savior of England and the courage that results from a clean conscience. Richard's first breaking is portrayed dramatically as he hears of Richmond's arrival and starts giving orders in his old resourceful way. But he tells Catesby to be gone and forgets to tell him what to do. He then forgets that he has just instructed Ratcliff to meet him at Salisbury. Plainly he is badly upset. Soon he has a conscience and is a prey to fear. He confesses:

> I have not that alacrity of spirit
> Nor cheer of mind that I was wont to have.
>
> (V.iii.73-74)

When the ghosts vanish, he is a broken man:

> O coward conscience, how dost thou afflict me! ...
> Cold fearful drops stand on my trembling flesh....
> I am a villain: ...
> I shall despair. There is no creature loves me.
>
> (V.iii.179-200)

To Ratcliff, who enters at this point, he confesses his terror. Only before the battle does he become his old self:

> Let not our babbling dreams affright our souls,
> For conscience is a word that cowards use, ...
> March on, join bravely, let us to't pell-mell;
> If not to heaven, then hand in hand to hell.
>
> (V.v.308-313)

In accusing Richard—or rather his creator—of inconsistency, I am well aware that I am contradicting many critics of weight. Obviously it would be most convenient for my thesis of Shakespeare's dramatic evolution if I could believe that Richard's attack of conscience is a genuine part of the total characterization and that, insofar as it is, he anticipates Macbeth. But I cannot find the evidence in the play. The closest approach to the conscience-stricken and suffering Richard of *The True Tragedie* seems to me to be Clarence as he tells of his dream, and he goes beyond that Richard in achieving something close to true penitence:

> O God! if my deep prayers cannot appease thee,
> But thou wilt be aveng'd on my misdeeds,

> Yet execute thy wrath in me alone!
> O, spare my guiltless wife and my poor children!
> Keeper, I prithee, sit by me a while.
> My soul is heavy, and I fain would sleep.
>
> (I.iv.69-74)

Edward, too, repents of Clarence's death and dies fearing the justice of God. By contrast with these men, Richard feels craven terror rather than the workings of conscience. Even in his last speech on the subject his conscience warns him that all men hate him for his crimes and desire vengeance. His despair is fear of the wrath of men, not that of God. Unlike Macbeth, he has no understanding of what he has done to himself. And, I repeat, the terror is first inspired by Richmond and is itself a dramatic device.

But Richard's last soliloquy does constitute an exception to the general tenor of his soliloquies and asides. These derive, of course, from the expository prologues and soliloquies of the villains in Seneca, but they also look forward to those of Hamlet and Macbeth. They are therefore of considerable interest. In that Richard's soliloquies merely reveal his motives and guide the audience in following his intrigues, they may be contrasted, for example, with Hamlet's. Both men are fundamentally alone in that for very different reasons they cannot trust their fellow human beings. They must therefore reveal themselves fully in soliloquies if they do so at all. But Hamlet's meditations are full of the torments of a man unsure of himself as well as of the world to which he stands opposed. They are the deepest probings of his soul. Richard's, except for his last confession that all the world stands against him, have no emotional content except glee. They are brisk and businesslike: "I am determined to prove a villain," he seems to say briskly; "now watch me do it."

In one respect, however, his soliloquies do anticipate the technique of *Othello* and *Macbeth*. Richard is quite as unrealistically objective and gifted at seeing his actions *sub specie aeternitatis* as Macbeth:

> And if King Edward be as true and just
> As I am subtle, false, and treacherous.
>
> (I.i.36-37)

Like Iago and Edmund, he knows that he is bad and his adversaries are good, though vulnerable. But his meditative speeches differ from theirs in lacking precisely the characteristic that enabled the great tragedies to hold the mirror up to nature: they stigmatize the action as sinful, but they make no attempt to relate it to those moral principles that it violates. Richard tells us that he will murder his brother; he never reflects on the evils of fratricide. He chuckles over his wooing of Anne and enumerates her late husband's virtues; but it never enters his mind to consider the rightness of marrying, to serve his ends, a woman whom he plans shortly to dispose of (I.ii.228-264).

Intellectual depth, in short, is not to be found in Richard, brilliant and clever as he is. That aspect of the play which looks toward the future Shakespeare—an aspect already, on my reading of his plays, characteristically Shakespeare—is to be found in the devices used to present Richard's life as part of a divine purpose. Richard's real antagonist is Providence, and an intention to construct the play in terms of a conflict between his devilish will and God's merciful providence may indeed have led to the simplification of his character upon which I have commented. Providence uses Richard upon both the individual and the social level. His crimes punish the guilty for their murders and their broken oaths; they also lead to the reunion of England. Shakespeare's problem was to give these concepts dramatic expression.

Such depth of meaning was, indeed, necessary if Shakespeare was to compete with Marlowe. Beside Tamburlaine's achievements Richard's were puny. He drove no pampered jades of Asia, and a single crown was the summit of his ambition. As a villain hero he was hopelessly outclassed. But meaning was more satisfying than melodrama and more in accord with the best critical theory; and Shakespeare provided it. For the intellectual dimensions of the play are achieved primarily by use of the Duchess of York and the queens Margaret, Elizabeth, and Anne. Margaret's presence in England, false to history, was Shakespeare's invention; so was his use of the women as dramatic symbols. Their great scenes are all original with him. Both curses and the notion that Richmond unified England by his marriage with the princess Elizabeth appear in Legge and *The True Tragedie*; the marriage, in fact, receives considerably more attention than in Shakespeare. What Shakespeare accomplished primarily by his handling of the queens was to make both the curses and the reunion of England structural principles operating to give unity and meaning to the play.

Any thoughtful Elizabethan, confronted with the spectacle of suffering and death caused by Richard's ruthless ambition, must inevitably ask why God permitted such things to be. One answer, the most obvious, might be that God could use even the devil for his purpose either to purify the good in the fires of adversity or to punish the sins of the wicked. The title page of the 1590 quarto of Marlowe's *Tamburlaine* reflects this explanation of a conqueror who "(for his tyranny, and terrour in Warre) was tearmed, The Scourge of God," and it has been argued, not to my mind altogether convincingly,[11] that Marlowe simply intended to portray him in terms of this orthodox concept. Such apparently was Shakespeare's view of Richard III. He was God's agent of punishment, although not God's servant; Margaret implies this view:

> Richard yet lives, hell's black intelligencer,
> Only reserv'd their factor to buy souls
> And send them thither.
>
> (IV.iv.71-73)

In exercising this function, Richard is part of a scheme of crime and punishment that is worked out in terms of a series of curses that are recalled as one by one the objects of the curses meet their death. Margaret sets the system in motion. As though to establish its validity, Richard reminds her of his father's curse after the murder of young Rutland and argues that "God, not we, hath plagu'd thy bloody deed" with the murders of her son and husband (I.iii.181). This view she accepts and proceeds in her turn to curse, in order, Edward IV, the young prince Edward, Queen Elizabeth, Rivers, Dorset, Lord Hastings, and Richard. For Buckingham she has a warning as much as a curse. Then finally she concludes by summarizing the view of events that must have been Shakespeare's:

> Live each of you the subjects to his [Richard's] hate,
> And he to yours, and all of you to God's!
>
> (I.iii.302-303)

On their way to execution Grey and Rivers recall her curse upon them for "standing by when Richard stabb'd her son" (III.iii.17). Then, as if to keep the theme before the audience, they also allude

---

[11]See Roy W. Battenhouse, *Marlowe's Tamburlaine: A Study in Renaissance Moral Philosophy* (Nashville, 1941), pp. 129-133, 169-174.

to her curse of Richard, Buckingham, and Hastings. Only a scene later Hastings laments:

> O Margaret, Margaret, now thy heavy curse
> Is lighted on poor Hastings' wretched head!
>
> (III.iv.94-95)

The guilt of these men for which they deserved death was a part of Margaret's curse, and no further moral exposition was needed. Not so with Buckingham. Margaret had treated him more gently than the rest:

> O princely Buckingham, I'll kiss thy hand. . . .
> Thy garments are not spotted with our blood.
>
> (I.iii.280-283)

So Shakespeare found it necessary to make Buckingham himself explain why he deserved to die. First, he lists those to whose murders he was, in effect, a party—Hastings, the princes, Grey and Rivers, King Henry and his son Edward, Vaughan, "and all that have miscarried"—and bids them for revenge mock his destruction (V.i.3-9). Then he remembers the oath to King Edward to be true to the princes and the queen's kinsmen. Only after he has done a thorough job of reminding the audience of his guilt does he recall Margaret's curse and quote her prophecy (V.i.26-27).

For Richard himself a more elaborate treatment is indicated. As the Duchess of York laments Clarence's death with his children, they are joined by Queen Elizabeth bewailing Edward, and there follows the first of the scenes of lamentation which the women contribute to the play. It is interrupted by Richard, who asks his mother's blessing and formally receives it upon his knees. The sequence from first wailing scene to blessing is obviously deliberate, for, by contrast, it underscores Richard's interruption of the last great scene of lamentation, this time to receive the Duchess' heartfelt curse, more terrible even than Margaret's because it comes from a mother:

> Therefore take with thee my most grievous curse,
> Which in the day of battle tire thee more
> Than all the complete armour that thou wear'st!
> My prayers on the adverse party fight;
> And there the little souls of Edward's children

> Whisper the spirits of thine enemies
> And promise them success and victory.
> Bloody thou art, bloody will be thy end;
> Shame serves thy life and doth thy death attend.
>
> (IV.iv.187-195)

The curses given and recalled undoubtedly make the play better "theater"—they add sensationalism in abundance. But that sensationalism was not conceived as mere blood and rant for their own sakes. The curses gave the deaths a deeper ethical significance. They made the play, in fact, a perfect example of the kind of dramatic treatment of history that showed how sins were punished and tyrants met their doom. They were a means of driving home the principle that men must pay for their sins and of making that principle operate in the structure of the play itself. Except for Clarence and Edward at the beginning of the play, and perhaps for Richard at the very end, the payment was, as yet, cruelly physical. But the careful workmanship expended upon the theme shows, I think, that Shakespeare's heart was in it and that his moral lesson was no perfunctory gesture.

We have noted that Puttenham, whose view is typical of his age, thinks of tragedy as dealing with evil kings, whose "infamous life and tyrannies were layd open to all the world, ... and their miserable ends painted out in playes and pageants, to shew the mutabilitie of fortune, and the just punishment of God in revenge of a vicious and evill life."[12] In *Tamburlaine* or *Sejanus*, whatever the intention of Marlowe or Jonson, the evil life and the ultimate fall are depicted; but, except that the portrayal of Sejanus' fall is a much more important part of the play and more artfully managed than anything in *Tamburlaine*, the spectators of both plays were left to infer for themselves any moral lessons that they might draw from it, at least as to universal principles at work. But Shakespeare extracted from Halle and further developed for himself a moral interpretation of the events that he portrayed as part of God's design not only for punishment of the guilty but also for reunion and pacification of England. This interpretation he worked into the dramatic structure as well as the dialogue of his play to a degree achieved, unless I am mistaken, by no other writer of *de casibus* tragedy. In other words, as a novice

---

[12]*The Arte of English Poesie*, in *Elizabethan Critical Essays*, ed. G. Gregory Smith (Oxford, 1904), II, 35.

tragedian he took more seriously than his contemporaries, and strove more artfully to obey, the primitive theory of tragedy that was then all he knew. Shakespeare's additions therefore prove not only that he was a superb dramatic craftsman but also that he was trying as best he knew how to teach as well as to delight—if delight be an appropriate word for the pleasure which a good performance of *Richard III* undoubtedly arouses.

The last great scene of lamentation is also the keystone in the dramatic structure by which the Duchess and the queens personify the other theme which gives depth of meaning to the play—the providential reunion of England under Richmond. This point has been so often made that it need only be glanced at. There are really three stages in this development. First, Margaret bursts in upon the Yorkist women, and, as symbol of the Lancastrians from whom she alone survives, she curses the Yorkist men, women, and children, but not until she has been thoroughly reminded of what they have suffered from her. Then, as Richard's crimes multiply but even before he has had the princes murdered, the Duchess, personification of the Yorkists as Margaret is of the Lancastrians, abandons Richard. To Dorset she gives her blessing: "Go thou to Richmond, and good fortune guide thee!"; to Anne she offers her prayers: "Go thou to Richard, and good angels tend thee!" (IV.i.92-93). When finally she joins Margaret in enumerating her parallel sorrows and betters Margaret in her vehement curse of Richard, the point has been made. The appearance of the ghosts of Richard's victims to Richard and to Richmond serves only to focus the blessings of all Englishmen upon Richmond and give the theme a final emphasis. Like the role of the women, it is Shakespeare's own contribution, an elaboration of Richard's dream mentioned in the chronicles and used, substantially unchanged, by Legge.

I have spoken of Margaret and the Duchess of York as personifications or symbols of Lancastrians and Yorkists. Insofar as they are merely symbols of the two themes which give philosophic depth to the play, the women are fundamental to the structure of the play as a whole but external to the main action involving the rise and fall of Richard the protagonist. They have no part in Richmond's landing, and they do little even to explain how he gathered followers. They are, in fact, background for that action, and they are part of it much

108

as the background for a portrait is necessary to outline the features by contrasting dark with light and to provide a clue to the expression that plays on the face. But, granted all this, the really significant fact as to Shakespeare's dramatic development is that they are characters in the play. Shakespeare might well have used the Senecan chorus to make his points in purely interpretive interludes. But he preferred to weave the larger historical and philosophic implications into the events of the play and to combine moral exposition with action. There results, perhaps, an ambiguity of structure. In one sense the antagonist is Richmond; in another and more fundamental sense the antagonist is God, whose captain Richmond accounts himself and whose designs the queens trace out. But the designs are a harmonious part of the entire play as in no other English drama that had so far been written. At a stroke Shakespeare had made obsolete the Senecan chorus and the pseudo-Senecan dumb show; he had also raised the fall of princes to a new dramatic height.

Romeo and Juliet is not only the most appealing of the early tragedies in its hold upon our imagination and sympathy. It is also the most original. Fundamentally it is a tragic love story without historical background or implications, a tragic romance in the proper sense of the word, resembling, in its earlier scenes, Shakespeare's romance comedies more than contemporary tragedy.[13] As such, its only predecessors among extant Elizabethan plays are the two versions of *Tancred and Gismund* by Wilmot and others (1566, 1591) and *Solyman and Perseda* (ca. 1590), but even the latter surrounds and almost buries the love story with the hazards of war.

From its romance background *Romeo and Juliet* inherits the reliance upon coincidence and chance that weakens its plot. Shakespeare obviously worked from Arthur Brooke's *Romeus and Juliet*, even if he knew the shadowy play to which Brooke alludes; furthermore, a play earlier than 1562 would have been something very different from Shakespeare's, undoubtedly like other plays of the period in confusion of structure and poverty of texture. But Shakespeare seems himself to have thought of his play as a tragedy in the *de casibus* tradition. He probably accepted the story as history, and his prologue sonnet (which parallels a very different sonnet intro-

[13]See Franklin M. Dickey, *Not Wisely But Too Well: Shakespeare's Love Tragedies* (San Marino, Calif., 1957), pp. 65-88.

ducing Brooke's story) describes the action as a fall from happiness due to fate and family:

> From forth the fatal loins of these two foes
> A pair of star-cross'd lovers take their life;
> Whose misadventur'd piteous overthrows
> Doth with their death bury their parents' strife.

Romeo, however, is also presented as morally responsible for what happens to him. To some extent, although very imperfectly, he is portrayed as contributing to his fall by his own deliberate acts, and the play therefore anticipates Shakespeare's mature tragedy of moral choice. But the three disparate elements—romance narrative, *de casibus* overthrow, and willful action—are in very unstable union. The play is, in fact, as artistically faulty as it is emotionally compelling.

In its concern with the larger background of fate and social order and in its emphasis upon moral responsibility, *Romeo and Juliet* is, of course, at one with *Richard III*. But Shakespeare was committed by his source to portraying, not a villain for whom death was a fitting punishment, but a tragic hero worthy of respect and deserving of pity. It is probably no accident that the "piteous overthrows" are described two lines later as "The fearful passage of their death-mark'd love." If Shakespeare had heard—as he very probably must already have heard—that pity and fear are the proper outcome of tragedy, he must have reflected that a Richard III could arouse terror, but only such pity as we may feel for a monster who discovers too late that "There is no creature loves me." This change from villain hero to romantic hero made all the difference in the world, dramatically speaking, and it enormously complicated the problem of portraying the protagonist as responsible for his downfall. That problem Shakespeare did not wholly solve. I suspect, furthermore, that he felt his way and learned as he wrote, often from hints in his sources. In *Richard III* the background that gives depth to the play was thoroughly consistent with the main action but did not need to be fused with it; in *Romeo and Juliet* there is, on the other hand, a serious inconsistency between background and foreground.

We have already noted that the Prologue blames the "piteous overthrows" of the young lovers on the stars and their parents' strife, the bulk of the sonnet being devoted to the family feud. These two themes are continued throughout the play.

The metaphysics of the play is not particularly sophisticated, and it is nowhere clear whether the stars symbolize blind fate or chance or whether they indicate, as in *Julius Caesar* and other later plays, the operation of natural forces which may be resisted or modified by human will. The same thing may be said of Fortune. Stars and Fortune (the latter borrowed from Brooke[14]) probably symbolize simply what we would call a hostile environment—forces of any kind operating as determining events. At any rate, references to them occur at key points in the play as comment upon the action. Before visiting the Capulets' party, Romeo reflects, in a speech given special emphasis by concluding a scene,

> my mind misgives
> Some consequence yet hanging in the stars
> Shall bitterly begin his fearful date
> With this night's revels.
>
> (I.iv.106-109)

"O, I am fortune's fool!" he cries after slaying Tybalt (III.i.141). Juliet, too, calls upon Fortune to be fickle once more and send Romeo back to her (III.v.60-64). But the clearest implication that the stars determine events is to be found in the last act. As he hears of Juliet's death, Romeo says: "Then I defy you, stars!" (V.i.24), and he views his death as a way to shake off "the yoke of inauspicious stars" (V.iii.111). It seems to me likely, however, that it is unwise to search the implications of Shakespeare's language too closely, simply because his language is not consistent. Against passages implying that the lovers are star-crossed must be balanced at least two direct statements that events are controlled by Providence. In fact, one would be tempted to say that Shakespeare accepted the orthodox notion that Fortune and the stars merely serve as names for man's inability to fathom God's providence, were it not that the passages cited above simply cannot be reconciled with this view. Friar Laurence, however, sees in Juliet's death the hand of God:

> The heavens do lour upon you for some ill;
> Move them no more by crossing their high will.
>
> (IV.v.94-95)

[14]Cf., e.g., Brooke, ll. 1667-72, with Shakespeare's *Romeo and Juliet* III.v.60-64; see Brooke's *'Romeus and Juliet' Being the Original of Shakespeare's 'Romeo and Juliet'*, ed. J. J. Munro, Shakespeare Library (New York, 1908), pp. l, liii.

Since this is indeed stern language to a family in grief, however excessive, it must mean what it says. The Prince, too, sees Providence at work:

> See, what a scourge is laid upon your hate,
> That Heaven finds means to kill your joys with love.
>
> (V.iii.292-293)

We must conclude, in short, that Shakespeare regarded his lovers as overthrown, in the best *de casibus* tradition, by hostile forces outside themselves, but that he made no attempt to define these forces in metaphysical terms. In clarity of meaning, the stars and Fortune are less satisfactory than the curses of *Richard III*.

The second of the Prologue's themes is, however, defined precisely; it, too, serves as background throughout the play, but it also becomes at one point a fundamental part of the main action. The frame setting is obvious. The play opens with a quarrel between the servants of the two families and the Prince's formal threat of punishment. This first quarrel is not in Brooke but is Shakespeare's own addition to the story on the basis of the later fight. The play ends with the feuding families, or the remnants thereof, once again assembled; but this time they mourn together as they hear the Prince promise that "Some shall be pardon'd, and some punished" (V.iii.308). All this would be mere setting for the main action, like the theme of the reunion of England in *Richard III*, were it not that Romeo's killing of Tybalt is, in fact, the turning point of the play; at that point not so much Tybalt as the feuding families become a kind of dramatic antagonist, and the conflict between young love and old hate is basic to the action.

The conflict between youth and age itself seems to have been constantly in Shakespeare's mind, even though it never comes to specific statement in the play.[15] Not only are Romeo and Juliet made younger than in the source, probably to make their haste and rashness more plausible, but the four parents are all presented in action as far older than the chronology of the play would indicate. Juliet's mother is under thirty; her father is at most middle-aged, but they

[15]Cf. John Erskine, "Romeo and Juliet," *Shakespearian Studies by Members of the Department of English and Comparative Literature in Columbia University*, ed. Brander Matthews and Ashley Horace Thorndike (New York, 1916), p. 219; Henry Edward Cain, "Crabbed Age and Youth in 'Romeo and Juliet,'" *Shakespeare Association Bulletin*, IX (1934), 186-191.

act much older, and the Montagues are tottering toward the grave. There is no effective communication between generations in either family.

So far I have deliberately isolated those elements in the play which seem to explain the downfall of the young lovers in terms external to them and without attributing to them any culpability. We should have to assume that Shakespeare had been attracted by a romantic story and, on the basis of hints in the source, had tried to present the action as a fall, from great happiness if not high station, in the fashion of *de casibus* tragedy, complete with references to Fortune and the stars. The result was structurally unstable but emotionally sound. A large proportion of readers and spectators, I am sure, have always interpreted the play in these terms and have wept over the needless sacrifice of young love to a cruel world. There can be no question, furthermore, that at crucial points the story loads the dice against Romeo and Juliet. They are the victims of a considerable series of coincidences and accidents which, by their very number, strain dramatic probability as well as verisimilitude to life. The stars seem, in fact, to be working overtime to cross the lovers.

There is, however, another aspect of the play which is apparent at first reading and grows in importance as one studies the text more closely. That is an attempt to show that Romeo and Juliet—Romeo especially—are in several ways morally culpable and are partly responsible for their own tragedy.

If I were asked to find a passage in which Shakespeare states the Christian view of man which seems to me to inform the mature tragedies and to dictate their plot structure, I could find no better than Friar Laurence's words before his first scene with Romeo. Romeo enters, in fact, while the friar is speaking, and I take this fact to be Shakespeare's way of making clear that this expository speech applies generally to all mankind but specifically to Romeo.

> O, mickle is the powerful grace that lies
> In plants, herbs, stones, and their true qualities;
> For nought so vile that on the earth doth live
> But to the earth some special good doth give,
> Nor aught so good but, strain'd from that fair use,
> Revolts from true birth, stumbling on abuse.
> Virtue itself turns vice, being misapplied;
> And vice sometime's by action dignified.

Enter ROMEO.
Within the infant rind of this weak flower
Poison hath residence and medicine power;
For this, being smelt, with that part cheers each part;
Being tasted, slays all senses with the heart.
Two such opposed kings encamp them still
In man as well as herbs, grace and rude will;
And where the worser is predominant,
Full soon the canker death eats up that plant.
(II.iii.15-30)

The last four lines are a clear statement of the internal conflict which makes all men potentially saints or sinners and of the chain of sin that operates in those governed by rude will. They undoubtedly describe Othello or Macbeth. To what extent do they describe Romeo?

If one looks for it, one finds a good deal of language in the play that stigmatizes the love between Romeo and Juliet as an outcropping of rude will. Everyone knows tags from the Prologue, but the sonnet spoken by the chorus at the beginning of Act II goes almost unnoticed. It is a clear warning, just before the balcony scene, that the love is on the level of the sensual appetite. Both the technical terms and the imagery are significant:

Now old Desire doth in his death-bed lie,
    And young Affection gapes to be his heir;
That fair for which love groan'd for and would die,
    With tender Juliet match'd is now not fair.
Now Romeo is belov'd and loves again,
    Alike bewitched by the charm of looks,
But to his foe suppos'd he must complain,
    And she steal love's sweet bait from fearful hooks.
Being held a foe, he may not have access
    To breathe such vows as lovers use to swear;
And she as much in love, her means much less
    To meet her new-beloved anywhere.
But passion lends them power, time means, to meet,
Temp'ring extremities with extreme sweet.

"Affection" is, of course, a technical term for a movement of the sensible appetite; "passion" denotes an inordinate or diseased appetite. "Extremities" implies the same thing. Both lovers are "bewitched" by external appearances, and Juliet is fearfully hooked like a fish. Shakespeare was exuberant in his use of language, but not reckless. This sonnet says, if any sonnet could, that the love is a sensual infatuation and not a rational love such as that which Othello and Desdemona are at such pains to describe (cf. I.iii.253-255, 262-266, etc.). Friar Laurence takes up the same theme: "Young men's love then lies / Not truly in their hearts, but in their eyes" (II.iii.67-68). The clearest statement of this theme is to be found, however, in Romeo's own words to Friar Laurence. The extravagance of language—"Heaven is here, / Where Juliet lives," and so on—shows the inordinate violence of his passion, and the friar quite properly calls him "Thou fond mad man"—"fond" meaning, of course, foolish (III.iii.29-30, 52). The counsel of reason he despises: "Hang up philosophy!" (l. 57). Finally, he openly admits the truth of Laurence's words:

> Wert thou as young as I, Juliet thy love,
> An hour but married, Tybalt murdered,
> *Doting* like me and like me banished,
> Then mightst thou speak, then mightst thou tear thy hair,
> And fall upon the ground, as I do now,
> Taking the measure of an unmade grave.
> (III.iii.65-70; italics supplied)

Later, the friar's long speech of consolation and advice gains the open-mouthed admiration of the nurse, but Romeo is quite unimpressed until she remembers to give him Juliet's ring. "How well my comfort is reviv'd by this!" he exclaims (l. 165).

Friar Laurence has a still more important function, however, in establishing the irrational violence, and therefore the culpability, of the haste with which Romeo acts. The point, too, is made throughout the play. Juliet herself introduces the theme during the balcony scene:

> I have no joy of this contract to-night;
> It is too rash, too unadvis'd, too sudden.
> (II.ii.117-118)

But Friar Laurence recurs to it repeatedly:

> Wisely and slow; they stumble that run fast.
> (II.iii.94)
> These violent delights have violent ends, ...
> Too swift arrives as tardy as too slow.
> (II.vi.9-15)

Finally, Romeo offers to kill himself, and Friar Laurence responds with a warning which is, in fact, a forecast of what happens at the end of the play but which Romeo spurns. The first few lines make the point, which the rest of the speech merely amplifies:

> Hold thy desperate hand!
> Art thou a man? Thy form cries out thou art;
> Thy tears are womanish; thy wild acts denote
> The unreasonable fury of a beast.
> Unseemly woman in a seeming man,
> And ill-beseeming beast in seeming both,
> Thou hast amaz'd me! By my holy order,
> I thought thy disposition better temper'd.
> Hast thou slain Tybalt? Wilt thou slay thyself,
> And slay thy lady that in thy life lives,
> By doing damned hate upon thyself?
>
> (III.iii.108-118)

Shakespeare here is merely improving upon a parallel passage in Brooke (ll. 1353-58), which no doubt suggested to him a device of which he was to become increasingly fond. Romeo's threatened suicide provides a kind of parallel to that which does, indeed, kill Juliet, and it enables the friar, in effect, to point out the irrationality of that later act and Romeo's responsibility for Juliet's death as well as his own. The concept that man acting irrationally is no man but a beast later became a staple of Shakespeare's thinking and of his imagery, especially in *King Lear*. Here it makes Romeo's moral responsibility for the tragic outcome of the play absolutely clear. Lest we should forget that responsibility, Romeo stigmatizes himself as a sinful madman when he advances to fight Paris. Shakespeare apparently wanted badly to make the point, since the speech to Paris causes an awkward pause in the rush of events:

> I beseech thee, youth,
> Put not *another sin* upon my head,
> By urging me to fury: O, be gone!
> By heaven, I love thee better than myself;
> For I come hither arm'd against myself.
> Stay not, be gone; live, and hereafter say
> A *madman's* mercy bid thee run away.
>
> (V.iii.61-67; italics supplied)

In the passages cited, however, Romeo's moral responsibility has been portrayed from without, so to speak, just as in *Richard III*. Except in the one short speech to Paris, where Shakespeare needed to remind the audience of the moral point made earlier by Friar Laurence, we are told that Romeo acts imprudently; we see no realization of that fact on his part. The rude will is undoubtedly present in abundance, and it brings the canker death. But grace, if encamped in Romeo, must be cowering within its tent. It offers no resistance to rude will. Shakespeare's failure to develop throughout the play the dramatic implications of Friar Laurence's figure of speech is, in fact, surprising, for the main tradition of Christian literary art, from the medieval debate on morality on, had centered not upon the external manifestations of man's disordered will but upon the inner conflict itself, upon the *psychomachia* between grace and rude will. This tradition was by no means dead.

At the time Shakespeare penned *Romeo and Juliet*, the greatest poetic achievement of the English Renaissance was unquestionably Spenser's *Faerie Queene*, of which the first three books were published in 1590. Spenser was deeply interested in contemporary affairs, and the warfare between Protestantism and Roman Catholicism is a subject of the poem. But for him that external conflict was but a symptom of the eternal warfare between good and evil which goes on in the soul of man. Confronted with the problem of giving tangible form to that internal conflict, Spenser chose allegory, and the forces struggling for the soul of Red Cross or Guyon are personified as enemies and allies of one sort or another. More important even than the battleground of England was the battleground of the human soul. Una is truth, primarily, and only secondarily Anglicanism; Duessa is all falsehood, and only in passing the whore of Babylon. If one sees human life in these terms (and Friar Laurence's words prove that Shakespeare already did), one must portray the inner struggle or be false to one's vision of life. I know of only two ways to give this struggle literary or dramatic expression—the method of allegory, which Spenser chose, or the technique of *exempla*, which must somehow be given universal application. But the use of examples inevitably raises the problem of presenting the interior struggle, and the only solution seems to be self-revelation of one kind or another, often as an interpretation of meaningful conduct. This method

Marlowe had already employed in the great opening soliloquy in *Faustus,* and Shakespeare must have known it. But in *Romeo and Juliet* he made only one tentative effort to show moral conflict within Romeo—tentative not only because it is confined to one crucial scene but also because even then the dramatic emphasis, and therefore the audience's attention, is inevitably upon the crowded and violent external action. The scene is, however, the turning point in the play.

The full implications of Romeo's refusal to fight Tybalt are lost, of course, upon all of us, for we have not been trained in the code of honor. Technically Romeo's action was exactly what Mercutio called it—a "calm, dishonourable, vile submission" (III.i.76). (I suspect, incidentally, that this is the only time in the play when anyone imputes calmness to Romeo.) Shakespeare implies, furthermore, that Romeo is acting calmly in full realization of his necessary course under the circumstances. But Mercutio has been developed by Shakespeare for just this moment. He is ignorant of Romeo's problem, and he is too impulsive to trust his friend's judgment. So he fights and is killed. Once more Romeo is tried when Tybalt returns, and this time he yields under extreme provocation indeed. But he knows that, in abandoning the mildness appropriate to his new relationship to Tybalt, he is yielding to rude will:

> Away to heaven, respective lenity,
> And fire-eyed fury be my conduct now!
>
> (III.i.128-129)

But, however briefly, heaven—or grace—has had its dramatic moment, and Shakespeare has suggested the kind of inner struggle and choice that he will later analyze so powerfully. He has understood, furthermore, that it must be centered upon a decisive action.

The passages cited are of extreme interest in another respect. In developing Romeo's moral responsibility and even a brief inner struggle, Shakespeare used methods that he was to employ throughout his tragedies to relate the action to fundamental moral principles. That Friar Laurence knows the medicinal properties of plants establishes him dramatically as a man of learning, but it also gives Shakespeare a chance to inject without strain a moral discourse that speedily becomes a guide to the audience in interpreting the action, a guide to which signposts are inserted at other points in the dialogue. As the friar tells Romeo not to kill himself like a young fool, Shakespeare manipulates the warning to make it fit later and more important events and couches it in terms of man's place in the hierarchy of nature in such a way as to guide the audience in judging Romeo's acts at the end of the play. Lest they forget, they are reminded by signposts just before the fight with Paris. Since no suitable minor character is present to label Romeo's conduct for what it is, the words must be given to Romeo himself, even though they imply a moral awareness on his part that he does not ordinarily possess. Before he fights Tybalt, Romeo also provides the audience with an ethical diagnosis of his action, but it is so skillfully inserted that it is in complete harmony not only with Romeo's character but also with the situation.

Despite these devices, however, the play completely lacks other more elaborate devices used in the mature tragedies to clarify and underscore the moral significance of the action. The passages pointing out Romeo's responsibility (Juliet's role in this matter is passive) are tucked in the middle of the play, and culpability is not stressed at key points as it is in the later plays. The Prologue is silent, and the Prince's moral judgment at the end is reserved for the families and the culprits. It is not, as in the later tragedies, a formal settling of accounts for Romeo and Juliet themselves. The play suffers, in short, from a kind of moral schizophrenia. The lovers are crossed by the stars, their families, and themselves; and the lines of moral responsibility are equally crossed. But, however briefly, in one key episode and fitfully elsewhere the tragic overthrow of Shakespeare's contemporaries gave place to the moral error, the *hamartia*, of his own greatest tragedies.

Richard II can be dealt with much more simply. It is an almost perfect example of *de casibus* tragedy in its formal structure and in its technical mastery. But only incidentally does it look toward the future rather than the past.

By abandoning the standard metaphor of Fortune's wheel, Shakespeare achieved another figure which not only implied that some must rise as others fall but also made explicit the balance of his play:

> Give me the crown. Here, cousin, seize the crown;
> Here, cousin,
> On this side my hand, and on that side thine.

Now is this golden crown like a deep well
That owes two buckets, filling one another,
The emptier ever dancing in the air,
The other down, unseen, and full of water.
That bucket down and full of tears am I,
Drinking my griefs, whilst you mount up on high.

(IV.i.181-189)

As Richard falls, so Bolingbroke rises; not only is the play as a whole
constructed on this principle, but the language and the imagery and
even the action of key scenes are adapted to it. At Flint Castle,
Richard talks of glistening Phaethon; then he comes down from the
wall himself to symbolize his fall. But, lest the structure be too
simple, he rises in our sympathy as he falls from power, and this
effect, too, Shakespeare was at pains to achieve. Only the talk of
Prince Hal and the handling of Aumerle's conspiracy seem to mar
the perfect unity and symmetry of the play. The former is an obvious
preparation for *1 Henry IV*, but the latter is actually a part of the
design, a perfectly acceptable part in terms of the dramatic tradition
in which Shakespeare was working. As we saw Richard begin his
descent by mismanaging the quarrel between Bolingbroke and Mowbray, so we watch Bolingbroke signalize his control by his swift
dispatch of the conspiracy.

In a more fundamental sense, too, the play is a masterpiece of
structure. Once again Shakespeare gives depth to his tragedy by
relating it to a fundamental problem—the nature of the kingship and
its authority. Here, however, the principles of political philosophy
are an integral part of the action in that they control the behavior of
important characters. Gaunt and York not only talk of the subject's
duty of obedience to his king, the Lord's anointed; Gaunt is true to
his principles, and York tries to be faithful as long as his weaker nature
and very weak position will admit. Once Bolingbroke is crowned,
he is loyal again, even to the injury of his own son. Carlisle, on the
other hand, has the more difficult role of making clear the king's
duty to himself and to his subjects. His warnings to Richard gain
additional emphasis from his final great act of devotion to the principle of the divine right of the kingship.

Carlisle's great speech on obedience has an even more important
function as one of the devices by which Shakespeare establishes

Richard's moral responsibility for his downfall and death. Unless I am mistaken, Richard has no long soliloquies or asides or even what I have called meditative speeches. There is no inner conflict, nor do we ever feel in touch with Richard's mind and soul as we do with Edward II's. Even when we least approve of Edward's actions, we understand and, to that extent, sympathize with him. Marlowe aimed higher than Shakespeare, though he missed his mark in the play as a whole. Yet we have a very clear impression of Richard's character and especially of the weaknesses that cost him his crown. Shakespeare achieved this effect by a masterly combination of significant words and actions on Richard's part and expository speeches by other characters, most notably Carlisle, whose devotion gives extreme force to his testimony. Richard shows his own ineffectiveness and excitability by his handling of the opening quarrel and his moods after the landing in England. His actions at Flint Castle and the deposition scene demonstrate his failure to think of the crown as a heavy responsibility rather than as a crutch or a toy. Gaunt, York, and Carlisle all reveal his sins and his follies. Even Northumberland underscores the hysteria of his conduct at Flint Castle.

> Sorrow and grief of heart
> Makes him speak fondly, like a frantic man.
>
> (III.iii.184-185)

Richard's histrionics, too, gain point as a revelation of how not to be a king when compared to the cool efficiency and self-control of Bolingbroke.

But Shakespeare achieves his surface polish only by dodging fundamental issues. We do not really know why Richard stopped the trial by combat or lightened Bolingbroke's banishment. To the end of the play we never know whether Bolingbroke set out to become king or merely took advantage of Richard's weakness. Others have theories about the obedience due a king. He has none, and a decision like that which cost Brutus endless agony is not even mentioned in the play, although he must logically have made it. Only in York and Carlisle do we see the rudiments of a genuine moral conflict, and their subordinate position, if not Shakespeare's wish, prevented any dwelling upon their problems.

In one important respect, however, the play does anticipate the future. The true punishment of Macbeth lies not in his final death but in the restless agony of his life after the murder of Duncan. Shakespeare was merely dramatizing the doctrine that the real punishment for our sins is that we have to live with what they do to us, sometimes through all eternity. So Dante conceived the circles of hell, and Shakespeare saw Macbeth as achieving his circle even before death. In Pomfret Castle Richard has time to reflect, within the shallow limits of his nature, upon his sins, and he produces some very neat epigrams: "I wasted time, and now doth Time waste me" (V.v.49). I find his attitudinizing not very moving, although brilliantly in character. Bolingbroke, on the other hand, says much less, but one feels that the process of atonement will be endless. The stylized ending of the play seems but the beginning of a punishment:

> Lords, I protest, my soul is full of woe
> That blood should sprinkle me to make me grow.
> Come, mourn with me for what I do lament,
> And put on sullen black incontinent.
> I'll make a voyage to the Holy Land,
> To wash this blood off from my guilty hand.
> March sadly after; grace my mournings here
> In weeping after this untimely bier.
>
> (V.vi.45-52)

I have indicated elsewhere that I think *Richard II* the most brilliantly structured of all the *de casibus* tragedies. As it weighs impartially a king who cannot rule and a usurper who can, it is magnificent art in the dramatizing of political ideas. But it is not a profoundly satisfying tragedy. In fact, one hardly feels it as tragic at all. The reason is simply that Richard is not a tragic hero in our sense of the word (as well as Aristotle's), whereas Romeo is. He is a part of the action physically but not emotionally. Not that he does not feel grief and pain—he does, in much very fine and often convincing rhetoric. But he does not develop or decay or even respond to his suffering in any fundamental way. He is acted upon, and he reacts only by attitudinizing. We do not enter into his inner agony, and he arouses in us little pity or fear. The surface hero of *Richard II*, like the surface villain of *Richard III*, represented a dramatic dead end. Even Jonson's *Sejanus* is less interesting technically, though it is, for me at least, as exciting a play as these.

Julius Caesar is separated from *Richard II* both by a considerable interval of time and by major developments in dramatic technique. If, with E. K. Chambers, we take *Richard II* as Shakespeare's first play in the season of 1595-1596 and *Julius Caesar* as the first product of 1599-1600, the two plays stand four years apart. These four years represented somewhat under a fifth of Shakespeare's active career as a playwright and somewhat over a fourth of the period spanned by the tragedies. They produced at least five of Shakespeare's greatest plays—*The Merchant of Venice* and *Much Ado about Nothing*, *1* and *2 Henry IV* and *Henry V.* It is no wonder, therefore, that *Julius Caesar*, standing near the midpoint of Shakespeare's tragic career, is a very different kind of play from *Romeo and Juliet* or *Richard II*. It is possible, in fact, that the four-year interval reflected a desire on Shakespeare's part to wait until he had acquired both an intellectual and a technical background more nearly adequate to the demands of tragedy as the highest form of drama and, as some said, of all literature.

The interval in time and in technique between *Richard II* and *Julius Caesar* must not blind us, however, to an even greater interval that separates it from the next tragedy which, in important respects, it anticipates. *Hamlet* came the next year, but *Hamlet*, for all its dazzling richness, grew out of the revenge play and was not constructed according to the formula of the other great tragedies. To find the fruition of what began in *Julius Caesar*, we must wait for *Othello*, which was (once again to follow E. K. Chambers' chronology) the second play of the season 1604-1605. This is an interval of five and one-half years. *Julius Caesar*, therefore, is probably closer in time to *Richard II* than to *Othello*. This fact has important consequences—consequences which I, for one, have previously overlooked in writing about the play.

Julius Caesar is, like *Richard III* and *Richard II*, a political play in that it deals with public figures engaged in governing a great nation and its events are conceived in political terms. Like *Richard II* it is also political in the more fundamental sense that the action is grounded in philosophic principles having to do with the relationship between authority and obedience and the consequences of disobedience. The two plays have in common, alone among the tragedies, a high proportion of speeches devoted either to expounding political principles or to relating those principles to events. Carlisle's great exposition of the Tudor commonplaces about the divine right of kings, passive obedience, and the evils of civil war is even balanced by Antony's soliloquy after Caesar's murder, which makes parallel points and draws from the same sources.[16]

Two major differences from *Richard II* immediately stand out, however, as soon as one begins comparing the political element in the two plays. Richard himself rhapsodizes about the divinity that hedges a king, but the real political sense in the play (as Shakespeare understood it) is talked by such subordinate figures as Gaunt, York, Carlisle, and even Bolingbroke and Northumberland. The only characters who act decisively on the basis of their views are again Gaunt and York, who refuse to disobey the king even to avenge their murdered brother, and Carlisle, who places his life in jeopardy rather than acquiesce in the deposition. York may be said once again to act on principle in betraying Aumerle's conspiracy to Bolingbroke. But neither Richard nor Bolingbroke is himself governed by any genuine thinking about first principles of political conduct. These affect the two leaders only via the secondary characters. Even Richard's surrender to Bolingbroke is dictated by desperation and hysteria rather than by his theory, which he expounds at such length, that God's ministering angels will protect a king. In *Julius Caesar*, however, the political speeches eventuate in action by Brutus and Caesar. Cassius' discourses on tyranny and freedom are part of his campaign to woo Brutus; aided by well-placed "anonymous" messages, they succeed. Brutus' meditation upon political ambition leads him to kill Caesar. Caesar's notion of a ruler's duty to prefer his subject's interests to his own prevents the unmasking of the conspiracy. And other examples could be cited. The political principles stated in *Julius Caesar* are, in short, more nearly central to the action than in *Richard II*. In fact, they dominate several of the decisive scenes.

If *Julius Caesar* differs from *Richard II* in making its political discourses the basis of action by major characters, it also differs from it in relating events in the political order to supernatural forces in a

---

[16]Cf. *Richard II* IV.i.134-149; *Julius Caesar* III.i.256-275. See Alfred Hart, *Shakespeare and the Homilies: And Other Pieces of Research into the Elizabethan Drama* (Melbourne, 1934), pp. 52-53.

way reminiscent of *Richard III*. But, whereas it improves upon *Richard II* in integrating political thinking into the action, its prodigies and omens, though more numerous, have less to do with the movement of the play than do the ghosts in *Richard III*. Even Caesar's ghost at Philippi contributes less to the meaning than the ghosts of Richard's victims. But this paradox, I am convinced, is true only from our point of view. For the exhalations, the fiery men, even the lion in the capitol and the frightful tempest represent Shakespeare's attempt to add a new dimension to his tragedy. As usual he makes clear his own meaning. Calpurnia puts the matter succinctly after reciting an awesome list of prodigies:

> When beggars die there are no comets seen.
> The heavens themselves blaze forth the death of princes.
>
> (*Julius Caesar* II.ii.30-31)

The unnatural and supernatural events of *Julius Caesar* belong in the same category as the cannibal horses and other portents in *Macbeth*. The storm of this play belongs with the stormy night of *Macbeth* and the storm on the heath of *King Lear*. They all represent Shakespeare's attempt to symbolize his belief that the social order is part of the order of nature, and that a breach of any part of nature's order will produce convulsions throughout the whole. The murder of a great ruler will be attended and even "blazed forth" by other equally unnatural phenomena. *Julius Caesar*, like the other tragedies mentioned, culminates the tendency that we noticed in its predecessors. Once again Shakespeare gives his action depth and significance by setting it against a larger background. That background now becomes the whole order of nature. The political principles are now part of the laws of nature.

The political context of *Julius Caesar* inevitably involved a major problem of dramatic structure for an Elizabethan writer. This problem Shakespeare was unable wholly to solve. The important Roman sources, not only Plutarch's *Lives* but also Lucan's *Pharsalia*, were strongly republican in sympathy. Caesar's career was based upon the murder of Pompey and the suicide of Cato, and his heirs destroyed Brutus. Both Cato and Brutus were Stoic saints in their devotion to principle and their contempt of fortune. But the fact of Caesar's greatness remained; in theory at least, the Kaiser—that is, the Caesar—

of the Holy Roman Empire was the greatest of living monarchs, and the real power of Charles V had not been forgotten. Shakespeare, furthermore, seems to have understood Tudor absolutism rather than Stoic republicanism. In his other plays Caesar is usually a symbol of greatness, his murder an ultimate crime.[17] It was simply impossible, furthermore, for Elizabethan dramatists to square the republicanism of Roman writers with Tudor ideas of history or of monarchy or of the European political system. In plays before *Julius Caesar* the solution, insofar as we have evidence, was a compromise.

The Latin *Caesar Interfectus* of Richard Eedes was performed at Christ Church College, Oxford, probably in 1582. Only its Epilogue survives.[18] That shows an imitation of Stoic prose, like that which Shakespeare attempted in Brutus' oration, and a deliberate attempt to hold the scales even between Caesar and Brutus: Caesar did badly to seize the state, well in that he seized it without bloodshed; Brutus did right in restoring liberty, wrong in thinking that it must be restored by the murder of Caesar. The moderation of Caesar's victory veiled the baseness of the crime; the ungrateful cruelty of Brutus shadowed the glory of his deed. Caesar bore himself well in a bad course, Brutus badly in a good cause. Antony urged Caesar on; Cassius, Brutus. Cassius was as much the better leader as Brutus was the better man. Brutus hated tyranny, Cassius the tyrant. Caesar's fortune was just if we regard him as a tyrant, unjust if we regard him as a man; but the immortal gods do not tolerate tyrants, even the best of them.

The Tragedie of Cæsar and Pompey Or Cæsars Revenge was not entered in the Stationers' Register until 1606, but it obviously belongs in the middle 1590's, both because of its imitation of the early revenge plays and because of its pedantry. It seems, indeed, to have been performed at Oxford. Discord and, at the end, the Ghost of Caesar serve as prologue, chorus between acts, and epilogue. The play presents the entire story from the battle of Pharsalia to the death of Brutus; it manages to include Caesar's refusal to kill Brutus, Caesar's love of Cleopatra (punctuated by amorous asides from

[17]Cf. *3 Henry VI* V.v.53; *All's Well That Ends Well* III.vi.56; *Cymbeline* III.i.2-11; but *As You Like It* V.ii.34.

[18]The Latin original is quoted in Boas, *University Drama in the Tudor Age*, pp. 164-165.

Antony), the murder of Pompey, the suicide of Cato, and the main episodes of Shakespeare's play, except that Antony has no funeral oration and goads the people on to revenge in a scene that he shares with Octavius. Caesar's ghost is built up into a standard revenge ghost. What is really interesting about the play is its point of view, which once again holds the balance even. Caesar's followers praise him, his enemies excoriate him. Only Brutus seems to speak impartially:

> To what a pitch would this mans vertues sore,
> Did not ambition clog his mounting fame.
>
> (ll. 210-211)[19]

Caesar, in effect, confesses to ambition:

> For *Pompey* though thou wert mine enemy,
> And vayne ambition mov'd us to this strife.
>
> (ll. 805-806)

It should be noted, furthermore, that Brutus simply assumes that Caesar is a tyrant as he resolves to kill him and has no doubts, as in Shakespeare.[20] Discord may perhaps be assumed to speak *sub specie aeternitatis*. She hates both Caesar and Brutus impartially:

> Now *Caesar* rides triumphantly through *Rome*,
> And deckes the Capitoll with Pompeys spoyle:
> Ambition now doth vertues feat usurp,
> Then thou Revengfull great *Adastria* Queene.
> Awake with horror of thy dubbing Drumm,
> And call the snaky furies from below,
> To dash the Joy of their triumphing pride,
> *Erinnis* kindle now thy Stigian brands,
> In discontented *Brutus* boyling brest,
> Let *Caesar* die a bleeding sacrifice,
> Unto the Soule of thy dead Country *Rome*.
>
> (ll. 1144-56)

Brutus is the "author of *Romes* liberty," but he is "proud" in his murdering hand and that hand will stab his "trayterous heart" (ll. 1770-80). At the end Discord summarizes, once again impartially:

[19]Quotations are from *The Tragedy of Caesar's Revenge*, Malone Soc. Reprints (London, 1911).

[20]He simply equates Caesar with Tarquin. Cf. ll. 1551-60.

> *Caesar* I pitied not thy Tragick end:
> Nor tyrants daggers sticking in thy heart,
> Nor do I that thy deaths with like repayd.
>
> (ll. 2549-51)

Caesar, in Discord's view, was a bloody, ambitious tyrant; but his murderers, including Brutus, also deserved to die. The play also portrays Caesar as a braggart (though what he says is accurate prophecy). He turns down the crown but adds:

> Content you Lordes for I wilbe no King,
> An odious name unto the *Romaine* eare,
> *Caesar* I am, and wilbe *Caesar* still,
> No other title shall my Fortunes grace:
> Which I will make a name of higher state
> Then Monarch, King or worldes great Potentate.
>
> (ll. 1504-09)

The title of the play indicates its debt to the tradition of Lucan, but its attempt to portray the action as a series of crimes and punishments—Caesar for Pompey, Brutus and Cassius for Caesar—is something less than sophisticated. In blaming all, it blames none effectively.

A case could perhaps be made that Shakespeare knew this play, largely on the basis of very close parallels in structure and management of details between its latter part and his play. But I doubt that it could be proved. *Caesars Revenge* seems to me useful primarily in illuminating Shakespeare's dramatic structure and his thinking.

The structure is much improved. Shakespeare's action is the assassination of Caesar and its consequences. He begins with events that move—or are used by Cassius to move—Brutus to join the conspirators, and he continues to Brutus' death, which ends the consequences of that action. But I suspect that even Shakespeare, at this point in his dramatic development, was not capable of rising completely above the habits of contemporary drama. We have noted that Elizabethan tragedies were sometimes governed, in their structure, by the need to present a traditional block of history. *Caesars Revenge* obviously attempts to do so. The story which Shakespeare knew was that of Caesar and Brutus.

Caesar's complicated personality and the circumstances of his death as presented by Plutarch must also have had for Shakespeare a compelling fascination. In his previous tragedy he had combined, in

128

effect, two stories: the life and coronation of Bolingbroke and the downfall and death of Richard II. These two actions were, of course, intimately related, and they could easily be managed in one drama, particularly if the death of Richard were reserved until after Bolingbroke had established himself by quelling a major conspiracy against him, and Richard's coffin were brought in as Bolingbroke settled accounts in the final scene. But the fact remains that Shakespeare, like his fellow playwrights, found adequate unity in a drama that had, in effect, two heroes. In *Julius Caesar*, though he condensed the action of the older play immeasurably, he kept something of the double focus of *Richard II*.

We can get a clearer notion of *Julius Caesar*, perhaps, if we create for it a title following a standard Elizabethan formula from Marlowe's *Edward II*: "The troublesome life and lamentable death of Julius Caesar with the tragicall fall of proud Brutus." To do this is simply to restate in dramatic terms the fact that *Julius Caesar* is closer in time to *Richard II*, in which the influence of Marlowe is strong, than to *Othello*, in which the tragical fall of the proud Moor furnishes the entire substance, as well as the basic action, of the play. But in dramatic structure as in time we are far more than halfway from *Edward II* to *Othello*. Though Caesar receives great attention, Brutus does provide the basic action of *Julius Caesar* and gives the play genuine unity. Shakespeare has eliminated everything from the traditional story before the hatching of the conspiracy against Caesar, and important events involving Caesar occur offstage while we watch Cassius work upon Brutus before our eyes. Most important of all, however, Brutus has been developed into a tragic hero of the Aristotelian type. To achieve this result Shakespeare almost completely eliminated the moral ambiguity which resulted from the sources and was present in *Caesars Revenge*. For him Caesar was, despite minor shortcomings, a great and just ruler; Brutus was guilty of a tragic error. I have argued elsewhere that Caesar, whatever his weaknesses and his braggadocio (and it is as nothing in Shakespeare compared to *Caesars Revenge*), is to be thought of as the legal ruler of Rome.[21] For Brutus to kill him is not only murder but regicide unless he can be proved a tyrant. He is therefore in the position of Richard II, except that he is undoubtedly a powerful and able ruler, a man who

[21]See *Shakespeare's Use of Learning*, pp. 226-239.

dominates all about him and not a weakling like Richard. No pilgrimage to the Holy Land will atone for Caesar's death. Brutus must die.

But all the sources presented Brutus as a great and good man, and Shakespeare was confronted with the task of showing how such a man would come to commit murder. Once again, as in *Romeo and Juliet*, he was faced with the problem of presenting a crucial act in terms of a crucial decision, and this time his technique, though not faultless, proved equal to the occasion. Largely, I think, upon the basis of Marlowe's *Faustus* and the whole tradition of the moralities upon which it, in turn, rested, Shakespeare evolved the method which remained characteristic of the great tragedies.[22]

Cassius is used, as in the dramatic tradition, to urge Brutus to action. But Brutus is already tainted. Just as Macbeth starts when the witches prophesy his kingship, so Brutus tells Cassius: "What you would work me to, I have some aim" (I.ii.163). Cassius' other role is Shakespeare's own creation and becomes another item of his method. The hero must not only be tempted, but that temptation must be linked to those appetites which might overturn reason. The particular action must be interpreted in the light of the accepted psychological and ethical system. So Cassius is given a soliloquy which amounts to a character analysis of Brutus plus a plan of campaign for subverting his "honourable metal" by appealing to his pride in "the great opinion / That Rome holds of his name" (I.ii.312-326).

The crucial and agonizing decision is made in the soliloquy that opens Act II (II.i.10-34). The decision itself, in contrast to Romeo's, now receives complete attention. Shakespeare is at some pains to show that Brutus' conclusion does not follow logically from his own statement of the evidence, for Caesar is to be killed lest he become what his behavior so far indicates he will not become:

> to speak truth of Caesar,
> I have not known when his affections sway'd
> More than his reason.
>
> (II.i.19-21)

Shakespeare reinforces his point that Brutus is the one who is being swayed by affection more than reason by having Brutus succumb

[22]Ibid., pp. 240-246.

only after another appeal to his pride. A letter—doubtless planted by Cassius—is brought to him, once again urging him to act; and only then does he resolve to do so. The execution of this design to show Brutus actually making a tragic error is by no means perfect. There is no bystander to point out to Brutus (and the audience), as Kent does to Lear, the fallacy of his position. To that extent Shakespeare is responsible for the hash which critics have sometimes made of the soliloquy and, in my view, of the play. We are only told, furthermore, that Brutus'

> state of a man,
> Like to a little kingdom, suffers then
> The nature of an insurrection.
>
> (II.i.67-69)

We do not feel his agony as we do that of Othello and Macbeth. But Shakespeare has moved his crucial action into the soul of Brutus, and he has anchored his tragedy to the Christian tradition that the warfare within the soul of man between grace (or reason) and rude will is the only action, in ultimate terms, that really matters. He holds his mirror up to the moral nature of the universe in the omens and prodigies; in Brutus' soliloquy and agony, he holds it up to the moral nature of man.

The fact remains, however, that the dramaturgy of Brutus' moral choice is not quite up to the conception. The play also has other serious flaws in dramatic technique. The worst of these is probably Antony's soliloquy after the murder of Caesar (III.i.254-275). It closely parallels the Bishop of Carlisle's great speech on rebellion in *Richard II* (IV.i.114-149) and, like it, is derived from the official Homilies. It must be taken, I think, as Shakespeare's attempt to place both the murder of Caesar and the subsequent civil war in the context of sound political principles. The murder of a ruler must lead to social chaos and to infinite misery, in classical Rome as in medieval England. But Antony hardly seems to us an objective judge under the circumstances, and his role in the play certainly does not invest him with the moral stature of the Bishop of Carlisle. So the speech has seldom received, in modern times at least, the attention due it.

The moral degeneration of Brutus also needs to be pointed out more clearly than by contrast with Cassius, who is made a stronger and better man toward the end of the play than at the beginning. The audience can hardly be expected to note the inconsistency when Brutus first upbraids Cassius for his way of getting money and then demands for his own use some of the ill-gotten gold, explaining self-righteously that he "can raise no money by vile means" (IV.iii.65-78). In fact, the entire degeneration of the conspirators, especially Brutus, needs to be underscored. For this function Shakespeare later used the hero himself, as in Macbeth's great soliloquies, or a clearly established protatic character like Enobarbus, who diagnoses Antony's downfall in purely expository speeches. Shakespeare also learned to use imagery and symbols: witness the blood in Macbeth. The gold just alluded to is, in fact, a faint promise of this kind of device, but much more stress would be needed to make it an adequate symbol of Brutus' self-righteous hypocrisy.

The most serious weakness of the play from the point of view of moral exposition is undoubtedly Brutus' own failure to recognize the enormity of his mistake. Here, too, Shakespeare made a beginning in his use of the ghost; but we miss the great speeches in which Othello or Lear or Macbeth confess their mistakes and survey the tragic consequences.

These and other means of relating the particular action to universal principles of human conduct Shakespeare subsequently developed. But the crucial step from an external to an internal action was taken in *Julius Caesar*. The play also developed methods of analyzing that action in terms of the moral laws of nature, just as it related the soul of man which took that action to the stars that blazed forth the death of a prince.

Chapter Four ✍ FORM AND PRESSURE:

SHAKESPEARE'S TRAGIC MATURITY

THE EARLY tragedies discussed in the preceding chapter had in common two characteristics that set them apart from contemporary plays: their much superior dramatic structure and their tending systematically to relate the particular action to a larger background, whether the designs of Providence or the nature of kingship. In these respects, as in others, they achieved an excellence unique in their time, though they merely exemplified standard forms of tragedy—revenge, *de casibus*, or historical narrative. But each had its peculiar excellences, and in each Shakespeare developed dramatic techniques of interest, some of which he discarded, but many of which remained a part of his art. It was therefore necessary to discuss each play separately.

After *Julius Caesar*, however, we confront a different situation. Shakespeare continued to grow in skill, and one can see that weaknesses of technique in one play were corrected in the next. In fundamentals, however, all the mature tragedies but *Hamlet* were developments of the tragic method first approximated in the handling of Brutus in *Julius Caesar*. Even *Hamlet* so largely employs the same view of human nature and the same techniques of presenting it that one is tempted, with many critics of standing, to try to analyze it in the same terms as one uses for the other great tragedies. I think myself, incidentally, that many of the critical problems that traditionally surround the play have resulted from yielding to that temptation. Be that as it may, it becomes possible to discuss a common structure and a large variety of techniques that are characteristic of most or even all of the later tragedies, and a different approach will therefore avoid repetition. This chapter will attempt to isolate and describe methods characteristic of the plays as a group. Later chapters will resume the survey approach and will concentrate upon what is especially important or even unique in individual plays.

I have suggested elsewhere that Shakespeare's great tragedies—*Hamlet, Othello, King Lear, Macbeth, Coriolanus,* and *Antony and Cleopatra,* especially the middle two—are in a sense problem plays.[1] In the romantic comedies and the plays based upon English history and even in *Romeo and Juliet,* Shakespeare was content to dramatize his source, preserving the narrative and only condensing or occasionally complicating it to dimensions suitable for an Elizabethan stage play and developing characters that would give some plausibility to the action. Romeo and Juliet, for example, were both made younger than in the sources partly, at least, to motivate their extreme haste and the violence of Romeo's emotional reactions. But the action was derived almost entirely from Brooke's *Romeus and Juliet.*

In the great tragedies, on the other hand, the source narrative is drastically reshaped to make the action conform to traditional diagnoses of human conduct. The new method, like much of the new technique, is apparent in *Julius Caesar.* We have noted that Shakespeare transformed Brutus from Plutarch's flawless patriot into a tragic hero whose *hamartia* was a moral error grounded in pride that made him responsible for the collapse of his party and his own death. Only minor changes in the source were needed. As the conspirators meet to plan their course of action, Brutus three times vetoes, for reasons reflecting vanity and impractical idealism, sound proposals made by Cassius; two of the proposals are in Plutarch, but Shakespeare supplied the motives that reveal Brutus' weakness.[2] Then Brutus fatuously advances as a reason for letting Antony deliver a funeral oration the very argument which Antony himself offers in Plutarch (III.i.245-246). The quarrel with Cassius over the ill-gotten gold combined two episodes separated by a considerable interval in Plutarch, so that the self-righteous inconsistency is Shakespeare's addition. The key soliloquies in which Cassius describes Brutus and Brutus considers killing Caesar are, however, not a change from Plutarch but simply the kind of addition that Shakespeare made continually in developing and motivating action implied in the source. They make clear the intent of the changes, which reinforce them. The skill with which Shakespeare reversed the characterization in

[1]*Shakespeare's Use of Learning: An Inquiry into the Growth of His Mind & Art* (San Marino, Calif., 1953), pp. 11-12.

[2]Ibid., pp. 234-235.

his source by adding a few speeches and altering a few details makes the play one of the best examples of the deftness with which he worked.

Any theory of what happened in *Hamlet* must rest on conjecture, and the deviations from the source in *Othello* are once again minor, although fundamental to Shakespeare's interpretation of the action.[3] But in *King Lear*, as we shall see, the entire last half of the play was written to motivate the moral regeneration of Lear and provide the tragic ending, and the parallel subplot was added. Macbeth's murder of Duncan was changed from an open revolt in alliance with Banquo to a secret crime, the object being to make the play a study of the causes and consequences of sin as it affects the mind and soul of the sinner.[4] In *Coriolanus* and *Antony and Cleopatra* Shakespeare once again confined himself to a few deft changes; these were adequate because Plutarch had already shaped the lives with care.

The extent of the changes does not really matter. What counts is that, because of them, each play became an *exemplum*, the value of which was guaranteed not by its fidelity to historical fact but by its truth to fundamental principles of human conduct as the Elizabethans understood them.[5] The mirror which is held up to nature presents not historical events but universal moral principles, and fidelity to history, or what Shakespeare understood as history, has been deliberately subordinated to faithful exemplification of the "moral laws / Of nature and of nations"[6] and even the supernatural laws of human salvation. The "true tragedy" of other Elizabethan dramatists gives way to the universal tragedy of Shakespeare.

In seeing man as part of the natural order of society and of the supernatural order of grace, Shakespeare was, of course, at one with his contemporaries. Their insistence that tragedy be concerned with the great and with historical events amounted, in fact, to demanding

---

[3] I have outlined my own view of *Hamlet* at some length in *Shakespeare's Use of Learning*, pp. 253-258, 329-346. For *Othello*, see pp. 277-278. The change in the ending is, of course, simply the telescoping of events that Shakespeare used throughout his career. It is true, furthermore, to the tragic ending of the source and does not affect the nature of the story.

[4] Cf. Henry L. Paul, *The Royal Play of Macbeth* (New York, 1950), pp. 183-203.

[5] Cf. Marion Hope Parker, *The Slave of Life: A Study of Shakespeare and the Idea of Justice* (London, 1955), p. 34.

[6] *Troilus and Cressida* II.ii.184-185.

that it concern itself with persons who moved in a larger context and, by their acts, partly determined that context for themselves and for others. Even the domestic tragedies, which provide the only exceptions to the exalted rank of Elizabethan tragic characters, see man as involved in the larger order of salvation and as tragic in his fall from grace. The sin of the criminal and, if it comes, his repentance are shown as affecting the spiritual lives of his accomplices and his associates. I suspect that it would have been impossible for an Elizabethan to concentrate completely upon an individual in the modern fashion simply because he could not conceive of human life apart from the meaning that it derived from its place in the larger order. Even the catechism that the child learned in his first days in school was conceived in those terms: "My dutye toward my neyghbor is to love hym as my selfe: And to do to all men as I would they should do unto me. To love, honour, and succour my father and mother. To honour and obey the Kyng, and his minysters. . . . To order my selfe lowly and reverently to all my betters. . . . and to do my dutye in that state of life, unto whiche it shal please God to cal me."[7]

Shakespeare was unique, therefore, not in seeing human tragedy as fundamentally involved in a larger order but rather in the skill and intellectual integrity with which he faced the dramatic consequences of that view. The following discussion will therefore pass over the Elizabethan concept of the great chain of being and resist the inevitable tendency to quote Ulysses' great speech on degree. These matters have been amply considered already. Attention will be focused, rather, upon the implications of the concept of order for Shakespeare's tragic technique.

Man's part in the universal order created by God affected him, broadly speaking, in three ways. As a physical animal he was subject to the forces of inanimate nature, which, by his reason, he could understand and in part control. As a rational animal he was involved in a social order and subject to its laws, which, as a creature endowed with reason and free will, he could obey or violate. As a being called to a supernatural end, he was involved not only in the bonds of human society but also in the divine plan of salvation. The first of these relationships, the physical, involved no problem for the drama-

[7]*The Prayer-Book of Queen Elizabeth 1559* (Edinburgh, 1911), p. 119.

tist, except, of course, for adapting the action to the physical limitations of the actor and the resources of the Elizabethan stage. These were not serious problems. The actors were well trained, and the stage was flexible. Poetry was quite adequate to describe what could not be presented or to take the place of stage lighting or to interpret and supplement sound effects.

Man's place in the social order presented, on the other hand, the fundamental problem of relating the action of the individual to the larger context without slighting either the individual or the social order. I do not mean, of course, the way in which the decision of the protagonist resulted in a physical act directed toward or against other people. That was simple enough to handle. I mean the problem of making the social order part of the dramatic action.

This problem has already been discussed in connection with *Richard II* and *Julius Caesar*. In the former the king's personal tragedy is brilliantly related to the system of political thought which, for Elizabethans, defined the relationship between king and subjects as part of a social order which was, in turn, part of the order of nature itself. The king had rights, to absolute obedience among others, but he also had heavy responsibilities for the welfare, both moral and physical, of his subjects. Richard is all too well aware of his rights but indifferent to his duties. In *Julius Caesar*, on the other hand, we lose the political thought in our distrust of Antony, and with it our ability to follow the action of the play as Shakespeare conceived it. Instead, we see Caesar and Brutus as vivid, if puzzling, character portrayals.

Among the later tragedies, *Lear* perhaps illustrates a narrow escape from the converse danger, in that the regeneration of Lear and Gloucester tends to be lost sight of as Shakespeare develops the social chaos to which their initial acts of folly have led. Lear's suffering is so great and so powerfully presented that we are in no danger of forgetting his tragedy; but we are likely to overlook the development of his character in the last half of the play and to slight Gloucester altogether. *Macbeth*, on the contrary, is thoroughly successful in maintaining a balance. Macbeth's personal tragedy is always in the foreground, but it never obscures the larger implications of that tragedy for Scotland.

Critics who have written about Shakespeare's concern with the order of nature in society have often overlooked the implications for the individual of the parallel and interrelated concept that man is a rational creature ordained to a supernatural end. Yet Shakespeare probably differs most significantly from his fellow dramatists in just this respect—that he was fully aware of the moral order as it operates in man and worked out his tragic structure in the light of that body of doctrine. The moral order is present even in *Titus Andronicus*; in his combination of greatness and tragic blindness to the claims of mercy, Titus is, in fact, closer to the great tragic heroes than any subsequent character before Brutus. But this aspect of the play is not a fundamental part of the action or perhaps even of the portrayal of Titus. In *Richard III* the moral order is omnipresent. But it is indicated symbolically by characters outside the main action and, in part, outside the world of nature. Only in the few speeches of terror that we noted toward the end of the play does it operate upon and within Richard. In the mature tragedies, on the other hand, it operates within the tragic hero, and often in other major figures as well, to provide the dynamics of character, so that human beings grow or degenerate inexorably as a consequence of their own moral actions. Brutus, once again, is the first example. His obtuseness in the conspirators' meeting shows how his egotism has grown in the brief time since he yielded to it in joining the conspiracy. "The acting of a dreadful thing" did not end, as he thought, the insurrection in his "state of a man" (*Julius Caesar* II.i.63-69). From then on he quarrels with his friends and destroys them by his unwise acts. But, as we noted in the last chapter, all this needs to be much clarified and emphasized to be as effective dramatically as it might be. It seems only a preliminary hint of what happens to Othello or Macbeth or Antony. There was nothing unusual about Shakespeare's view of the moral order; it was a commonplace of his age. But his exemplification of it in tragedy was almost unique. Since it is the key to the structure and the technique of his great tragedies, and it is not a commonplace of our age, it requires a few words of explanation.

To summarize briefly, the end of human life for the Aristotelian tradition is happiness, which consists in action perfectly in accord with man's nature as a rational being. Christian thinkers, following Augustine, redefined happiness as beatitude, which consists in the intellectual contemplation and love of God. The Shorter Catechism of the Westminster Assembly (pub. 1648), though in general specifically Calvinistic, begins with a famous restatement of this universally accepted doctrine: *"Question. What is the chief end of man?* A. Mans chief end is to glorifie God, and to enjoy him for ever."* But this goal, unlike Aristotle's, is an impossibility in this life, where the intellectual apprehension of God must remain imperfect as contrasted with the immediate apprehension enjoyed by angels and by the saved in heaven. Possession of the infinite God remains man's goal, however, and such is his nature that he can never be satisfied with less than that infinity. Lacking it, his life will be one of restless and ill-directed striving. This concept is, of course, the theme of George Herbert's poem "The Pulley." But this final end must be achieved by means which become in themselves intermediate ends, and so on down the ladder. Human life was therefore viewed by thinkers in this tradition as a series of choices of intermediate ends all governed by man's ordination toward the final end of the possession of God, which, in turn, determined the scheme of values by which subsidiary ends were chosen.

This Christian doctrine therefore meant that life became a series of choices, and it provided the moral standards by which these choices were governed, since man was bound not only to obey the direct commands of God but also to live in conformity with that nature which was God's instrument—including his own human nature. To live rightly was therefore to live in accordance with the commands of God and the laws of nature as interpreted by right reason. Because of man's ordination to God, the moral life became the significant life, and, for a writer who took the Christian view seriously, tragic action inevitably occurred in a moral context.

But man was also a creature of habit. Each correct choice involving a moral issue fortified a habit of virtuous action. An incorrect or immoral choice, on the other hand, made easier the next false choice, and, unless the chain were broken, a habit of sin would result. Man, as a creature desiring the infinite good, would choose what seemed to him a good. Finding no satisfaction in the false good that he had chosen, he would keep striving and each false choice would lead him farther from his goal and make him more frustrated, until finally he might approach the ultimate frustration of complete privation of God. Such is Macbeth's state toward the end of the play, although

139

even then he must face the ultimate horror that, in the hell which he has made of himself, the privation of God is not complete and he still can know what he has lost. He is involved in the "strange desolation" imagined by Fulke Greville (whose "fatall mirrour" is, of course, God, the perfect exemplar by contrast with which man reveals his sinfulness):

> And in this fatall mirrour of transgression,
> Shewes man as fruit of his degeneration,
> The errours ugly infinite impression,
> Which beares the faithlesse downe to desperation;
>> Depriv'd of humane graces and divine,
>> Even there appeares this *saving* God of mine.
>
> In power and truth, Almighty and eternall,
> Which on the sinne reflects strange desolation,
> With glory scourging all the Sprites infernall,
> And uncreated hell with unprivation;
>> Depriv'd of humane graces, not divine,
>> Even there appeares this *saving* God of mine.[8]

The actual psychology of moral choice—or, for that matter, of any deliberate choice by man—can be summarized briefly. Any act is always directed toward what seems good. Man's appetite, which since Adam's fall has not been subject to his reason and will, is inevitably aroused by any apparent good and solicits the will to act to achieve that good. But will can act only with the consent of reason; and if reason remains in full and effective control, so that it can restrain the will unless the good proposed is in fact the highest good in terms of ultimate values, a sound choice must result. But the reason may fail and assent to a lesser or apparent good for one or more of three reasons: (1) ignorance of what is involved (such a choice is morally culpable, of course, only if the ignorance is culpable in that it involves matters of which the individual ought to have knowledge); (2) such continuous and violent soliciting of the will by a passion—that is, excessive appetite—that reason yields assent improperly, especially if the lesser good is apparent and the greater lies hidden; (3) a wrong habit resulting from a series of false choices. Shakespeare's use of passion psychology has been thoroughly ex-

[8]*Cælica*, Sonnet XCIX, in *Poems and Dramas of Fulke Greville, First Lord Brooke*, ed. Geoffrey Bullough (Edinburgh, [1939]), I, 144.

plored by scholars,[9] but far less attention has been paid to the ethical system of which it is a part. For the latter we need not go beyond Shakespeare: he has himself presented a more than adequate exposition of the entire process in the Trojan council scene of *Troilus and Cressida*, and Hector even provides a brief summary in technical terms of what is happening (II.ii.168-188). The ever-present danger that men may choose falsely by preferring appearance to reality is the point of one of the most quoted lines in all Shakespeare, though often its context is forgotten:

> One touch of nature makes the whole world kin,
> That all, with one consent, praise new-born gawds,
> Though they are made and moulded of things past,
> And give to dust that is a little gilt
> More laud than gilt o'er-dusted.
>
> (*Troilus and Cressida* III.iii.175-179)

The contrast between appearance and reality is an omnipresent theme in Shakespeare, simply because it is a fundamental problem of his ethics and psychology.

To give dramatic form to this psychology, Shakespeare worked out a structural pattern for the mature tragedies except *Hamlet* that I have outlined elsewhere.[10] The hero is confronted with a crucial temptation to choose a lesser or apparent good, which is being urged upon him by his own appetite, by one or more human beings who have their own reasons for wishing him to choose falsely, and in *Macbeth* by supernatural forces of evil as well. Brutus is motivated by pride and solicited by Cassius to join the conspirators and thereby substitute the apparent good of saving Rome from tyranny for the real good of the moral order. In most of the tragedies, though not in *Julius Caesar*, the good is also represented by an important character, Banquo being the clearest example. The hero then works out his crucial choice to a wrong and potentially tragic conclusion in an important scene of the play, as we have noted in discussing Brutus'

[9]The pioneer works seem to have been Ruth Leila Anderson's *Elizabethan Psychology and Shakespeare's Plays*, University of Iowa Humanistic Studies, Vol. III, No. 4 (Iowa City, 1927), and Lily B. Campbell's *Shakespeare's Tragic Heroes: Slaves of Passion* (Cambridge, Eng., 1930), which, despite questionable interpretations, remains the most important discussion of the subject.

[10]*Shakespeare's Use of Learning*, pp. 248-250. For a parallel analysis of the same structure, see John Vyvyan, *The Shakespearean Ethic* (London, 1959), pp. 13-14.

key soliloquy (II.i.1-58). The crucial choice leads to an act of far-reaching consequences, and the hero falls to destruction as a result. In all the plays but *King Lear* the downfall of the hero's fortunes is less important than the disintegration of character which results from the initial violation of his moral nature in the false choice. Lear and Gloucester, however, find moral cleansing in the frightful suffering that they undergo, and a fundamentally different kind of action results in the last half of the play.

This structure is essentially a way of dramatizing in terms of a specific *exemplum* and realistic characters the *psychomachia* of Christian tradition that had also been basic to the morality plays. But Shakespeare's use of an *exemplum* is both intellectually sounder and dramatically more effective, as comparison with *Everyman* will show. The morality play treated all forces disposing man to sin as allegorical abstractions, whether they were in fact the solicitings of his own appetite or external agents tempting him by arousing his appetite. Goods and Good Fellowship are parallel figures in the allegory. Shakespeare distinguished between internal and external causes. The promptings of appetite in Brutus (analogous to Goods) are described by Cassius or revealed by Brutus in what he says and does. Cassius himself, as well as other conspirators, is Good Fellowship in action, appealing to Brutus' pride and tempting him to murder. In *Macbeth* the range of possibilities for evil is completed, and the devil himself intervenes (as he does in some of the moralities) when not only Lady Macbeth but the witches as instruments of Satan work upon the desire for the crown that is already present in Macbeth's appetite. Banquo is like Knowledge in that he reminds the audience as well as Macbeth what the latter ought to know, but in his purely human relationship to Macbeth he has no allegorical analogue in *Everyman*, though such a character—called, perhaps, Good Counsel—might logically appear as an opposite for Good Fellowship. Much of this dramatic development is present in Marlowe's *Dr. Faustus*, though the Good and Evil Angels are closer to the morality play than anything in Shakespeare, and the Old Man is far more of a symbol than Banquo or even Edgar. But Marlowe fails to make his play a convincing *exemplum* in that Faustus' choice of magic is motivated by a general desire for knowledge and power and not by an overwhelming desire for a specific goal, such as the destruction of

Caesarism or the crown of Scotland, to get which he sacrifices his immortal soul. The play therefore lacks the dramatic climax, as well as the concentration, which Shakespeare's tragedies achieve. It also has much less impact upon the audience. Shakespeare carried the dramatic development much farther than Marlowe—but only, it must be said in fairness to Marlowe, after an interval of ten years.

In this deliberate and thoughtful use by Shakespeare of traditional psychology and ethics lies, I think, the explanation for his writing what I have called quasi-Aristotelian tragedy. In a rationalist ethical system like that which Shakespeare inherited, a sin would necessarily involve an error of judgment, unless due to culpable ignorance; and the false moral choice of his heroes is, in fact, simply a special type of Aristotle's *hamartia*, or "missing the mark." The heroes themselves conform to Aristotle's description of the ideal tragic protagonist. As soon as Shakespeare visualized tragedy in terms of a moral choice, two further consequences followed. For him, as for Aristotle, action came to involve a crucial movement of will as well as the physical activity that resulted. Further ancillary decisions and deeds were inevitably involved, and character revealed itself in action. It was the act of will, furthermore, that determined the tragic outcome, and the play became a matter of motivating the choice and showing its results. This scheme imposed upon the tragedy a unity such as few of Shakespeare's contemporaries achieved. *Sejanus* and *Othello* are both great plays written not more than a year apart. Jonson and Shakespeare were both skilled dramatic craftsmen, and both achieved unusual unity. But Jonson saw drama as history, and the unity of *Sejanus* is that of historical narrative—it has an arbitrary beginning and an inevitable end but no middle. Shakespeare saw drama as moral philosophy, and *Othello* has a true beginning, a middle, and an end. His point of view, moreover, furnished Shakespeare not only with a principle of unity but also with a standard of magnitude. For Jonson, as we have seen in Chapter ii, the problem was simply how much activity could be presented in a given time. For Shakespeare the magnitude of the play lay in the fundamental importance of the moral choice—lay, in other words, in an action that determined the outcome of a great man's life with respect to his full potentialities as a man.

In dramatic terms, the climax of the play—the middle—might be the act of will or it might be the resulting deed. The formula was by no means inflexible. The climax might even involve, as in *King Lear*, a second great decision that initiated a regenerative process. But the middle did mark a genuine turning point in the action of the play, and its presence was the logical outcome of a principle of organization that determined the structure of the entire play. The principle, to repeat, was that the play was centered about a crucial moral choice that led to the hero's death in this life and often, as we shall see, to eternal death or eternal life in the world to come. The action, therefore, was necessarily of great magnitude.

It has been impossible to discuss the dramatic action without mentioning the world to come simply because Shakespeare, like his contemporaries, saw man as part of the supernatural order of grace as well as the order of nature. Beatitude and eternal life were supernatural ends in the strict sense that they transcended the order of nature and were impossible of achievement within it. The theology of salvation, as such, was therefore of no direct concern to a tragedy centered in this life, though numerous allusions to it occur in Shakespeare. But it was, in fact, impossible that a fallen son of Adam should conduct his life without yielding to omnipresent temptation. The order of grace must therefore operate in the moral order of this life to temper and correct the rigors of the order of nature; to this extent it became a concern of serious drama. I am no theologian, and I have no intention of trying to write a summary of Renaissance theology which would be beyond my competence. But even without expert knowledge of religious doctrine one can detect several results of this system of ideas at work in Shakespeare's tragedies.

If, for the moment, I spend more time on Shakespeare's use of the order of grace than on his handling of the order of nature, I do not in any way mean to imply that the order of grace dominates his thinking except in the sense that it provided the ultimate values. Shakespeare's tragedies are of this world and centered therein. But students seem to me to have paid ample attention to his concern with order and degree and too little to his account of repentance and regeneration or their absence. Correcting the critical balance will involve an opposite imbalance in this immediate context.

We have already noted that one sinful act inevitably made easier the next and that, if the chain were not broken, a habit of sin would be established and a steadily increasing perversion of the moral nature would result, as it does in Macbeth. Since it was inevitable that fallen man should sin, the outlook would have been indeed gloomy had it not been for the Christian doctrine of repentance. The grace of God was continually calling even the hardened sinner to repent, often by reminding him, like Macbeth, of what he had lost. Elizabethan discussions of repentance, most notably that in the official Homilies, are specific and detailed. Whatever the cause that first moved the sinner to repent (it might even be fear), four parts must be present if the repentance were to be valid and the chain of sin to be broken. These were contrition, confession, faith in God, and amendment of life, although with respect to the last a genuine intention would be adequate if death prevented performance.

Although penance was no longer regarded as a sacrament, it played almost as great a part in the Anglican spiritual regime as in the Roman Catholic. But Protestant teachers had endeavored to safeguard it against pre-Reformation abuses by several very specific provisos that are important for understanding Shakespeare's text. Whereas attrition—that is, fear of the consequences of sin—had been adequate if perfected by the sacrament of penance, the Reformers, who denied to penance the status of a sacrament, quite logically demanded full contrition—that is, heartfelt sorrow for sin simply because it offended God—as a condition of valid repentance. The emphasis was upon public rather than private confession, and amendment of life must include an attempt at reconciliation with the wronged person and restitution of goods unlawfully taken.

The operation of these ideas should be immediately apparent to any student of Shakespeare. Mowbray says to John of Gaunt:

> Once did I lay an ambush for your life,
> A trespass that doth vex my grieved soul;
> But ere I last receiv'd the sacrament
> I did confess it, and exactly begg'd
> Your Grace's pardon; and I hope I had it.
> (*Richard II* I.i.137-141)

Malcolm reports of Cawdor:

> But I have spoke
> With one that saw him die; who did report
> That very frankly he confess'd his treasons,

> Implor'd your Highness' pardon, and set forth
> A deep repentance. Nothing in his life
> Became him like the leaving it.
>
> (Macbeth I.iv.3-8)

Cawdor had merely availed himself of the opportunity, never denied to an Elizabethan criminal, to make his peace with God by public confession, so that the execution itself might become an act of atonement and a means of salvation. He had confessed his sins, sought reconciliation, and intended an amendment of life. Shakespeare lets important matters rest while Hamlet and Laertes exchange forgiveness in preparation for death. When Iago declares, "From this time forth I never will speak word," Lodovico immediately retorts: "What, not to pray?" (*Othello* V.ii.304-305).

But Claudius most clearly illustrates this body of doctrine as he prays (*Hamlet* III.iii.36-72). He is contrite because he has offended God: "O, my offence is rank, it smells to heaven." He confesses explicitly to "A brother's murder." He has adequate faith:

> What if this cursed hand
> Were thicker than itself with brother's blood,
> Is there not rain enough in the sweet heavens
> To wash it white as snow?

But, as Claudius recognizes throughout his prayer, these three parts are not enough without amendment of life, and that involves restitution

> Of those effects for which I did the murder,
> My crown, mine own ambition, and my queen.
> May one be pardon'd and retain th' offence?

Claudius also knows and states one further principle. The sinner who rejected the call of grace thereby hardened himself in sin and made his spiritual state even more desperate: "O limed soul, that, struggling to be free, / Art more engag'd!"

In the closet scene, Hamlet himself describes how repentance may form a habit of virtue like the contrary habit of sin.

> Assume a virtue, if you have it not.
> That monster, custom, who all sense doth eat,
> Of habits evil, is angel yet in this,
> That to the use of actions fair and good

He likewise gives a frock or livery,
That aptly is put on. Refrain to-night,
And that shall lend a kind of easiness
To the next abstinence; the next more easy;
For use almost can change the stamp of nature,
And either master the devil or throw him out,
With wondrous potency.

(III.iv.160-170)

The order of grace therefore operated to give man the spiritual strength needed to break through the workings of nature within himself and to begin a new life. Even more important, it could turn the misfortunes and suffering of this world into a means of purification. Suffering itself was a part of God's design and might be a purgatorial experience in the proper meaning of that term, purifying man for the life to come. We shall have occasion to examine the full implications of this concept when we come to *King Lear,* for the notion that man achieves spiritual vision through suffering is a premise of the action of the play. For the moment it will suffice to note Othello's brief allusion to suffering as a means of testing mankind:

Had it pleas'd Heaven
To try me with affliction; had they rain'd
All kind of sores and shames on my bare head,
Steep'd me in poverty to the very lips,
Given to captivity me and my utmost hopes,
I should have found in some place of my soul
A drop of patience.

(IV.ii.47-53)

This view of suffering had, in general, two important consequences for Shakespeare's drama. It led him to emphasize the virtue of patience, to which Othello alludes, and to avoid the easy poetic justice sometimes advocated by critics and practiced by dramatists.

The Christian who believed that the plans of a just and beneficent God were being worked out in time was committed to seeing the finger of God not only in the pattern of history but in the events of his daily life. Sir Walter Raleigh in his *History of the World,* for example, and Shakespeare in his chronicle plays were at one in seeing providence constantly at work. But, on these premises, the Christian's only proper attitude in adversity was patience and resignation to the will of God, since any other attitude implied rebellion against

147

the divine plan. Raleigh's wonderful letter to his wife written in 1603 on the night before he expected to be executed exists to show his patience. Its testimony of Elizabethan attitudes is the more meaningful because he has sometimes been thought to be more skeptical than most of his contemporaries.

And seeing itt is not the will of God, that I shall see you any more in this life, beare itt patiently, and with an heart like thy selfe....

Teach your sonne alsoe to love and feare god whilst hee is yett younge, that the feare of god may growe upp with him; and the same God will bee a husband to you, and a Father to him, A husband, and a Father, which Cannot bee taken from you.[11]

What of Shakespeare? Some years ago J. V. Cunningham collected examples to prove that the following lines from *Hamlet* merely state a commonplace of contemporary preaching on patience and resignation to the will of God:

There's a special providence in the fall of a sparrow. If it be now, 'tis not to come; if it be not to come, it will be now; if it be not now, yet it will come; the readiness is all. Since no man has aught of what he leaves, what is't to leave betimes?

(V.ii.230-235)[12]

Bertram Joseph sees in these words, and in the lesson which they show Hamlet to have learned, the theme of the play.[13] I remain unconvinced as to the theme, but the doctrine is undoubtedly there. Similarly Gloucester comes through suffering to the same view:

> Henceforth I'll bear
> Affliction till it do cry out itself
> "Enough, enough," and die.
>
> (*King Lear* IV.vi.75-77)

After Gloucester lapses, Edgar urges upon him the same view in words that more nearly parallel Hamlet's:

> What, in ill thoughts again? Men must endure
> Their going hence even as their coming hither;
> Ripeness is all.
>
> (V.ii.9-11)

[11]*Sir Walter Raleigh: Selections from His Historie of the World, His Letters, etc.,* ed. G. E. Hadow (Oxford, [1926]), pp. 181, 183.

[12]*Woe or Wonder: The Emotional Effect of Shakespearean Tragedy* (Denver, 1951), pp. 9-14.

[13]*Conscience and the King: A Study of Hamlet* (London, 1953), pp. 130-151.

But these views are only expressed in *Hamlet*; in *King Lear* they are basic to the play.

Shakespeare's acceptance of this view saved him, I think, from the shallow poetic justice advocated by contemporary critics and practiced by many dramatists. A drama that shows events "agreeable to the merits of Vertue and Vice" or "more just in Retribution and more according to Revealed Providence"[14] is obviously no mirror of nature. Cordelia does not deserve to die, but frequently neither does the man who is killed, in indescribable agony, on the field of battle or in the flaming wreckage of an automobile. A tragic art—or a view of life that really means something—must be tough enough to face these facts. Whether or not Shakespeare's solution is adequate or convincing, he does make the attempt. Bradley recognized this aspect of his art clearly: "Shakespeare was not attempting to justify the ways of God to men, or to show the universe as a Divine Comedy. He was writing tragedy, and tragedy would not be tragedy if it were not a painful mystery."[15] But Bradley seems to me wrong in continuing: "Nor can he be said even to point distinctly, like some writers of tragedy, in any direction where a solution might lie." Shakespeare, I grant, does not dwell upon the point. I doubt that it ever occurred to him that the ways of God to man needed justifying; though Lear does undertake, by mending his own ways toward his fellow men, to "show the heavens more just" (III.iv.36). In making his proud attempt, Milton was of a later and more skeptical generation. What really needed justifying, in Shakespeare's view, was the ways of man to God. But Shakespeare does face the problem of undeserved suffering.

Shakespeare, I think, accepted the notion that man's place in the order of nature means that some men must suffer for the sins of others, just as many small trees may be crushed in the fall of a mighty oak; but he also accepted the belief that this is part of God's plan, and that man's place in the order of grace means that his sufferings, even though undeserved, may be a means of salvation for himself and for others and, in terms of the still larger order of nature and grace, may

[14]Francis Bacon, *Advancement of Learning*, in *Critical Essays of the Seventeenth Century*, ed. J. E. Spingarn (Oxford, 1908), I, 6.

[15]A. C. Bradley, *Shakespearean Tragedy: Lectures on Hamlet, Othello, King Lear, Macbeth* (London, 1905), p. 38.

therefore be a good. Such, at least, is the meaning I find in *Hamlet* and *Lear* and *Coriolanus*.

Shakespeare's acceptance of the Christian order of grace also added a new dimension to the outcome of four tragedies and, in fact, to the entire action as directed toward that final outcome. The Christian was ordained not only to a life of trial and preparation in this world of nature but also to the supernatural end of salvation in the world to come. Death was therefore not the end, as we noted in discussing Elizabethan tragedies, and man might also be viewed in terms of his supernatural ordination. The tragic hero's *hamartia*, his tragic error, must destroy him in the order of nature, or there would be no tragedy. The emphasis in Shakespeare is very decidedly on the order of nature and on the mystery of human suffering. Death is the inevitable tragic outcome of the action, and it is never minimized.

But man's supernatural end is not forgotten. Hamlet's problem is repeatedly viewed in terms of the world to come. Even though Shakespeare cannot quite reconcile his new Hamlet with the barbaric conventions of revenge tragedy, his final judgment is Horatio's "Good-night, sweet prince, / And flights of angels sing thee to thy rest!" (V.ii.370-371). Othello, on the other hand, speaks of that "demi-devil" that "hath thus ensnar'd my soul and body" (V.ii.301-302). *Macbeth* involves a thorough study of the interaction of man's appetite and supernatural forces of evil, and the last half of the play is worked out in terms of the concept of the chain of sin. We have read carelessly indeed if we are not sure that the "dead butcher and his fiend-like queen" (V.viii.69) are damned. A Shakespearean tragedy therefore has three possible outcomes. It may be purely secular, as most of them are, and view death as the end of the action. It may still concentrate upon this world but also imply that the hero's death is for all eternity—that he is damned. Or it may present the hero as somehow undergoing a moral regeneration even in his tragic agony, so that death is the door to eternal life; in doing so, it may still focus on the order of nature, but it will have to pay considerable attention to the order of grace and its values. We are told that Romeo and Juliet will be remembered in Verona, but we are given no hint of their future life. Even though Richard III, on the other hand, is repeatedly described as of the devil's party, no attention is paid to his eternal destiny as such, the final emphasis of the play being on the reunion of England. We are left in no doubt, however, that Othello and Macbeth feel themselves doomed to hell. We are told to hope that Hamlet will be with angels, and I shall argue that, in this respect, Lear is to be classed with Hamlet. Despite Cleopatra's talk of "immortal longings," her heaven is only an amorous paradise. In *Antony and Cleopatra* and *Coriolanus* we return to the secularism of their sources and of Shakespeare's early tragedies.

There have been so many speculations about the "dark" period of Shakespeare's tragedies and problem comedies that I hesitate to add another. The fact remains, however, that the plays from *Hamlet* to *Macbeth* have in common more than a preoccupation with human sin. If we accept E. K. Chambers' chronology, *Hamlet, The Merry Wives of Windsor, Troilus and Cressida, All's Well That Ends Well, Measure for Measure, Othello, King Lear*, and *Macbeth* were written between 1600 and 1606. Of these *The Merry Wives* carries the old favorite Falstaff into a style of comedy that is not even typical of Shakespeare at any period. It must be left out of account. The rest all reflect an unusual preoccupation not only with human sin but with the entire philosophical and theological system of ideas in terms of which thoughtful Elizabethans interpreted human conduct. *Hamlet* shows, not only in action but also in elaborate speeches of moral exposition, how "reason panders will" (III.iv.88) and how repentance may begin a new and better life. *Troilus and Cressida* expounds Elizabethan cosmology and moral psychology. *Measure for Measure* talks about the doctrine of atonement and exemplifies repentance and growth in virtue. *King Lear* is a full-scale study of man's relationship to the order of nature and of the moral regeneration by which he may transcend it. *Macbeth* is the best *exemplum* in all literature of how, in the Christian view as Shakespeare inherited it, man falls into sin and degenerates as the chain of sin increasingly binds him. Similar preoccupations appear, though with less emphasis and less didactic exposition, in *All's Well* and *Othello*. It is the tragedies of this period that relate the hero's life and death explicitly to the world to come. Surely this part of Shakespeare's dramatic career might well be called his philosophical or better yet his metaphysical period, since metaphysics implies a view of eternity as well as of time. In these years I, for one, find not only Shakespeare's intellectual energy but also his technical virtuosity as a playwright at their peak.

151

But it is high time that I added a qualification, lest I seem to be converting Shakespeare into a Christian apologist rather than a dramatist. As a matter of fact, such a result would do violence to my concept of Shakespeare the man as well as to the playwright. Most Elizabethans were Christians intellectually, whatever their moral commitment, in a fashion impossible today for the devoutest nun, simply because the fundamental Christian assumptions had not been seriously challenged. As a boy, I spent a great deal of time with my grandmother. She was not a naïve or inexperienced woman. She had attended a "female seminary" and was relatively well educated; she had lived in the midst of war and had taken her part in smuggling prisoners and ammunition. But it was obvious to me even as a boy that, in matters religious, there was a gulf between us. She belonged to an age of faith; I was growing up in an age of doubt. I suspect that Shakespeare had similar attitudes and that, in this respect, my grandmother can lead me to him, except that two centuries of considerable skepticism separated even her acceptance of Christian assumptions from his.

I have no idea, of course, whether Shakespeare was a Christian as churches define the term. There is, as I read his plays, no evidence that he was personally a pious man, although his language is occasionally devout. What I must insist is that he was intellectually a Christian not only as none of us can ever be but also as none of us can even imagine. There are literally hundreds of scriptural echoes and precise doctrinal allusions in his plays to reflect his saturation in the Christian culture of his day. He continued to study the Bible and occasionally other religious documents throughout his career. That point no longer needs argument. Whether he was Anglican or Roman Catholic, whether he was devout or a nominal conformist, does not really interest me. I am merely concerned to show that he accepted the beliefs of his age and that these beliefs often govern the structure of his plays and are therefore a necessary key to their meaning. If I have not demonstrated that he took seriously the ideas that he accepted, I have written in vain, and so have many other contemporary students of his works.

The plays, in brief, reflect an intense attempt to face the implications of philosophical and theological ideas and to work them out in the drama. This same disposition to pursue ideas to their logical consequences also helped to produce a plentiful indulgence in anachronisms. Or so they seem to us. But, if we are more sophisticated than Shakespeare historically, we are less tutored metaphysically. Obviously if the Christian concept of the universe was valid at all, it was valid universally. Lear and Cleopatra differed from Queen Elizabeth not in the laws of nature to which, as rational creatures, they owed obedience, but only in the fullness of their understanding of those laws. Like her they also owed obedience to the will of God, and they stood in need of his grace. Like her they might even feel their imperfection and their need; it was their misfortune that, unlike her, they had access to no revelation of the supernatural order of grace and no means of calling upon the help of God, as opposed to their false gods. So Shakespeare applied to pre-Christian plays not only the natural order which he accepted but also the moral order, including fundamental Christian teaching. When he made Antony say of Cleopatra, "O this false soul of Egypt! this grave charm, . . . / Whose bosom was my crownet, my chief end" (IV.xii.25-27), he surely expected the audience to judge Antony's conduct in the light of their superior knowledge that man's chief end is God and not a creature, however bewitching. Gloucester, as we have seen, learns to substitute for the Stoic solution of suicide the Christian virtue of resignation, though he cannot appeal to religious teaching as Hamlet does. But the Fool is intended, among other functions, to show that all things, even including time, are upside down in Lear's former kingdom. He is therefore allowed to refer in explicit terms to the Christian order.

Shakespeare's notion that tragedy should hold the mirror up to nature also led him to reverse, in practice, the famous commonplace of Donatus that tragedies begin in calm and end in tempest. Actually the remark was not a very good one; even with respect to classical drama it sacrificed truth to rhetorical antithesis.[16] It was, however, more nearly applicable to Elizabethan narrative tragedy, which often took as its starting point the beginning of broils. It describes perfectly Shakespeare's own *Richard II* and even *Richard III* or *Romeo and Juliet*. But, if one believes in an ordered universe and writes drama in such terms, universal order must ultimately triumph over

[16]Cf. Madeleine Doran, *Endeavors of Art: A Study of Form in Elizabethan Drama* (Madison, 1954), p. 107.

man's disorder. Such is Shakespeare's mature view, and his tragedies do in fact begin in disorder and end in order. The most notable example is, of course, *Macbeth*, which opens upon the end of a witches' sabbath in a storm amid civil war and closes with a restoration of God's grace and the order of nature to Scotland:

> this, and what needful else
> That calls upon us, by the grace of Grace
> We will perform in measure, time, and place.
>
> (V.viii.71-73)

But the formal restoration of legal authority and order forms the conclusion to all his mature tragedies, except for *Coriolanus*.

Shakespeare's view of tragedy compelled him, in short, to relate his fundamental action to the order of nature and, in some plays at least, to the order of grace. To that extent it helped to mold his thinking and thereby his plots. But its concomitant principle, that he must couple the general notion with the particular example, had fundamental consequences as it affected his method of writing the plays. It involved, in fact, a heroic problem of dramatic exposition. Not only must he take care that his audience followed the story, but he must also make sure that the judicious, at least, saw the action in terms of its larger implications and arrived at the proper ethical judgment. The spectators must be led to maintain a kind of double relationship to the play. They must be absorbed in its events and must feel themselves at one with the protagonist in his problems and his suffering. But at the same time they must remain apart from the action so that they could judge it. Their interest in the play was based upon anticipation and not suspense, since they knew the general outline and the outcome of the story, or, if they did not know, Shakespeare was at pains to forewarn them. Their continuing attention therefore depended in part upon their feeling of superiority to the protagonist. They shared his knowledge and his emotions, but above and beyond these they possessed a superior insight that enabled them to see his mistakes as he made them and to feel pity for his errors as well as for his suffering. That insight the dramatist must convey without making the action lose plausibility or the protagonist seem merely stupid. The problem was difficult, and Shakespeare did not always solve it completely, even in his greatest plays. Untutored spectators, for example, have been known to anticipate Emilia in calling Othello a fool.

Like all the great dramatists who have tried to deal in universals, Shakespeare inevitably relied upon artistic conventions. These have been seriously misunderstood, especially in what seems to me one of the best but also one of the most exasperating introductions to the interpretation of Shakespeare, namely L. L. Schücking's *Character Problems in Shakespeare's Plays*. So often Schücking is right in the general principle that he enunciates and wrong in his interpretation of specific passages! Apparently he was misled by reading and judging Shakespeare in terms of the naturalistic drama of the nineteenth century. He therefore regards the drama as centered in the portrayal of character and sees any use of conventions as evidence of a primitive art. If we grant, however, that Shakespeare was primarily concerned with universal patterns as exemplified in a given action, that for him poetry was perhaps more philosophic than philosophy rather than more historical than history, then the drama must to some extent be conventional and symbolic, because in no other way can it rise to the required level of generalization. Its conventions, or at least many of them, are not primitive survivals in a dramatist still relatively unsophisticated, as one can see by comparing them with medieval techniques from which they often descend. They are the symbols of a mind that operates on the level of moral equations. The all-important equation, furthermore, consists in the developing action, and the characters are merely the variables with which it operates. Schücking's book was brilliant in its revelation of Shakespeare's methods (I found it a landmark in my own study of Shakespeare), but it looked in the wrong direction. It should have been entitled "Expository Problems in Shakespeare's Plays," and it should have focused upon the problem of revealing the full meaning of the action.

Schücking's treatment of Lady Macbeth is a case in point. He is expanding and qualifying his general proposition, which is absolutely sound, "that the first mention in the drama of things which are important for the action or the characterization of the central figure must never be allowed in the interest of the characterization of secondary figures to distort the representation of the facts."[17]

[17]*Character Problems in Shakespeare's Plays: A Guide to the Better Understanding of the Dramatist* (London, 1922), p. 71.

After quoting Lady Macbeth's soliloquy that Macbeth is "too full o' the milk of human kindness" (I.v.18), he argues that she is right as to his actual behavior but wrong in the reasons to which she ascribes that behavior. "Besides, is it true that Macbeth would have liked to attain his ends 'holily', that he is free from criminal inclinations, that his mind is 'full o' the milk of human kindness'? Obviously not. . . . His inhumanity and cruelty most distinctly appear in his treatment of the innocent Banquo."[18] But Shakespeare is not trying to build a consistent and static portrait of Macbeth. He is concerned with presenting an action that turns upon the fall of man into sin and reveals its terrible consequences. He wishes to show us Macbeth as he was initially, so he uses Lady Macbeth as a means both of presenting Macbeth's character and of analyzing it with unrealistic ethical acumen. Macbeth is not free from criminal inclinations—no son of Adam is. He has the disordered appetites of fallen man, but, as men go, he is great and good. He is restrained by his essential humanity, by the precepts of religion, and by fear which is the outcome of prudence and foresight. He is, in other words, Everyman raised to a higher power of capacity for good or evil. The consequence of his fall is that he becomes cruel and inhumane—loses, in fact, his essential humanity because he has dared do more than may become a man and has become, as he prophesied, "none." What Lady Macbeth says is thoroughly consistent with what we see and hear of him at the opening of the play. She functions, therefore, as a means of exposition at the outset, just as she performs a similar role in interpreting action later in this play. The problem throughout is not to present a character sketch but to show character revealing itself in action and developing or degenerating as a consequence of that action. The action is therefore the play, and Shakespeare's attempt to show action as involving change of character enormously complicated his expository problem. Lady Macbeth's various expository speeches are signposts along Macbeth's road to hell, and they show the rate of his progress.

I have dwelt on Schücking's fallacy, not because I want to castigate what seems to me a great book, but because I want to illustrate the complexity of Shakespeare's problem. The conventions that he used in trying to solve that problem are neither naïve nor primitive,

[18]Ibid., p. 81.

156

unless one regards the attempt to write philosophic drama as itself naïve. To a considerable extent Shakespeare merely used devices which were part of theatrical tradition, adapting them to his purpose by keeping his eyes fixed on what he was trying to accomplish. In certain respects, however, he developed habits of organizing and presenting his material that were more distinctively his own. The techniques to be considered will be grouped roughly into these two categories.

Shakespeare's adaptation of traditional devices to his dramatic purposes involved, generally, the application of two principles which are themselves, logically but not in origin, a result of his attempt to write philosophic tragedy. These were the strict subordination of characters to the action and the use of all characters to interpret the action to the audience.

If the dramatic end was to present an action of magnitude, the dramatis personae functioned as means to that end, and almost automatically they arranged themselves in each play into a hierarchy. At the top was the protagonist, great both in social rank and in capacity for good or evil, whose fatal moral act was central to the action of the play. Below him stood the antagonist or antagonists, one or more characters (Iago, Lady Macbeth, Goneril and Regan) who wished the hero to make a false choice and functioned as human agents of temptation. The use of the word "antagonist" is primarily justified in terms of the inner moral conflict. Throughout much of the play Lady Macbeth is her husband's support and ally; but there is no doubt that she is a moral antagonist if the action be viewed as the destruction of his moral nature and his immortal soul. The same thing is true, of course, of Iago; but so much of the play is concerned with Othello's inner conflict and Iago is so clearly a villain from his first line that we feel no temptation to think of him as other than antagonist. Farther down in the hierarchy come minor characters who frequently arrange themselves, either as means of exposition or as tools in the action, on the side of the protagonist or of the antagonist.

From this hierarchical arrangement of characters resulted the principle that a character on any level was, so to speak, expendable in the interests of a higher level. Othello and Macbeth are the protagonists of their respective plays, and at the outset they must be characterized fully enough to motivate the action and to make plausible the intertwining developments of character and action. Since the spotlight is upon them, they must behave consistently and their motives must be adequate. That is, they must be dramatically probable. Iago and Lady Macbeth, as antagonists, must be developed enough to make plausible their roles, but their fundamental alignment on the side of evil is simply assumed as a postulate of the action. Motives are therefore suggested but not developed. Their probability or integrity as characters is sacrificed, furthermore, in the interests of explaining the hero. Both display a quite unrealistic understanding of the hero's good qualities and an even more unrealistic disposition to label those qualities as good. To move on down, Banquo lives to make clear how Macbeth is succumbing to evil, and he dies for the same reason. Roderigo and Cassio are relatively undeveloped and are strictly expendable, morally and physically, as part of the antagonist's schemes. On a still lower level, we never give a second thought to the sleeping grooms whom Macbeth polishes off; they have never become persons, or even dramatis personae, at all. As I have tried to suggest by my examples, this hierarchy of value operates with respect to amount of character development, consistency of characterization, and claim upon the audience's attention and emotions, as well as in many other equally obvious ways.

In speaking of Iago and Lady Macbeth, I have already glanced at a second principle resulting from the attempt to write philosophic drama. All the main characters and all the supporting expository characters are endowed with an understanding of moral principles, an ability to analyze action, and an extraordinary insight into the hero's nature. All this is completely unrealistic, but it is vitally necessary if the dramatist is to relate his action to first principles. It has caused, I think, a good deal of confusion. Macbeth lays the reasons for not killing Duncan on the line so neatly that critics accustomed, unlike Shakespeare, to a morality based upon sentiment rather than reason have doubted that he had a conscience. For a rational ethic, prudence and conscience work in alliance, and prudential motives for doing good are as sound as any other—are, in fact, the soundest of all, for prudence is one of the four cardinal virtues. But few men in any age analyze the warnings of their conscience as exactly as Macbeth does in coupling his particular action to the general principles that it violates. Enobarbus is a notorious example of an expository character who analyzes the hero's behavior in almost clinical terms; Iago is less technical but equally specific about the errors of judgment that will make Othello his dupe.

But this kind of ethical writing was by no means confined to Shakespeare. It occurs in many other writers of his period. One might accuse Hamlet of lecturing Gertrude during the closet scene in unrealistically technical language, but the ultimate source of the episode in Belleforest is equally technical and considerably more long-winded. I recall a passage in Thomas Lodge's *The Famous, true and historicall life of Robert second Duke of Normandy* in which Robert, defeated and wounded by the Duke of Constances, undergoes a repentance that is traced in detail and is exactly in accord with theological teaching up to the final restitution of what he had wrongfully taken.[19] Robert's previous career would hardly have involved either leisure or inclination to master so precisely the theology of repentance.

I should be careful to point out, furthermore, that neither the sacrificing of minor characters to exposition nor unnatural clarity of analysis is confined, in Shakespeare, to his great tragedies. There is, in fact, nowhere in the tragedies so outrageous an inconsistency of characterization as the way in which Vernon is made to praise Prince Hal (*1 Henry IV* V.ii.52-69) or the French to magnify Henry V (*Henry V* II.iv). Iago never reveals himself so clearly as Richard III in his opening soliloquy. What is unique in the tragedies, and what reflects the pressure of an attempt to write basic principles into the plays, is the consistency and, be it said, the smoothness with which the two techniques operate. In these fundamentals, as in the details of technique presently to be discussed, Shakespeare merely adapted and developed what he had found in other writers and used in his own earlier plays. But what a development!

The actual devices for interpreting his action to the audience which Shakespeare adapted from himself and from other writers may perhaps be grouped as conventional characters, conventional speeches, and conventional plot elements.

The most obvious and the most ancient example of the conven-

[19]London, 1591, pp. 13-16.

tional character is variously called a protatic or expository character or a dramatist's mouthpiece. Actually, however, the function is more pervasive than the character, since anyone from the protagonist on down may at times be used to guide the audience in following or interpreting or evaluating the action. We have noticed, for example, how Romeo is given a few lines just before he kills Paris to indicate that he is acting in sinful fury (V.iii.59-67). The facility with which some of Shakespeare's major characters slide in and out of this interpretive role has been at times a source of confusion as to the meaning of the play. The clumsiest use of this device in the tragedies, if I am right in my interpretation of *Julius Caesar*, is Antony's soliloquy after the murder of Caesar (III.i.254-275), discussed in Chapter iii. Iago's protatic function is actually less consistent with his character than Antony's, since we do not ordinarily expect the mean-spirited to recognize nobility; but dramatically it is much safer and more effective, since we are quite prepared to believe the antagonist when he praises the protagonist, whereas we suspect his motives when he accuses the hero of wrongdoing. Antony himself illustrates this principle. Critics have largely ignored his soliloquy on the murder, as we noted; but they have all given due weight to his final speech in praise of Brutus. Doubts of Lady Macbeth's testimony favorable to Macbeth, when expressed, have been based, like Schücking's, upon the action of the play rather than upon her motives.

The use of a protatic character of lower rank than an antagonist can be illustrated by Horatio and Banquo. The former exemplifies a different problem—that of using a character to give a variety of information without producing an inconsistency. Shakespeare may actually have ignored the problem. At any rate, Horatio lectures Bernardo and Marcellus (and the audience) on the characteristics of the late king, of whom he later says to Hamlet, "I saw him once." In the latter scene he figures as a visitor from Wittenberg whose presence in Elsinore astonishes Hamlet (I.ii.160-176). But changing Horatio into a stranger enables Hamlet, in turn, to give him (and the audience) a good deal of useful information.

Banquo is much better integrated into the play, and he is used more skillfully to guide the audience in watching Macbeth's reactions to the ghost and in judging them by sound principles. In accordance with Shakespeare's habit of making sure that the audience does not

miss a significant action, Banquo calls attention to Macbeth's first
sign of horror:

> Good sir, why do you start, and seem to fear
> Things that do sound so fair?
>
> (I.iii.51-52)

After explaining to the audience the source of the witches' knowledge, he warns Macbeth that

> oftentimes, to win us to our harm,
> The instruments of darkness tell us truths,
> Win us with honest trifles, to betray 's
> In deepest consequence.
>
> (I.iii.123-126)

In doing so, he underscores the fallacy of Macbeth's argument in his
next speech that the "supernatural soliciting / Cannot be ill" (ll.130-
131) because it commences in a truth. Then, once again, he calls attention to significant action—Macbeth's preoccupation with the
witches' prophecy. Throughout the scene he is pointing out to the
audience the correct interpretation of events and is enabling them
to perceive, in the light of their superior understanding, the errors
of a man too much "rapt" in his own surmises to heed Banquo's
warnings.

Horatio and Banquo also illustrate a second kind of conventional
character—one who makes the dramatist's point by the contrast between his actions or reactions and the hero's. Shakespeare had used
this device to good effect in *1 Henry IV*. There Hotspur illustrates
both the military prowess which Hal must achieve and the stubbornness and rashness which he must avoid if he is to be a great leader;
Falstaff exemplifies both the rich humanity to which Hal must respond and the immoral self-indulgence and cynicism that he must
deny. Horatio and Banquo, because they function in tragedy, are
simpler character foils in that they need only illustrate the moral
norm from which the hero deviates: Horatio, the moral poise of a
man who is not passion's slave; Banquo, rectitude and loyalty to one's
sovereign. Perhaps the best examples of this device in Shakespeare
are to be found in *Coriolanus*. Menenius Agrippa is both the voice
and the example of tolerant wisdom; he is also a salty character in
his own right. Volumnia is a more subtle use of the same device in

that she has made Coriolanus what he is; she therefore is doubly meaningful when she reproves Coriolanus for adhering too stubbornly to the principles which she taught him.

Most difficult of all Shakespeare's conventional characters to isolate and describe are a group which may be thought of as personifying or symbolizing a force at work in the play. The borderline between realism and allegory was never sharp in the Elizabethan mind, and symbolism was a fundamental part of the medieval tradition. Nowhere in the tragedies do we find a character like "Rumour, painted full of tongues" of *2 Henry IV*. But the medieval morality has certainly left traces in the handling of characterization. I am not referring to obvious survivals of such stock characters as the vice or the clown. I am thinking, rather, of the effect produced by the basic structure as the morality dramatized the *psychomachia* in man by lining up its allegorical figures on the side of good and evil. In Shakespeare, the basic conflict still rages within the soul of the hero, but the forces lined up in opposition are now dramatis personae. In many of them, however, the symbolic function as a force making for good or evil is only slightly disguised by the name of the character.

Kent, for example, is a developed character as well as a personification of proper loyalty to one's king; on the other hand, the servant of Cornwall who dies trying to prevent the blinding of Gloucester is simply a symbol of the point at which the moral law demands something more than mere obedience, even from a servant. But, in the larger sense, the principle of good and evil in strife for the human soul accounts for Shakespeare's failure to motivate both his villains and his completely virtuous characters. Iago, Edmund, Goneril and Regan, and Lady Macbeth have personality; they also have complexity, as one sees if one tries to name them in the fashion of figures in a morality—jealousy, ambition, lust, and pride. The fact that none of them can be described by a single epithet illustrates, among other things, what Shakespeare has gained by his method. But they are, nevertheless, forces for evil whose character is a postulate of the drama, as is their interest in subverting the hero. Once again Shakespeare seems to have grown in skill. Cassius is used to seduce Brutus into murdering Caesar; he is a complex, well-motivated character, and later in the play he is actually used as a moral norm to show, by contrast, what has happened to Brutus. But our interest in him and our sympathy for him toward the end of the play confuse its total meaning. The simplicity of the roles assigned to Iago and Edmund obviously makes for dramatic clarity, but the two characters lack depth. Goneril and Regan gain interest from their more complex relationships as sisters, wives, and rivals in love, but their role as evil forces in the play is nevertheless unambiguous. The pattern developed for them remains in the tribunes of *Coriolanus*. But the ambiguity—or perhaps I should say double nature—of Cleopatra's role once again produces confusion of meaning, which has been reflected in the critical tradition, even as it produces more striking drama.

The virtuous characters require less comment. Dramatists, like other writers, have always found the bad people more likely to yield excitement than the good. Desdemona is purely passive; Banquo and Enobarbus are primarily expository. In *Coriolanus* the exposition of good is divided between Menenius and Volumnia, and the good characters gain in strength and dramatic importance as contrasted to the preceding. Only in *King Lear*, however, is there a complete pairing of forces in the strict morality-play tradition, as Cordelia and Kent and Edgar line up against the sisters and Edmund. The emergence of strong forces for good in *King Lear* and *Coriolanus* is, of course, no accident. For only in these plays does the good, to some extent and in some sense, win out. How important that extent and that sense are will become apparent, I hope, during the discussion of the plays. The point that I want to make now is that the good of Cordelia, like the evil of Edmund, is simply assumed and is not explained. But she is thoroughly human, and, as a virtuous human being should, she grows toward perfection during the play.

Shakespeare obviously believed, like his contemporaries, that man is continually tempted to sin not only by his own appetite and other human beings but also by the devil and his instruments. The supernatural forces, like human beings, could damage man's soul only by proposing an object to his appetite and seducing him to that consent of will which was part of every sinful deed. In other words, the demon who possessed a man could no more damn him by driving him to involuntary acts than could his human enemy who killed him in battle. But he might masquerade as a ghost and frighten him into suicide, a damnable act, as Horatio warns Hamlet (I.iv.69-78). The ghost in *Hamlet*, like so much else in that play, is uncertain in that his true nature, as opposed to the truth of his revelation, is never revealed. The witches in *Macbeth*, however, are worked out in accordance with the orthodox theories to which Banquo alludes. Shakespeare makes clear, incidentally, that he thinks of them as witches and nothing more.[20] They are servants of the devil as a result of the compact which has won them the service of their familiar devils in animal form, and they serve the purposes of supernatural evil in characteristic fashion by proposing an object to Macbeth's appetite. They are symbolic in the sense that they typify one of the forces for evil which the baptismal service calls "the devil, the world, and the flesh." But, like the human agents of evil, they function as persons and not as allegorical symbols.

The Fool in *King Lear* is, of course, much more nearly symbolic than any of the characters so far discussed. Often he seems to say openly what Lear is beginning to understand but is too proud to acknowledge. In a morality play he might have been called Conscience or Understanding. In general, however, he functions as the voice of reason and common sense in a world turned upside down, so that men who should be wise are fools, as he points out, and professional fools are wise. He is one of the many paradoxes of the play, and the paradox implicit in his role is itself a symbol of the complete upsetting of the whole order of nature which occurs as part of the action. But he is also a devoted servant of Lear, and as such he is a real person as well as a dramatis persona.

In short, these characters are symbolic only in that they grow out of and fit into a pattern conceived in abstract terms. They are, however, in no sense symbols themselves, and they function not as allegory but as persons of the drama. Shakespeare's method was to illustrate general principles and to state them through the mouths of his characters, not to portray them allegorically as Spenser did.

The term "conventional speeches" to describe another category of expository devices is to some extent misleading. In enunciating fundamental principles and relating the action to them, Shakespeare relied heavily upon the actual dialogue of the drama. Sometimes a mere phrase places the action in perspective. When Lady Macbeth

[20]Cf. Paul, *The Royal Play of Macbeth*, pp. 158-160, 195.

says of the murder, "What, in our house?" Banquo supplies perspective: "Too cruel anywhere" (II.iii.93). In the next scene, Ross discourses more elaborately to a convenient "Old Man"—that is, to the audience:

> Ah, good father,
> Thou seest the heavens, as troubled with man's act,
> Threatens his bloody stage. By th' clock 'tis day,
> And yet dark night strangles the travelling lamp.
> Is't night's predominance or the day's shame
> That darkness does the face of earth entomb,
> When living light should kiss it?
>
> (II.iv.4-10)

Here Ross not only relates events to an outraged natural order but also makes explicit part of the symbolism of the play, which is, in fact, the traditional symbolism of light in all its implications as good and dark as evil. Other examples occur that are more specific and detailed but, for that very reason, less typical of Shakespeare's normal practice.

In dialogue, as in characterization, Shakespeare was apparently willing to sacrifice consistency of detail to the total meaning of the drama. The parents in *Romeo and Juliet*, for example, are described as far older than allusions to various ages in the play, if worked out mathematically, will permit them to be. What matters is not the mathematics but the contrast of youth and age. Lady Macbeth's much-discussed infant surely belongs in this category (I.vii.54-58). The speech occurs during the crucial scene of moral choice, and Macbeth has decided to "proceed no further in this business" (l. 31). Lady Macbeth replies with standard feminine arguments: Don't you love me enough? Are you a coward? To reinforce the latter, she imagines the most frightful act to which a woman might nerve herself and talks of dashing her own child's brains out. Shakespeare intends not only that she shall use an extreme argument upon Macbeth but also that we shall see that, in her desire to overcome his moral scruples, she is desperate to the point of hysteria. Once the point is made, we hear no more of Lady Macbeth's children, and the play surely implies that her having any is out of the question.

In *King Lear*, however, there may be an intentional inconsistency that escapes a modern reader. As Schücking pointed out, we must surely take at face value any statement made in a play unless we have somehow been specifically warned that the speaker is lying to secure his own ends. But the principle would obviously not apply if a child, for example, talked of himself as a man. As he prepares to divide his kingdom, Lear implies that he is an extremely old man:

> and 'tis our fast intent
> To shake all cares and business from our age,
> Conferring them on younger strengths, while we
> Unburden'd crawl toward death.
>
> (I.i.39-42)

Later he calls himself "Fourscore and upward" (IV.vii.61). This is in part his apology for being weak and confused, and Shakespeare notoriously uses statements of age loosely to emphasize a point. But modern productions of the play usually present him as extremely old. If, as seems likely, Burbage played Lear, he had played Hamlet only five years previously and Othello just the preceding season. He was undoubtedly a vigorous man. It is an obvious inference from Shakespeare's carelessness in alluding to ages that what really counted was how the actor looked on the stage. If Lady Capulet looked middle-aged, it would not matter in the least that statements about Juliet's age and her own age at Juliet's birth added up to twenty-eight. But if Burbage looked fifty or even sixty, and Lear implied that he was broken with age, the effect would be totally different. Lear's divesting himself of responsibility while insisting upon the trappings of royalty would not only be hideous rashness, as Kent calls it, but the selfishness of a spoiled man, such as Lear shows himself in other respects. It seems to me very likely that Burbage did produce an effect considerably short of extreme old age. Such an impression would increase Lear's moral responsibility for his own tragedy in divesting himself of authority; it would also leave the actor more opportunity than most performances now allow him to weaken under suffering and to become, at the end of the play, "a very foolish fond old man" (IV.vii.60) in the full meaning of that phrase.[21]

The effect just suggested would make Lear's statements about his

[21]I owe this suggestion to my student Carolyn French. It is elaborated in her unpublished Stanford University dissertation "*King Lear*: Poem or Play?" (1958).

166

age stand out as contrary to fact and derive their meaning from that contradiction. This is not, it must certainly be granted, Shakespeare's normal way of guiding the audience. Comments inserted in the dialogue are often so deft, in fact, that they escape notice. But every reader or spectator of Shakespeare's tragedies has been struck by the insertion of long soliloquies or considerable asides into the action. From the viewpoint of dramatic technique they are an important characteristic of his plays at certain periods in his career. From my present point of view, however, they are merely striking examples of what I should call the meditative or expository speech. If the purpose is to enlighten the audience as to the character's mental processes, it makes little difference in expository method, as opposed to dramatic realism, whether another character is present or even whether he is supposed to be listening or not. Iago's speeches on self-love and self-control (*Othello* I.iii.312-337) are addressed to Roderigo and are dramatically plausible as part of a dialogue; Edmund's speeches on his bastardy (*King Lear* I.ii.1-22) and on his scorn of his father's superstition (I.ii.128-145) are soliloquies. But dramatically both pairs serve exactly the same function—that of describing a villain whose inordinate self-love or pride indicates a fully developed habit of sin, so that his reason is thoroughly enslaved to his baser nature.

Dramatically, of course, these speeches derive from the too obvious exposition of medieval drama and from the conventional prologues and soliloquies in Seneca. They seem to us extremely artificial in their length and in their careful rhetorical structure. But it is possible to overestimate both their dependence upon dramatic tradition and their artificiality for Shakespeare's audience.

The soliloquy or long meditative speech was actually just as important a part of Elizabethan prose fiction as of Elizabethan drama. Any number of examples could be cited from prose romances of an important character who responded to some crisis by a formal meditation on the pros and cons of a course confronting him or, if the situation were desperate enough, a listing of the cons. These are related, of course, to the moral discourses that are an important part of Lyly's *Euphues* and of euphuistic romances in general. The handling of such soliloquies can be indicated by a passage from John Dickenson's *Arisbas, Euphues amidst His Slumbers:*

Drowned in this déepe meditation, he procéeded pensive, but he had not walked farre, when he espied a faire broade Oake, whose spatious branches environd the ground lying underneath with a shady circle. There hée determined to rest awhile his bodie wearied by long journeyes, and somewhat disburthen his soule by displaying his sorrowes. Thether he came, downe he sate, and fixing his eyes on the starrie concave, began thus to utter passionate complaints, not limiting his laments with distinct clauses, for his mone admitted no methode.[22]

This example has been selected because the apology for lack of rhetorical structure implies the norm. Actually Arisbas' moan, which lasts for a page or more, involves considerable method.

Robert Greene provides in *Philomela: The Lady Fitzwaters Nightingale* (1592) an example of what was intended as a soliloquy but involuntarily became a meditative discourse. Il Conte Phillippo Medico of Venice, jealously believing his wife unfaithful, caused her to be banished. Her beauty inflamed Tebaldo, the master of the boat on which she sailed, and he approached her cabin intent upon having her—by rape if necessary. But just at that opportune moment she began a protracted discourse (three pages long) on her virtue and her present perilous state and then concluded with a song to her lute preferring death to unchastity.[23] Fortunately, her voice had not been weakened by her suffering, and Tebaldo overheard all through the door. He was so moved by her rhetorical catalog of her woes that he offered her his strictly platonic assistance, and he and his wife cared for her.

This is more artificial as a plot device than anything in Shakespeare, but the formal meditation, especially if the rhetoric was good enough, obviously had great attraction for Elizabethan readers. I suspect that it did not seem so remote from life to them as it does to us and that it may even have had a kind of practical interest for some of them. Elizabethan schoolboys were taught to write themes subjecting all kinds of fantastical situations to rhetorical analysis, and the habit persisted. We still have, either as state papers or as private relics, a number of similar discourses in which a state official summarized a political problem or an educated man a personal situation.

[22]*Arisbas, Euphues amidst His Slumbers: Or Cupids Journey to Hell* (London, 1594), sig. B2.

[23]In *The Life and Complete Works in Prose and Verse of Robert Greene, M.A.*, ed. Alexander B. Grosart (London and Aylesbury, 1881-86), XI, 174-179.

In method, and sometimes even in rhetoric, these are like the discourses of the romances and, barring verse, like the speeches in Shakespeare's plays. As so often in art, a convention flourished because it had real meaning for the reader or spectator. The more educated among Shakespeare's audience, at least, would automatically have followed the design and the content of his great speeches.

Two characteristics of these speeches are of importance in connection with our analysis of Shakespeare's technique of relating action to moral principles. The first of these has already been glanced at several times—namely, that the clarity of moral perception or the power of analysis in philosophic terms generally present in these discourses is often not otherwise characteristic of the speaker and is sometimes even inconsistent with the general impression that he produces. We accept Hamlet as introspective, and his soliloquies seem in character. They are, in fact, generally concerned with a moral issue or state of mind and are not means of forwarding the action of the play. It is therefore easier to accept them as brooding for its own sake. Macbeth, on the other hand, is represented as strong in imagination but weak in ratiocination, and the warnings of his conscience usually present themselves to him as visual images—most notably, the bloody dagger. We are not prepared, therefore, to accept as characteristic of him the close reasoning of his first great soliloquy (I.vii.1-28), beginning "If it were done when 'tis done, then 'twere well / It were done quickly." But Shakespeare had both to show that Macbeth had already yielded to temptation to the point of being willing to "jump the life to come" and to provide the audience with a sure understanding of the enormity of Macbeth's sin. The first part of the speech is therefore out of character in the exactness of its ethical analysis, although the violent images of the latter part—the naked newborn babe, heaven's cherubin horsed, the tears that drown the wind—revert to Macbeth's normal manner.

The structure of these speeches is a second characteristic more important than their verisimilitude. Most of them will bear examination as means of relating a particular problem to universal principles. What is perhaps Shakespeare's commonest method—derived, no doubt, from his rhetorical training, for it occurs as early as Portia's great mercy speech—can be illustrated from Macbeth's words mentioned just above. The speech needs to be quoted:

If it were done when 'tis done, then 'twere well
It were done quickly. If the assassination
Could trammel up the consequence, and catch
With his surcease success; that but this blow
Might be the be-all and the end-all here,
But here, upon this bank and shoal of time,
We'd jump the life to come. But in these cases
We still have judgement here, that we but teach
Bloody instructions, which, being taught, return
To plague th' inventor. This even-handed justice
Commends th' ingredients of our poison'd chalice
To our own lips. He's here in double trust:
First, as I am his kinsman and his subject,
Strong both against the deed; then, as his host,
Who should against his murderer shut the door,
Not bear the knife myself. Besides, this Duncan
Hath borne his faculties so meek, hath been
So clear in his great office, that his virtues
Will plead like angels, trumpet-tongu'd, against
The deep damnation of his taking-off;
And pity, like a naked new-born babe
Striding the blast, or heaven's cherubin hors'd
Upon the sightless couriers of the air,
Shall blow the horrid deed in every eye,
That tears shall drown the wind. I have no spur
To prick the sides of my intent, but only
Vaulting ambition, which o'erleaps itself
And falls on th' other—

(*Macbeth* I.vii.1-28)

The issue is stated twice, first as a general principle, and then in terms of the specific problem—whether to kill Duncan. The second formulation adds the important "We'd jump the life to come," which limits the question to this world. Macbeth then proceeds to list reasons why the deed will not be the end of the matter: (1) he will teach others how to assassinate himself; (2) the circumstances of the deed, done by a kinsman, subject, and host, and Duncan's own character will arouse universal pity for Duncan and horror of Macbeth. Obviously the deed will not be the end of the matter, and Macbeth concludes quite logically that he can find no spur to drive him on except his own ambition. "Vaulting ambition" he takes, like all Elizabethans, to be sinful, and his words to Lady Macbeth, "We will proceed no further in this business" (l. 31), state his decision to act upon his logic. Her methods of confusing the issue need not concern us here. It has been made clear that Macbeth acts unwisely, even in human terms, in killing Duncan; and the audience has been effectively reminded of the general principles of conduct in the light of which Macbeth's actions are to be judged.

The most brilliant use of this same structure is to be found in Hamlet's "To be, or not to be." Yet the speech has often been misread, partly because its logical structure has not been understood. Hamlet, like Macbeth, states his problem first in general terms, here philosophical, and then as a specific problem:

> To be, or not to be: that is the question.
> Whether 'tis nobler in the mind to suffer
> The slings and arrows of outrageous fortune,
> Or to take arms against a sea of troubles,
> And by opposing end them.
>
> (III.i.56-60)

But his counsel, to use the Thomistic term for this kind of meditation preliminary to an act of will, involves both sides of the question. A sleep that ends our troubles is to be desired. But is death an end? Like sleep, it may involve dreams, and that is why men do not commit suicide as an easy way out of their burdens. Furthermore, the undiscovered country of death, as our conscience warns us, may bring greater ills. So "enterprises of great pith and moment"—like attempting revenge upon Claudius, almost certainly at the cost of Hamlet's life—"lose the name of action" (ll. 86-88).

The initial formulation in abstract terms involves a kind of metaphysical pun that provides the answer to the question. Shakespeare did not expect his audience to be metaphysicians, but he could be sure that the judicious among them knew that nonbeing is possible only through the withdrawal of that God "in whom we live, and move, and have our being" and that hell is simply the absence or privation of God. To formulate Hamlet's problems in terms of being and nonbeing was to settle it, and the last part of the soliloquy merely explores the implication of the initial statement. It might be argued that what is obviously a "loaded" statement of the issue implies that Hamlet was, in effect, finding an excuse for not acting. I do not think so. It means, rather, that Shakespeare the dramatist was making Hamlet his mouthpiece to summarize for the audience the implications of taking arms to achieve revenge, which they knew to be sinful, on the promptings of a ghost who pretended to be from "The undiscover'd country from whose bourn / No traveller returns" (ll. 79-80) and who therefore might very well be an instrument of Satan.[24] But Shakespeare the dramatist is also at work making the speech reflect Hamlet's own emotional bias as he confronts not an agonizing problem but an agonizing uncertainty as to what his problem is.

Almost all the major soliloquies have a logical or rhetorical pattern, and generally it involves some relationship between present action and eternal verities. But I know of no other structure used several times as is that just described. Macbeth's speech beginning "Is this a dagger which I see before me" (II.i.33-64) may be taken as an example of a structure resulting from a special purpose. The dagger that Macbeth sees is first established as a visual illusion and then as a symbol of the murder that he is about to commit. The meaning of that symbol is made clear by the alternatives:

> Mine eyes are made the fools o' th' other senses,
> Or else worth all the rest.

(ll. 44-45)

They are worth all the rest, for the speech proceeds to relate the impending murder to the death of nature as order and moral law. This murder is therefore associated with witchcraft, murder personified, and rape as destroying the order of nature by supernatural or natural means. But Macbeth follows his other senses rather than his eyes, and Duncan goes "to heaven or to hell" (l. 64). The images used are hackneyed to a degree, but therein lies their point. They are commonplace *exempla*, and their very triteness makes clear that Macbeth's crime makes him at one with all sinners. Only his evil deed is his own; his path to moral ruin is that of every man who sins and does not repent. The soliloquy is not a meditation upon a course of action. It expresses the warnings of Macbeth's conscience, which relates his deed to the commands of God and nature. It also makes sure that the spectators will see the crime with eyes like his—eyes worth all the rest.

[24]See Schücking, *Character Problems in Shakespeare's Plays*, pp. 117-118, for consequences of failing to see Hamlet's words as, among other things, a reminder to the audience of accepted demonology.

A third, and perhaps the most important, method by which Shakespeare relates the particular action to universal principles—the use of conventional plot elements—has already been noted in the discussion of symbolic characters above. In view of this anticipation, bare mention here will suffice. The typical structure of Shakespearean tragedy is itself a means of relating a given action to a general pattern. As soon as subordinate characters line up on opposite sides and the hero is confronted with a problem, we know that we stand in the framework of the Christian warfare against the devil, the world, and the flesh. We know what the odds are and what the consequences of moral error will be. The struggle against "the flesh," moreover, is clearly defined. For Shakespeare is usually careful to label the hero's weakness in terms that are technical although generally understood. Brutus is noble, but his "honourable metal may be wrought" (I.ii.313); that is, his very confidence in his rectitude is a weakness. Othello is

> of a free and open nature,
> That thinks men honest that but seem to be so,
> And will as tenderly be led by th' nose
> As asses are.
>
> (I.iii.405-408)

Macbeth has "Vaulting ambition." Antony "dotes" upon "a gipsy's lust" (I.i.10). And so on. There is nothing subtle about the motivation of Shakespeare's tragedies. They derive their power, rather, from the clarity with which they mirror well-known formulations of human conduct that had themselves grown out of, and been tested by, centuries of experience.

So far, in considering Shakespeare's adaptation of his methods to his view of tragedy, I have discussed his use of three kinds of dramatic device—protatic characters, meditative or expository speeches, and a traditional plot organization. I want now to turn to a variety of changes from his earlier practice, or at least developments therefrom, which may also result from his attempt to solve the problem basic to his view of tragedy—namely, that of relating the particular action to universal principles. I shall consider, first, a change in characterization, then new techniques in presenting the action, and finally an increased reliance upon philosophic and religious formulations.

If one were asked, in the fashion of nineteenth-century students of Shakespeare, to contrast Hamlet and Macbeth as persons rather than as dramatis personae, one would make certain obvious generalizations. The former is a man of thought, the latter a man of action; but Hamlet is actually the braver of the two; and so on. Such comparisons are not very profitable. But a more basic contrast would soon become apparent. If one plays this game, one can say much more about Hamlet than about Macbeth. It was, in fact, such characters as Falstaff and Hamlet that first led to the game's being played, for they are many-faceted personalities, and the dramatist's delight in his creatures seems to have led him to multiply facets beyond the needs of the drama. Frequently, in fact, the facets reflect so many sidelights as to confuse the pattern of the drama itself. Hamlet is, however, the last of these characters. The principal figures in later plays seem to be restricted to essentials. We know, for example, that Macbeth is brave and humane but subject to ambition; that Lear is old and spoiled and proud and wrathful. We do not know very much more. What has happened, I think, is that the characters have been simplified to those traits strictly necessary to the meaning of the play, and Shakespeare's attention has been centered upon the design of the action in terms of ethical principles rather than upon characterization for its own sake. This simplification leads both to clarity of design and to concentration of the audience's attention upon the theme or problem of the play. It therefore parallels, and is a consequence of, the change in Shakespeare's technique of using sources that I mentioned earlier. Where his attention had formerly been directed toward creating characters who would conceal weaknesses in the source plot, it was now focused upon organizing the plot in terms of a specific theme or themes. Portia and Shylock so interest us that we overlook Shakespeare's failure to provide time for the bond to be forfeited; insofar as critics have become interested in Lady Macbeth (and her children) except as means to an end, they have misdirected their attention and have misunderstood the play.

If I am right in assuming that this simplification resulted from an attempt to focus attention upon the theme or meaning of the play, it was corollary to a pattern in the action that produced the same effect. If one is trying to explain a difficult principle, one strips it to its essentials and then selects examples that cover the ground as fully as possible. For example, a professor trying to illustrate consonant shifts in Indo-European languages would select words, if possible, that involved no exceptions or confusing secondary principles. He would also push his exploration of various languages to the farthest possible limits of the Indo-European system. Shakespeare did somewhat the same thing. He not only simplified his characters; he also pushed the action to extreme poles of virtue and vice. A gentleman tells Lear:

> Thou hast one daughter
> Who redeems Nature from the general curse
> Which twain have brought her to.
>
> (IV.vi.209-211)

One test case is enough to vindicate man's moral capacity, whether the twain who have brought the curse be Goneril and Regan or Adam and Eve. Shakespeare, I am sure, meant "twain" to be ambiguous and to imply those responsible for the "general curse" on all mankind. He also intended his tragedies to provide test cases. Othello, for example, is "one not easily jealous, but, being wrought, / Perplex'd in the extreme" (V.ii.345-346). So far apart are his poles of trust and jealousy, in fact, that critics have simply refused to believe Shakespeare—or rather Othello speaking for his creator—and have argued that he was by temperament or background disposed to jealousy. On the other hand, they have credited Lear's initial pride and wrath but have overlooked his final humility and patience. Others besides Schücking have disputed Lady Macbeth's diagnosis of her husband, doubting that the brave and humane man of whom she speaks could have become the cowardly butcher that he is toward the end of the play. But Shakespeare, unlike his critics, believed that all men participated in Adam's fall and that only by perpetual vigilance could the greatest and best among them avoid utter moral destruction. This traditional view he tried to underscore by representing the greatest and best falling to utter ruin, and he makes them explicitly recognize the extent of their downfall. The only exceptions to the latter generalization are Brutus and, as usual, Hamlet. "The wheel is come full circle," says Edmund (King Lear V.iii.174). This complete overturn was in the medieval tradition. It was also a staple of A Mirror for Magistrates. Shakespeare apparently regarded

175

it as essential to the mirror for mankind which his tragedies provided. But his action differs fundamentally from that of medieval "tragedy." The hero's downfall results not from the caprice of fortune but, at least in part, from his own error. In that respect, Shakespeare's "mirror" is more consistently faithful to the moral order in which he believed than medieval "tragedies" or even than the *Mirror for Magistrates*.

Shakespeare not only simplifies his action and pushes it to extremes of moral degeneration; he also underscores the fundamental action by paralleling it in the subplot. Almost from the beginning of his career, Shakespeare experimented with doubling plot elements. In the great tragedies, however, the parallels are better integrated into the dramatic action. I mean by action, of course, the hero's crucial choice and its causes and consequences. The most obvious examples of this device hardly need comment. Laertes stands to Hamlet as Hamlet stands to Claudius; but Laertes chooses to attempt revenge for his father by violence and treachery and in the process loses not only his life but also his integrity as a man. Gloucester finds in his sons the same poles of goodness and evil that Lear finds in his daughters; like Lear, though in his lesser way, he atones for his first error by learning patience and humility. The same kind of device is used more subtly in other tragedies. Banquo, too, hears flattering promises from the witches; he, too, is tempted, but unlike Macbeth he does not yield. Octavia, in her attempt to be faithful to her husband and her principles, underscores Antony's betrayal of wife and duty. In all the plays but *Lear* the point at which the subordinate action ceases to parallel the main one furnishes a signpost to the audience pointing out the path of reason and morality. In *Hamlet*, where the subplot illustrates the wrong path, Laertes' failure is apparent as soon as he confronts Claudius. In *Lear*, on the other hand, the parallel between main action and subplot continues to the end, but in the last half of the play Gloucester's halting regeneration is described in simple expository terms by Edgar and by Gloucester himself as a kind of guide to the more important change in Lear which is worked out in action.

Another and very different way of relating the action to universal principles was to present it within a frame of reference well known to the audience. For a variety of reasons Shakespeare had at his disposal schematized bodies of knowledge far exceeding in number and clarity anything available to a modern writer. For one thing, traditions of popular instruction dating from the Middle Ages, when few could read and books were scarce, still operated. Knowledge was reduced to headings, which were then memorized. For another, popular attention was fixed upon a small number of religious and political problems which were intensely debated. These issues were likewise reduced to first principles and carefully explained. We need only recall the absolute uniformity of grammar-school education, with its strong moral and religious bias; the enforced reading of the official Homilies at all church services, services which Englishmen were compelled by law to attend; and the debates carried on in the pulpit and in the religious books which provided the major output of Elizabethan printing presses. All these developed popular understanding of a body of religious and political doctrines, of the heads under which they were discussed, and of the first principles upon which they were grounded.

Shakespeare uses these formulations of knowledge at all levels in his plays. Hamlet's first words to the Ghost, for example—"Be thou a spirit of health or goblin damn'd" (I.iv.40)—immediately place the action in the context of accepted demonology and of a hot religious issue of the day, since the true spirit of the departed, as opposed to an angel or devil masquerading as such, could return only from purgatory, and purgatory was disallowed by Protestants. In *Tarltons Newes Out of Purgatorie*, a popular jestbook of 1590, the first big joke is that the ghost of the famous clown Richard Tarlton is returning from purgatory, when everyone knows that purgatory does not exist and ghosts cannot return:

With this he drewe more neere me and I starting backe cried out: *In nomine Jesu*, avoid sathan for Ghost thou art none, but a very divell (for the soules of them which are departed) if the sacred principles of Theologie be true) never returne into the world againe till the generall resurrection: for either are they plast in heaven, from whence they come not to intangle themselves with other cares, but sit continuallye before the seat of the Lambe singing *Alleluia* to the highest, or else they are in hell: and this is a profound and certain Aphorisme, *Ab inferis nulla est redemptio*. Upon these conclusive premises, depart from me Sathan the resemblance of whomsoever thou doost carrye. At this pitching his staffe downe on the end & crossing one leg over an other, he answered

177

thus: why you horson dunce, think you to set *Dick Tarlton Non plus* with your aphorismes?[25]

The knowledge demanded for an understanding of *Hamlet* is all assumed in this passage. *Macbeth* relies on more demonology, this time as it related to witchcraft. Banquo's exposition of accepted principles to be applied in dealing with witches is so adequate, however, that a modern audience has no trouble in grasping the full implications of what is happening.

We have already noticed Shakespeare's use of the chain of sin in *Macbeth* and of the steps of repentance in *Hamlet*. The two bodies of doctrine are, in a sense, converse parts of the Christian moral psychology of habit. For one act of sin might begin a chain unless repentance intervened to restore the human soul to its proper orientation toward God and to begin, if possible, the development of a habit of virtue. Shakespeare needed only to relate his action to this body of ideas, often by a mere reference, to give the audience an easy clue to the interpretation of events. Macbeth says:

> I am in blood
> Stepp'd in so far that, should I wade no more,
> Returning were as tedious as go o'er.

> (III.iv.136-138)

The whole speech of which this is a part is, incidentally, another perfect example of the kind of expository analysis of action which Shakespeare gives to his characters for the benefit of the audience. The lines quoted are derived from a famous *sententia* from Seneca's *Agamemnon*,[26] but they are used to place the following action squarely within the context of the chain of sin.

Traditional Aristotelian ethics, often derived from Cicero's *Offices*, might be used in the same way. The concept of virtue as a rational norm between cowardice and rashness is implied by Antony's boasts and Enobarbus' comment:

[25]Richard Tarlton, *Tarltons Newes Out of Purgatorie. Onelye Such a Jest as His Jigge, Fit for Gentlemen to Laugh at an Houre, &c.* (London, [1590]), pp. 2-3.

[26]"Per scelera semper sceleribus tutum est iter" (l. 115). See Francis R. Johnson, "Shakespearian Imagery and Senecan Imitation," in *Joseph Quincy Adams Memorial Studies*, ed. James G. McManaway et al. (Washington, D.C., 1948), pp. 50-52.

Ant.　Do so, we'll speak to them; and tonight I'll force
The wine peep through their scars. Come on, my queen;
There's sap in't yet. The next time I do fight,
I'll make Death love me; for I will contend
Even with his pestilent scythe.

　　　　　　[Exeunt all but Enobarbus.]
Eno.　Now he'll outstare the lightning. To be furious,
Is to be frighted out of fear; and in that mood
The dove will peck the estridge; and I see still
A diminution in our captain's brain
Restores his heart. When valour preys on reason,
It eats the sword it fights with. I will seek
Some way to leave him.
　　　　　　　　　　　　　　　　(III.xiii.189-201)

Antony's courage is based upon desperation and wine, not reason; it is therefore the rashness of a hunted man, as Maecenas also recognizes in the next scene. The same set of ideas is basic to the characterization of Macbeth. We first hear of him as an extraordinarily brave man. But from the murder of Duncan he becomes a prey to fear, which his visit to the witches changes to false confidence. But his false courage speedily turns to cowardice when he learns that Macduff "was from his mother's womb / Untimely ripp'd," and then to the rashness of desperation when Macduff warns him of the consequences of yielding (V.viii.4-34).[27] For Macbeth the rationality necessary to true bravery has been destroyed by his reliance upon the "juggling fiends . . . / That palter with us in a double sense" (ll. 19-20). It has been destroyed not only in the limited contest of one battle but in the larger area of his whole life. And the confession just quoted is a kind of belated acknowledgment that Banquo's warning was sound when he first encountered the witches:

　　　And oftentimes, to win us to our harm,
　　　The instruments of darkness tell us truths.
　　　　　　　　　　　　　　　　(I.iii.123-124)

The echo is not only a masterly dramatic stroke; it is also an example of Shakespeare's habit of underscoring the entire action with a parallel detail. For the entire play has witnessed Macbeth's degeneration from a brave man into a cowardly butcher as a part of his still greater loss of that noble rationality which should determine "all that may become a man" (I.vii.46).

[27]Cf. Campbell, *Shakespeare's Tragic Heroes*, pp. 208-239.

Other echoes of traditional ethics occur in Shakespeare. Kent is a perfect exemplar of the duties of a counselor to his king. He is bound to give Lear sound advice, even at the risk of his own life:

> Thinkest thou that duty shall have dread to speak
> When power to flattery bows? To plainness honour's bound
> When majesty falls to folly.
>
> (I.i.149-151)

Enobarbus finds too late that he cannot break the bonds imposed by the same code of fidelity to an erring master, and his suicide is the result.

King Lear especially, because of its enormously complicated plot, compelled Shakespeare to make constant use of this device of expecting the audience to interpret details of the play in the light of their philosophical and theological training. I have argued elsewhere that the action of the play must be interpreted in terms of the accepted theory of nature and of two well-known perversions of that theory represented by Gloucester and Edmund. John F. Danby has proposed a somewhat different reading that also demands knowledge of the same body of theory.[28] In fact, the word "nature" occurs constantly throughout the play, always so used that a full understanding of its implications is vital to following the play. In the exchange between Gloucester and Edmund on "These late eclipses in the sun and moon" (I.ii.112 ff.), Gloucester shows himself a superstitious old fool in accepting astrological determinism, whereas Elizabethans knew that the stars incline but cannot compel. In contrast, he shows himself in the same speech to be familiar with the accepted categories of distributive justice (presumably to facilitate Shakespeare's task of stating one aspect of his theme). Edmund, on the other hand, is shrewd and completely right about the eclipses. His irrationality is on a higher level, in that he completely fails to understand his obligation as an individual to live according to nature's laws. In short, not only what the characters say, but their very failure to say what sound learning dictated, is part of Shakespeare's exposition of his meaning. Reliance on the audience's knowledge of simple and popular summaries of technical religious and philosophical concepts could go no farther.

[28]*Shakespeare's Doctrine of Nature: A Study of King Lear* (London, 1949).

As *King Lear* shows, the importance of the conventional ways of thinking discussed, and others like them that could be cited, is not primarily that they enable us to interpret individual lines or even scenes. It is rather that they functioned as a means of communication between Shakespeare and his audience. When Enobarbus described Antony as "frighted out of fear" or Kent refused to hold his tongue or Edmund accused his father of making the stars guilty of man's disasters, the audience gained a means of understanding Antony or Lear or Gloucester and, through them, the action of the play that was more effective than long passages of exposition. Shakespeare was enabled to use shortcuts in expressing his meaning just as a mathematician may speak of π or a physicist may denote various constants by symbols. As we shall see in examining individual plays, our ignorance of these dramatic symbols, or more often our failure to heed them, has led to much misunderstanding of Shakespeare. It has led, I think, to a still greater oversight, and that is to our ignoring the extent to which Shakespeare's tragic art is itself made possible by the system of philosophy and ethics upon which it rests. Shakespeare could concentrate upon effective drama because he took for granted a set of values and a system of ideas. Too often the modern writer has to begin from scratch. Still more often he ignores the philosophic problems implicit in his action and keeps busy telling a story which tells us little about life.

We should perhaps note in passing that Shakespeare's attempt to square his action with contemporary doctrine may sometimes have led him to ignore dramatic structure. Many a critical shaft has been directed at the long scene in *Macbeth* between Malcolm and Macduff at the English court. Schücking, for example, argues that Shakespeare reverted to the loose structure of the chronicle plays and inserted it because it was in the source and therefore part of the story.[29] But, under James I, rebellion was a ticklish subject for a dramatist to handle, at best, and he had to make sure of his ground. An attack upon Macbeth was justified only if he was incontrovertibly a tyrant and those involved had never sworn allegiance to him.[30] Malcolm and Macduff had fled Scotland before Macbeth was crowned. The scene under discussion is devoted to establishing beyond a doubt that

[29]*Character Problems in Shakespeare's Plays*, pp. 144-146.
[30]Cf. Paul, *The Royal Play of Macbeth*, pp. 195-196.

Macbeth is a tyrant in the technical sense. As the evidence is presented, he is called a tyrant for the first time in the play, and he is regularly described by that term during the remainder of the play.

In concluding this general discussion of Shakespeare's tragic technique, I am well aware that I have devoted myself to what I have called the philosophic aspect of Shakespeare's plays as opposed to the poetic or purely dramatic—to his problem of relating his action to eternal truths as opposed to his job of writing an effective and exciting stage play. But the former aspect of his art seems to me to need stressing, just because the latter has already received so much attention. No one doubts that he was a great poet or theatrical craftsman. But it is still somewhat daring to claim that he was a careful, if not an original, philosophic thinker. These aspects of his art therefore require emphasis. I hope that they even justify adding another book to the already groaning shelves of Shakespeare collections.

There is, however, another caution that needs to be added. Nothing could be more untrue to Shakespeare's own thinking and to his dramatic method than to assume a dichotomy between the thinker and the playwright. Shakespeare, I am sure, was at one with his age in assuming that poetry must teach and delight and move to virtue. This did not mean, however, that he longed to express his personal vision or emotional tension, as L. C. Knights, for example, seems to think,[31] but had to put it in the straitjacket of intellectual concepts. It means that for him certain great truths illuminated life fundamentally and that he saw his daily experiences in the light that they shed. The problem of relating the particular action to the general concept was not a duty to be faced. It was simply the problem of revealing fully the meaning that he saw in life. Exploring that meaning must have been necessary to his sense of workmanship, or artistic satisfaction, whether it was embodied in the laws of nature or the drunken ribaldry of the Porter. Even that ribaldry might—and did—have meaning as part of a larger order. Shakespeare, I am sure, wrote philosophic drama not because he had to but because he wanted to. Therein lay the reason for his triumphant success.

[31]"On Historical Scholarship and the Interpretation of Shakespeare," *Sewanee Review*, LXIII (1955), 223-240.

Chapter Five ⚬ THE RACK OF THIS TOUGH
WORLD: *HAMLET* AND *KING LEAR*

To PAIR *Hamlet* and *King Lear* for purposes of discussion no
doubt seems odd. *Hamlet* apparently belongs to the season of
1600-1601, *King Lear* to 1605-1606. The former is a revenge play in
a Christian setting, the latter a cosmic tragedy in a pagan world. But
a closer look will reveal, I trust, that the two plays have important
characteristics in common. They have, first of all, the crowded
structure characteristic of Elizabethan tragedy as opposed to the
almost classical simplicity of action in *Othello* and *Macbeth*. Not
only do more events happen and more people become enmeshed in
the main plot, but each play has a subplot, paralleling the main plot
in theme and in events, that adds further complexity of structure
and meaning. This complication of events includes an exciting
scheme and counterscheme and is attended by marching and counter-
marching. All Shakespearean tragedy has its share of sensational
episodes, but *Hamlet* and *King Lear* easily exceed the normal quota.
These superficial parallels are reinforced by deeper resemblances.
Othello and *Macbeth* are clearly centered about a single crucial
choice. John F. Danby comments that "*King Lear* makes more use
of deliberate choice as a means of characterization than any other
of Shakespeare's plays with the possible exception of *Antony and
Cleopatra*."[1] *Hamlet* has the same atmosphere of continuous deciding,
except that the deciding too often stops short of decision. This is
obviously true of Hamlet himself, but it also applies at times to
Claudius and Gertrude and even Laertes. Finally, both plays make
specific use of the doctrine of repentance, both conceive of man as
scourge and minister of God, and both explicitly state a concept of
patience and resignation originating in Christian doctrine.

Isolating these similarities, however, reveals fundamental differences which make it logical—though no doubt startling—to think of
Hamlet as apprenticeship and *King Lear* as achievement. On the

[1]*Shakespeare's Doctrine of Nature: A Study of King Lear* (London, 1949), p. 40.

183

level of dramatic technique *King Lear* is a much more adroit and polished play than *Hamlet*. Not only its tremendous physical activity but also its even more marked growth and decay of the inner man are revealed primarily by action or dialogue incidental to action, often in the form of brief comments. There are few of the expository or meditative speeches so characteristic of Hamlet, and those that appear, like Edmund's, are short and to the point. Expository functions are better distributed among the characters, and no character is sacrificed to the needs of exposition as is Horatio. Loose ends have been found in *King Lear* in plenty,[2] as in all Shakespearean plays, but they are incidental to crowded action rather than to clumsy exposition. This contrast in dramaturgy is even more striking on the level of ideas. Both plays devote a large amount of space to intellectual concepts. In *Hamlet* these passages tend to be outright philosophizing, and they are often attached to the surface of the play. That is, they neither interpret events in progress nor motivate actions to come. In *King Lear*, on the other hand, the philosophy not only interprets and motivates action but is basic to the entire structure of the play. It looks, in short, as though Shakespeare foisted the contents of his teeming mind upon *Hamlet* but drew *King Lear* out of the deepest recesses of his intellect.

The following discussion of the two plays will concentrate upon this problem of the relationship between thought and action as, in turn, an aspect of the larger problem that confronted Shakespeare of relating dramatic action to moral principles. This basis of selection has the incidental advantage that it avoids tackling the meaning of *Hamlet* but necessitates an interpretation of *King Lear*, and this difference is, in turn, a result of the different use of ideas in the two plays.

In writing *Hamlet*, Shakespeare apparently built upon a revenge tragedy of the late 1580's which had the staple characteristics of the type and was, like *The Spanish Tragedie*, by Kyd. Since I have elsewhere attempted an elaborate reconstruction of the old play, I will not repeat myself here.[3] It is enough to remark that the old play was

---

[2]Cf. A. C. Bradley, *Shakespearean Tragedy: Lectures on Hamlet, Othello, King Lear, Macbeth* (London, 1905), pp. 256-260.

[3]*Shakespeare's Use of Learning: An Inquiry into the Growth of His Mind & Art* (San Marino, Calif., 1953), pp. 251-265, 329-346.

apparently first-class melodrama. The problems with which it confronted the revenger were largely external, but it derived from the ultimate source in Belleforest a closet scene that involved an elaborate analysis, in technical terms, of the psychology of Gertrude's infatuation with Claudius and of the justice of Hamlet's punishing the murderer of his father. This scene operated powerfully upon Shakespeare's imagination, and traces of it are to be found not only in his closet scene but in three other passages: in Hamlet's first soliloquy (I.ii.149-153), in his soliloquy after watching Fortinbras and his army (IV.iv.32-66), and in his only discussion of the propriety of his taking revenge upon Claudius (V.ii.63-70).[4] Like other revenge tragedies the old play involved a doubtful revelation of guilt that needed to be tested, a revenger who suffered terrible agony of soul and lacerated himself emotionally because of his inaction, and a final revenge achieved during festivities that involved death for the revenger and maximum slaughter of other characters. From the native heritage it drew its emphasis upon a crowded narrative of events and upon death as the final outcome; from Seneca it derived the theme of revenge and many of its dramatic trappings. Philosophizing and ethical commentary are not absent from *The Spanish Tragedie*, but they are certainly not its distinguishing traits. Doubtless the old play was as "talky" as our present *Hamlet*; but, except for the closet scene, its great speeches probably declaimed hysterical emotion and self-laceration with all the resources of Elizabethan rhetoric and Senecan commonplaces. It was, however, superb theater! Few plays of its period—probably none except *The Spanish Tragedie* and *Tamburlaine*—have left so many traces.

When Shakespeare went to work upon the old Hamlet play, he was obviously master enough of his craft as a playwright to retain all its theatrical effectiveness and make it even more thrilling. That is obvious to anyone who sees a good performance of *Hamlet*. But Shakespeare also wrote into the play a tremendous body of ideas—so many, in fact, that Hamlet seems one of the most intellectual characters in all literature. In fact, one important historical interpretation of the play—that associated with Schlegel and Coleridge—views it as the tragedy of a sensitive man of thought. I am not concerned with an attempt to interpret the play, except, perhaps, to argue that no

4Ibid., pp. 262-265.

interpretation is possible on the premise that the play is an integrated work of art; but I do want to point out that the ideas, whether expressed by Hamlet or others, are largely extraneous to the action of the play.

The best way to make clear what I mean by extraneous is to illustrate what I should regard as a genuinely relevant use of intellectual concepts. Most commonly this takes the form of straight exposition by a character of the principles upon which he is operating. In giving Reynaldo instructions to spy upon Laertes, Polonius states the theory underlying his method:

> See you now,
> Your bait of falsehood takes this carp of truth;
> And thus do we of wisdom and of reach,
> With windlasses and with assays of bias,
> By indirections find directions out.
>
> (II.i.62-66)

This speech gains point, of course, when Polonius' attempts by indirections to find directions out lead him to "loose his daughter" (II.ii.162) to Hamlet or to arrange an interview between Gertrude and Hamlet while he hides behind an arras. Later in the same scene Polonius explains to Ophelia—that is, to the audience—the basis for his diagnosis that Hamlet suffers from love madness:

> This is the very ecstasy of love,
> Whose violent property fordoes itself
> And leads the will to desperate undertakings
> As oft as any passion under heaven
> That does afflict our natures.
>
> (II.i.102-106)

A far more important and elaborate example of the same method is to be found during Laertes' attack upon Claudius. In rushing in to demand satisfaction for Polonius' death, Laertes spouts out the consequences implicit in the kind of headlong fury into which he has fallen. He indicates the lack of moral principle which makes him become an easy tool for Claudius, and, by contrast, he also defines the moral considerations which have made it necessary for Hamlet to move cautiously. "The undiscover'd country" (III.i.79) has no puzzles for Laertes' will!

> To hell, allegiance! Vows, to the blackest devil!
> Conscience and grace, to the profoundest pit!
> I dare damnation. To this point I stand,
> That both the worlds I give to negligence,
> Let come what comes; only I'll be reveng'd
> Most throughly for my father.
>
> (IV.v.131-136)

Hamlet's praise of Horatio is a diagnosis of the ideal man in philosophical and psychological terms:

> Since my dear soul was mistress of my choice
> And could of men distinguish, her election
> Hath seal'd thee for herself; for thou hast been
> As one, in suffering all, that suffers nothing,
> A man that Fortune's buffets and rewards
> Hath ta'en with equal thanks; and blest are those
> Whose blood and judgement are so well commingled,
> That they are not a pipe for Fortune's finger
> To sound what stop she please. Give me that man
> That is not passion's slave, and I will wear him
> In my heart's core, ay, in my heart of heart,
> As I do thee.
>
> (III.ii.68-79)

This speech has a specific function, however, in that it marks Horatio's emergence as the confidential friend in whom Hamlet can confide for the audience's benefit, and it also establishes Horatio as a moral norm with whom Hamlet may be contrasted. The contrast is not, however, developed.

Each of the passages quoted interprets a particular act in terms of general principles of human conduct; yet each seems probable in its dramatic context. A subtler use of general principles is to be found in the efforts of Claudius and Gertrude to console Hamlet in the court scene that follows the first appearance of the ghost. The queen is quite right in reminding Hamlet that "all that lives must die" (I.ii.72), and her new husband is on equally sound ground in pointing out that excessive grief is "unmanly" and "shows a will most incorrect to heaven" (ll. 94, 95). Everything they say is true. It is also appropriate to the dramatic situation in that it establishes Hamlet's alienation from those around him. But we are already aware that a ghost is abroad, and Claudius has himself told us that "discretion fought with nature" (l. 5)—that is, expediency with moral law—to the point that he combined "mirth in funeral" and "dirge in marriage" (l. 12). We also know that the devil can cite scripture to his purpose. Shakespeare makes doubly sure that we remember this principle by having Hamlet guide us with several asides. So we conclude, quite rightly, that Claudius is a most clever hypocrite and a man from whom any crime may be expected—no mean antagonist for Hamlet. Shakespeare had used this method in making Richard quote scriptures; he was to develop it still further in *King Lear*, where the concept of nature as law and order is basic to the play and the characters' misuse of that concept reveals their weakness or, in Edmund's case, their villainy. All these devices are rooted in the notion that the will might become so habituated to evil that the reason was its willing tool and could draw all its resources, even its knowledge of sound moral principles, to the service of evil.

In contrast to the passages just cited, many statements of theory in the play are merely digressions. Among the most interesting of these are a group concerned with dramatic theory that are largely irrelevant to the context. Horatio's remark that the ghost "harrows me with fear and wonder" (I.i.44) has already been noted (Ch. ii) as perhaps indicating Shakespeare's knowledge of theory as to the outcome of tragedy. It is not at all improbable as a reaction to the situation; neither is Horatio's final description of the tragic spectacle as one of "woe or wonder" (V.ii.374).[5] Hamlet's somewhat confused statement about the "vicious mole of nature" that brings general censure even to those otherwise as pure as grace (I.iv.23-38) is a perfect description of the tragic hero that Shakespeare was beginning to portray, and one is therefore tempted to align it with the utterances on dramatic theory; yet it is completely irrelevant and was cut out in the acting version preserved in the Folio. All the instructions to the players, except that they play "The Murder of Gonzago," are, strictly speaking, unnecessary. But they tell us most of what we know about Shakespeare's views on playing, including Hamlet's preference for a play that was "caviare to the general" (II.ii.457) and his view that the mirror should be held up to nature.

For the ordinary student of Shakespeare, Hamlet's soliloquies

[5]Cf. J. V. Cunningham, *Woe or Wonder: The Emotional Effect of Shakespearean Tragedy* (Denver, 1951), pp. 21-23.

come very close to being Hamlet; in fact, they form a large part of the total impact of the play. Certainly they do more than anything else to make Hamlet seem thoughtful and introspective. Two of them are primarily dramatic exposition, even though they are given a veneer of introspection. The speech beginning "O, that this too too solid flesh would melt" (I.ii.129-159) actually defines Gertrude's relation to her late husband, makes explicit just how o'er-hasty her marriage to Claudius was, and reminds the audience that cohabitation with the brother of a deceased husband is incest. "O, what a rogue and peasant slave am I!" (II.ii.576-634) begins that process of self-castigation for delay in which all revenge-tragedy heroes indulged, however necessary the delay may have been, but it also explains how the play will test Claudius' guilt and why additional proof is needed because the ghost may be a devil working upon Hamlet's melancholy. The remaining soliloquies have nothing whatever to do with events in the play. "To be, or not to be" might be argued to explore a course of action that Hamlet rejects and therefore to be relevant; but he does not actually reject the idea of killing Claudius, and a drama constructed on the principles of working out alternative lines of action that the protagonist does not for the moment follow would get nowhere at great length—as revenge plays sometimes do. In that the course rejected for the time being is to take revenge, the speech is merely another example of the self-laceration characteristic of revenge tragedy; so is the last soliloquy, "How all occasions do inform against me" (IV.iv.32-66). What Shakespeare did was to take the lament and self-castigation for inactivity conventional in revenge tragedies and to convert them into a series of meditations in which one follows the movements of a quick and informed mind working with principles intellectually but not dramatically relevant to events in the play. The soliloquies do not interpret dramatic action; rather they portray what might plausibly have gone through Hamlet's mind under the circumstances. In this respect they are like much modern fiction and help to give the play its "modern" quality. But they are deliberation that does not lead to decision, and in that respect they differ fundamentally from the soliloquies in *Julius Caesar* and *Macbeth* or from Edmund's first soliloquy in *King Lear*. They also differ from Hamlet's words over the king at prayer, which lead to a genuine act of will (III.iii.73-96).

189

The most spectacular example of dramatically irrelevant learning is, of course, the closet scene. Elizabethans, as everyone knows, held eloquence in great respect; they were convinced that, among its other powers, it might move the guilty to repent. A considerable list of scenes could be collected from Elizabethan and Jacobean drama in which a powerful exhortation moves a guilty soul to fear of God and repentance. In the old *King Leir*, the murderer sent by Gonorill and Ragan is so moved by the eloquence of Leir and Perillus (Kent) that, at an opportune clap of thunder, he lets fall his daggers at their feet (IV.vii.254-294). The scenes that most closely rival Shakespeare's are those between Melantius and Evadne in Beaumont and Fletcher's *The Maides Tragedy* and between Hippolito and Bellafront in Dekker's *The Honest Whore*. Both date from some years later than *Hamlet*. The closet scene in the old Hamlet play may have been the first of these sensational dramatic exhortations. Shakespeare's closet scene, in which a grief-stricken son confronts an adulterous and incestuous mother, remains among the most effective of them all theatrically. Hamlet's exhortation is not only among the most theatrical; it is indubitably the most learned. If we may infer from elements in Belleforest that carry through into Shakespeare, he found a great deal of passion psychology in his source play. This he retained (cf. III.iv.65-88), providing for the traditional view of sin a brilliant summary in the phrase "reason panders will." He added moral theology, particularly the discussion of repentance (ll. 144-159) and of habit (ll. 161-169). He was apparently at great pains to back up, or perhaps atone for, the theatrical effectiveness of the scene with a maximum of sound moral instruction. He produced a dramatic sensation. But it is almost pointless! In earlier versions of the story Gertrude had allied herself with Hamlet, although it is doubtful how much her aid amounted to. I am convinced myself that she became his supporter in Shakespeare's first version.[6] But in our present play they arrive at no genuine understanding; Gertrude, though acknowledging her guilt, makes no promises except not to betray Hamlet, nor do we see any evidence later that she has actually taken the steps that Hamlet prescribes. The killing of Polonius is, of course, necessary to future action. Otherwise the scene provides us with a chance to

[6]*Shakespeare's Use of Learning*, pp. 344-346.

see the ghost once more and to watch Hamlet round upon his mother in language offensively specific. But that is all, and lecturing Gertrude gets the play nowhere.

The closet scene may serve, in fact, to suggest a difficulty in the construction of the play more fundamental than the intrusion of irrelevant learning. The system of Christian thought which plays so large a part in the language of the play is simply not reconciled with the action as a whole. It is used, rather, as a means to brilliant improvisations that add power to individual episodes. But it is not applied as a consistent basis for the action or as a thorough judgment upon it. The play oscillates between Christian morality and the code of the vendetta.

Shakespeare's handling of the ghost perhaps furnishes the best example of brilliant use of conventional learning to solve a problem of motivation inherent in the conventions of the revenge play. In *The Spanish Tragedie* the first accusation of Lorenzo and Balthazar comes in an anonymous letter written in blood which Hieronimo finds, and this doubtful accusation of guilt requires further proof and therefore agonizing delay. In the old Hamlet, the revelation was undoubtedly made by a ghost. Possibly that ghost was there treated in Christian terms; more probably Shakespeare added this dimension, since it is not in the analogous *Der bestrafte Brudermord*.[7] At any rate, developing the ghost in theological terms added a most compelling reason to doubt its word, since it was probably a devil. The ghost's nature is carefully established by standard expository devices. Bernardo describes it as "like the King that's dead" (I.i.41). Horatio addresses it as *usurping* "that fair and warlike form" (ll. 46-47); or again, "Stay, illusion!" (l. 127). After it leaves, Horatio speaks of it as an elemental demon "Whether in sea or fire, in earth or air" (l. 153). Marcellus adds further lore, stigmatizing it as an unwholesome thing. When Hamlet himself confronts the ghost, he pursues the same line:

> Angels and ministers of grace defend us!
> Be thou a spirit of health or goblin damn'd,
> Bring with thee airs from heaven or blasts from hell,
> Be thy intents wicked or charitable.
>
> (I.iv.39-42)

[7] Ibid., pp. 335-336, 256-258.

"I'll call thee Hamlet," he says (l. 44), implying a polite fiction. Later Horatio fortifies the impression by attributing to it the standard devices used by devils in luring men to destroy themselves by suicide (ll. 69-78).

All this is a commonplace of recent Shakespearean criticism. But it has not often been noticed, I think, that Shakespeare, having made clear the possible interpretations of the ghost, now uses the ghost not only to explain what has happened but also to reveal what is happening to Hamlet. The scene between Hamlet and the ghost can profitably be compared with that between Macbeth and the witches, where Shakespeare improved his technique for relating time to eternity by having Banquo stand by as an expository character. In *Hamlet* he counted on the audience's knowledge of demonology. The ghost, like the witches, is working on something already well established in Hamlet's mind. As its revelation progresses, Hamlet exclaims, "O my prophetic soul! / Mine uncle?" (I.v.40-41). But the point is lost as excitement mounts. Macbeth, on the other hand, indicates his already existing ambition only by a start and by fear, but Banquo calls both of these to the audience's attention so effectively that they are seldom, if ever, overlooked in the interpretation of the play. As Hamlet responds emotionally to the ghost's narrative, he is temporarily won over and rejects the notion that it may be a devil:

> O all you host of heaven! O earth! What else?
> And shall I couple hell? O, fie!
>
> (ll. 92-93)

He tells Horatio: "It is an honest ghost" (l. 138). From then on, he tends to accept the ghost when excited, to doubt it when calm. This shifting in Hamlet's attitude toward the ghost becomes, if the audience views it as probably diabolical, a means of showing Hamlet's inner turmoil and distress and a proof of the danger that the ghost may indeed be a devil working upon his melancholy, as he fears. In other words, if Shakespeare first gave the ghost a theological setting, as I think probable, he wonderfully improved upon his source both in motivating Hamlet's delay and in revealing his inner distress.

The shift from revenge ghost to probable Christian devil therefore strengthened the play immeasurably up to the proof of Claudius' guilt. But it thereupon raised several new problems which Shakespeare ignored. In the first place, Hamlet and the audience knew as well as Banquo that "to win us to our harm, / The instruments of darkness tell us truths" (*Macbeth* I.iii.123-124). The nature of the ghost and of its motives therefore became of primary importance. Nor could its desire to damn Claudius for all eternity, however standard a part of revenge plays, be reconciled with Christian principles. All this Shakespeare brushed aside, as Hamlet exclaims: "O good Horatio, I'll take the ghost's word for a thousand pound. Didst perceive?" (III.ii.297-298). Hamlet seems, in fact, to be completely in the ghost's power:

> 'Tis now the very witching time of night
> When churchyards yawn and hell itself breathes out
> Contagion to this world. Now could I drink hot blood,
> And do such bitter business as the day
> Would quake to look on. Soft! now to my mother.
> O heart, lose not thy nature! Let not ever
> The soul of Nero enter this firm bosom;
> Let me be cruel, not unnatural.
> I will speak daggers to her, but use none.
> My tongue and soul in this be hypocrites.
>
> (III.ii.406-415)

This is hardly the sweet prince whom flights of angels sing to rest. His problem is regarded as solved, when, in terms of the moral values associated with the ghost, it had only begun. Not the truth of the ghost's revelation, but its very nature as a guide to its motives, was fundamental to Hamlet's problem. What kind of ghost it was Shakespeare never tells us.

The ghost had provided a brilliant motivation for delaying the revenge up to the middle of the play. At that point Shakespeare still had half a play, crowded with episodes, but provided with no sustained explanation of why Hamlet failed to kill Claudius. He seems to me to have improvised. If I am right, it is no accident that there is much more use of the Christian system in the last half of the play and that it is even less integrated with the plot than is the Christian background of the ghost. Shakespeare needed it to provide the appearance of motivation. In view of Claudius' more than frank confessions and his complete honesty with himself and his audience, we hardly need to be told that he is in a state of sin. His prayer, in which he labors powerfully to repent and fails, demonstrates Hamlet's willingness to kill him and provides a compelling reason for not doing so (I take Hamlet's reason as sound). But the elaborate revelation of just how far toward repentance he has moved and why he must sink further into sin serves no purpose that could not have been achieved by a few lines on his knees, except to titillate the audience as he comes close to repenting and to provide ironic commentary upon Hamlet's decision to make sure that he will be damned. The real trouble with the scene, however, is that the kneeling figure grappling in orthodox Christian terms with the problem of repentance is morally superior to the prince whose only desire is to send him to hell. This may be one reason why many critics have hesitated to take Hamlet's stated motives seriously. We cannot reconcile them with the sweet prince of Shakespeare and of our own sympathies. So the contrast here posed between a Claudius developed in Christian terms and a revenge-play Hamlet merely underscores the contradiction between the revenge-play Hamlet of this and similar scenes and the Christian Hamlet shortly to be discussed. As Claudius kneels in prayer beneath Hamlet's drawn sword, Christian logic panders vengeful will, and theology panders melodrama.

In the closet scene a totally different Hamlet emerges—a Hamlet who reappears at intervals throughout the remaining episodes of the play. This Hamlet has been the subject of an interesting essay by Fredson Bowers called "Hamlet as Minister and Scourge,"[8] which develops the implications of Hamlet's comment on the body of Polonius:

> For this same lord,
> I do repent; but Heaven hath pleas'd it so,
> To punish me with this and this with me,
> That I must be their scourge and minister.
> I will bestow him, and will answer well
> The death I gave him.

(III.iv.172-177)

Bowers sees this speech as a key to the play, of which the killing of Polonius is the climax or turning point. His thesis, as I understand it, is as follows. Since the ghost was permitted by God to return from purgatory, its revelation was a command to act as God's minis-

[8]*PMLA*, LXX (1955), 740-749. See also the sequel "The Death of Hamlet: A Study in Plot and Character," *Studies in the English Renaissance Drama*, ed. Josephine W. Bennett et al. (New York, 1959), pp. 28-42.

ter in punishing Claudius and restoring order to Denmark. But Hamlet must await the opportunity which God will provide for him to "contrive a public vengeance which will demonstrate him to be a minister of Heaven's justice" (p. 744). In the meantime, he must resist the strong emotions which urge him to a personal revenge of blood. In resisting the temptation to kill Claudius at prayer, he acts properly. But in killing Polonius, he yields to the temptation to take private vengeance and kills the wrong man, thereby setting in motion retribution against himself. He acts, in effect, as God's scourge upon Polonius—that is, as a wicked man used by God to punish another's sins. His use of the word "scourge" is a confession that he has done wrong. ". . . Hamlet is not only punished *for* the murder of Polonius but *with* his murder, since Polonius was not his assigned victim; hence this fact is the evidence for Heaven's displeasure at his private revenge. The punishment *for* the murder will come, as indeed it does" (p. 746). Hamlet thereafter resigns himself to the will of God, and in due time his opportunity to punish Claudius without personal guilt does come, when Claudius has been publicly revealed as the murderer of Gertrude. But he must suffer death for the killing of Polonius, as he recognizes in forgiving Laertes.

This interpretation of the lines in their immediate context seems to me unquestionably sound. But I should offer two objections to his suggestion that Hamlet's words interpret the first half of the play. First, it seems most unlikely that Shakespeare would expect his audience to assume that a public act of justice instead of a private vengeance was required, at least for the reasons stated. They might indeed expect a public killing because of the traditions of the revenge tragedy or the requirements of good theatrical spectacle. But Shakespeare was at great pains to make clear to them that the ghost must be interpreted in theological terms. Would he not have taken equal pains to make clear that Christian and legal morality operated to govern the circumstances of Claudius' punishment, if he had expected the audience to think in those terms? The ghost, who gives rather specific directions on the point, tells Hamlet that he is bound to revenge. And Hamlet, in his most agonized soliloquy, cries, "O, vengeance!" and speaks of himself as prompted to his revenge (II.ii.610-613). Nowhere does he talk of a public as opposed to a private killing or even of punishment as opposed to revenge. His problem, insofar as he delimits it, is simply whether the ghost abuses him to damn him and how to find "grounds / More relative than this" (ll. 632-633).

To solve the problem of the ghost's nature, Bowers makes a tacit assumption that a ghost might return from purgatory. To repeat his words:

> Moreover, it has not been well considered that if the Ghost is a spirit of health, it could not escape from purgatory under its own volition in order to influence affairs on earth. Since divine permission alone could free the Ghost to revisit the earth, the Ghost's demand for the external punishment of Claudius, and its prophecy of the internal punishment of Gertrude, is not alone a personal call but in effect the transmission of a divine command, appointing Hamlet as God's agent to punish the specific criminal, Claudius. (pp. 744-745)

The ghost, it is true, represents himself as coming from purgatory, but, for many of the audience if not for Shakespeare, that would cast further doubt upon his *bona fides*. Only Catholics accepted purgatory, and Papists were even more dangerous than devils, because more numerous and closer at hand, and equally given to equivocation. Everyone but the ghost—including Hamlet—speaks explicitly in terms of heaven and hell. Surely, if Bowers' interpretation had been intended, Hamlet could have been spared a few lines, among his many, to reflect that the ghost might have been loosed from purgatory to bear a divine command. Hamlet's description of himself as scourge and minister, like so much of the Christian thought in the play, seems to me brilliant improvisation based upon a detail from the source play.

Bowers is surely right, however, in pointing with other critics to the new Hamlet, who, after his return from England, resigns himself to the will of God, confident that heaven is ordinant (V.ii.48). But I suspect that once again Shakespeare was grafting an intellectual explanation upon a preexisting plot. A few scars remain to show the graft.

Certainly Hamlet's last words before he leaves Denmark do not sound like waiting for the proper time:

> I do not know
> Why yet I live to say, "This thing's to do,"
> Sith I have cause and will and strength and means
> To do't....

> O, from this time forth,
> My thoughts be bloody, or be nothing worth!
> (IV.iv.43-66)

Granted that Hamlet may have succumbed to temper in fighting
Laertes in Ophelia's grave, his expression of regret to Horatio—not,
be it noted, to Laertes—offers his passion as justification for his conduct but does not condemn it. His words are surely not those of
a man dedicated to patience:

> But I am very sorry, good Horatio,
> That to Laertes I forgot myself,
> For by the image of my cause I see
> The portraiture of his. I'll court his favours.
> But, sure, the bravery of his grief did put me
> Into a tow'ring passion.
> (V.ii.75-80)

Hamlet, it is true, has returned from England convinced that heaven
was ordinant in revealing the command that he be disposed of and
even in his having his father's signet to forge a new command that
Rosencrantz and Guildenstern be killed, "Not shriving time allow'd"
(l. 47)—a command more worthy of the revenge Hamlet than of
God's minister. If we accept Bowers' theories, we must also infer
that Hamlet expects an ordinant "heaven" to set a time for his revenge or, granted this idea, we must say punishment. But he is also
convinced that he should kill Claudius—in fact, must kill him immediately:

> And is't not to be damn'd,
> To let this canker of our nature come
> In further evil?
> (V.ii.68-70)

To Horatio's warning that the time will be short, he replies: "the
interim is mine." But since his return from England he has done
nothing with it.

An examination of the subplot does not clarify the problem.
Laertes has no doubt who killed Polonius or that he was morally culpable. He moves straight against Claudius, is won over to him, and
becomes his tool. It is he, not Hamlet, who displays patience in the
sense of genuine self-control as he waits for the chance promised by

197

Claudius (cf. IV.v.210; V.i.317-322). Then his action seems to fail as signally as Hamlet's inaction. But he is equally successful in achieving vengeance and kills fewer innocent bystanders in the process.

In short, Hamlet's "the readiness is all" (V.ii.233) obviously summarizes a whole literature of Christian commonplaces upon patience and resignation to the will of God.[9] But in its dramatic context it is not a guide to the action of the last part of the play, except in that Hamlet uses it to justify risking his life before he has accomplished his mission. The suggestion may startle admirers of Shakespeare, but it is possible that he found himself with a crowded and exciting plot —Hamlet's escape and return, Ophelia's madness and suicide, and a fight in a grave—but without an explanation why his hero took no decisive action. He found a kind of explanation in religious concepts and trusted the excitement to cover up its inadequacy. Or, to put the matter in other terms, he created an emotionally convincing Hamlet who talks of, and believes in, Christian resignation. That Hamlet fascinated Shakespeare, just as he fascinates us. But he did not grow out of the plot of the play, and he does not explain it.

A similar objection can be made to the fencing match. Hamlet begs Laertes' pardon in words that are obviously meant to be sincere and to place his death in that context of forgiveness and reconciliation demanded by religious teaching. But he excuses himself on the grounds that madness made him do the things for which Laertes demands satisfaction. Nowhere else does he admit to madness (mere distraction would not free him of moral responsibility), and the killing of Polonius was obviously not an act of madness. In other words, the satisfaction that he offers is false, even though he goes through the motions of reconciliation. We are confronted, I think, by three alternatives: Shakespeare may intend Hamlet to seem a hypocrite, but this is untenable in the light of the play as a whole and of what immediately follows in the final scene; we may disregard the remarks about madness and take seriously only what agrees with our theory of the play, but on this principle interpretation of *Hamlet* or of any other play would be a matter of whim; we may assume that Shakespeare meant us to accept Hamlet's request as sincere but that, as often in other plays where he was not concerned with a pattern of meaning, he was careless of consistency in detail (the lapsing

[9]See the discussion, already cited, in Cunningham, *Woe or Wonder*, pp. 11-14.

198

of the bond in *The Merchant of Venice* would be the most obvious parallel). This last seems to me the only possible alternative. Laertes' final offer to exchange forgiveness is, in contrast to the explanation by Hamlet that we have just discussed, simple and sincere, and so is Hamlet's response.

This final exchange of forgiveness leads dramatically to Horatio's final benediction: "Good-night, sweet prince, / And flights of angels sing thee to thy rest!" (V.ii.370-371). These lines, like other summary speeches after the hero's death, presumably represent the interpretation that Shakespeare wishes us to form of Hamlet. Having submitted himself to the will of God, he may expect salvation. But this outcome, however kind and charitable and agreeable to the sympathy that we have developed for Hamlet, is not a logical outcome of the action in the terms in which it has been conducted. The interior state necessary to salvation in the terms so carefully outlined by Claudius to himself or by Hamlet to Gertrude has not been revealed to us. We have seen an attempt at reconciliation on a false basis; we have seen no genuine contrition even for the death of Polonius, not to speak of Rosencrantz and Guildenstern. Horatio's hope is not necessarily unfounded, but it is not founded on the action of the play. There is no need, of course, that it should be, unless we are arguing for a particular kind of play which, on my reading, *Hamlet* is not.

The explanation that Hamlet, in the last half of the play, has resigned himself to the will of God and is waiting for a providential opportunity to punish Claudius agrees with important statements in the play, and *King Lear* shows that Shakespeare believed in patience as a virtue; but this philosophy is not really reconciled with the action of *Hamlet* or with much of its text. In *King Lear*, on the other hand, Shakespeare treated the events as cause, and patience both as effect and as a means to growth of character. To that extent *King Lear* makes the explicit philosophy a part of the action as *Hamlet* does not.

Another three-way contrast involving *Hamlet*, *King Lear*, and other mature tragedies is indicative, I think, that Shakespeare found no profound meaning in the action of *Hamlet*. This point will have to be discussed at some length in connection with *King Lear*, but it can be mentioned here. Most of the great tragedies end with speeches in which the ranking survivor takes charge, allots rewards and punishments to the other survivors, and restores order. In *King Lear* this speech is moved a few lines earlier, and emphasis is upon King Lear at the end of the play. The final emphasis is also upon Hamlet. Horatio summarizes quite accurately, point by point, the main events of the play (V.ii.390-397). Fortinbras praises Hamlet as likely "To have prov'd most royally" (l. 409) and arranges for his body to be borne off. However, except that Fortinbras claims the crown, there is no settling of accounts or restoration of order as in *King Lear* and the other plays. We are reminded, furthermore, that Lear has been stretched upon the rack of this tough world, and our attention is turned to what the play means about evil and suffering. Any such attempt as in *King Lear* to give a total meaning to the play, either by restoring the social order or by raising the question of ultimate meaning, is absent from *Hamlet*. We hear only what has happened to the prince or what he might have been. The play is about the life and tragical death of Hamlet. Shakespeare's mature art is to be found in the poetry, the masterly handling of details, and above all the character drawing. The dramatic structure is that of his source and of the tragical histories of his contemporaries.

The view that *Hamlet*, as a revenge play, is fundamentally in the tradition of narrative tragedy seems to me also to explain the inability of critics to analyze the play in the Aristotelian terms applicable to the other great tragedies. There is, in fact, no real moral choice or tragic *hamartia*, just as there is no clearly defined tragic weakness in Hamlet himself.[10] What confuses the issue in *Hamlet* is that there is a great deal of counsel of the sort that ought to lead to choice. But the only meditation leading to decision is that over the king at prayer, sometimes regarded as the climax of the play. It is, however, only a decision not to kill the king at that time, which is, from Hamlet's point of view, sound. It does not determine the whole course of the play, nor does it constitute a tragic error, however unfortunate for Hamlet the consequences of his failure to kill Claudius may be. In this respect Hamlet is actually like Bolingbroke. He does things that imply important decisions, but the decisions are, for the most part,

[10]See Cunningham, *Woe or Wonder*, pp. 126-129, for an interesting interpretation of Hamlet's problems as a choice, first of end in terms of fact and then of means to the end. The classic summary of theories as to Hamlet's tragic flaw is, of course, Bradley's (*Shakespearean Tragedy*, pp. 91-108).

not written into the action of the play. The difference is, of course, that Bolingbroke is an opportunist of few words. Hamlet meditates continuously, and that habit has been taken by an important critical tradition to be his tragic weakness. But, despite one or two passages that can be taken to support this view, it is not written into the play, nor can one apply the test that the tragic flaw should lead to tragic error. *Hamlet* is, at least in its exciting rush of events and its failure to organize them into a clear pattern, the greatest of Elizabethan narrative tragedies.

If the structure looks to the past, both in Elizabethan drama and in Shakespeare's own development, the tremendous burden of thought imposed upon the play looks to the future. Revenge was, I suspect, for Shakespeare a dramatic theme unworthy of serious effort. The problem of sin and evil in the world moved him profoundly; so apparently did the problem of human integrity, if we may judge by the Christian overtones of the last half of the play and by its three separate treatments of repentance in formal terms. In *Hamlet* Shakespeare failed to make his borrowed plot and his moral interests coalesce. In *King Lear* he succeeded brilliantly.

But, before turning to *King Lear*, I must face a final question. If I had my choice between first-class performances of *Hamlet* and *King Lear*, which would I attend? I do not know, since I have never seen a great performance of *King Lear*. But I suspect that most people would choose *Hamlet*, and I am not sure that I would not do the same. Why, on my showing, is *Hamlet* so effective a play? Partly, I think, because Shakespeare made a virtue of necessity. His imagination worked at white heat, as it never did again, not upon the plot —which was good enough for his purposes as it stood—but upon the agonies of baffled humanity. If Hamlet drifts, so do most of us in this tragic world. And Shakespeare keeps him intensely alive at every minute, even if that life is often at the expense of dramatic unity. In this respect *Hamlet* has the virtues of some modern novels, plus rhetorical precision and poetic power to which they cannot pretend. These virtues of mastery in character drawing and in development of detail are not those of Aristotelian tragedy or of classical art of any kind, but they are nevertheless very real, and, granted Shakespeare's superior powers, they are those of Elizabethan drama as a whole.

Christian ideas of repentance and of patience and resignation may not be well integrated in the last half of *Hamlet,* but their presence undoubtedly shows that they interested Shakespeare profoundly, not only as a view of life but as having dramatic possibilities. These same ideas very probably first attracted him to the old *True Chronicle History of King Leir, and his three daughters, Gonorill, Ragan, and Cordella.* It had been played for Henslowe in 1594 and entered in the Stationers' Register a month later, although it was not actually published until 1605. The process by which it was developed from Holinshed and other sources need not concern us, except in one respect. Unlike Shakespeare's play, it was completely anachronistic in that both Leir and Cordella refer to Christian doctrines and the action of the play is explained in terms of concepts that Shakespeare explored in *Hamlet.* The following summary of the play is intended not so much to show the extent to which Shakespeare derived his plot from the old play as to suggest how the ideas mentioned are developed in context.

At the opening of the play, Leir wishes to marry off his daughters and resign his cares. Gonorill and Ragan are quite willing to take the kings of Cornwall and Cambria respectively, but Cordella refuses to wed. Leir plans to ask each daughter to profess her love and obedience as a means to trap Cordella into marrying the man he chooses. Skalliger, a scheming courtier without analogue in Shakespeare's play, hastens off to betray Leir's scheme to the older girls, who fall in eagerly. Perillus, Shakespeare's Kent, concludes the scene:

> Thus fathers think their children to beguile,
> And oftentimes themselves do first repent,
> When heavenly powers do frustrate their intent.
>
> (I.i.91-93)[11]

The play does not show Cordella being informed of the trap, but doubtless we are to assume that she senses it. She behaves as in Shakespeare's play:

> I cannot paint my duty forth in words,
> I hope my deeds shall make report for me:
> But look what love the child doth owe the father,
> The same to you I bear, my gracious lord.
>
> (I.iii.78-81)

[11]Quotations are from *The Chronicle History of King Leir: The Original of Shakespeare's 'King Lear',* ed. Sidney Lee (New York, 1909).

Leir flies into a rage, but his curse is without the references to nature so prominent in Lear's lines.

> Peace, bastard imp, no issue of King Leir,
> I will not hear thee speak one tittle more.
> Call not me father, if thou love thy life,
> Nor these thy sisters once presume to name:
> Look for no help henceforth from me nor mine;
> Shift as thou wilt, and trust unto thyself:
> My kingdom will I equally divide
> 'Twixt thy two sisters to their royal dower,
> And will bestow them worthy their deserts.
>
> (I.iii.113-121)

Cordella's final words strike a religious note characteristic of her entire role:

> Now whither, poor forsaken, shall I go,
> When mine own sisters triumph in my woe?
> But unto Him which doth protect the just,
> In Him will poor Cordella put her trust.
> These hands shall labour, for to get my spending;
> And so I'll live until my days have ending.
>
> (I.iii.129-134)

The next act is largely fantastic romance. The King of Gallia comes disguised to Britain to see whether the local beauties deserve their reputation. He brings along Mumford, a bluff and amorous courtier whom Shakespeare would have found irresistible in his earlier plays. Disguised like pilgrims, they encounter Cordella lamenting her fate:

> Oh, father Leir, how dost thou wrong thy child,
> Who always was obedient to thy will!
> But why accuse I Fortune and my father?
> No, no, it is the pleasure of my God:
> And I do willingly embrace the rod.
>
> (II.iv.24-28)

Gallia overhears her lament, finds her to his liking (she still has on her costly robes and is no Cinderella), and marries her forthwith. In the meantime, Cornwall and Cambria have ridden to Leir's court in almost ridiculous haste and have drawn lots for halves of the kingdom.

With the third act Leir's troubles begin, but he has already undergone a complete transformation. He is the perfect example of patience! Perillus describes events in soliloquy:

> He sojourns now in Cornwall with the eldest
> Who flatter'd him, until she did obtain
> That at his hands, which now she doth possess:
> And now she sees he hath no more to give,
> It grieves her heart to see her father live.
> Oh, whom should man trust in this wicked age,
> When children thus against their parents rage?
> But he, the mirror of mild patience,
> Puts up all wrongs, and never gives reply:
> Yet shames she not in most opprobrious sort
> To call him fool and dotard to his face....
> His pension she hath half restrain'd from him,
> And will, ere long, the other half, I fear.
>
> (III.i.5-21)

Later Gonorill twists even Leir's mild efforts to excuse her behavior into further grievances. Leir, however, recognizes that he deserves punishment, and we encounter a significant allusion to the overturning of nature:

> Thus, say or do the best that e'er I can,
> 'Tis wrested straight into another sense:
> This punishment my heavy sins deserve,
> And more than this ten thousand thousand times:
> Else aged Leir them could never find
> Cruel to him, to whom he hath been kind.
> Why do I over-live myself, to see
> The course of nature quite revers'd in me?
>
> (III.iii.37-44)

Leir reverts to the same themes when Perillus attempts to comfort him:

> If they, which first by Nature's sacred law
> Do owe to me the tribute of their lives; ...
> Do now reject, contemn, despise, abhor me,
> What reason moveth thee to sorrow for me?
>
> (III.iii.81-88)

> Oh, how thy words add sorrow to my soul,
> To think of my unkindness to Cordella!
> Whom causeless I did dispossess of all.

Upon th' unkind suggestions of her sisters:
And for her sake, I think this heavy doom
Is fallen on me, and not without desert.

(ll. 94-99)

Meanwhile Cordella, sad in Gallia despite her husband's unfailing kindness, explains her feelings:

I cannot want the thing but I may have,
Save only this which I shall ne'er obtain,
My father's love, oh, this I ne'er shall gain.
I would abstain from any nutriment,
And pine my body to the very bones:
Barefoot I would on pilgrimage set forth
Unto the furthest quarters of the earth,
And all my life-time would I sackcloth wear,
And mourning-wise pour dust upon my head:
So he but to forgive me once would please,
That his gray hairs might go to heaven in peace.
And yet I know not how I him offended,
Or wherein justly I have deserved blame.
Oh, sisters! you are much to blame in this,
It was not he, but you that did me wrong:
Yet God forgive both him, and you, and me;
Even as I do in perfit charity.
I will to church, and pray unto my Saviour,
That ere I die, I may obtain his favour.

(IV.i.14-32)

Gallia (who has one's sympathy in his lugubrious marriage, although that is doubtless not what the dramatist intended) tells Cordella to forget her father, but she appeals to nature:

Yet pardon me, my gracious lord, in this:
For what can stop the course of Nature's power?
As easy is it for four-footed beasts,
To stay themselves upon the liquid air,
And mount aloft into the element,
And overstrip the feather'd fowls in flight:
As easy is it for the slimy fish,
To live and thrive without the help of water:
As easy is it for the blackamoor,
To wash the tawny colour from his skin,
Which all oppose against the course of nature:
As I am able to forget my father.

(IV.iv.34-45)

Gallia sends a messenger to inquire about Leir, but the latter fails to find Leir and is detained in Cornwall.

When Cornwall, worried by Leir's absence, sends a messenger to Ragan to inquire about him, Gonorill intercepts the messenger and gets him to promise even to kill Leir if Ragan so wishes. Ragan so instructs him, and he is prevented only by the eloquence of Perillus and divine intervention in the form of thunderclaps. This scene constitutes a final revelation of Leir's change of heart. Thinking the murderer sent by Cordella, he prepares to die willingly:

> Because my daughter, whom I have offended
> And at whose hands I have deserv'd as ill,
> As ever any father did of child,
> Is queen of France, no thanks at all to me,
> But unto God, who my injustice see.
> If it be so that she doth seek revenge,
> As with good reason she may justly do,
> I will most willingly resign my life,
> A sacrifice to mitigate her ire:
> I never will entreat thee to forgive,
> Because I am unworthy for to live.
> Therefore speak soon, and I will soon make speed;
> Whether Cordella will'd thee do this deed?
>
> (IV.vii.136-148)

Learning that Gonorill and Ragan seek his life, he resigns himself to death:

> Ah, my true friend in all extremity,
> Let us submit us to the will of God:
> Things past all sense, let us not seek to know;
> It is God's will, and therefore must be so.
> My friend, I am prepared for the stroke:
> Strike when thou wilt, and I forgive thee her,
> Even from the very bottom of my heart.
>
> (IV.vii.211-217)

Leir gives one more proof of his moral regeneration by urging the murderer to kill him but to spare Perillus. After their escape, Perillus suggests that they go to Cordella in Gallia. The dialogue develops once again the theme of natural bonds and adds the concept of grace:

> *Per.* ... Now let us go to France, unto Cordella,
> Your youngest daughter; doubtless she will succour you.
> *Leir.* Oh, how can I persuade myself of that,

Since the other two are quite devoid of love;
To whom I was so kind, as that my gifts
Might make them love me, if 'twere nothing else?
   Per. No worldly gifts, but grace from God on high,
Doth nourish virtue and true charity.
Remember well what words Cordella spake,
What time you ask'd her, how she lov'd your grace,
She said, her love unto you was as much,
As ought a child to bear unto her father.
   Leir. But she did find, my love was not to her,
As should a father bear unto a child.
   Per. That makes not her love to be any less,
If she do love you as a child should do.
(IV.vii.317-332)

As Leir and Perillus wander in distress, Leir once again laments his unnatural conduct:

I, like an envious thorn, have prick'd the heart,
And turn'd sweet grapes, to sour unrelish'd sloes:
The causeless ire of my respectless breast,
Hath sour'd the sweet milk of Dame Nature's paps.
(V.iii.66-69)

After Leir and Perillus reach France, Leir prepares for death from hunger (Perillus has even offered to feed him from his own arm) and makes his confession:

Well, unkind girls, I here forgive you both,
Yet the just heavens will hardly do the like;
And only crave forgiveness at the end
Of good Cordella, and of thee, my friend;
Of God, whose majesty I have offended,
By my transgression many thousand ways.
(V.iv.58-63)

(Presumably Leir's somewhat smug assurance that God will not forgive Gonorill and Ragan was intended by the dramatist as a moral judgment for the benefit of the audience and not as evidence that Leir's forgiveness was insincere; other playwrights, like Shakespeare, had their problems of exposition.) But Cordella and her husband have gone picnicking in disguise. They overhear Leir, decide not to reveal themselves, but use the basket lunch to succor the old man. Cordella asks Leir to tell the cause of his sorrows. He does at length, concluding:

And now I am constrain'd to seek relief
Of her, to whom I have been so unkind;
Whose censure, if it do award me death,
I must confess she pays me but my due:
But if she shew a loving daughter's part,
It comes of God and her, not my desert.

(V.iv.193-194)

Cordella reveals herself and kneels before him, but he kneels, too:

Oh, stand thou up, it is my part to kneel,
And ask forgiveness for my former faults.

(V.iv.205-206)

There follows a kind of ritual of kneeling, in which Leir, Cordella, the King of Gallia, and Mumford all join. The natural and proper kneeling of the younger three is intended, by contrast, to emphasize the act of contrition involved in Leir's kneeling to Cordella, father to child. As compared with Shakespeare's parallel scene, it is badly overdone; but it makes the same point and provided Shakespeare with the device.

The rest of the play is irrelevant for our purpose. Leir's party, as we may call them, invade Britain, take a British town by surprise, and route the forces of Cambria and Cornwall—that is, Mumford chases the two kings from the stage. So Leir is restored without benefit of tragic bloodshed.

The old play was obviously a strange compound of pseudohistory and outright romance. It was an even stranger blend of fairy tale and Christian piety. But it had several characteristics that stimulated Shakespeare's imagination. In the first place, its central contrast between unpaternal father and filial child was explicitly stated in terms of the obligations of nature. The laws of nature had recently preoccupied Shakespeare in *Troilus and Cressida*[12] and were still in his mind; a suggestion would set him thinking how they might be used more fully. Leir himself must have appealed to Shakespeare in two ways. First of all, he was an interesting dramatic problem. The old play simply presented him as proud and wrathful in the opening scenes and thereafter penitent, humble, and patient in adversity. It

[12]*King Lear* may almost be thought of as dramatizing Ulysses' speech on degree (*Troilus and Cressida* I.iii.75-137), *Othello* and *Macbeth* of Hector's on the corruption of nature by affection (II.ii.173-193).

208

made no attempt to explain or motivate this change, which had in itself the stuff of great drama. The problem of motivating the moral regeneration of Leir was like that which Shakespeare had faced in the three plays dealing with Henry V. He had found in *The Famous Victories* and in popular legend a dissolute prince who became a model king. This development he had tried, not wholly successfully, to portray dramatically. But he was now far better equipped, both as a playwright and as a thinker, to tackle the change in Lear. Furthermore, the Leir of the latter part of the old play illustrated exactly those elements of Christian doctrine that Shakespeare had written into Hamlet. He was scourged by his older daughters and ministered to by Cordella. Patience in adversity and resignation to the will of God, explicitly recognized as such, could hardly be carried further. Then, the old playwright had worked overtime to demonstrate that Leir's repentance was valid by showing contrition, confession overheard by Cordella herself, and reconciliation accompanied by an act of atonement. But these virtues rang false. They were too unmotivated and too complete. The old Leir should have revealed himself even in his repentance; this he did not do, and his virtue became cloying. He lost humanity as he took on grace. All this Shakespeare could rectify. Cordella's conduct illustrated both the law of nature and love that transcends the law. But she, too, needed to be made a human woman with less sanctimonious profusion of utterance. Her dutifulness protested too much.

Much of the play was too childishly like a fairy tale for Shakespeare's purposes. Cinderella appeals to us, but we should find a responsible king who wages war unsuitable as her prince charming. A country picnic in disguise does not belong in a tragedy. All these elements, as well as Leir's clever scheme to trap Cordella and the improbably happy ending, Shakespeare eliminated. But beneath them he saw a story of sin and redemption. He stripped the play to these essentials and began afresh.

In building *King Lear*, Shakespeare apparently faced several problems in retaining the intellectual element that interested him in the old play. One of these was to relate the entire play, and not merely the relationship between Lear and Cordelia, to the laws of nature. He actually produced, at any rate, a play which is very nearly the ultimate attempt in all drama to hold the mirror up to nature. A whole series of natural relationships become involved—those between parents and children, husband and wife, ruler and subject, master and servant in the social order; those between man and nature and between the very forces of nature themselves. But there is no need to list these relationships here, for we shall find them listed in the play.

The change portrayed in Leir was not to be explained in terms of the order of nature, however, since it involved breaking the bonds of habit and making a new man. The changes were to be accounted for only by the strength that came to man in the order of grace, and Shakespeare found himself not only with a potential tragic action in natural terms but also with a morality-type action in which Everyman repents, is saved, and is received by the angels in heaven. As O. J. Campbell has pointed out, the parallel is even closer, for Everyman, too, is deserted by his fair-weather friends and sustained in adversity by those whom he has neglected.[13] Shakespeare was therefore committed to a double action if he were going to convert the old play into genuine tragedy. On one level the very nature whose laws had been disobeyed must visit upon the guilty the inevitable consequences of disobedience. The happy ending of the old play was false philosophically as well as dramatically. But on another and higher level there must come, to Lear at least, a new vision and a new character. This illumination must somehow grow out of the same forces that brought disaster. The answer, of course, lay in the Christian concept that God permits suffering to try and to refine the natures of men. The suffering that destroys in the order of nature may purge in the order of grace and bring salvation.[14] Shakespeare therefore found himself committed, by the logical implications of his source and of the view of man which he accepted, to conducting his action both in the order of nature and in the order of grace. In some aspects the closest analogue among plays that he knew was Heywood's *A Woman Kilde with Kindnesse*, produced in 1603; but the main action of that play was so directed toward the salvation of Mistress Frankford's soul that her loneliness and her suffering were

[13]Oscar James Campbell, "The Salvation of Lear," *ELH*, XV (1948), 93-109.

[14]Campbell remarks (ibid., p. 104) that ". . . Lear's purgatorial experiences result in a form of salvation more Christian than Stoical." Paul N. Siegel develops similar ideas in "Adversity and the Miracle of Love in *King Lear*," *Shakespeare Quarterly*, VI (1955), 325-336.

minimized. The tragic fact of suffering and death Shakespeare refused to take lightly.

Working out his action in Christian terms involved, for Shakespeare, another problem that the old playwright simply ignored. The references to God and Providence in the old play are so explicitly Christian in tone and context that they are completely false to the pre-Christian setting of the play. Shakespeare, however, faced this problem of chronology. That he did so shows, incidentally, that, however naïve historically he may sometimes have been, he was less so than some of his contemporaries. Actually he eliminated specifically Christian language and substituted references to the forces of nature and the divinities that personified those forces. The ethical principles associated with Christianity he regarded as universally valid. They applied in pre-Christian, as in Christian, Britain, even though men had no name to call them by or did not even recognize their existence. "The wages of sin is death" is a formulary of the New Testament, but the law of nature that it stated was as old as Adam. Only the Fool uses specifically Christian language, and he illustrates, in an extreme form, the paradox that runs through the play. Where daughters rule and kings obey, all nature is upside down, so that rulers are fools and fools are wise. This reversal, of which the Fool is the dramatic symbol, extends in him even to time. "This prophecy," he says, "Merlin shall make; for I live before his time" (III.ii.95). He also speaks of grace, though he lives before Christ.

In developing *King Lear*, Shakespeare used other versions of the story, especially Holinshed and Spenser, as well as Sidney for the subplot. I do not mean to imply that he depended exclusively upon the old play for his material. Obviously he did not do so. I am only trying to suggest that the intellectual content of the old play must have fascinated him and that it posed the problems which he solved as I have indicated. This seems to me, at least, to be a logical inference from parallels of thought running through *Hamlet*, *King Leir*, and Shakespeare's *King Lear*.

The plot of *King Lear*, insofar as it operates in the order of nature, is a thorough working out of the concept that nature is order until man's folly destroys the equilibrium. From an initial disturbance there follows, like waves from a stone thrown into water, an ever-ramifying series of evils that produce chaos, and finally this chaos

> Must make perforce an universal prey,
> And last eat up himself.
>
> *(Troilus and Cressida* I.iii.123-124)

But the good are eaten along with the bad.

Lear's abdication of his kingship and his treatment of Cordelia are false to three obligations which he owes in nature: a king should rule; a father should guide and cherish children, even when they go astray, just as children must love and protect their parents no matter how badly they have been mistreated; and an old man should be wise. All these natural principles are underscored repeatedly by Kent and the Fool: "Thou hadst little wit in thy bald crown when thou gav'st thy golden one away. . . . thou mad'st thy daughters thy mothers . . ." (I.iv.177-188). Both of these protatic characters also call Lear a fool in so many words, not once but often. His tragic flaw is therefore a combination of pride and wrath; his tragic error is to lay down his authority while trying to preserve the trappings of royal power and to cast out his youngest daughter, preferring her false elder sisters. By relaxing his authority, Lear gave full rein to the vicious natures of his daughters, which he should have controlled. By the middle of the play they have cast him out into the storm, and the first movement of the plot, the downfall of Lear, is complete. But "appetite, an universal wolf," makes the sisters desire more than authority; they also lust for Edmund, and that lust turns them against each other, until they die by poison and suicide even as their armies are victorious in war. In this second movement of the plot, Lear's folly, through the sisters, ramifies into social chaos, as wife turns against husband, sister against sister, and man against man. Even inanimate nature participates in the confusion, and the storm on the heath is, for Shakespeare, at once symbol of the tempest within Lear's mind and manifestation of the agony of outraged nature. But love, as the bond among men and the principle of harmony in all nature, also begins to work; and Cordelia, true to the laws of nature and the promptings of love, returns to aid Lear. Though she fails to save Lear and herself, her efforts merge in the larger struggle that leads to the restoration of order in a suffering world, and to that extent her sacrifice is not in vain, even in the order of nature.

The subplot parallels this development closely. Gloucester, as a weak and sensual man, is the victim of Edmund's machinations rather than the furious cause of his own undoing, as is Lear. But his rejection of Edgar leaves him finally blind and an outcast, to be cared for by the child whom he has wronged. Edmund is destroyed in the counteraction, as are the sisters, but he falls before the brother whom he has betrayed.

As usual, Shakespeare states explicitly what happens during the play; and, as always in this play, the speaker understands clearly what is happening to other people and how they are at fault, but he is blind to his own true role in what is occurring. Gloucester tells Edmund:

These late eclipses in the sun and moon portend no good to us. Though the wisdom of nature can reason it thus and thus, yet nature finds itself scourg'd by the sequent effects. Love cools, friendship falls off, brothers divide: in cities, mutinies; in countries, discord; in palaces, treason; and the bond crack'd 'twixt son and father. This villain of mine comes under the prediction; there's son against father: the King falls from bias of nature; there's father against child. We have seen the best of our time; machinations, hollowness, treachery, and all ruinous disorders, follow us disquietly to our graves.

(I.ii.112-124)

Both main plot and subplot, when analyzed in these terms, fall into two halves; for the sisters and Edmund, whose rise and fall approximate that characteristic of Shakespeare's other tragedies, are clearly not the protagonists. Even on this level the organization of the play is, in fact, philosophic; and the storm on the heath is the climax of the play because the action, to use Shakespeare's terms, is really the rise and fall of appetite, that universal wolf who eats all else and then must eat himself—in short, the development of chaos and its self-destruction. The metaphysical basis of the play has determined its organization, though only in conjunction with a totally new kind of structure arising from the moral regeneration of Lear and Gloucester.

This second level of action in the play may be summarized briefly: through the purgatorial experience of suffering and of having brought home to them their own error, both Lear and Gloucester find redemption, not in the order of nature by understanding the full extent of their errors and being restored to their first estate, but in the order of grace by growing in humility and patience—by discovering, as Edgar puts it, that "Ripeness is all" (V.ii.11).

In roughly the first two acts of the play, the regenerative action is the same as that on the level of nature. The mistreatment that drives Lear forth into the storm affects him spiritually as well as physically. The violence of his wrath seems partly a response to doubts of his own wisdom that the Fool expresses openly and repeatedly. But during the storm on the heath Shakespeare begins to devote attention to the process of Lear's regeneration even while he shows the forces of anarchy gathering power in his former kingdom. On this level the storm brings with it the moral choice, not for evil but for good, and when Lear finds himself at one with poor naked wretches and tears off his clothes—the "lendings" that symbolized his illusion that he was apart from other men and from human nature—the turning point has been reached and his regeneration has begun. The fact that Lear's first act of outright madness is his first act of spiritual wisdom erects into dramatic structure the paradox already implicit in the Fool's role in the play—that the wise are foolish and the foolish wise. During his reunion with Cordelia (IV.vii) Lear twice speaks of himself as old and foolish, and this admission is itself intended as proof of his growth in moral insight. In the soliloquy in which Edmund explains his designs against Edgar, he plans to practice upon his brother's "foolish honesty." But the wheel comes full circle, and the foolishness of Edgar confounds the wisdom of Edmund. An equation of the subtle wisdom of this world with foolishness in the light of eternal values seems written into the play.

The source of this paradox, as of so much else in Shakespeare, is probably to be found in the Bible.[15] At the beginning of First Corinthians, Paul is concerned to vindicate Christianity against the charge of being ridiculous. This he does by boldly enunciating the paradox that the wisdom of this world is folly in the sight of God and returning to the point several times (the quotations are from the Geneva version, which Shakespeare habitually used by the time he wrote *King Lear*):

But God hath chosen the foolish things of the world to confounde the wise, and God hath chosen the weake things of the world, to confound the mightie things.

(I Cor. i.27)

[15] I owe this suggestion to two graduate students, Richard Kraus and Carolyn French; the latter's dissertation "*King Lear*: Poem or Play" (1958) has already been mentioned.

But the naturall man perceiveth not the things of the spirit of God: for they are foolishnesse unto him: neither can hee knowe them, because they are spiritually discerned.

(I Cor. ii.14)

Let no man deceive himselfe. If any man among you seem to be wise in this world, let him be a foole, that hee may be wise. For the wisedome of this worlde is foolishnesse with God: for it is written, He catcheth the wise in their owne craftinesse.

(I Cor. iii.18-19)

Feste, the fool in *Twelfth Night,* appropriately enough echoes the last of these passages, proving, incidentally, that Shakespeare knew them and had been interested by their paradox. What he says describes exactly the role of the Fool in *King Lear*:

Wit, an't be thy will, put me into good fooling! Those wits, that think they have thee, do very oft prove fools; and I, that am sure I lack thee, may pass for a wise man; for what says Quinapalus? "Better a witty fool than a foolish wit."

(*Twelfth Night* I.v.35-40)

The importance of the paradox for Shakespeare's age is indicated by the use which Erasmus makes of it in his *Praise of Folly*. Toward the end the work grows more serious, at least in the object of its attack, and Erasmus describes the folly of various learned scholars who spin webs of false learning out of a few words of Scripture to justify, among other things, the burning of heretics. With these he contrasts the humility of St. Paul (I quote Sir Thomas Chaloner's version, first published in 1549):

But now at last I leape backe agayne to sainct *Paule,* & *Gladly* (sayeth he) *yee do beare wyth unwyse men,* speakyng it by hym selfe) also in an other place, *receive you me, as unwise that I am?* & further, *I speake not this precisely as upon Gods precept, but rather in my owne unwysedome.* Than againe, *we* (sayth he) *are become fooles for Christes sake:* Do you heare now how great prayses of Follye this so great an autour alleageth, yea and that more is, hee playnely enjoyneth Follie unto us, for a thing most necessarie, and right, importyng to salvation: *For who so semeth* (sayeth hee) *to bee wyse amonges you, let hym become a foole, to the ende he bee wyse in deede.* How saye you my Maisters, woulde yee any more evydent proofes than this, or an other example also in Lukes Gospell, where *Jesus* calleth the two Disciples *fooles,* with whome hee joyned company by the way?[16]

[16]*The Prayse of Follie* (London, 1577), sigs. Nviv-Nvii.

There is every probability that *King Lear* is Shakespeare's dramatizing of this paradox, and it is even probable that Feste's casual lines germinated in Shakespeare's mind into Lear's Fool and into this aspect of the play. *Twelfth Night* stands, in the accepted chronology of the plays, next to *Hamlet,* in which we have noted other ideas fundamental to the structure of *King Lear.*[17]

The fundamental action of the play whose hero is King Lear is his moral awakening, though it be to foolishness in the eyes of the world; and the climax of the play on this level, as on the level of nature, is conceived in philosophic terms. It is not the deed but the moral act of will that counts fundamentally, and after this reversal Lear gains in moral stature, though not in strength or even in wisdom as the world counts it. But, just as Shakespeare rejected the unmotivated character reversal of the old play, he was too wise to present Lear —or Gloucester—as undergoing a complete change. Both have their relapses into the old man, Lear even in the final scene of the play.

The progress of the subplot is similar, though the turning point comes later in the play, symbolized by the blinding that leads to moral sight. Let me add, parenthetically, that it is perhaps not fanciful to see in Gloucester's blindness a parallel to that loss of natural sight which Spenser attributes to the hermit Contemplation as he gazes on things heavenly. The hermit's blindness derives from the mystical tradition that darkness to things of this world must precede the divine illumination. Perhaps Shakespeare, too, thought of that notion as he read the story in Sidney's *Arcadia* from which he derived his subplot, including the blinding, even though Gloucester's moral vision is at best partial and imperfect.

Before we trace Shakespeare's handiwork in the regeneration of Gloucester and Lear, some generalizations may be made about his exposition on this level of action. In this redemptive action, the morality structure of this play, as of all the tragedies of moral choice, becomes especially apparent. The forces for good and evil are clearly aligned—Cordelia, Kent, and Edgar on one side; Goneril, Regan, and Edmund on the other. Edgar and even Cordelia come closer than any other characters in Shakespeare to personifying moral forces: Edgar is analogous to Knowledge in *Everyman,* Cordelia is

[17]E. K. Chambers assigns *Twelfth Night* as last in 1599-1600, *Hamlet* as first in 1600-01 (*William Shakespeare: A Study of Facts and Problems* [Oxford, 1930], I, 270).

Love. Even the sisters approximate Lust, and Edmund is still Ambition, though with them the morality-play analogy breaks down because they are too much involved in the subordinate counteraction to act directly upon Lear and Gloucester.

Once again the action is pushed to extreme limits as if to provide a test case. In fact, Shakespeare says as much, for we have noted in an earlier chapter the remark that Cordelia

> redeems Nature from the general curse
> Which twain have brought her to.
>
> (IV.vi.210-211)

The curse from which she redeems nature is that brought by Adam and Eve, not Goneril and Regan. Just as pride, wrath, and lust in an almost ultimate form operate in the natural action, so their opposites —humility, patience, and love—here persist in the face of extreme obstacles. In Cordelia and Edgar love persists, as Lear and Gloucester recognize, in defiance of the normal human inclination to resent evils suffered.

But the redemptive power of humility and patience is isolated in another way. Gloucester is weak and broken, confused in thought if not in mind. Lear is, as he confesses, "a very foolish fond old man" (IV.vii.60). Certainly he never atones for his sins by understanding their full measure or by doing anything positive, except to ask forgiveness and to be patient. That he has wronged Cordelia and neglected his subjects he knows. But nowhere does he imply any recognition that his abdication of his proper authority had led to the chain of evils from which he and his friends and kingdom suffer. Shakespeare seems, in short, to be saying that humility and patience will redeem even those who are incapable of full understanding —that salvation is possible to those who become as little children, provided, however, that their sufferings have left them incapable of bearing the burdens of men. Kent and Edgar must "the gor'd state sustain" (V.iii.320).

A final characteristic of the redemptive action harks back to Hamlet's description of himself as "scourge and minister." The two sisters and Edmund function as heaven's scourges to punish Lear and Gloucester, and Edmund as a further means to overcome Goneril and Regan. There is, furthermore, textual warrant for believing so. In the Folio, Edgar says of his father to the dying Edmund:

217

> The Gods are just, and of our pleasant vices
> Make instruments to plague us:
> The darke and vitious place where thee he got,
> Cost him his eyes.
>
> (V.iii.170-174)

Instead of "plague" the Quarto reads "scourge." But the concept is surely present even in the Folio version.

There is no question that Edgar and Cordelia are heaven's ministers in the regeneration of Gloucester and Lear. Edgar says, in fact, that he not only led his father and begged for him but also "sav'd him from despair" (V.iii.191). The significance of this remark will be discussed later. As befits Gloucester's weaker nature, Edgar's ministry is one of instruction, and, for the modern mind, the bogus miracle of Gloucester's jump at Dover pushes the principle far indeed. But it is appropriate to the superstitious nature that Gloucester has shown from the start and to the moral blindness of which the physical is a result and a symbol. Spiritually, too, he must be led by the hand. It is also dramatically sound even if somewhat dubious theologically. Gloucester is brought to salvation, as to destruction, by a stratagem. He is of the weaker sort whose faith must be confirmed by miracles. Lear is made of sterner stuff, and he needs only Cordelia's love and the assurance of her forgiveness. Just as he precipitated his own fall, so he finds through suffering his own way to rise.

Shakespeare's dramatic presentation of the regeneration of the two old men makes brilliant use of the parallel subplot. Gloucester's fall was, to some extent, a result of Lear's and it followed in the play. But Gloucester's need to be taught by Edgar enables Shakespeare to explain briefly, through expository speeches given to Edgar, the principles involved. For this reason, as well as to concentrate the final lines of the play upon Lear, the structure shifts, and in the last two acts events in the subplot precede the parallel action in the main plot. We can therefore see Lear exemplifying those virtues that Edgar has already instructed Gloucester to practice. The subplot is used once again to underscore the main plot, this time by outlining schematically in doctrinal terms what the main plot presents only in action. Because the subplot parallels the main plot to the very end, whereas that in *Hamlet* deviates as Laertes pursues his violent course to revenge, it can be used far more subtly and effectively to point up the contrast between Gloucester and Lear. What really gives Lear tragic stature is not his kingship or even his titanic wrath in the first half of the play. It is the moral strength with which he fights his way through to regeneration. It is too simple to say that the Fool symbolizes the workings of Lear's own mind. He is a dramatic character, and he interacts with Lear dramatically. We feel that he tortures Lear because he is saying what Lear is himself coming to realize, and that Lear's anguished replies are the real indications of what is going on within him. The storm, he says, is as nothing to his inner tempest (III.iv.12-14). So Lear needs no Edgar to lead him. He needs only Cordelia to ratify the peace to which his struggle has led by granting him love and forgiveness—to provide the reconciliation which makes perfect the repentance that he has himself achieved. For these reasons it will be appropriate to trace what happens to Gloucester before considering Lear.

Gloucester's redemption is worked out generally in terms of the traditional teaching on repentance that Shakespeare used in *Hamlet*. The steps, to repeat, are contrition, confession, faith, and amendment of life. Faith, in the Christian sense, would be an anachronism; its place is supplied by belief in an ordered universe and an acceptance of what life brings. In a sense, the theological virtue of hope is substituted for that of faith.

In the first scene of Act IV, Gloucester enters blinded and led by an old man. He first demonstrates his unselfishness and thoughtfulness by urging the old man to leave him:

> Thy comforts can do me no good at all;
> Thee they may hurt.
>
> (IV.i.17-18)

The man's retort, "You cannot see your way" (l. 19), leads to a crucial speech already mentioned. It constitutes both a statement of contrition and a confession that he has wronged Edgar:

> I have no way, and therefore want no eyes;
> I stumbled when I saw. Full oft 'tis seen,
> Our means secure us, and our mere defects
> Prove our commodities. O dear son Edgar,
> The food of thy abused father's wrath!
> Might I but live to see thee in my touch
> I'd say I had eyes again!
>
> (IV.i.20-26)

219

Gloucester says this, of course, completely unaware that he is talking in front of Edgar. The latter tells us, moreover, that he did not reveal himself to his father until he was armed for his final combat with Edmund (V.iii.192-195), but he gives no explanation why he concealed his identity. This detail is curious and becomes more so when compared with Cordella's failure in the old play to reveal herself until Leir has made full confession of his faults and with Shakespeare's far better managed scene in which Lear also confesses before recognizing Cordelia. It can hardly be chance that Shakespeare twice followed the device that he found in *King Leir*. I can only conjecture that he regarded it as a means of guaranteeing the *bona fides* of the repentance, especially the genuineness of contrition, in that Lear and Gloucester both felt impelled to confess their sorrow and their unworthiness before accepting aid even from an unknown human being. Certainly Edgar and Cordelia were spared any suspicions that their parents were merely seeking aid.

To return to Gloucester's "pilgrimage," he still lacks the faith needed to make any positive effort; he is, in fact, in that state of profound skepticism which Shakespeare's age called despair:

> As flies to wanton boys, are we to th' gods,
> They kill us for their sport.
>
> (IV.i.38-39)

> 'Tis the time's plague, when madmen lead the blind.
> Do as I bid thee, or rather do thy pleasure;
> Above the rest, be gone.
>
> (ll. 48-50)

When next he appears, he has come to the point of knowing what he needs—patience—but is still in despair. In fact, he is proceeding to suicide, guided now by Edgar, who explains that he is trifling with his father's despair to cure it (IV.vi.33-34). For an Elizabethan, suicide was a probable outcome of despair. One thinks, once again, of *The Faerie Queene*. There Despair tried to persuade Red Cross to suicide and would have succeeded had not Una snatched away the knife and reminded her knight of his part in heavenly mercies. The Romeo who plans suicide is "desperate" (V.iii.59), and Horatio's "toys of desperation" clearly involve suicide (I.iv.69-88). Gloucester prays:

> O you mighty gods!
> This world I do renounce, and in your sights
> Shake patiently my great affliction off.
> If I could bear it longer, and not fall
> To quarrel with your great opposeless wills,
> My snuff and loathed part of nature should
> Burn itself out. If Edgar live, O bless him!
> Now, fellow, fare thee well.
>
> (IV.vi.34-41)

This speech is a perfect example of Shakespeare's trick of making a character reveal his own moral error, and, as so often in this play, the result is achieved with maximum economy. The wills of the gods are indeed "opposeless," and Gloucester is not behaving "patiently" in that he is trying to thwart them. Therein lies the error of his ways.

The supposed miracle provides him with the faith he needs:

> *Edg.* ... It was some fiend; therefore, thou happy father,
> Think that the clearest gods, who make them honours
> Of men's impossibilities, have preserv'd thee.
> *Glou.* I do remember now. Henceforth I'll bear
> Affliction till it do cry out itself
> "Enough, enough," and die. That thing you speak of,
> I took it for a man; often 't would say,
> "The fiend, the fiend!" He led me to that place.
> *Edg.* Bear free and patient thoughts.
>
> (IV.vi.72-80)

Gloucester, in short, has accepted the parallel principles of patience and resignation to the will of God. But Shakespeare expects no miracles in human nature, even if he provides them in drama, and Gloucester weakens at the first approach of danger:

> *Edg.* Away, old man; give me thy hand; away!
> King Lear hath lost, he and his daughter ta'en.
> Give me thy hand; come on.
> *Glou.* No further, sir; a man may rot even here.
> *Edg.* What, in ill thoughts again? Men must endure
> Their going hence even as their coming hither;
> Ripeness is all. Come on.
> *Glou.*   And that's true too.
>
> (V.ii.5-11)

Presumably his assent lasted until his death, for we hear ultimately not only that Edgar has saved him from despair but that, after a final reconciliation with Edgar,

> his flaw'd heart,
> Alack, too weak the conflict to support!
> 'Twixt two extremes of passion, joy and grief,
> Burst smilingly.
>
> (V.iii.196-199)

The regeneration of Lear actually has its preparation early in the play, as Lear begins to realize the danger of his wrath. After his terrible curse upon Goneril, his attitude toward Regan is strangely resigned. Clearly he is breaking as he gives way to tears, but he also grasps his need: "You heavens, give me that patience, patience I need!" (II.iv.274). In the storm scenes Shakespeare traces, though hastily as so crowded a play requires, a profound evolution in Lear. We first hear from the handy and inevitably expository "gentleman" that Lear is trying to outscorn the elements; and we shortly see him, in no patient mood, calling upon the storm to avenge him:

> And thou, all-shaking thunder,
> Strike flat the thick rotundity o' th' world!
> Crack nature's moulds, all germens spill at once
> That makes ingrateful man!
>
> (III.ii.6-9)

But soon a new note appears. He is "more sinn'd against than sinning" (l. 60), and the implied confession is significant. When next he appears, the tempest in his mind is working a further change. He realizes that he has taken too little thought of "poor naked wretches" (III.iv.28) and that his pomp has shielded him from truth:

> O, I have ta'en
> Too little care of this! Take physic, pomp;
> Expose thyself to feel what wretches feel,
> That thou mayst shake the superflux to them,
> And show the heavens more just.
>
> (III.iv.32-36)

He has even been responsible for his daughters:

> Is it the fashion, that discarded fathers
> Should have thus little mercy on their flesh?
> Judicious punishment! 'Twas this flesh begot
> Those pelican daughters.
>
> (III.iv.74-77)

And he tears off his clothes that he may become at one with other men.

So far Lear has achieved some realization of his errors. From this point on his development is presented primarily in terms of his relationship to Cordelia, and this limitation of vision is appropriate as his body and his wits both weaken. It also enables Shakespeare so to conduct the action that humility and patience may be presented as an integral part of the drama rather than being mere statements superimposed upon the play, as in *Hamlet*. From here on the development parallels and follows Gloucester's progress through the steps of repentance, but it is presented in much greater detail. As befits his greater nature as a man, Lear also feels more keenly and reacts more intensely.

Before presenting Lear, however, Shakespeare must attend to an important detail, and the care that he expends upon it is typical of the attention that he has lavished upon the regenerative action of the play. If Lear's repentance is to have meaning, he must, of course, be morally responsible. A madman cannot repent in any meaningful sense. We first have a short expository scene (IV.iv) in which a doctor assures Cordelia that "repose," provoked by his drugs, "Will close the eye of anguish" and restore Lear's "bereaved sense." Before Lear awakes in the profoundly moving scene of his reconciliation with Cordelia, the expository doctor once again assures her that Lear has "slept long" and

> Be by, good madam, when we do awake him;
> I doubt not of his temperance.
>
> (IV.vii.23-24)

Lear's awakening, building slowly to the climactic recognition of Cordelia, is constructed not only to produce maximum dramatic impact but also to convince us that Lear is indeed returning to his right mind, however enfeebled he may be. His puzzled doubts show that he sees things as they really are.

In portraying Lear himself, Shakespeare, as so often with an important bit of action, instructs us how to interpret it; and we first hear of Lear's contrition from Kent before we see it:

> A sovereign shame so elbows him. His own unkindness,
> That stripp'd her from his benediction, turn'd her
> To foreign casualties, gave her dear rights

> To his dog-hearted daughters,—these things sting
> His mind so venomously, that burning shame
> Detains him from Cordelia.
>
> (IV.iii.44-49)

This account prepares for Lear's first words in the presence of Cordelia, whom he does not yet recognize. They are a statement of his full contrition.

> You do me wrong to take me out o' th' grave.
> Thou art a soul in bliss; but I am bound
> Upon a wheel of fire, that mine own tears
> Do scald like molten lead.
>
> (IV.vii.45-48)

As Cordelia kneels for his paternal blessing, in a ritual familiar to Elizabethan parents and children, Lear also kneels. His puzzled "Methinks I should know you" (l. 64) shows that, halfway through his speech that follows, he still does not recognize Cordelia. The kneeling is the automatic response of a man who knows, in his contrition and his complete humility, that he is unworthy of such honor from any human being. The recognition comes as he kneels. It is followed by confession and an offer to accept, as penance, even death at Cordelia's hands.

> Be your tears wet? Yes, faith. I pray, weep not.
> If you have poison for me, I will drink it.
> I know you do not love me; for your sisters
> Have, as I do remember, done me wrong:
> You have some cause, they have not.
>
> (IV.vii.71-75)

> You must bear with me.
> Pray you now, forget and forgive; I am old and foolish.
>
> (ll. 84-85)

But the full measure of Lear's faith and patience is revealed only after he and Cordelia are captured. Here the sequence of action on the Elizabethan stage, one scene following another without interruption, is crucial to the meaning. In the preceding scene, Edgar has left Gloucester in the shade of a tree. He rushes back to report that Lear and Cordelia are captured and to take his father with him in flight. But Gloucester refuses to budge. "A man may rot even here," he says, in a return of his former despair. "What, in ill thoughts again?" Edgar chides him impatiently. Then comes the speech already quoted, ending "Ripeness is all. Come on." Gloucester assents, and they flee. Edgar's whole exhortation that "Men must endure" is obviously intended by Shakespeare as the key to what immediately follows. As Edgar and Gloucester exit through one stage door, Lear and Cordelia are led in through another as prisoners. Cordelia is cast down, she says, not for herself but for Lear. He replies:

> No, no, no, no! Come, let's away to prison;
> We two alone will sing like birds i' th' cage.
> When thou dost ask me blessing, I'll kneel down
> And ask of thee forgiveness.
>
> (V.iii.8-11)

> Upon such sacrifices, my Cordelia,
> The gods themselves throw incense. Have I caught thee?
> He that parts us shall bring a brand from heaven,
> And fire us hence like foxes. Wipe thine eyes;
> The good-years shall devour them, flesh and fell,
> Ere they shall make us weep. We'll see 'em starv'd first.
>
> (ll. 20-25)

The last lines show that the old Lear is not wholly dead—the Lear who curses Goneril and kills the slave that hangs Cordelia. More important still, as he comforts Cordelia, the relationship intended by nature is restored.

This brings us to the final scene of the play and its problem of the death of Cordelia.

The last scene of *King Lear*, like the end of all Shakespeare's tragedies, is full of slaughter. In the order of nature the cataclysm that Lear began leads ultimately to the deaths, reported or occurring during this scene, of Gloucester, Regan, Goneril, Edmund, Cordelia, and Lear. The order of nature is restored at a fearful price, as that action draws to its tragic close. What of the regenerative action? It is, in fact, paramount, and the scene closes with the final testing of Lear. I suggest that the handling of this scene, including the death of Cordelia, is the logical outcome of principles of structure that have operated all through the play.

I have discussed *King Lear* as though the actions in the orders of nature and of grace were separate, at least in the last part of the play, and to some extent they are. But the two philosophic lines and the

225

two lines of action both fuse in the storm scene; they also fuse at the end of the play. The key is simply Shakespeare's habit of pushing his action to extremes. In the world of inexorable natural laws, violation of these laws must lead to the suffering of the innocent as well as of the guilty. In the Christian tradition the final means of salvation for all men was the death of an innocent victim, and for the individual, too, death may be the final means to victory. It would certainly be in accord with the contrasts and the paradoxes of the play if the final penalty that Lear must pay for his sins, the death of Cordelia, were the means to his final insight, so that punishment ends only as illumination is complete. Her death is Cordelia's last contribution: As expendable lesser character, she proves that a just moral order is itself part of that order of nature which Lear has destroyed; as minister, she leads her father to his last insight.

Once again Shakespeare's preparation is careful, though extremely brief. Lear enters with Cordelia in his arms, but in his anguish he imagines that she may be alive and demands a looking glass to test her breathing. But the bystanders turn their minds (and the spectators') to another issue, the Last Judgment. "Is this the promis'd end?" says Kent (l. 263). "Or image of that horror?" echoes Edgar. "Fall, and cease!" agrees Albany (l. 264)—that is, as the Arden edition glosses, "Let the heavens fall, and everything come to an end."[18] I have stressed these three speeches because they provide—and, I think, were carefully calculated to provide—the context for Lear's next words, which state a major proviso:

> This feather stirs; she lives! If it be so,
> It is a chance which does redeem all sorrows
> That ever I have felt.
>
> (V.iii.265-267)

In this world, the poor old man is deceived, as he will be yet once more. But what of "the promis'd end"?

Shakespeare reserved this question, I think, for the conclusion of his play. To do so, he has departed from his normal practice in ending a tragedy, and thereby he has given maximum emphasis to the circumstances and meaning of Lear's death. In *Othello* the speech in which Lodovico takes control, punishes the guilty, and restores

[18]Ed. Kenneth Muir (London, 1952).

226

order concludes the play; so does the parallel, though more elaborate, restoration of "measure, time, and place" by Malcolm in *Macbeth*. In *King Lear* the same function is allotted to Albany as the ranking survivor.[19] He takes control, offers to restore Lear to the kingship, rewards Edgar and Kent, and promises to deal with other friends and foes. But he does not end the play. Instead he abruptly transfers the audience's attention to Lear, no doubt pointing as he speaks: "O, see, see!" (l. 304).

Let us now turn with the spectators to Lear's final lines, for Shakespeare has compressed a great deal into a short space:

> And my poor fool is hang'd! No, no, no life!
> Why should a dog, a horse, a rat, have life,
> And thou no breath at all? Thou'lt come no more,
> Never, never, never, never, never!
> Pray you, undo this button. Thank you, sir.
> Do you see this? Look on her, look, her lips,
> Look there, look there!
>
> (V.iii.305-311)

Lear recurs to the problem that bothered Gloucester. It is, in fact, the inevitable and the ultimate human question in the presence of suffering and death. It was also the question of Christ on the cross: "My God, my God, why hast thou forsaken me?" That Lear asks it only proves that he is human. Shakespeare was no Stoic; the tradition in which he believed had never denied the reality of human agony or refused to forgive the doubts and protests of the suffering. It had never asserted, furthermore, that an answer to the problem of evil was to be found in the order of nature. Lear responds, therefore, with an answer of faith. He thinks he detects breathing, and the Lear who humbly thanks a bystander for undoing a button has come a long way from the Lear who disowned Cordelia. "Look on her, look, her lips," he cries, and he dies in an ecstacy of joy, thinking that Cordelia lives.[20] This, too, Shakespeare has prepared for.

When Edgar finally revealed himself to Gloucester, so he has told us only a few lines earlier, his father's tired heart, "'Twixt two

[19]In this, as in the preceding point, I differ from Geoffrey Bush, who states succinctly an alternative reading; cf. *Shakespeare and the Natural Condition* (Cambridge, Mass., 1956), pp. 16-17.

[20]Bradley's interpretation has been almost universally accepted. See *Shakespearean Tragedy*, p. 291, and for the parallel in Gloucester's death, p. 294.

extremes of passion, joy and grief, / Burst smilingly" (V.iii.198-199). Gloucester grieved for what was past, joyed to know that Edgar lived. Surely the subplot has once again been used to prepare for and to illuminate by explicit statement the actions of Lear. Shakespeare was true to his history. This play is pre-Christian in time, and the word salvation is never uttered; but it is, as we have seen, profoundly Christian in thought. In its earlier action the professed fool was wisest of all. So now is the foolish, fond old man. His last illusion, like his first act of madness, expresses a profound moral insight. We are surely intended to believe that his dying vision is clear[21] and that at the promised end will come the "chance which does redeem all sorrows." This may not be our answer to the problem of suffering, but it is the Christian answer, and apparently it was Shakespeare's. Cordelia lives, and so, we may believe, does Lear. He has been stretched long enough upon the rack of this tough world, not so much because he can endure no more as because he has become patient and resigned, perfected in the "ripeness" that is all. He is a higher kind of man for the stretching!

Presenting this crowded series of events and relating them to the metaphysical and religious principles which gave them meaning confronted Shakespeare with a problem of dramatic exposition unique in the history of the theater. Something of his technique we have already seen in discussing his use of the subplot, but there is much more to be noticed. I mean by exposition, of course, the technique by which a dramatist reveals to the audience his interpretation of the action; I am not thinking of the narrower sense in which the term is applied to a part of the play that explains the necessary background. Shakespeare tried to make clear his meaning by developing to their highest efficiency devices that he used in all the great tragedies. *King Lear* is, in fact, the ultimate Shakespearean tragedy not only in its full presentation of the metaphysical system of nature and the theological doctrine of grace that he strove to mirror, but also in its supreme exemplification of his characteristic dramatic craftsmanship.

Most striking of these techniques of exposition is the extent to which the play depends for its meaning upon the audience's under-

[21]Cf. Nerissa's "holy men at their death have good inspirations" (*Merchant of Venice* I.ii.30-31).

standing of the concept of nature taken for granted in Shakespeare's time. The action obviously flows from violation of the laws of nature by four characters (if I may take Goneril and Regan as one) and from obedience to these laws by two others. Except for Gloucester's speech quoted above (I.ii.112-127), there is no full-scale exposition of natural order like that given to Ulysses in *Troilus and Cressida*. The various evil characters talk about nature endlessly, but they reveal their own errors and their motivation by their misunderstanding of nature. In *Hamlet* Shakespeare established a normal interpretation of the ghost and then used as a means of dramatic exposition Hamlet's approximation to or deviation from that norm as already understood by the audience. In *King Lear* knowledge of nature and the laws subsumed under it is simply taken for granted.

To speak first of Cordelia and Edgar, who obey their obligations as children, Shakespeare contented himself with revealing their attitude by Cordelia's original statement that she loves Lear according to her bond, no more no less, and then showing the sincerity of their emotional reaction to their fathers' suffering. No more was needed, and the effectiveness of his restraint is in marked contrast to the saccharine tedium of disquisitions in the old play. Cordelia and Edgar present what they do as an outcome of what they feel, and their lines are devoted to explaining their feelings. We are convinced that they act from love more than from duty, and Shakespeare's technique is eminently effective. There was no need to tell Elizabethan audiences the obligations of children toward their parents. The catechism had attended to that when they were children.

Of the evil characters, Goneril and Regan were the simplest dramatically for similar reasons. Their conduct was outrageously unfilial and violated the same principles that Cordelia and Edgar obeyed. It was necessary only for Shakespeare to have other characters, and Lear himself, comment from time to time. But Lear's more violent outbursts are so clearly an outcome of his own predicament that they can hardly be called expository in the sense in which I am using the term.

The other three characters presented a more complex problem, since each errs not because he disobeys nature but because he misunderstands what it involves. Edmund, Gloucester, and Lear are the most complex characters in the play, in ascending order, and each reveals his own weakness in what he has to say about nature. It is these three, therefore, who push to the limit Shakespeare's technique of using deviations from an established norm as a means of characterization. At the same time, by their very talking about nature they emphasize the metaphysical basis of the play. Dramatic economy is at work as one aspect of craftsmanship.

Edmund, like all Shakespeare's villains, is motivated fundamentally by inordinate self-love. In contrast to Lear, he is so habituated to his sin of pride that he needs no reassurance from others. His self-confidence is complete, and he sees himself as the measure of all things. He therefore takes nature to be the promptings of his own will; he confuses nature, the instrument of God, with his own fallen nature.[22] His denial of primogeniture is an obvious hint to the audience, for a universal custom was evidence of a natural law. "The general and perpetual voice of men is as the sentence of God himself."[23] Edmund, in short, reveals himself as a villain habituated to sin in his first soliloquy:

> Thou, Nature, art my goddess; to thy law
> My services are bound. Wherefore should I
> Stand in the plague of custom, and permit
> The curiosity of nations to deprive me,
> For that I am some twelve or fourteen moonshines
> Lag of a brother? Why bastard? Wherefore base? . . .
>   I grow; I prosper.
> Now, gods, stand up for bastards!
>
> (I.ii.1-22)

Edmund's bastardy is itself a dramatic signpost reinforcing the point of his soliloquy. A bastard is not invariably a villain in Elizabethan drama—witness Shakespeare's own Philip Faulconbridge in *King John*. But Don John in *Much Ado about Nothing* can illustrate a likelihood that bastards are up to no good. Like him, Edmund is also in the tradition of the dramatic machiavel villain. The more experienced playgoers in the audience probably had no trouble placing him in the line of Barabas or Richard III soon after he appeared. His bastardy was one hint; his soliloquy itself was another, for it

[22]Cf. Danby, *Shakespeare's Doctrine of Nature*, pp. 31 ff.

[23]Richard Hooker, *Of the Laws of Ecclesiastical Polity*, Bk. I, Ch. viii, sec. 3, in *The Works of . . . Richard Hooker*, ed. John Keble (Oxford, 1888), I, 227.

clearly belongs, like the great soliloquy in which Richard III presents himself to the audience at the beginning of his tragedy, to the conventional type in which the villain proclaims his evil intentions. Such signs to the audience are a part of Shakespeare's technique, as of Elizabethan drama in general; and the point is worth mentioning, because no example was noted during the earlier discussion of Shakespeare's techniques. But another villain's introductory soliloquy will shed further light on the use of such hints. Aaron in *Titus Andronicus* is established as evil not only by his soliloquy but by the fact that he is a member of a race well represented among the villains of drama. Othello, however, is also a Moor. But his character is presented with extreme care, and it is possible, furthermore, that Shakespeare intended the prevailing reputation of Moors to be part of the background which the audience brought to his play and to make dramatic capital out of contradicting a common impression, just as two other plays, Robert Wilson's *Three Ladies of London* (1581) and Robert Daborne's *A Christian turn'd Turke* (1610), exploit the shock value of a Jew and a Turk, respectively, who give Christians a lesson in virtue and fidelity to their religion. The reader who recalls how various enemies of the recent past—Germans, Japanese, or Russians, for example—have been treated on the stage or screen will have no difficulty in understanding what happened on the Elizabethan stage and why an established character type would be reversed for dramatic effect. All signposts of the type being discussed were therefore subject to important exceptions, but they did establish a probability: a hint would stigmatize a bastard or a Moor as a villain, whereas elaborate care would be needed to make the audience accept him as virtuous. It is no accident, therefore, that Edmund is a bastard and that he begins his active participation in the play with a soliloquy.

Gloucester is a more complicated character than Edmund. As the victim of a tragic error, he must inevitably be without the singleness of purpose and of nature characteristic of a villain, whose soul, though misdirected, is undivided. Gloucester's weakness seems to be sensuality. As befits a sensual man, he sees not only the begetting of Edmund but the universe itself in terms of his reaction of the moment. Of order and purpose superior to himself he has no understanding. The problems implicit in Edmund's bastardy he dismisses with singular heartlessness and selfishness: "Though this knave came something saucily to the world before he was sent for, yet was his mother fair; there was good sport at his making, and the whoreson must be acknowledged" (I.i.21-24). If he has any consistent attitude toward nature or, to put it in other terms, any philosophic notion of the scheme of things, it is that the external world is irrational and hostile—that he is the victim of blind fate. The destruction of social order that he describes in the speech already quoted, he attributes to astrology: "These late eclipses in the sun and moon portend no good to us" (I.ii.112). At this, Edmund, who knows with the audience that the stars incline but do not compel, comments: "An admirable evasion of whoremaster man, to lay his goatish disposition on the charge of a star!" (I.ii.137-139). But Gloucester's ultimate expression of his personal fallacy (not, as some writers have thought, Shakespeare's) is, as we have already noted, his anguished cry of despair:

> As flies to wanton boys, are we to th' gods,
> They kill us for their sport.
>
> (IV.i.38-39)

Lear's error is quite simply to see himself as above the order of nature. This refusal to see that nature imposes, even upon a king, obligations as well as privileges, is an extreme manifestation of inordinate self-love or pride. This pride is the source of all Lear's sins, as it is the source of all sin in the Christian ethical tradition. Lear's attitude toward nature is the clearest revelation of his character, and it appears constantly in his savage bursts of wrath in the early part of the play. To Cordelia he says in the first heat of his wrath:

> Here I disclaim all my paternal care,
> Propinquity and property of blood,
> And as a stranger to my heart and me
> Hold thee from this for ever.
>
> (I.i.115-118)

That is, he formally attempts to break the bond of nature which binds him to Cordelia and which is above his control. Even more terrible is his curse of Goneril, in which he bids nature itself to withdraw from his offending daughter:

> Hear, Nature! hear, dear goddess, hear!
> Suspend thy purpose, if thou didst intend
> To make this creature fruitful!
> Into her womb convey sterility!
> Dry up in her the organs of increase,
> And from her derogate body never spring
> A babe to honour her!
>
> (I.iv.297-303)

Lear knows, in short, that there is an order of nature, but he does not know that it applies even to himself. This he has to learn.

This use of the philosophic basis of the play as a means of interpreting character and action extends, however, beyond self-revelation. As part of the almost incredible dramatic economy of the play, all characters are to some extent expository. They are endowed with an extraordinary clarity of vision in evaluating the actions of others but, for the most part, with complete blindness in looking upon themselves. We have already noted that Gloucester describes the theme of the play, stating quite accurately what is happening in Britain, oblivious that he has radically mistaken what has happened to him. Edmund corrects Gloucester, but not himself. Kent and the sisters quite accurately diagnose Lear's wrath and folly; but Kent is blind to the savage temper that lands him in the stocks (from any point of view except his own and Lear's, he deserves to be there), and the sisters fail to see their own faults that destroy them.

All the characters, major and minor, tend to speak in terms of the order of nature and thereby to reinforce the theme of the play as well as to judge and interpret details of action. Albany tells Goneril:

> That nature which contemns its origin
> Cannot be bordered certain in itself.
> She that herself will sliver and disbranch
> From her material sap, perforce must wither
> And come to deadly use.
>
> (IV.ii.32-36)

"Some good I mean to do," says Edmund, "Despite of mine own nature" (V.iii.243-244). Edmund and Edgar are given, as we have noted in another context, a final judgment upon the action of the subplot and indirectly of the whole play. Edgar thinks primarily of his father:

My name is Edgar, and thy father's son.
The gods are just, and of our pleasant vices,
Make instruments to plague us.
The dark and vicious place where thee he got
Cost him his eyes.

(V.iii.169-173)

Edmund, true to his own nature to the end, thinks immediately of himself:

Thou'st spoken right, 'tis true.
The wheel is come full circle; I am here.

(V.iii.173-174)

The ultimate example of this habit of thinking in terms of order and disorder is, of course, the Fool; occasionally he speaks directly: "Let go thy hold when a great wheel runs down a hill, lest it break thy neck with following; but the great one that goes upward, let him draw thee after" (II.iv.72-75). But clear statements of this sort are hard to find among his lines. More often he speaks in riddles or figurative language. It is a commonplace that the basis of his quips is some kind of inversion: "Why, this fellow has banish'd two on's daughters, and did the third a blessing against his will" (I.iv.114-116); "Good nuncle, in; ask thy daughters' blessing" (III.ii.11-12); (on Kent in the stocks) "Horses are tied by the heads, dogs and bears by th' neck, monkeys by th' loins, and men by th' legs" (II.iv.7-9). But this trait of his humor appears most clearly in his songs, many of which turn on some kind of denial of the usual.

The Fool illustrates still a third method, in addition to relying upon knowledge of philosophy and recognition of dramatic signposts, by which Shakespeare reinforces his meaning—a method that is even more important in *Macbeth*—namely, the choice of imagery. Once again the images in *King Lear* tend to be derived in some way from the concept of natural order, so that philosophy and figure blend to the point that one is often put to it to distinguish what is philosophic statement and what is figure of speech. When Gloucester says, "I stumbled when I saw" (IV.i.21), he is twisting a simple statement of fact into a figure of speech that becomes a profound confession. More technical is the constant comparison of the sisters to animals, particularly animals of prey. So Lear calls Goneril "Detested kite" and refers to her "wolvish visage" (I.iv.284-330). Gloucester speaks

234

of her "boarish fangs" (III.vii.58). This is based, of course, upon the principle that man is a rational animal and that when he ceases to act rationally—and therefore naturally—he becomes no better than a beast—worse, in fact, for he is being false to his nature. Albany makes explicit this principle. After calling the sisters "Tigers, not daughters" (IV.ii.40), he continues to Goneril:

> See thyself, devil!
> Proper deformity seems not in the fiend
> So horrid as in woman.
>
> (IV.ii.59-61)

The ultimate example of this blending of philosophy and imagery is, of course, the storm on the heath. It is a real force in the play, and its buffets beat Lear at once into madness and moral sanity. But it is also a figure of action, if not of speech, in that it symbolizes the tempest within Lear (as he himself implies) and the convulsion that has produced chaos in the whole order of nature. But for Shakespeare the social and the physical orders were part of one nature and one order of law. So the disorder of the elements is not only a symbol of social chaos. It is a partial manifestation of natural chaos as well. It is a kind of cosmic synecdoche.

In his attempt to show an ultimate disruption of the order of nature, Shakespeare did not restrict himself, however, to literal or figurative statement. He constructed his very action in such a way as to imply the operation of ultimate forces throughout all nature. From his source he took over the technique of motivating the action in terms of the fundamental passions that lead men astray or of their healing opposites. Lear is driven by pride, in the Christian tradition the cause of all sin, and by wrath. Gloucester has been prey to lust; the sisters and Edmund destroy themselves at its urging. In the classification of passions going back ultimately to Plato's *Republic* but still in use, say, in Burton's *Anatomy of Melancholy*, the passions are categorized into those related to wrath and those related to love, or lust, as inordinate love may be called.

Not only do these archetypal passions operate, but they are manifested in an extreme form. Lear is false not to one natural obligation but to all possible natural obligations attaching to him as king, father, and old man. His pride is terrible, and so is his wrath. All the resources of Shakespearean rhetoric are expended upon his terrible curses. This aspect of Lear is, in fact, the most notable contrast to the old play. Leir shows anger and refers later to his ire; but in dis-inheriting Cordella, he is mild-mannered indeed as compared to Lear. There is nothing in the old play comparable to the dreadful curses upon Goneril, for Leir has already become patient. Lust, for obvious dramatic reasons, is harder to push to the limit, but Shake-speare does his best both in the actions of the sisters and in their words. This heightening of emotional tension has two results. It gives the play maximum impact as an *exemplum* of the evil effects of wrath and lust. But it also poses a test case of the power of suffering to chasten and enlighten the human spirit. It is no surprise that Glou-cester should profess patience or waver in his resolution. He is at best unsteady, easily led, quick to weaken. But the chastening of Lear is as terrible, in its way, as the pride and wrath of which he is purged. If Lear can acquire patience, any man can; and that is the point that Shakespeare makes, just as he tells us that if Othello can become a monster of jealousy so can the best of us, and we, like Macbeth, can fall from goodness to destruction.

Shakespeare is also at pains not to distract our attention from the point of his moral lesson. For, in marked contrast to his earlier prac-tice, especially in Hamlet, he strips both Lear and Gloucester to mental essentials. We know that Lear is proud and wrathful. We watch him learn the meaning of care for others and acquire humility and patience. But he has no personal traits like Hamlet's sardonic humor, his streak of perverse cruelty, his habit of using whirling words in excitement, his liking for bawdy jests, and so on indefinitely. Lear is a towering figure of a man, but he towers undifferentiated by petty details. Gloucester actually has more individuality than Lear in his puzzled weakness and his fundamental kindliness, but he, too, is not a richly developed character. In following his growth in patience, as in watching Lear's, we are not diverted from the main line of action.

This simplicity and universality of *exemplum* is developed also by the use of thematic doubling. If Lear is led by his violent passions to misjudge his daughters, so is Gloucester persuaded by his weaker sensuality and credulity to misjudge his sons. Strong and weak, wrathful and lustful—in fact, all of us—are alike in danger if we relax our vigil.

So Shakespeare holds the mirror up not only to the whole order of nature's laws but to the full range of their power upon mankind. But he uses still another method of making his points—namely, dramatic irony or poetic justice. These, I take it, are expository devices, a means of underscoring a point, and not a view of life. The blinding of Gloucester is so appropriate a punishment for a lustful man that it emphasizes the weakness ultimately responsible for his destruction. It is possible that Shakespeare derived the idea from the official Homilies, for the "Third Part of the Sermon against Adultery" mentions that "Among the Locrensians, the adulterers had both their eyes thrust out."[24] This detail is, however, one of a series of punishments and is not stressed. So obvious an example of poetic justice would no doubt have occurred to Shakespeare as he read Sidney, but he may well have developed it as he wrote. Lear loses his reason as an appropriate outcome of his failure to use it; he is accompanied by his Fool as he had been led by his folly. Edmund is killed by the brother upon whose "foolish honesty" he had practiced. And examples can be multiplied throughout the play. But they cannot be found at the end of the play, and that point needs to be emphasized. In the old play Leir regained his kingdom and Cordella presumably returned in happiness to France. That was poetic justice. But in Shakespeare Lear and Cordelia both die, the latter by what is no more than a trick of fate. That is life. The ending of the play shows that Shakespeare had not subscribed to Bacon's theory that "because *true Historie* propoundeth the successes and issues of actions not so agreable to the merits of Vertue and Vice, therefore *Poesie* faines them more just in Retribution and more according to Revealed Providence."[25] He was quite capable of using poetic justice to make a point; he refused to regard it as a principle of nature to be mirrored in the fundamental structure of his play. He distinguished between neatness of moral exposition and perversion of moral truth.

In still another respect Shakespeare shaped his action in conformity with the nature of man (and of all things) as he understood it. He inherited from Aristotle and the schoolmen a thoroughly teleological view of nature. All things moved toward a destined end; the nature

[24]*Certain Sermons . . . 1574* (Cambridge, Eng., 1850), p. 131.

[25]*Advancement of Learning*, in *Critical Essays of the Seventeenth Century*, ed. J. E. Spingarn (Oxford, 1908), I, 6.

of a thing was itself that property inhering in the thing that impelled it toward the end for which it was created, man's nature being his rational soul. As Shakespeare's contemporary Hooker put it: "all other things besides [God] are somewhat in possibility, which as yet they are not in act."[26] As a corollary, if a living thing, including man, failed to grow, it inevitably decayed. In any of Shakespeare's heroes moral decay is an inevitable result of the tragic false choice that initiates a chain reaction. So Brutus loses his peace and his clarity of mind, Othello his noble calm, and Antony his military judgment. In these men there is clearly a decay of the moral nature, and in Macbeth the chain of sin produces an almost complete degradation. But the four heroes mentioned are the only characters in their respective plays who change fundamentally during the course of the action, except that Lady Macbeth breaks under strain rather than evolving from bad to worse as does her husband. In all three plays the minor characters are static, no different at the end than at the beginning. But in *King Lear* almost every character undergoes some kind of change. In this respect, too, Shakespeare did his uttermost to hold the mirror up to nature. Only Edmund, who remains from first to last an opportunist villain except for his belated attempt to save Lear and Cordelia, is a static character, and even he learns finally that "The wheel is come full circle." Goneril and Regan sink from bad women to monsters, and Cornwall is dragged with them, finally to be slain by a servant. Edgar gains strength and wisdom, and Kent acquires patience and resignation along with his master. The regeneration of Gloucester and Lear has been discussed. But what of Cordelia?

Few of Shakespeare's characters have caused more divided reactions than Cordelia has aroused by her part in the opening scene of the play. Some critics have seen in her a model of rectitude and sound moral principles. Such, indeed, she is, for everything she says is absolutely true and her principles are impeccable. But others find her hard and unyielding—a chip off the old block in her stiff-necked pride in her superior virtue. So, I confess, she impresses me. Which did Shakespeare intend her to be? Did his skill fail him as he tried to motivate Lear's titanic wrath? I think not. The key to Cordelia is Isabella in *Measure for Measure*, and especially the way in which

[26]Hooker, *Of the Laws of Ecclesiastical Polity*, Bk. I, Ch. v, sec. 1, in *Works*, I, 215.

Shakespeare manipulates his plot to make her kneel to ask forgiveness for Angelo who has wronged her. *Measure for Measure* makes it perfectly clear that Isabella, for all her virtue, is an imperfect character and that the measure which she needs to apply to herself is a measure of Christian charity. Even righteousness must be informed by charity, which is the love of God and, for his sake, of his creatures. In *King Lear* there is a scene (IV.iii) in which thirty-three lines are given to an account of Cordelia's reaction to news of her father's suffering. We are told that she combines "patience and sorrow" (l. 18). But why is this scene inserted in so crowded a play, especially since Cordelia herself has only about six times as many lines in the whole play? It has, I think, two purposes: it shows the moral norm of patience which Lear, too, must achieve; but it also shows that Cordelia has grown in charity if not in rectitude. In other words, she, like Isabella, has measured her righteousness and found it wanting; she has learned to weep tears of sympathy even for the father who wronged her. A few of those tears would have become her in her first scene, not at her banishment from court but at her estrangement from Lear. The old play was right in making her wish forgiveness, but its verbosity is far less effective than Cordelia's simple words when next she sees her father:

> O, look upon me, sir,
> And hold your hand in benediction o'er me.

(IV.vii.57-58)

Cordelia develops, therefore, not in the natural virtue of justice, which included for Shakespeare the bond between child and parent,[27] but in the theological virtue of charity or love. Her growth is rather in grace than in wisdom, and it brings us once again face to face with the second level of action in the play.

The interpretation of *King Lear* just proposed is one that has developed through many years of teaching, discussion with graduate students, and reading of contemporary scholarship. If it is sound, two conclusions seem to me to follow. *King Lear* is, first of all, the ultimate Shakespearean tragedy—ultimate both in its holding the mirror up to nature (and grace) and in its pushing characteristic

[27]Cf. Hardin Craig, "The Ethics of King Lear," *Philological Quarterly*, IV (1925), 97-109.

techniques and habits of mind as far as art would permit. This I have several times implied. But it is, secondly, in the paradox that it is a profoundly Christian tragedy about a pre-Christian world, undeniable proof that it is possible to write Christian tragedy. This has been denied by many critics—not least by A. C. Bradley in writing about Shakespeare. But no one can deny that *King Lear* is tragedy, though he may deny, with many critics, that it is Christian. I have stated my reasons, as best I could, for thinking their position untenable. On the other hand, much as *King Lear* may resemble a morality play in its structure, it differs profoundly in never neglecting the tragic suffering of those who find regeneration or the tragic waste of those who sink from sin to sin. The vision of reality that obliged Shakespeare to hold the mirror up to both nature and grace also led him to solve a major critical problem and to write a genuinely Christian tragedy of redemption as he was to write in *Macbeth* an ultimate tragedy of damnation.

Chapter Six ❧ THE WAY TO DUSTY DEATH:
OTHELLO AND *MACBETH*

To PAIR *Othello* and *Macbeth* for purposes of discussion is un-
conventional, but it is not unreasonable. They were written, apparently, in adjacent seasons (*Othello*, 1604-1605; *Macbeth*, 1605-
1606), and only *King Lear* may have intervened between them. In
structure they both rely upon a single plot centering in the temptation and fall of a great and good but less than perfect human being.
In each the fatal choice of evil is made in a single scene, and in each
the grounds and the process of that choice are more simply and explicitly presented than in *King Lear*. Each of them leaves the hero
"ensnared" in soul as well as body, and they are, in a sense, tragedies
of damnation. So much is obvious. But a subtler relationship exists.
If one conceives of Shakespeare as a dynamic playwright, constantly
thinking and experimenting dramatically—and it must surely be
obvious that I hold such a view—then it seems likely that ideas and
problems implicit in *Othello* are worked out to better solution in
Macbeth. But there is no such clear reworking of the same specific
concepts as that which connects *Hamlet* and *King Lear*. The line of
development lies, rather, toward a better adjustment in *Macbeth* of
dramatic structure to the same ways of viewing human nature under
temptation and degeneration.

There are, of course, striking parallels between *Macbeth* and
Hamlet or *King Lear* and *Othello* that might have been pursued.
The former are alike in the tremendous poetic power of the great
soliloquies, although, as I have tried to indicate, the resemblance
can be pushed too far. Parallels in characterization have been drawn
between Macbeth and Hamlet themselves. Iago and Edmund are
conceived in almost identical terms. But the parallels are, I think, less
striking than those between *Othello* and *Macbeth*. Certainly they
are less significant for my particular purposes.

Othello is, in structure, so much simpler than *Hamlet* or *King

Lear that it presents few difficulties, but a brief summary of the plot as I see it will indicate how Shakespeare makes his points and perhaps clarify the discussion to follow. The dramatic exposition has, as usual, the double purpose of presenting events leading up to the main action and developing the characterizations needed to make that action probable. Events are swiftly presented. Othello has stolen Desdemona from her father's house and married her. Roderigo has also wooed Desdemona but been rejected by her father. Iago is fleecing him under pretense of furthering his suit. Cassio has been preferred over Iago as Othello's lieutenant, and Iago bears, or pretends to bear, deep resentment. All this comes out as the Duke summons Othello to consult about the defense of Cyprus and Brabantio calls Othello to account for the theft of his daughter. The upshot of the exposition is perhaps contained in Brabantio's grim warning to Othello:

> Look to her, Moor, if thou hast eyes to see;
> She has deceiv'd her father, and may thee.
>
> (I.iii.293-294)

Much more time is spent upon exposition of character. Shakespeare uses his regular technique of establishing minor characters, letting them describe the hero or villain, and then making him exemplify in action what the audience has been told about him. Roderigo's opening lines contain a strong hint that Iago has been taking his money and double-crossing him. Iago follows through by pointing out that his service to Othello is motivated purely by self-interest and that he is a dissembler:

> In following him, I follow but myself;
> Heaven is my judge, not I for love and duty,
> But seeming so, for my peculiar end;
> For when my outward action doth demonstrate
> The native act and figure of my heart
> In compliment extern, 'tis not long after
> But I will wear my heart upon my sleeve
> For daws to peck at. I am not what I am.
>
> (I.i.58-65)

Roderigo is too dull to see that the same principles govern Iago's service to himself. But Iago is already established as a man motivated by self-love or pride, chief of the seven deadly sins.

Later this characterization is made still more explicit in language that glances at the technical definition of pride as inordinate self-love: "since I could distinguish betwixt a benefit and an injury, I never found man that knew how to love himself" (I.iii.313-315). In Iago's next speech Shakespeare proceeds to establish him as a villain in that he has become so habituated to evil that his reason is completely subservient to his will and the slave of his evil purposes. His moral nature is completely perverted:

> Virtue! a fig! 'tis in ourselves that we are thus or thus. Our bodies are our gardens, to the which our wills are gardeners; so that if we will plant nettles or sow lettuce, set hyssop and weed up thyme, supply it with one gender of herbs or distract it with many, either to have it sterile with idleness or manured with industry, why, the power and corrigible authority of this lies in our wills. If the balance of our lives had not one scale of reason to poise another of sensuality, the blood and baseness of our natures would conduct us to most preposterous conclusions; but we have reason to cool our raging motions, our carnal stings, our unbitted lusts, whereof I take this that you call love to be a sect or scion.
>
> (I.iii.322-337)

Shakespeare, in short, has elaborately diagnosed Iago for the audience in terms of the theology and psychology of the day. Iago's motto, like Satan's, might well be: Evil, be thou my good. But he also does evil with a malevolent glee that makes him an individual human being and a powerful stage personality—as well as a dramatic offspring of Richard III.

Through Iago we are introduced to Othello. First we learn that because of the wars in Cyprus,

> the state,
> However this may gall him with some check,
> Cannot with safety cast him.
>
> (I.i.148-150)

Then we see Othello self-assured in the presence of Brabantio's threats:

> My services which I have done the signiory
> Shall out-tongue his complaints.
>
> (I.ii.18-19)

There is also a note of proud superiority to those about him that looks to the future: "Keep up your bright swords, for the dew will rust them" (I.ii.59). His response to Brabantio's tirade is similar:

243

> Hold your hands,
> Both you of my inclining, and the rest.
> Were it my cue to fight, I should have known it
> Without a prompter.
>
> (I.ii.81-84)

Othello's account of his wooing is intended, I think, to establish two points. First, both Othello and Desdemona make clear that their love has been of slow growth and is no mere sensual infatuation:

> 'Twas pitiful, 'twas wondrous pitiful.
> She wish'd she had not heard it; yet she wish'd
> That Heaven had made her such a man. She thank'd me,
> And bade me, if I had a friend that lov'd her,
> I should but teach him how to tell my story,
> And that would woo her. Upon this hint I spake:
> She lov'd me for the dangers I had pass'd,
> And I lov'd her that she did pity them.
> This only is the witchcraft I have us'd.
>
> (I.iii.161-169)

Desdemona reverts to the same theme:

> My heart's subdu'd
> Even to the very quality of my lord.
> I saw Othello's visage in his mind,
> And to his honours and his valiant parts
> Did I my soul and fortunes consecrate.
>
> (I.iii.251-255)

The point just made is, of course, a commonplace of Shakespearean criticism. But the lines immediately following those just quoted seem to me intended to convey an implication that has been overlooked:

> So that, dear lords, if I were left behind,
> A moth of peace, and he go to the war,
> The rites for which I love him are bereft me,
> And I a heavy interim shall support
> By his dear absence.
>
> (I.iii.256-260)

Desdemona is quite clear that if she stays in Venice she will lose "The rites for which I love him" and bear "a heavy interim." The meaning of these lines must have been perfectly clear, if not to us, to an audience whose pledge of marriage ran: *"And the man taught by the Priest, shal say. With this ring I the wed: with my body I the worship: and with all my worldly goodes, I the endow."*[1] The contrast to this in Othello's lines that follow immediately is surely intentional, for he is either fooling himself or trying to deceive the council when he denies that his "appetite" is involved:

> I therefore beg it not
> To please the palate of my appetite, . . .
> But to be free and bounteous to her mind.
>
> (I.iii.262-266)

Granted the character established for him already and later confirmed by Iago, Othello is misjudging himself. In other words, the contrast between Desdemona's simple statement of fact and Othello's alleged concern only with her mind is deliberate. Othello foolishly thinks that he is not as other men and is underrating the physical commitments of marriage and the emotional complications following therefrom.

In portraying Othello as in effect failing to understand the full range and implications of love, Shakespeare is not only building toward the panic that seizes Othello when Iago's insinuations force him to think in physical terms but also using one of the character contrasts of which he is so fond. For Iago, too, is equally one-sided in his view of human relationships. If Othello sees only a marriage of true minds, Iago thinks only in terms of carnal appetite. Depth of affection he cannot understand, and it is this blindness that destroys him when Emilia, true to Desdemona, convicts him of lying, preferring truth to the marital obedience that he expected:

> 'Tis proper I obey him, but not now.
> Perchance, Iago, I will ne'er go home.
>
> (V.ii.196-197)

During most of the play, however, the contrast between Othello's idealism and Iago's carnality serves primarily to define the difference and the superiority of understanding that is one aspect of Othello's proud and excessive self-confidence.

To return to Othello's account of his wooing and marriage, this

[1] *The Prayer-Book of Queen Elizabeth 1559* (Edinburgh, 1911), p. 124.

blindness to realities appears in his immediately handing Desdemona
over to Iago:

> A man he is of honesty and trust.
> To his conveyance I assign my wife.
>
> (I.iii.285-286)

The first line is, the audience knows, untrue. It is not impossible
that Othello's unfortunate choice of the word "conveyance," with
its connotations of betrayal, was intended to underscore to the audience his reckless self-confidence.

Iago returns to this point in his soliloquy outlining his schemes.
Othello is not only free and open but lacking in prudence and cir-
cumspection:

> The Moor is of a free and open nature,
> That thinks men honest that but seem to be so,
> And will as tenderly be led by th' nose
> As asses are.
>
> (I.iii.405-408)

The exposition makes a second point about the marriage that
suggests complications. It is, to some extent, unnatural in its unit-
ing people of different social and ethnic background. It is also improbable because of Othello's ugliness. Brabantio simply assumes
that Desdemona's love for Othello is so unnatural as to prove that
she has been drugged or bewitched (I.ii.62-76). He repeats his
charge to the Senators:

> She is abus'd, stol'n from me, and corrupted
> By spells and medicines bought of mountebanks;
> For nature so prepost'rously to err,
> Being not deficient, blind, or lame of sense,
> Sans witchcraft could not.
>
> (I.iii.60-64)

> Of spirit so still and quiet that her motion
> Blush'd at herself; and she, in spite of nature,
> Of years, of country, credit, everything,
> To fall in love with what she fear'd to look on!
>
> (ll. 94-98)

Othello argues that Desdemona was won by the strangeness of his
life, and she, by implication, assents to her father's description of
him by saying that she saw his "visage" in his mind. The marriage is,

in short, potentially subject to tensions of misunderstanding and physical repulsion. Roderigo is quite prepared to grant Iago's argument that trouble is inevitable:

If sanctimony and a frail vow betwixt an erring barbarian and a super-subtle Venetian be not too hard for my wits and all the tribe of hell, thou shalt enjoy her; therefore make money.

(I.iii.361-365)

Othello is therefore strong and noble but overconfident. Notice that not a word has been said about any tendency toward jealousy. Shakespeare clearly did not intend us to think of him in those terms. His tragic flaw is self-confidence and the liability to self-deception that follows from an excess thereof. Like most human beings, he is proud, and to that extent he is Everyman. To regard him, with some critics, as predisposed by race or climate to jealousy is to weaken the force of Shakespeare's *exemplum*.

The action of the play, Othello's tragic misjudgment of Desdemona and its consequences, is cast in the traditional pattern of the subornation of reason by passion, the passion being in this case jealousy, as Iago explicitly tells us.

If my analysis is correct, the opening wedge is Othello's misunderstanding of his own marriage. Desdemona has become, in fact, his god, and he dotes upon her. The contrast between what he said to the Senators and what he professes to her when she arrives in Cyprus is revealing, and Shakespeare has chosen his words with care to define Othello's moral error. They substitute Desdemona for God as the object of man's soul and specifically deny that even the beatific vision will bring equal comfort:

> To see you here before me. O my soul's joy!
> If after every tempest come such calms,
> May the winds blow till they have waken'd death!
> And let the labouring bark climb hills of seas
> Olympus-high, and duck again as low
> As hell's from heaven! If it were now to die,
> 'Twere now to be most happy; for, I fear,
> My soul hath her content so absolute
> That not another comfort like to this
> Succeeds in unknown fate.

(II.i.186-195)

247

Desdemona, by contrast, speaks sound doctrine and, incidentally, echoes the Confirmation service:

> The heavens forbid
> But that our loves and comforts should increase,
> Even as our days do grow!
>
> (II.i.195-197)

Othello says Amen to her words but reiterates his heresy and adds an implication that his comfort is of the flesh as well as of the mind:

> Amen to that, sweet powers!
> I cannot speak enough of this content;
> It stops me here; it is too much of joy.
> And this, and this, the greatest discords be
> That e'er our hearts shall make!
>
> (II.i.197-201)

As he puts it finally, "I dote / In mine own comforts" (ll. 208-209), and for once he is right about his feelings. A perversion of his moral nature has set in. This passage shows perfectly Shakespeare's way of giving dialogue meaning by making it allude to accepted doctrines in terms of which it must be judged. Spenser portrayed exactly the same perversion of the marital relationship in Book III of *The Faerie Queene*, "Of Chastity." Amoret and Scudamore represent an excessive delight in the pleasures of marriage that must be corrected by spiritual discipline. Shakespeare was writing into his play a commonplace of his age, but his technique enabled him to make in a few lines a point that Spenser's allegory pursues at some length.

The rest of the action is more easily summarized. Othello's reaction to Cassio's brawl (II.iii.204-209) shows that he is less imperturbable than he had supposed; his concern for Desdemona further shows his uxoriousness, in that awakening her becomes a final ground for his punishment of Cassio:

> Look, if my gentle love be not rais'd up!
> I'll make thee [Cassio] an example.
>
> (II.iii.250-251)

Iago, ever the skillful opportunist, now sees a means of working upon Othello. Like all Shakespeare's villains, he outlines his strategy in advance. (Note that he has expository soliloquies in both the first and third scenes of this act.) Since he is speaking alone, we must, I

248

think, take his words as an accurate diagnosis of Othello's situation as well as of his own schemes. Notice that he reverts to the theme of Othello's lines quoted earlier in saying that Othello places his love for Desdemona above his duty to God:

> For 'tis most easy
> Th' inclining Desdemona to subdue
> In any honest suit; she's fram'd as fruitful
> As the free elements. And then for her
> To win the Moor, were't to renounce his baptism,
> All seals and symbols of redeemed sin,[2]
> His soul is so enfetter'd to her love,
> That she may make, unmake, do what she list,
> Even as her appetite shall play the god
> With his weak function. How am I then a villain
> To counsel Cassio to this parallel course,
> Directly to his good? Divinity of hell!
> When devils will the blackest sins put on,
> They do suggest at first with heavenly shows,
> As I do now; for whiles this honest fool
> Plies Desdemona to repair his fortune
> And she for him pleads strongly to the Moor,
> I'll pour this pestilence into his ear,
> That she repeals him for her body's lust;
> And by how much she strives to do him good,
> She shall undo her credit with the Moor.
> So will I turn her virtue into pitch,
> And out of her own goodness make the net
> That shall enmesh them all.
>
> (II.iii.345-368)

The climax of the play comes in Act III, Scene iii. It opens with Desdemona almost nagging Othello for Cassio. Othello's mind is on other things. Even so, he apparently means his repeated "I will deny thee nothing" (ll. 76, 83), and he follows her exit, not with an expression of irritation, but with Shakespeare's adaptation of a famous passage in Ovid:

> Excellent wretch! Perdition catch my soul,
> But I do love thee! and when I love thee not,
> Chaos is come again.
>
> (III.iii.90-92)

[2]Cf. Richmond Noble, *Shakespeare's Biblical Knowledge and Use of the Book of Common Prayer as Exemplified in the Plays of the First Folio* (London, 1935), p. 218.

Othello's marriage has thrown him so far off balance, in short, that Desdemona—and her charms—have become for him all the world and heaven itself. Upon this background Iago works by keeping Othello's mind upon the physical aspects of his marriage and upon the improbability that Desdemona should continue to love a man black, ill-favored, and alien as he is. This seems to me the real point of Othello's blackness. It does not denote a race or climatic background predisposing a man to jealousy. Evidence for such psychology can easily be found in Elizabethan treatises, but Shakespeare does not develop the point in his play. Othello's color simply means that, once he starts thinking in sensual terms, as he does repeatedly in this scene, the probabilities are all against him, and he needs only minor prods by Iago to convince himself. His jealousy is rooted in insecurity.

Iago—that is, Shakespeare—makes this point in trying to prepare us to accept the rather flimsy plot device of the handkerchief:

> I will in Cassio's lodging lose this napkin,
> And let him find it. Trifles light as air
> Are to the jealous confirmations strong
> As proofs of holy writ; this may do something.
> The Moor already changes with my poison.
> Dangerous conceits are, in their natures poisons,
> Which at the first are scarce found to distaste,
> But with a little act upon the blood
> Burn like the mines of sulphur. I did say so.
> (III.iii.321-329)

The scene ends as Othello and Iago swear vengeance in a ridiculous travesty of a solemn religious oath (III.iii.460-469), and Othello departs to furnish himself "with some swift means of death / For the fair devil" (ll. 477-478). Chaos has indeed come—at least in Othello's moral nature. Having made Desdemona everything, he now has nothing.

The remaining action of the play represents the steady degeneration of Othello's moral nature resulting from his false moral choice of vengeance. At first his nature is in tumult. He strikes Desdemona, flies into a passion, and is incapable of facing the issue with Desdemona. Characteristically, Shakespeare makes Othello show his state by having him describe the moral norm of patience, including explicit reference to Job, and then refuse it:

250

> Had it pleas'd Heaven
> To try me with affliction; had they rain'd
> All kind of sores and shames on my bare head,
> Steep'd me in poverty to the very lips,[3]
> Given to captivity me and my utmost hopes,
> I should have found in some place of my soul
> A drop of patience; but, alas, to make me
> The fixed figure for the time of scorn
> To point his slow and moving finger at!
> Yet could I bear that too, well, very well;
> But there, where I have garner'd up my heart,
> Where either I must live or bear no life;
> The fountain from the which my current runs
> Or else dries up; to be discarded thence!
> Or keep it as a cistern for foul toads
> To knot and gender in! Turn thy complexion there,
> Patience, thou young and rose-lipp'd cherubin,
> Ay, there look grim as hell!

(IV.ii.47-64)

Here, too, Shakespeare implies that the root of Othello's desolation lies in his uxoriousness, and once again he uses oblique scriptural references to make his point. Treasures are to be garnered up in heaven; and it is God in whom we live and move and have our being. Richmond Noble has called attention to the derivation of the next lines from Proverbs v.15-18, quoting the Genevan version: "Drinke the water of thy cisterne, and of the rivers out of the middes of thine owne well. Let thy fountaines flowe foorth, and the rivers of waters in the streetes. But let them bee thine, even thine onely, and not the strangers with thee. Let thy fountaine bee blessed, and re-joyce with the wife of thy youth."[4] Noble adds that the Genevan annotates, "Thy children which shall come of thee in great abun-dance, shewing that God blesseth mariage and curseth whoredome." But Shakespeare perverts the passage to his own purpose. In Proverbs the man is the fountain from which flow children; here Desdemona is the fountain from which flows Othello.

As Othello pulls himself together, he becomes so habituated to the control of passion that he begins to act like his own self, except that

[3]Cf. ibid., p. 219.
[4]Ibid., pp. 67-68.

the premises of his action are false. He sees himself as called to justice, and the promptings of mercy as those of appetite:

> Yet she must die, else she'll betray more men.
> Put out the light, and then put out the light.
> If I quench thee, thou flaming minister,
> I can again thy former light restore,
> Should I repent me; but once put out thy light,
> Thou cunning'st pattern of excelling nature,
> I know not where is that Promethean heat
> That can thy light relume. When I have pluck'd the rose
> I cannot give it vital growth again,
> It needs must wither. I'll smell it on the tree.
> Oh, balmy breath, that dost almost persuade
> Justice to break her sword! One more, one more.
> Be thus when thou art dead, and I will kill thee
> And love thee after. One more, and that's the last;
> So sweet was ne'er so fatal. I must weep,
> But they are cruel tears. This sorrow's heavenly;
> It strikes where it doth love. She wakes.
>
> (V.ii.6-22)

He makes sure that Desdemona, like every doomed Elizabethan criminal, has a chance to make her peace with God. He thinks himself rational, but Desdemona points out the symptoms of his error:

> That death's unnatural that kills for loving.
> Alas, why gnaw you so your nether lip?
> Some bloody passion shakes your very frame.
>
> (V.ii.42-44)

But Othello's moral perversion is not yet complete. Desdemona, in her dying words, had lied to protect him:

> *Emil.* O, who hath done this deed?
> *Des.* Nobody; I myself. Farewell!
> Commend me to my kind lord. O, farewell!
>
> (V.ii.123-125)

Yet he can muster no faith in her mercy or, since she has been his god, in the mercy of God:

> Where should Othello go?
> Now, how dost thou look now? O ill-starr'd wench!
> Pale as thy smock! when we shall meet at compt,
> This look of thine will hurl my soul from heaven,
> And fiends will snatch at it. Cold, cold, my girl!

Even like thy chastity. O cursed, cursed slave!
Whip me, ye devils,
From the possession of this heavenly sight!
Blow me about in winds! roast me in sulphur!
Wash me in steep-down gulfs of liquid fire!
O Desdemon! dead, Desdemon! dead!
Oh! Oh!

(V.ii.271-282)

Like Gloucester, Othello takes refuge from despair in suicide. His final words are not of penitence but of self-justification, and he remains proud and uxorious to the end:

Then must you speak
Of one that lov'd not wisely but too well;
Of one not easily jealous, but, being wrought,
Perplex'd in the extreme.

(V.ii.343-346)

I kiss'd thee ere I kill'd thee: no way but this,
Killing myself, to die upon a kiss.

(ll. 358-359)

Like several of Shakespeare's dying heroes, Othello isolates quite accurately the cause of his downfall: he loved "too well" and was jealous. His death is magnificent, but there is no reason to doubt his own statement that Iago has ensnared not only his body but also his soul. The chain of sin has led to damnation.

Shakespeare's method of indicating Othello's probable damnation is, incidentally, an improvement in dramatic technique upon Horatio's flights of angels. No human being can anticipate the judgment of God or circumscribe his mercy, as Shakespeare well knew. Dante notwithstanding, it verges upon blasphemy for a poet to visit eternal punishment even upon what he has created. But he may surely attribute spiritual insights to his creatures, whose mental life, like their dramatic, is of his making. In restricting himself to a conviction within Othello and Macbeth that they have destroyed both soul and body, Shakespeare is on sounder ground both dramatically and theologically.

In its expository methods, as in its structure, *Othello* is one of the simplest of Shakespeare's plays. The main burden of foretelling the action of the play is carried by Iago's soliloquies. Like the soliloquies of all Shakespeare's villains, they explain schemes of action but do not debate their merit. Incidentally, they tell us much of what we know about Othello and all we know about Iago except for the very important lectures to Roderigo on self-love. But the soliloquies are primarily examples of Shakespeare's habitual technique of telling the audience what is going to happen before they see it occur.

This same combination of preparation and action is characteristic of other persons in the play. Othello himself describes his intentions before he faces the Senators and before he murders Desdemona. Cassio tells us of his weak head before the brawl occurs.

Attention has already been called to the extent to which Othello reveals his own deviation from the moral norm either by statements so worded that they imply the norm or by significant action underscored by other characters such as Desdemona. Except for Iago, Emilia is, however, the only other character in the play who explicitly judges the action. Toward the end of the play, she not only makes clear to Othello the trap into which he has fallen but serves, though briefly, as Shakespeare's mouthpiece to comment on Othello's folly. Her repeated epithets of *fool, gull, dolt* are more than personal abuse of Othello. They stigmatize his conduct as that subordination of reason to passion which, for Shakespeare, is at the root of most human sin.

Shakespeare uses, in short, the methods of making clear his meaning that had served him almost from his earliest plays. The simplicity of the methods is doubtless an outcome of the simplicity of the play, not only structurally but intellectually. Dignity and self-assurance are easy to reveal in action, if a few signposts are provided for the audience. Jealousy is even easier to reveal. Only loving "too well" required a more subtle method of revelation, and it is significant that this aspect of Othello's character has been relatively unnoticed. To make clear the intellectual basis of the play, Shakespeare had only to manipulate his dialogue in such a way as to relate the action to two schemes of conduct. The first of these was the traditional psychology that explained how passion might overcome reason and bring about a false judgment of the evidence. The point of the play is not that Othello acts on insufficient evidence. What happens is that his passion is so aroused that he is simply incapable of evaluating evidence rationally. The second scheme was the chain of sin that led the sinner from his first evil act (in Othello purely an act of will) through a series of ever-easier immoral acts to final impenitence and despair. Both systems of ideas were well known, and a few explicit statements inserted in the lines assigned to Iago and Othello were all that Shakespeare needed.

All this has merely been, I suspect, a roundabout way of saying that *Othello* makes its powerful impact upon our emotions rather than upon our intellect. It has, in fact, several serious weaknesses from our point of view that have worried both critics and audiences. I believe that it may have had still other defects from Shakespeare's point of view. These shortcomings are worth noting, because they have undoubtedly been corrected in *Macbeth*. Whether the improvement was partly accidental or resulted from Shakespeare's own critical judgment of his earlier play, it is, of course, impossible to tell.

The first, and from any point of view the least serious, of these weaknesses in *Othello* is the length of its dramatic exposition. It is like some of the earlier plays and like *Coriolanus* among the tragedies in that it takes the entire first act to get the play started. But events are managed superbly, and the important expository scene, the third, has been so well prepared for by Iago's revelations and Brabantio's wrath that it moves at a high level of excitement. Desdemona's arrival raises the interest to its peak, as we watch her confront her father and the Senators. Only Iago's scheming with Roderigo and his final soliloquy seem an anticlimax. The difficulty of this long exposition consists not in the scenes themselves but in their effect upon the structure of the play, which they crowd badly. The arrival in Cyprus and the initiation of Iago's schemes require the second act and part of the third. These, too, are quite legitimate. But the final result is that the crucial action of the play, Othello's succumbing to jealousy, has to be crowded into one scene.

The green-eyed monster's conquest of Othello has always seemed, I suppose, the chief weakness of the play. Shakespeare's intention seems obvious enough. Iago is represented as so stimulating Othello's sensual imagination with suggestions of Desdemona's infidelity that passion overturns reason and jealousy takes control. As Shakespeare tells us, a man in this state is incapable of examining evidence critically and any trifle will serve. The management of the scene is based

255

upon the system of psychology generally understood in Shakespeare's day and almost universally accepted. In this respect the technique is no different from that of numerous other scenes in Shakespeare which depend for their full meaning upon the audience's ability to interpret the lines within an indicated context of ideas. Numerous conventional signposts both of jealousy and of yielding to passion are written into the scene, primarily in the direction taken by Othello's mind and in the violence of his interjections toward the end of the scene.

The original audience undoubtedly found the psychology of the scene perfectly sound as a diagnosis of a pathological state of mind. They were also quite prepared to see a man's honor as residing in his wife's fidelity and to understand the violence of Othello's feelings as a soldier as well as a lover. But for them, as for us, the primary emphasis of the scene was upon sexual jealousy—witness Othello's wish that he had been left in ignorance. So much can be said in Shakespeare's defense.

But Elizabethan psychology was thoroughly realistic, and Elizabethans were shrewd observers of human nature. Probably, in fact, they were closer observers than we are, simply because they had fewer distracting interests. The haste of Othello's fall must have seemed very nearly as improbable to them as it does to us if they examined the play critically. This is a big "if," for there is no question that numerous problems detected by critics scrutinizing a text at leisure pass unnoticed in the excitement of production. In this case, however, the "if" seems to me valid. For the audience, on one level of attention, must react to the same stimuli as Othello if they are to find him worthy of sympathy and not a fool. The double level of attention that Shakespeare habitually demands operates here as in few other scenes. The audience have been amply warned of Iago's schemes, and they must always remain aware that Iago is lying for his purposes and judge Othello's decisions in the light of their superior knowledge. But, if the play is to be convincing as drama, they must also feel something of Othello's horror and distress, if not his jealousy. This kind of reaction takes time in an audience as well as in a human being, and it seems to me that Shakespeare manipulates his puppet too fast for the audience to follow on this level of empathy, especially since their reactions have been slowed by their knowledge of Iago's motives. Elizabethan drama is full, it is true, of scenes involving even faster and cruder shifts of character. Ctesiphon's decision not to kill Cyrus in *The Warres of Cyrus* (ca.1588) or Syphax's two changes of mood in Marston's *Sophonisba* (ca.1605) might be instanced. But these and similar plays are completely without either the richness of motivation or the intellectual analysis of the action that characterizes *Othello*. Shakespeare's tragedies demanded of the audience a high level of critical attention, and he was artistically obliged to satisfy the higher standards which he himself aroused, at least in the judicious. Syphax is merely an amorous blackamoor; Othello is a human being whom Shakespeare expects us to observe as an *exemplum* of our own ways of life. If we respond as he asks, he must face the consequences.

I am arguing, in other words, that we cannot interpret Shakespeare in the light of his fellow dramatists, as E. E. Stoll tried to do in dealing with this particular scene,[5] simply because Shakespeare set himself very different standards. There is ample evidence that his audience knew that his plays were different, even if they did not understand precisely why. I am prepared myself to assume that Shakespeare had some notion of the "why" and that he judged his own work accordingly. Compressing Othello's temptation and fall into one scene strained even dramatic probability, and it is very likely that Shakespeare was as quick to note this defect as subsequent critics have been. Unlike them, he was in a position to do something about the matter, at least in later plays.[6]

I assumed above that Othello's striking Desdemona, his killing her under the illusion of justice, and his final suicide represent a steady degeneration of his character in accordance with the operation of the chain of sin. If Shakespeare intended him as an *exemplum* of the effect of irrational and violent passion upon a human being, these and similar acts must fall within this concept of human behavior, the only one known to Shakespeare that was applicable to this situation. They do conform to the theory, but we must place this interpretation upon them rather than being guided to it by the

---

[5]*Shakespeare Studies, Historical and Comparative in Method* (New York, 1927), pp. 93-100.

[6]Cf. the handling of Iachimo's "proof" of Imogen's unchastity in *Cymbeline*, where Posthumous and the Philario keep demanding more proof (II.iv.66-146).

play. Our attention is so focused upon Iago's double-dealing with Roderigo and upon Desdemona's agonized attempts to understand what is wrong that Othello's acts stand in isolation rather than coming as part of a developing character pattern. The emphasis is upon events rather than upon the tragic decline of Othello. Shakespeare is once again writing in the tradition of narrative tragedy. Not that the exciting events are a dramatic weakness—far from it. But our failure to keep one eye steadily upon Othello is a weakness if Shakespeare was interested in holding the mirror up to nature rather than merely writing exciting drama. The problem was to keep the excitement but to add a fuller revelation of Othello's inner decline, so that the spiritual despair and suicide seem an inevitable outcome of the action —so that we are really prepared emotionally and intellectually to believe Othello when he tells us explicitly that he is damned. The murder of Desdemona gives us no trouble. It follows logically from Othello's mistaken interpretation of the facts and his false premises as to his moral duty. But the play's final judgment upon Othello does give us trouble—unless, as has generally happened, it goes unnoticed. This weakness, too, I think Shakespeare noticed and made a mental note to correct.

If one assumes, as I do assume, that Shakespeare was trying to give his action meaning in universal terms, one must recognize that, judged in comparison with Shakespeare's other great tragedies, *Othello* is only partly successful. I think it possible that, if we find the play weak in motivation, Shakespeare was dissatisfied with it as a moral *exemplum* holding the mirror up to nature.

All that we really know about Othello is neatly summarized in his final evaluation of himself (V.ii.339-351), already quoted in part. He has "done the state some service, and they know't." His proud assurance of his merit has been unshaken by recent events, for which he remains fundamentally impenitent in the sense of recognizing his need for forgiveness. Though unused to weep, he says that he sheds tears for Desdemona; but he speaks of "these unlucky deeds," hardly an expression of overpowering remorse or a confession. He "loved not wisely but too well." He was "not easily jealous, but being wrought, / Perplexed in the extreme." Just as in *King Lear*, Shakespeare has simplified the issues and pushed the action to the extremes that befit a test case. A nature "Whom passion could not shake"

(IV.i.277) becomes a raving monster of jealousy; a man inherently noble becomes a murderer and suicide. If Othello can fall before Iago because his rational guard is down, who cannot succumb to the wiles of Satan and satanic men? To this extent the play is a moral *exemplum*.

The particular action involving the fall of Othello is also related to general patterns of psychology and theology by its explicit background of passion psychology and its specific allusion to Othello's damnation. To that extent it exemplifies the operation of general laws of human nature and of human salvation. But its exemplification is limited and negative—by implication only. It is sometimes described as a domestic tragedy and compared to other examples of the type. And such a comparison can be instructive, though the premise seems to me invalid, for *Othello* as completely avoids the homiletic emphasis of *Arden of Feversham* or Heywood's *A Woman Kilde with Kindnesse* as it lacks the philosophic exposition characteristic of *Hamlet* or *Macbeth*. There are no voices warning of the consequences of sin or exhorting the sinner to repent. There is no manipulation of the action with reference to man's supernatural end of salvation such as is omnipresent in Heywood and present in the other domestic tragedies. References to religious doctrine are few indeed, though important. For these differences most of us are, I suppose, profoundly grateful. But another is still more important. Othello operates in a historical setting and is an important officer of the Venetian state. This circumstance places the play in the main line of Elizabethan tragedies. The differences from typical domestic tragedies show that Shakespeare was writing his own particular kind of tragedy, which does not become domestic merely because Desdemona is murdered by her husband in her bed.

But, if *Othello* does not have the overt didacticism of domestic tragedy, neither does it have the elaborate philosophic exposition characteristic of Shakespeare. Othello's attitude toward Desdemona is, as we have noted, shown to be inordinate by use of figures drawn from religious teaching, so that he ascribes to her a place in his life that properly belongs to God. But these figures are used to guide us in judging Othello, and only tangentially do they relate the play to a larger scheme of values. The same thing is true of Othello's remark that chaos will follow the end of his love. We know that another scheme of values is involved, but we are not told specifically what that scheme of values is. Othello's deeds are linked to passion psychology but not to the moral laws of nature and of nations that they violate. Shakespeare neglects, in particular, to make clear the moral fallacies involved in Othello's assumption that he must kill Desdemona "else she'll betray more men," although he does point out that Othello is deluded in thinking that reason governs him. No real attempt whatever is made to relate Othello's disorder to the entire order of nature. The mirror is held up only to limited aspects of man's nature, not to Nature itself, which has less part in this play than in any of the mature tragedies. *Othello* is, in fact, the single exception to the elaborate and detailed relating of the particular action to larger issues that appears even in Shakespeare's earliest tragedies. This characteristic of the play does not make it less effective from our point of view, but, unless we have misread the evidence of Shakespeare's way of thinking, it must have made him less satisfied with his handiwork. In *Macbeth* he achieved the same unity and clarity without so limiting his view.

Since the appearance of Walter Clyde Curry's *Shakespeare's Philosophical Patterns,* no one has had the slightest excuse for misunderstanding *Macbeth,* and there is no need to attempt an interpretation of the play here. I wish, rather, to show how *Macbeth* supplements *Othello* as a key to Shakespeare's technique, whether or not he was consciously correcting weaknesses that he had detected in the earlier play. There is, in fact, some danger that I may lay too much stress on the parallels and contrasts between it and *Othello* and ignore *Macbeth*'s relationship to the other tragedies. To minimize that tendency, we may note in passing one respect in which *Macbeth* avoids weaknesses inherent in *Hamlet.*

In its unity of action (in all senses of the latter word), *Macbeth* is obviously at opposite poles from *Hamlet* among Shakespeare's tragedies. Its action is simply the yielding of a great and good man to temptation and the degeneration of his moral nature resulting from his first deed of sin. To center this action within the soul of Macbeth, Shakespeare substituted for the open revolt in Holinshed a secret murder from an earlier part of the Scottish history.[7] The

[7] For a more detailed analysis of Shakespeare's use of his sources, see Henry N. Paul, *The Royal Play of Macbeth* (New York, 1950), pp. 183-225.

theme of *Macbeth* is therefore the causes and consequences of human sin, of which the story of Macbeth is an *exemplum*. This theme dominates the entire play. Its opening shows temptation at work upon Macbeth, who is a brave and kind man but, like all fallen sons of Adam, subject to the promptings of appetite—in this case desire for the crown. The promptings of his own fallen nature are powerfully seconded by Lady Macbeth and deliberately used by the witches as instruments of Satan. So all possible forms of temptation —external and internal—converge upon him. The murder of Duncan is kept off the stage as an intentional device, I am sure, to concentrate our attention upon Macbeth's reaction to his deed and upon the initiation within him of a chain of sin as this murder, like all his subsequent crimes, leads only to greater frustration rather than greater satisfaction. In contrast, we see the deaths of Banquo and of Lady Macduff and her children, so that we may feel the full horror of Macbeth's descent into sin. And we watch Macbeth's progressive decline not only as it is manifested in his deeds but as he feels it in his heart. In fact, we see the latter part of the play primarily through his disillusioned eyes.

The theme is never lost sight of. Macbeth's great soliloquies or meditative speeches, in contrast to Hamlet's, are tightly linked to the action of the play. Before the murder of Duncan, they establish the right course of action which Macbeth rejects and reveal the full horror of his crime; after the deed, they describe with unequaled power the desolation of his soul. It is instructive, for example, to compare two soliloquies analyzed earlier as having the same rhetorical structure, Hamlet's "To be, or not to be" and Macbeth's "If it were done when 'tis done" (I.vii.1-28). Both speeches consider lines of conduct which the protagonist decides not to follow. But Hamlet's decision not to take arms against a sea of troubles, as we noted, has no fundamental relationship to the course actually taken by the play. It is merely a further revelation of Hamlet's inner distress. Macbeth's soliloquy, on the other hand, reveals the course which he should have followed and thereby clarifies the exact nature and extent of his sin. It also foretells the moral forces that will and do punish violation of the moral laws to which it refers. It thereby establishes a moral frame of reference for the play. The imagery, too, centers our attention upon the theme of the play, as it operates in terms of such archetypal symbols as light and darkness and blood. In short, the tremendous imaginative power at work in *Hamlet* darts off in all directions; that in *Macbeth* converges always upon a single focus.

In this unity of action and of thought *Macbeth* is, of course, much closer to *Othello* than to *Hamlet*. For this reason a close comparison of the two former plays seems to me likely to reveal much more as to the nature and development of Shakespeare's tragic technique, and it will therefore be pursued at some length. For *Macbeth* develops tendencies apparent in *Othello* while correcting what Shakespeare may possibly have felt to be its weaknesses.

In handling the dramatic exposition in *Macbeth*, Shakespeare reverted to the device that he had used so brilliantly in *Hamlet*. The witches, like the ghost, are used for a preliminary scene that captures the audience's attention and sets the mood of the play. Macbeth's character and his position in Scotland are revealed in a second scene. The action of the play begins in the third scene, when the witches powerfully reinforce the temptation already present in Macbeth's appetite; the fourth scene narrows his range of choice by denying him further hope that he may legally inherit the throne. With the fifth scene Lady Macbeth is laying plans for the murder, and by the end of the act the crucial moral choice has been made and the die is cast. In *Macbeth*, therefore, the exposition moves very swiftly, and exposition and action are to some extent intermingled, so that the line between them is blurred.

This interweaving of exposition and the temptation which begins the action is a means to blurring another, and more important, dividing line that is sharply drawn in *Othello*. We know the precise conversation during which Othello first conceived a doubt of Desdemona's fidelity. We have no idea when Macbeth began to think longingly of the crown of Scotland. Shakespeare avoids the improbable haste of Othello's yielding to Iago by several times representing stage action in *Macbeth* as the culmination of a process that has long been at work. Macbeth's start and his fear when the witches first mention the kingship are carefully pointed out by Shakespeare, through Banquo, and Macbeth's way of demanding to know more drives home the point. When he remarks, after being saluted as Thane of Cawdor, "The greatest is behind" (I.iii.117), we know what his mind is working on during the trance to which Banquo shortly calls attention. Shakespeare's art is deliberately vague. Temptation, we are sure, has been at work upon Macbeth for some time, so that the witches but tell him what he has dimly hoped. How long and how seriously Macbeth had thought of the kingship we have no need to know. Shakespeare has succeeded in giving to what happens in the play the plausibility of background and of mature deliberation.

Lady Macbeth gives us a similar hint that she and Macbeth have discussed the murder itself, and she cannot be referring to recent events. For she says of the occasion when Macbeth broke the enterprise to her,

> Nor time nor place
> Did then adhere, and yet you would make both.
> They have made themselves, and that their fitness now
> Does unmake you.
>
> (I.vii.51-54)

That is, they first discussed the murder before they knew of Duncan's impending visit. In terms of the play, this must mean before Macbeth saw the witches. But Shakespeare does not indicate when, and it would have defeated his purpose to do so. Lady Macbeth may conceivably be misrepresenting the letter of Scene v as a proposal to seize the crown, but that is unlikely, since characters invariably tell the truth about events of which the audience does not otherwise have knowledge and Shakespeare could easily have given her an allusion to the letter to show that she was misrepresenting it. What is intended, I think, is another hint that temptation has long been at work and that what we are seeing is merely the final and decisive discussion of a series. At any rate, we are quite prepared to accept Macbeth's decision to murder Duncan, even though fewer lines have been devoted to his temptation than to Othello's.

This solution involved, of course, a corollary danger which we have already noted. If critics have refused to be convinced that the noble Moor of the first scenes could succumb to jealousy as he does, they have denied that the tempted Macbeth of this scene could have been the good man praised by Duncan and his nobles and stigmatized by his wife as trying to live "holily." But this difficulty inheres, I think, in our habit of seeing men as black or white, in terms perhaps ultimately derived from Calvinism, rather than as soldiers in an ever undecided moral warfare, the traditional view that Shakespeare undoubtedly accepted.

Othello's repeated admission that he is damned comes as something of a shock. It is, in fact, so little prepared for that it has often been disbelieved. But no one has ever overlooked the full extent of Macbeth's downfall. The difference is partly one of space, but primarily one of dramatic method. The peace of Macbeth's soul is actually destroyed the moment he agrees to kill Duncan, and his soliloquy on the dagger at the beginning of Act II shows how swiftly disintegration of the moral man is setting in. When we are denied the death of Duncan and see only Macbeth and his wife reacting to the blood, the symbol of sin, our eyes are riveted upon Macbeth; and we watch the blood incarnadine his life, if not the multitudinous seas. By contrast Othello's moral degeneration begins only with Act IV, and the crucial deed, the murder of Desdemona, still remains to be done. So Shakespeare has far less space in which to present his decline. But that seems to me less important than the difference of technique. When we watch Iago using Roderigo to murder Cassio and failing in his stratagem, and even when we hear Desdemona agonizing with Emilia over the change in Othello, we are interested in these scenes for their own excitement or as part of the progress of events in the play. By contrast Macbeth dominates every scene of any importance during the last half of the play except that in which Lady Macduff and her son are murdered. He is as omnipresent in the scenes in England as in those in which he is physically present. By keeping the dialogue centered upon his tyrannies, Shakespeare manages to develop the counteraction without once diverting attention or emphasis from Macbeth. Only in the final lines of the play does Malcolm emerge in his own right.

Most effective of all, however, in centering our attention upon what is happening to Macbeth the human being are his own descriptive speeches, to which we will return later. Though short as major speeches in the plays go, in imaginative power and density they are unequaled. A few such lines can hold our attention upon Macbeth through all the confused fighting. Shakespeare's poetic gifts are thoroughly devoted to his central meaning. These speeches reveal a further contrast between Othello and Macbeth, one central to Shakespeare's purpose. Othello is thoroughly deluded by his pas-

sion of jealousy. He thinks that he is behaving justly, even gener-
ously, toward Desdemona; his deeds he calls unlucky. Macbeth, on
the other hand, represents a different order of moral understanding
altogether. His clarity of perception is perhaps unrealistic, but it is
what makes his tragedy so compelling. Just as he murdered Duncan
in full knowledge of his sin, so he knows just what he has lost as he
sinks to destruction. *Othello* is primarily the story of a man who,
through misunderstanding, killed his wife; *Macbeth* is the tragedy
of a man who, in full knowledge of what he was doing, destroyed his
own soul.

There is a still larger sense, however, in which the play *Macbeth*
is the tragedy of every man who, neglecting the principles of
morality and the voice of conscience, falls from the high estate for
which he was destined into the slavery of sin. A careful reading of
the play makes clear that this larger meaning was constantly in
Shakespeare's mind as he wrote. The minute attention to giving the
action a universal significance and a setting in the whole order of
nature differentiates *Macbeth* fundamentally from *Othello* and
relates it, in important characteristics, to *King Lear*.

Once again, as in both *Othello* and *King Lear*, the action is pushed
to extremes. In the first scenes Macbeth is the savior of Scotland,
trusted completely by Duncan and his nobles. At the end he has so
utterly destroyed himself as a man that he, alone among Shakespeare's tragic heroes, is denied even the dignity of dying bravely.
He offers craven submission to Macduff and then fights only when
threatened with public exhibition as a tyrant (V.viii.11-29).

Shakespeare has been at pains, however, not only to reveal the
extent of Macbeth's fall but also to relate his particular act to all
human sin. One notices this if one compares the play with its source.
There the wife of Donwald, who nags him on to the secret murder,
is driven by ambition, and so is Donwald. In Shakespeare, on the
other hand, the passion of ambition is mentioned only in passing,
and the emphasis in the crucial scene of moral choice (I.vii) is upon
the sophistication of reason that, in traditional Christian psychology,
was a fundamental part of that willful choice of a lesser or transitory
good involved in each sinful act by a man possessing adequate knowledge and not already enslaved by habit. Macbeth's desire for the
crown is stated but not emphasized. To him the issue is "this business."

The poetry of the play is expended not upon the gorgeous trappings of royalty but upon his relationship to the moral law and to his own conscience. Lady Macbeth is given no enticing description of the crown but only bad logic. She actually inveigles Macbeth into the murder, if we may believe her words, first by demanding that he do it to show that he is really a man and that he loves her, and then by showing him how he can get away with it.[8] Shakespeare seems primarily concerned to show that her logic, like all arguments for sin, is sophistic. Macbeth takes an absolutely sound position:

> I dare do all that may become a man;
> Who dares do more is none.
>
> (I.vii.46-47)

When he allows Lady Macbeth to drive him from that position with a clever sophistry and a violent example of her own courage, he is lost. Shifting his ground from the moral rectitude of the deed to its feasibility completely undermines him.

This emphasis of the play upon the nature and process of sin rather than upon ambition as a cause of sin is further reinforced by the choice of blood as the central symbol in the play. A crown might well have symbolized ambition, as it does, for example, in Marlowe's *Tamburlaine*—"The sweet fruition of an earthly crown" (II.vii.29);[9] and it would have been no trick for Shakespeare to make explicit Marlowe's implied contrast between an earthly crown and the crown of life. But blood was the symbol of murder and of all guilt—"His blood be on us, and on our children" (Matt. xxvii.25). So blood operates in the play to show that guilt is ineradicable. "A little water clears us of this deed," says Lady Macbeth (II.ii.67); but when we last see her, she is still trying to wash away the smell of blood, to "sweeten this little hand" (V.i.57-58). Blood also makes graphic the operation of the chain of sin. The blood on Macbeth's hand cannot be washed away, as he knows with a moral insight denied to Lady Macbeth. So he does not try. Instead he strives to find happiness or even release in a mounting series of crimes. "Blood will have blood," he says, and later in the same scene he plans to wade still further in blood (III.iv.122, 136-137).

[8]Cf. J. V. Cunningham, *Woe or Wonder: The Emotional Effect of Shakespearean Tragedy* (Denver, 1951), pp. 123-126.

[9]*Tamburlaine the Great: In Two Parts*, ed. U. M. Ellis-Fermor (London, 1930).

Another of Macbeth's speeches unites the imagery of blood with the whole system of images that relate the specific actions of the play to the cosmic forces of evil. Light and day have been symbols of knowledge and right conduct and God from earliest times; so have their opposites darkness and night been associated with ignorance, sin, and such supernatural forces of evil as ghosts and witches. These, in turn, are related by Macbeth to the chain of sin within himself:

> Come, seeling night,
> Scarf up the tender eye of pitiful day,
> And with thy bloody and invisible hand
> Cancel and tear to pieces that great bond
> Which keeps me pale! Light thickens, and the crow
> Makes wing to th' rooky wood;
> Good things of day begin to droop and drowse,
> Whiles night's black agents to their preys do rouse.
> Thou marvell'st at my words, but hold thee still;
> Things bad begun make strong themselves by ill.
>
> (III.ii.46-55)

In this use of imagery to place the action of the play in its metaphysical context, *Macbeth* is, of course, completely removed from *Othello* and at one with *King Lear*, which uses, as we have seen, an elaborate system of images to indicate the reversal of natural order in Lear's former kingdom.

Macbeth also shares with *King Lear* its use of several other expository devices to give the action universal significance and to establish the moral norm. The most obvious is its doubling of plot elements to achieve contrasts. A subplot paralleling the entire main action is impossible in so close-packed a play, but situations can be, and are, duplicated. Of the first Thane of Cawdor Duncan observed:

> There's no art
> To find the mind's construction in the face.
> He was a gentleman on whom I built
> An absolute trust.
>
> (I.iv.11-14)

Only two scenes later he once again misplaces his trust:

> Where's the thane of Cawdor?
>
> (I.vi.20)

> We love him highly,
> And shall continue our graces towards him.
>
> (ll. 29-30)

267

But Shakespeare was interested, I am sure, in more than this obvious parallel. For, of the two, Macbeth proved ultimately the worse. The first Cawdor at least repented and confessed his sins, so that "Nothing in his life / Became him like the leaving it" (I.iv.7-8). The grace of repentance was denied to Macbeth, and his death was the sorry ending of a wasted life. This contrast is the first of the devices by which Shakespeare keeps us in mind of that order of grace in which Macbeth forfeits his rightful destiny.

In these opening scenes Duncan himself illustrates how a good king should govern, accepting the love and service of his subjects, punishing the guilty and rewarding the deserving, making provisions for an orderly succession to the throne. The King of England raises the example to a higher level, as he bestows the grace of healing upon his subjects. Duncan the ideal king is Shakespeare's invention, for Holinshed presented him as a feeble ruler deserving scant sympathy and no esteem.

The parallels between Banquo and Macbeth are obvious and have already been alluded to. The important point to be noticed, I think, is the extraordinary skill and economy with which Shakespeare combines in the one role the functions of dramatic mouthpiece and character contrast. In the second scene with the witches Banquo states sound principles that should have governed Macbeth's interpretation of the witches' prophecy. He also calls the audience's attention to Macbeth's significant actions as well as to his fallacies. But he turns out to be more than a wooden figure of perfection. He, too, is tempted, as any man so placed must be. But he knows how to resist temptation even to calling for aid upon powers, the order of angels appointed to resist demons:

> A heavy summons lies like lead upon me,
> And yet I would not sleep. Merciful powers,
> Restrain in me the cursed thoughts that nature
> Gives way to in repose!
>
> (II.i.6-9)

When last we see him, he is still thinking of the prophecy:

> Thou hast it now: King, Cawdor, Glamis, all,
> As the weird women promis'd, and, I fear,
> Thou play'dst most foully for't; yet it was said
> It should not stand in thy posterity,
> But that myself should be the root and father

268

Of many kings. If there come truth from them—
As upon thee, Macbeth, their speeches shine—
Why, by the verities on thee made good,
May they not be my oracles as well,
And set me up in hope? But hush! no more.

(III.i.1-10)

He is, in short, not a superman but only a good man insofar as fallen
human beings can be good—a man who knows his need for aid in his
warfare against the world, the flesh, and especially the devil. He
is what Macbeth once was and might have remained, even though
tempted. The contrast is not only implied by the structure of the
play but also made explicit by Macbeth:

> Our fears in Banquo
> Stick deep; and in his royalty of nature
> Reigns that which would be fear'd. 'Tis much he dares;
> And, to that dauntless temper of his mind,
> He hath a wisdom that doth guide his valour
> To act in safety. There is none but he
> Whose being I do fear; and, under him,
> My Genius is rebuk'd, as, it is said,
> Mark Antony's was by Caesar.

(III.i.49-57)

The comparison is reinforced by the final irony that Macbeth has
given his "eternal jewel" "to the common enemy of man" only to
make Banquo's children kings (ll. 64-70). The contrast between
Macbeth and Banquo is needed to complete the meaning of the play.
Banquo shows how Macbeth might have saved himself in life, as
Cawdor showed how he might have redeemed himself in death.

Macbeth is like Julius Caesar and King Lear in that the action of
the play is shown as destroying the entire order of nature. The "rough
night" for which Lennox cannot recall a fellow (II.iii.66-67) parallels the tempest described by Casca in Julius Caesar (I.iii.3-13) or the
storm on the heath. The unnatural darkness, the owl that killed a fal-
con, and the cannibal horses (II.iv) are at one with the burning
hand, the lion in the capitol, and the men all in fire of Julius Caesar
(I.iii.15-32). The obscure bird that clamored all night in Scotland
(II.iii.64-65) is related to the owl that hooted at noonday in the marketplace of Rome (I.iii.26-28). All these omens proclaim the murder
of a king as so dreadful and unnatural that it is attended and signal-

ized by other violations of nature. All this is, of course, on the surface of Shakespeare's thought, and it involves converting metaphysics into symbolism.

But *Macbeth* also resembles *King Lear* in a more sophisticated use of the order of nature that involves explicit reference to the operation of nature's laws. The witches are thought of as knowing the future because their familiars can look into the seeds of time—that is, the operation of nature in created things (I.iii.58).[10] But Macbeth is well aware that, in attempting to use the witches, he is substituting for obedience to the order of nature an appeal to forces that seek to destroy that order. He sees the witches not as understanding the germens or seeds of time but as "tumbling" them.

> I conjure you by that which you profess,
> Howe'er you come to know it, answer me!
> Though you untie the winds and let them fight
> Against the churches; though the yesty waves
> Confound and swallow navigation up;
> Though bladed corn be lodg'd and trees blown down;
> Though castles topple on their warders' heads;
> Though palaces and pyramids do slope
> Their heads to their foundations; though the treasure
> Of nature's germens tumble all together,
> Even till destruction sicken.
>
> (IV.i.50-60)

This speech, because it shows so clearly that Macbeth knows what he is doing, is an important milestone on his road to hell.

This concern for relating events to the order of nature shows most clearly, as one would expect, in the handling of Duncan's murder. Not only do the unnatural events that attend it stigmatize it as unnatural, but Macduff becomes so involved in describing the murder as a violation of the laws of nature and of God that he neglects to make his meaning perfectly clear and Lennox has to gloss: "Mean you his Majesty?" (II.iii.75). Killing Duncan, Macduff implies, has produced an ultimate confusion in the order of nature—that is, chaos; it has also involved dreadful sacrilege against the God whose anointed minister the king is:

> Confusion now hath made his masterpiece!
> Most sacrilegious murder hath broke ope

[10]Cf. Curry, *Shakespeare's Philosophical Patterns* (Baton Rouge, 1959), pp. 29-49, especially 46-49.

The Lord's anointed temple, and stole thence
The life o' th' building!

(II.iii.71-74)

Through all the rhetoric one fact emerges. For Shakespeare the violation of nature's laws and the sacrilege are what need to be emphasized at this crucial point—not the killing of Duncan the human being. The manipulation of language in this speech is similar, in its purpose, to phrasing Lear's dreadful curses in terms of the operation of nature. Both relate the particular violation of nature to all violations of nature. Macbeth's sin is also specifically described as breaking the sacred law of God.

Macbeth has still another characteristic in common with *King Lear* in that its action is related not only to the order of nature but also to that of grace. In *Macbeth*, of course, the references can be specific because Shakespeare is dealing with a nominally Christian kingdom. They take a variety of forms. The imagery of light has already been mentioned in contrast to that of sin and darkness; and it plays an important, although relatively minor, part. "Stars, hide your fires; / Let not light see my black and deep desires" (I.iv.50-51), says Macbeth, as he hears Duncan nominate Malcolm Prince of Cumberland. They do indeed hide themselves, for Banquo observes as he enters Macbeth's castle: "There's husbandry in heaven; / Their candles are all out" (II.i.4-5).

More important are various explicit references in the play to the order of grace and salvation. The dying repentance of Cawdor has several times been mentioned. Just before Macduff hears of the murder of his wife and children, in a scene intended to reveal what the tyranny of Macbeth has done to Scotland, there stands, in pointed contrast, a description of England under a king who is the Lord's anointed indeed and from whom flow healing and grace:

> *Doct.* Ay, sir; there are a crew of wretched souls
> That stay his cure. Their malady convinces
> The great assay of art; but at his touch—
> Such sanctity hath Heaven given his hand—
> They presently amend.
> *Mal.*   I thank you, doctor.
>   [*Exit Doctor.*]
>
> *Macd.* What's the disease he means?
> *Mal.*   'Tis call'd the evil:

271

A most miraculous work in this good king;
Which often, since my here-remain in England,
I have seen him do. How he solicits Heaven,
Himself best knows; but strangely-visited people,
All swoll'n and ulcerous, pitiful to the eye,
The mere despair of surgery, he cures,
Hanging a golden stamp about their necks,
Put on with holy prayers; and 'tis spoken,
To the succeeding royalty he leaves
The healing benediction. With this strange virtue,
He hath a heavenly gift of prophecy,
And sundry blessings hang about his throne
That speak him full of grace.

(IV.iii.141-159)

This order of grace, as well as the order of nature, Malcolm sol-
emnly promises, in the last words of the play, to restore to Scotland:

this, and what needful else
That calls upon us, by the grace of Grace
We will perform in measure, time, and place.
So, thanks to all at once and to each one,
Whom we invite to see us crown'd at Scone.

(V.viii.71-75)

As befits a study of sin, however, the most eloquent and moving
references to the order of grace are contained in those speeches of
matchless poetry in which, toward the end of the play, Macbeth reveals his desolation. The ultimate horror of the hell on earth that he
has created for and of himself lies in the knowledge of what he has
lost; his most terrible scourge is that in his wasteland the privation
of God is not quite complete.

I have liv'd long enough. My way of life
Is fallen into the sear, the yellow leaf;
And that which should accompany old age,
As honour, love, obedience, troops of friends,
I must not look to have; but, in their stead,
Curses, not loud but deep, mouth-honour, breath
Which the poor heart would fain deny, and dare not.

(V.iii.22-28)

To-morrow, and to-morrow, and to-morrow
Creeps in this petty pace from day to day
To the last syllable of recorded time;
And all our yesterdays have lighted fools
The way to dusty death. Out, out, brief candle!

> Life's but a walking shadow, a poor player
> That struts and frets his hour upon the stage
> And then is heard no more. It is a tale
> Told by an idiot, full of sound and fury,
> Signifying nothing.
>
> (V.v.19-28)

The idiot is Macbeth himself, and he knows it!

In discussing the purposes of expository passages, so much has been said about the techniques being used that little more comment is needed. The main burden of relating the action of the play to fundamental moral principles is carried by Macbeth, and Shakespeare's incredible skill is shown, among other ways, in making Macbeth's speeches arise naturally out of the action and yet put that action in its moral context. But the method is itself adjusted to the action, as the degenerating Macbeth shifts from the statement of moral truths to palpable fallacies. In the first part of the play, as we have noted, Shakespeare attributes to Macbeth explicit statements of sound moral principles or graphic images of the horror aroused in his conscience by the deed he contemplates. Even after the murder he still understands perfectly the implications and the consequences of what he has done. But as he sinks further into sin, his reason, like that of all Shakespeare's villains, is sophisticated so that it assents to crime and becomes the tool of the sinful will. This is more skillfully indicated in *Macbeth*, I think, than in any other Shakespearean tragedy. The method is to make him state, as premises of his thinking or even of his action, propositions that contradict moral truths he had uttered earlier in the play. Take, for example, the scene in which the ghost of Banquo appears. Macbeth, horrified by the ghost, states the assumption that underlay his hiring the murderers:

> The time has been,
> That, when the brains were out, the man would die,
> And there an end; but now they rise again.
> With twenty mortal murders on their crowns,
> And push us from our stools. This is more strange
> Than such a murder is.
>
> (III.iv.78-83)

This is poles apart, in meaning and in moral penetration, from his earlier fear that heaven's cherubin would blow Duncan's murder in every eye (I.vii.16-25). Later on, he cowers before the ghost, exclaiming:

273

What man dare, I dare.
Approach thou like the rugged Russian bear,
The arm'd rhinoceros, or th' Hyrcan tiger;
Take any shape but that, and my firm nerves
Shall never tremble. Or be alive again,
And dare me to the desert with thy sword;
If trembling I inhabit then, protest me
The baby of a girl. Hence, horrible shadow!
Unreal mock'ry, hence!

(III.iv.99-107)

Here he remembers too late, and uses as an excuse for cowardice, the principle that he had stated and then violated in agreeing to kill Duncan: "I dare do all that may become a man." But Horatio and Hamlet regarded facing even a ghost as becoming a man. So would Macbeth if his conscience were clear. In view of what he had said about Duncan's blood, he is singularly naïve in asking Lady Macbeth's doctor:

Canst thou not minister to a mind diseas'd,
Pluck from the memory a rooted sorrow,
Raze out the written troubles of the brain,
And with some sweet oblivious antidote
Cleanse the stuff'd bosom of that perilous stuff
Which weighs upon the heart?

(V.iii.40-45)

Still further examples could be adduced. The wages of sin included, for Macbeth, not only a murderer's hand and heart but also a murderer's mind.

As commonly in Shakespeare's plays, the burden of outright moral exposition is lightened by relating the action to well-understood patterns of conduct, so that an allusion or two will suffice to clarify the meaning. The schemes of thought used in this play come from a variety of sources. From folklore, I am sure, comes the appearance of Banquo's ghost at the banquet to which he was invited. Like the Commandant's ghost in *Don Giovanni*, he exemplifies the principle that sooner or later one's sins will find one out, but he appears in accordance with the poetic justice so dear to folk tales. From Tudor political theory, and perhaps especially from the official Homilies, comes the view of the kingship implicit in Macbeth's attitude toward the murder, in Macduff's report of it, in the discussion between Malcolm and Macduff, and in Malcolm's final words.

In the opening scene of the play Macbeth shows courage in the presence of the enemy and equally rational terror in the presence of murder; toward the end he oscillates between rashness and terror. His behavior is grounded in the Aristotelian concept of bravery as the rational norm between cowardice and rashness. To risk one's life to preserve one's country is rational and brave; to jeopardize one's immortal soul for any earthly gain whatever is irrational and fool-hardy—more than becomes a man. To trust in the promises of witches is foolish rashness; to attempt surrender to a man whose wife and children one has murdered is so unwise as to be pure cowardice. Then to fight wildly, when all other hope is gone, is the rashness of despair, not the courage of reason. Macbeth's incapacity to act rationally in situations demanding courage is of a piece with his loss of moral understanding. It is part of his penalty for violating the laws of his own human nature. It is, in fact, one more example of the theological-psychological principle which operates throughout the last half of the play and to which repeated allusions have been made—namely, the chain of sin, in which each false choice of an apparent good makes easier the reason's acquiescence in another, so that blood will have blood.

In the last analysis, therefore, *Macbeth* stands in meaning and in perfection of technique, as it does in date of composition, beside *King Lear*. As a tragedy of damnation, it presents a simpler problem. The way to dusty death can be the way to spiritual death as well, and Shakespeare could concentrate upon a single action. He needed only to show the laws of nature and of God which Macbeth violated and the extent of his spiritual tragedy in this world as a preparation for his ultimate tragedy to come. Hell, for Shakespeare as for Milton and for all Christian thinkers, was the absence of God, and Macbeth caused that privation to begin in this world. In *King Lear*, on the other hand, Shakespeare had to show both the way to dusty death and discipline for eternal life. His action therefore had to be double, and his problem of exposition was more severe. But each play is almost perfect in its kind, and each holds the mirror up with great fidelity to the nature that Shakespeare understood and believed in. Though we may not believe in an eternal hell or even in an order of grace, it also holds the mirror up to the nature presented to us by our own experience; but that is another problem and another subject.

Chapter Seven ❧ THE WORLD OPPOSED:
ANTONY AND CLEOPATRA AND *CORIOLANUS*

No two of Shakespeare's tragedies seem more dissimilar, on first reading, than *Antony and Cleopatra* and *Coriolanus*. The former is a tale of true but sullied love that sprawls over half the Roman world and through innumerable episodes. The latter dramatizes the heroic pride of Coriolanus as it brings about his rise to greatness and his fall. But Shakespeare has written something much subtler and potentially more genuinely tragic than a *de casibus* play, for Coriolanus neither achieves nor really wants power. He allows himself to be propelled into a political contest for which neither his training nor his temperament have fitted him and in which he must be false either to the mother who has made him what he is or to his own nature. The two plays do have much in common, however, as a brief comparison will indicate.

No one, I take it, will dispute A. C. Bradley's judgment that both plays represent a falling off from the four great tragedies of Shakespeare's prime. To these four I would add *Julius Caesar*. *Antony and Cleopatra* has flashes of magnificent poetry and several fine scenes, but in dramatic clarity and in emotional impact it cannot stand beside *Othello*, which is also a tragedy of one that loved not wisely but too well—if such is the judgment, and this uncertainty is part of our trouble with the play, that Shakespeare intended us to form of *Antony and Cleopatra*. On the stage, certainly, it has had no such record of successful or even triumphant performances as *Othello*. Coriolanus stands beside Brutus and King Lear in the pride that caused his downfall, and he is allied to King Lear in his wrath. He never sins so outrageously as Lear, but even before the storm scenes we feel a sympathy for the old king that we never develop for Coriolanus. *Antony and Cleopatra* displays great imaginative control in individual scenes; it suggests, however, that Shakespeare lacked either the time or the creative energy to weld its fine details into a successful whole. *Coriolanus* is without the imaginative insight and poetic power needed to enlist our sympathy for the hero and, in so doing, to arouse our highest interest in the play. These remarks, or others tending to the same conclusion, are to be found repeatedly in critical discussions of the plays. They do not mean that the plays lack greatness. It would be hard to find their equals in dramatic power among the plays of Shakespeare's contemporaries, though perhaps not impossible. I think immediately, for example, of Webster's *The Duchess of Malfi* (1614), which is no weaker than *Antony and Cleopatra* in structure and comparable in dramatic impact, or of *The Maides Tragedy* by Beaumont and Fletcher (ca. 1610), which is far better constructed, would probably be more exciting on the stage, but is ethically wrongheaded rather than merely confused. Both are very great plays. But to equate them with a tragedy by Shakespeare implies that he is writing well below his peak. It also suggests a falling off in those qualities that make him unique in his age. This is exactly what has happened, as will appear if we examine briefly specific techniques in which *Antony and Cleopatra* and *Coriolanus* differ from the preceding tragedies.

Both plays, to begin with the most obvious parallel, revert to the episodic structure characteristic of the chronicle histories or narrative tragedies.[1] In fact, one has to go even beyond Shakespeare's early chronicle plays to the work of his contemporaries to parallel the fashion in which one short scene follows another in *Antony and Cleopatra* with only a single episode in each. "Episode" is, in fact, too precise a word, for many scenes contain no action whatever and merely present a curious detail or some character trait to the audience. Other related techniques characteristic of the chronicle play also pervade *Antony and Cleopatra*, but they will be reserved for detailed consideration later. *Coriolanus* is much more tightly structured, but the same tendency to fall into a string of short, loosely connected scenes is to be found just after the dramatic exposition in the first act and in the interval between Coriolanus' departure from Rome and his union with Tullus Aufidius. Those in the first act provide one reason why, in performance, the play gets off to such a slow start.

Even more significant of a change in Shakespeare, though less

[1]Cf. A. C. Bradley, *Shakespearean Tragedy: Lectures on Hamlet, Othello, King Lear, Macbeth* (London, 1905), p. 3.

damaging on the modern stage than the episodic structure, is the much restricted focus as compared with the preceding tragedies. This may seem a startling remark to make of *Antony and Cleopatra*, which moves all over the Roman world. But the extended background of the action is purely geographical. Though kings and kingdoms are lightly tossed about by Antony and the world is almost as lightly tossed away, no disruption of the order of nature follows, and the social order, as it involves first principles of human conduct, is barely mentioned. A few references do indeed imply the extended view of earlier plays. In the first scene, for example, Antony is called "The triple pillar of the world" (l. 12), and he assures Cleopatra that their love can be bounded only by finding a new heaven and a new earth. This is, however, only the hyperbole characteristic of so much Elizabethan dramatic—and nondramatic—rhetoric. Shakespeare does not intend us seriously to infer that their love is beyond the bounds of nature or contrary to it. Therein lies the difference from *Othello*, wherein a specific moral judgment in terms of ultimate values is indicated to the audience as Othello prefers his love and happiness in Desdemona to love of God and the bliss of heaven. A moral judgment like that in *Othello* is surely implied, however, when Antony laments that Cleopatra's "bosom was my crownet, my chief end" (IV.xii.27). But our attention is directed less toward the equation of Cleopatra with the true crown of life and with God —"man's chief end"—than toward the range of implications—not only sensual satisfaction but also nourishment, rest, and above all softness—underlying Shakespeare's choice of "bosom." Though *Othello* is less explicitly concerned with "the moral laws of nature" than either *King Lear* or *Macbeth*, they are, nevertheless, an omnipresent background to the play. The passage cited is almost unique in *Antony and Cleopatra*. Therein lies a major difference.

The kind of extended background that we are discussing may, however, take other forms than specific references to a metaphysical system. Cleopatra says of Antony:

> He was dispos'd to mirth, but on the sudden
> A Roman thought hath struck him.

> (I.ii.86-87)

"These strong Egyptian fetters I must break," he echoes in the same scene (I.ii.120). In her monument Cleopatra resolves to die "after the high Roman fashion" (IV.xv.87). These and similar allusions imply a contrast between two ways of life that opens endless vistas into two fundamental aspects of human nature itself. It is tempting to pursue these, as students of the play have done. But Shakespeare does not really develop this contrast as a means of organizing his play (consider, for example, the "Egyptian" episode on Pompey's galley), nor does he work it out in explicit statements or even in sustained imagery. If we develop casual allusions in the play into a view of polarities in man, we are relying upon our own imagination, not Shakespeare's.

Even less needs to be said of Coriolanus. Menenius Agrippa's pretty tale how "all the body's members / Rebell'd against the belly" (I.i.99-100) seems to open up Shakespeare's favorite theme of the consequences of civil strife. Throughout the play, however, Patricians and Plebeians alike are governed by political expediency, and, except tangentially in one or two remarks by Coriolanus, there is no appeal to principles of conduct. Coriolanus is concerned with adapting his course of action, as befits the inordinate self-love which is his tragic flaw, to his own nature, not to Nature. The impending downfall of Rome is seen as retribution visited upon the Tribunes and their dupes, not as potentially the destruction of European civilization that it would have entailed. There is no attempt whatever to establish all that Rome stood for as implicit in the action of the play. Bradley was surely right in noting that "the forces that meet" in most of the great tragedies "stretch far beyond the little group of figures and the tiny tract of space and time in which they appear" but that "of this effect there is very little in Coriolanus."[2] The play is the weaker for its absence.

A third weakness has a far more serious effect upon our reaction to the plays. What interests us about Hamlet or Othello or Macbeth or Lear is primarily their inner life of the mind. But the dramatic development that reached its climax in the complex growth and decay of characters in *King Lear* reached another peak in *Macbeth* and then ended. Antony or Coriolanus is the same man at the end of the play as at the beginning, and we know him only from without. Compare, for example, Antony with Othello. We watch Othello fall

[2]*Coriolanus*, The British Academy Shakespeare Lecture No. 2 (New York, 1912), p. 4.

into Iago's trap, abuse and kill Desdemona, and then commit suicide. But we trace with him every reaction of his mind as he succumbs to doubt and self-deceit and finally to a monstrous illusion as to his duty. We also suffer with him the agony of destroyed self-confidence and hope. We are told at the beginning of the play that Antony is "a strumpet's fool" (l. 13), and we watch him act like one throughout the play, with occasional periods of attention to his own interest. In death as in life he is still Cleopatra's toy. The understanding of himself that he displays in his outburst to Scarus (IV.xii) is only more extended, not more penetrating, than what he says in the second scene of the play. In similar fashion, the opening speeches about Coriolanus establish him as proud, and Tullus Aufidius is still describing him in the same terms at the end of the play. The characters of Antony and Coriolanus are static and are established initially as postulates of the play. They are revealed in action, but they do not develop or degenerate through action, though Antony loses his judgment under the stress of defeat. (I think that Cleopatra, too, remains the same, though she is a more complicated problem, to be discussed after analysis of the play.) We cannot say of these, moreover, as we can of many Greek plays, that we are dealing only with the outcome of a series of events and that the character is therefore portrayed in the state at which he has finally arrived—that Antony is analogous in being passion's slave to the Othello who kills Desdemona or that Coriolanus is like the bewildered and overly proud Brutus of events just preceding Philippi. For both plays tell a complete story involving a considerable period of time and a complicated series of loosely connected events—more time and events than *Othello* and more events, at least, than *Macbeth*.

Character, moreover, is revealed in these plays by devices external to the hero. Those used are standard parts of Shakespeare's dramatic technique. Antony and Cleopatra are both labeled before they first appear, and their acts are subject to a running commentary by others, most notably Enobarbus but including even Octavius and Pompey. Enobarbus' death is simply his final comment upon his master, and so, apparently, is that of Eros. But what does it mean, and how are we to reconcile the two? One difficulty is that the implications of words and deeds are not always consistent. Being provided no insight into the hero's own mind by which to test or interpret what others say and do, we are left confused as to what interpretation Shakespeare wished us to place upon Antony's death, and we are even more puzzled about Cleopatra's. We sorely miss the careful soliloquies and asides of earlier plays and the revelation of motives contained in them. There are more of these devices, however, than one recalls after even a careful reading. Their ineffectiveness is, of course, related to the lack of inner life, whether as cause or effect one can only guess. There is only one soliloquy in *Coriolanus*.[3]

Coriolanus, however, makes brilliant use of character contrast in establishing Menenius Agrippa as a moral norm and voice of wisdom. But Volumnia is its real triumph. She has made her son what he is, and her disapproval of his excesses is therefore doubly meaningful. Shakespeare needed only to have Coriolanus underscore her role, as he does: "I muse my mother / Does not approve me further" (III.ii.7-8). This remark is part of an aside (or a speech tantamount to an aside, though a noble is present), one of several such which occur at crucial points in the play and provide us with more genuine self-revelation by Coriolanus than by Antony. But even his soliloquy at Antium (IV.iv) comments on his past acts rather than revealing an inner struggle. Only by implication does it point out how unnatural is his course of action.

Granted such methods of character portrayal and such static characters, it is almost surprising that Shakespeare still preserves much of the formula developed for the tragedies of moral choice. Each of these plays involves a crucial choice by the hero at the climax of the play; *Coriolanus* adds a second at the end of the play as outcome of the first. In each play there is an alignment of characters on both sides of the question to be decided, and the question is elaborately posed. But there are new elements in the choice itself. It can no longer determine the hero's fundamental alignment with the forces of good and evil, for that is already determined and, with it, the ends toward which his life is directed. Cleopatra is Antony's chief end from first to last, and Coriolanus has been bred for military prowess and the consulship—not in themselves false goals. The choices that determine the outcome of the plays involve only means: how to preserve the military control which is necessary to Antony's

3Ibid., pp. 5-6.

possession of Cleopatra; how to campaign for the consulship. Both choices have moral implications, but they are not essentially moral. Only when Coriolanus must decide between achieving his revenge and preserving his country does the choice become one of ends conceived in moral terms—and then Coriolanus seems to yield rather because he cannot disobey his mother than because he is convinced by her moral arguments. All this is not to say that the choices are necessarily less effective dramatically. That in *Antony and Cleopatra* fails because the exposition of the play has prepared us for a more fundamental and more difficult choice between Cleopatra and something that we might call Rome or duty or even Antony's better self. But this choice is almost ignored; we learn of it incidentally in a conversation between Octavius and his sister (III.vi). The choice whether to fight by sea or land, though it is elaborately developed (III.vii-x) and given a climactic position in the play, is in fact an anticlimax; and it seems merely another episode in the play, which lacks a true dramatic climax and becomes merely a series of events. The choice in *Coriolanus*, on the other hand, involves a genuine inner conflict between the hero's knowledge of himself and his utter dependence upon his mother for moral support. It leads not to a decisive act but to a decisive failure to follow the course of action chosen. As such, it is novel and dramatically interesting. It also provides a strong and effective climax to the play. The two plays both differ from the other tragedies of moral choice, therefore, but not because their variations upon the formula necessarily deprive it of dramatic impact. They differ because the choice is not fundamental to a dramatic action centered primarily within the soul of the hero and involving a reversal in his character as well as, ultimately, in his external fortunes. In these plays the reversal is only in the hero's fortunes.

Antony and Cleopatra and *Coriolanus* are alike—to summarize what has been said—because they themselves represent a reversal in Shakespeare's dramatic development. The falling off in dramatic power is surely related to a change in dramatic technique. In the preceding tragedies Shakespeare had developed a carefully organized plot to present a hero whose inner conflict was related to the laws of Nature and of Heaven itself. In his sin he opposed what was good in himself and therefore all that was ultimately good—wife, family, friends, king, universe, and God himself. In these two plays Nature and God have disappeared; so has the hero's desire for another and better way of life. He is still the center of a sweeping tragedy. Half to half the world is opposed, and he is the sole question. But only the world is opposed.

Granted, however, that *Antony and Cleopatra* and *Coriolanus* have interesting characteristics in common, the fact remains that they are fundamentally different plays. It is high time to examine them individually and to place the emphasis upon what Shakespeare accomplished rather than upon what he did not try to do.

Antony and Cleopatra was probably produced early in 1607. If so, it perhaps followed *Macbeth* by about a year and preceded *Coriolanus* by about the same interval. The best clue to Shakespeare's interest is the closing speech assigned to "Caesar"—that is, of course, Octavius Caesar. For our purposes it must be read in the light of the summary speeches that preceded it in Shakespeare's dramatic development. At the end of *Macbeth* Malcolm is concerned to reward those who have aided him, call home the exiles, punish the guilty, imply a verdict upon the "dead butcher and his fiend-like queen," and restore to Scotland a rule of order and divine grace. Even at the end of *Timon of Athens*, which may have preceded *Antony and Cleopatra* (though E. K. Chambers places it with *Coriolanus*), Alcibiades passes judgment upon Timon and promises to heal the corruption of Athens. Octavius' interest is very different. He first attends to a necessary chore and clears the stage of corpses. Then he continues:

> She shall be buried by her Antony;
> No grave upon the earth shall clip in it
> A pair so famous. High events as these
> Strike those that make them; and their story is
> No less in pity than his glory which
> Brought them to be lamented. Our army shall
> In solemn show attend this funeral;
> And then to Rome. Come, Dolabella, see
> High order in this great solemnity.

> (V.ii.361-369)

Earlier Octavius had lamented Antony's greatness and left the only moral judgment to Maecenas: "His taints and honours / Wag'd equal with him" (V.i.30-31). Now he neither establishes his authority in Egypt nor judges the dead lovers. What he does say, in effect, is this: They are unique in their fame. Such important events affect even those who cause them. Their story is as pitiful as my achievement is glorious. Then he gives orders that their funeral shall be worthy of their fame. The entire emphasis is upon the fame of the lovers and their pitiful story—for I take Shakespeare to intend that our pity should be equal in quantity to our estimate of Augustus Caesar's glory, not that we should think Octavius' bragging ill-timed, though even his boast implies that the greatness of his conquest derived from the greatness of the conquered. In the final words of his play, therefore, Shakespeare directs our attention simply to the story of famous lovers whose piteous overthrow he has narrated. He gives us no hint of any thesis or any purpose that has ordered his telling of the story. He neither calls them dead lechers nor implies that for their love the world was well lost. Their story is its own justification and its own reward.

This final emphasis is a clue not only to Shakespeare's interest but also to his dramatic method. The episodic nature of the play has already been mentioned. Its forty-two scenes (to accept the arrangement of the new Arden edition, the Folio text being without scene divisions) are unique in Shakespeare and fortunately rare in Elizabethan drama. But modern scene divisions as such are meaningless in terms of the Elizabethan theater and should be minimized in performances today. What really counts is that many of the snippets of dialogue marked off by subsequent editors actually indicate an episode or a bit of information without close relation to what precedes or follows, so that the flow of action is fragmented and the spectator is asked to shift his attention too often. Shakespeare tried to crowd too many interesting details into his play because they were in his source, not because they were vital to an established theme. It is in this deference to the source narrative that the play really reverts to the technique of the tragical histories.

It was apparently Shakespeare's interest in the story for its own sake that led to still other resemblances to tragical history. The most obvious of these is a tendency to pursue side issues. The scene in Pompey's galley (II.vii) perhaps serves some useful purpose in characterizing the triumvirate and the world in which they operate. A director can even stage it to show Octavius coolly standing aside from the others. But mostly it is just a rousing scene. Menas' proposal that he cut the cable and carry off the guests, since it is rejected, has nothing to do with the conflict betwen Antony and Octavius. In that it presents Octavius and his party as singularly imprudent and the other Romans as ready, like Antony, for drunken revelry, it runs counter to the main impression established by the play. But Shakespeare even goes on to indicate that, after Pompey refuses his offer, Menas leaves him as one too stupid to deserve a follower. All this is interesting but irrelevant.

The scene in which Ventidius refuses to pursue his victory over the Parthians lest he offend Antony (III.i) can be defended. It is a cynical commentary upon the character and motives of both Octavius and Antony, and it shows how the pettiness of leaders frustrates the virtues of their followers. In the former effect, however, it undercuts Enobarbus' death, and the latter point is made repeatedly in subsequent scenes. As an example of political acumen it doubtless interested Shakespeare and therefore went into the play. The death of Enobarbus, though apparently intended to strengthen our sympathy for Antony, seems to be developed for its own sake. He tells us in one scene (IV.vi) that he will seek a ditch in which to die, apparently of a broken heart. The point has been made quite adequately, but later (IV.ix) two soldiers watch him lament his revolt against Antony and die. This scene, in which nothing else occurs, is one of too many short episodes that follow one another too rapidly.

Another of these episodes is the departure of "the god Hercules, whom Antony lov'd" (IV.iii.16). Music is heard, and a trio of expository soldiers tells the audience what is happening. As one in a series of omens of disaster like those in *Julius Caesar* or *Macbeth*, it would have been strikingly effective. It might also have occurred during a scene depicting Antony's downfall. As it stands, it is merely a picturesque but isolated detail, and it illustrates another weakness sometimes encountered in the tragical histories—a tendency to include vivid or picturesque details in the source without really forming them into any line of action.

It is possible, however, to exaggerate the extent to which the episodic development of the play parallels the narrative techniques of the looser tragedies of the age. They do present, after all, a rush of action; and events, though sometimes unrelated, come thick and fast. In all too many scenes of *Antony and Cleopatra* nothing whatever happens. People merely talk about what is happening or about each other. Much of the fragmentation of the play results, in fact, from excessive resort to purely expository devices that are, in themselves, good and are used repeatedly in the great tragedies. If Shakespeare wants to make a point, he throws in a short scene in which several characters talk briefly for the instruction of the audience. So far, so good. But then another such scene follows, and another!

Take, for example, Act III. In the first scene, already alluded to, Ventidius explains that he has defeated the Parthians and killed the king's son but will not advance farther. In the next scene Agrippa and Enobarbus discuss the Triumvirs, mostly Lepidus; then Octavius and Antony say farewell, to the accompaniment of asides intended to establish the hollowness of their affection. In the third scene a messenger describes Octavia to Antony. In the fourth we learn that Octavius and Antony are preparing for war, and Octavia leaves Antony to attempt a reconciliation—the first episode in the act that genuinely advances the action of the play. The next scene is purely expository. We learn that Lepidus has been disposed of and Antony's navy is prepared to move against Octavius Caesar. In following scenes we hear that Antony has returned to Egypt, and we are necessarily given an account of the battle of Actium. But we do at least see Antony make his fatal decision to fight by sea. For long stretches, however, the play might be described as a conversation piece, though much of the conversation is very good. This effect cannot result from a reversion to early techniques. Every one of the expository devices used in these scenes had done excellent service in the preceding tragedies. Shakespeare's excessive reliance upon them here can be ascribed only to his failure to work out a sound dramatic structure for his play—that is, to haste or to fatigue.

A sound dramatic structure in the fashion of the mature tragedies would have required that Shakespeare narrow the action to a single theme—say the destruction of a great soldier by sensual love—and then select episodes that would pose the issue, force Antony to a decisive choice and a decisive act, and illustrate the degeneration of his character and his fortunes under Cleopatra's spell. A moral judgment would inevitably be involved in the choice of a controlling theme. But such a play would have to omit much of Plutarch's account. Worse still, it would not be the tragical history of Antony *and* Cleopatra. The play does look, however, very much as though Shakespeare had started to write such a tragedy and for some reason had shifted to a narrative approach, though retaining much of the basic pattern of his tragedies of moral choice. At any rate, the guidelines such as Shakespeare provided in all his tragedies are in this play as likely to mislead the audience as to aid it in understanding the play. Perhaps the metaphor would be improved by saying that he provided guideposts but did not line them up.

The dramatic exposition sets up a perfectly clear issue. Philo's first words tell us that Antony's dotage "O'erflows the measure"—that is, that his love has passed the limits of reason and become a passion subordinating "his captain's heart" to "a gipsy's lust" (ll. 1-10). These terms will do very well to describe the conflict posed—between Antony's captain's heart and his lust for a gipsy. Shakespeare is using a favorite device of his; so Antony promptly illustrates the point made. A messenger from Rome arrives, but lust—described in matchless poetry, though the imagery clearly equates Antony as he is with beasts as opposed to men—controls the captain's heart and the messenger goes unheard. Cleopatra is even used to urge Antony to hear the messenger and thereby emphasize his dotage. This Antony, in short, is not Antony the reasonable creature and captain—as Philo explains. In the next scene Antony states the choice before him even more effectively himself, a messenger being used once more as a symbol that equates his duty to himself as a man with his duty to Rome. This time Rome wins; and the battle within seems not yet lost:

> Let him appear.
> These strong Egyptian fetters I must break,
> Or lose myself in dotage.
>
> (I.ii.119-121)

Antony resolves on Rome and breaks the news to Cleopatra in the next scene. But the odds are still with her, as his final words to her show:

> Our separation so abides and flies,
> That thou, residing here, goes yet with me,
> And I, hence fleeting, here remain with thee.
>
> (I.iii.102-104)

287

The next scene is devoted to establishing the Roman Antony. For the recital of his faults by Octavius, his rival, in effect diminishes them in our eyes, and we are strongly impressed later in the scene by Octavius' recital of Antony's achievements and his obvious need of Antony's help to meet Pompey. Lest we be convinced that Antony will become true Roman, the next scene shows Alexas presenting to Cleopatra a pearl that he has sent, with a significant message:

> "Good friend," quoth he,
> "Say the firm Roman to great Egypt sends
> This treasure of an oyster; at whose foot,
> To mend the petty present, I will piece
> Her opulent throne with kingdoms. All the East,
> Say thou, shall call her mistress."
>
> (I.v.42-47)

The strongly sensual, not to say sexual, atmosphere of this scene, like the soothsaying that opens the second scene, establishes all too clearly the lure that recalls the not-so-firm Roman to Egypt. Lest we miss the point, in another purely expository scene Pompey establishes the strength of the temptation:

> but let us rear
> The higher our opinion, that our stirring
> Can from the lap of Egypt's widow pluck
> The ne'er lust-wearied Antony.
>
> (II.i.35-38)

Throughout these scenes Cleopatra is established as a clever, infinitely varied, and alluring woman. But she is in no sense developed as a protagonist of stature equal to Antony's. She is the tempter, he the tempted; and our attention is focused upon him by the devices that Shakespeare customarily employs. Until Antony's suicide—or, at any rate, until his final defeat—Cleopatra's role is analogous to that of Lady Macbeth. It is more protracted because the conflict never really comes to decision; after Macbeth kills Duncan, Lady Macbeth has accomplished her role as temptress, and Shakespeare must find a new dramatic function for her. It is a very minor one, and she drops from sight. A similar problem may very well have led Shakespeare to alter the design of his play. Cleopatra could not be allowed to drop from sight; so the original design was abandoned. For the conflict between the Roman captain's heart and the gypsy's lust is not brought to the decisive dramatic climax for which the background has been so carefully laid. We see Antony accept Octavia as his wife, but the effect is somewhat lessened by the short scene with the soothsayer (II.iii). Shakespeare's attention is distracted by a detail that must have interested him strongly, since he alluded to it in *Macbeth* (III.i.56-57): Antony's demon—"that thy spirit which keeps thee"—is noble and courageous when he is alone but near Caesar "Becomes a fear" (ll. 19-22). But this is not the real point of the scene. In a short soliloquy Antony admits that the soothsayer has spoken true and concludes:

> I will to Egypt;
> And though I make this marriage for my peace,
> I' th' East my pleasure lies.
>
> (II.iii.38-40)

Later we hear Octavius tell his sister that Antony has gone to Egypt and has given Cleopatra the kingdoms that he promised her (III.vi). This act is indeed decisive in its effect upon Antony's fortunes, and Shakespeare's handling of events is quite adequate for a tragic narrative of the love of Antony and Cleopatra. But it is not adequate to the dramatic preparation, nor to the relationship between Antony and Octavia that is established in several scenes. Above all, it cannot, so soft-pedaled, provide an adequate climax for the play.

The climax Shakespeare apparently tried to develop in his treatment of the battle of Actium. Here he used the technique of the tragedies of moral choice, with the fundamental difference that the choice involves a matter of tactics—whether to fight by land or sea —and not the basic orientation of a human soul toward good or evil. The choice is of means, not ends, and results from the perversion of Antony's moral nature instead of determining it.

The choice to fight by sea occurs in the very next scene (III.vii) after we learn that Antony has returned to Cleopatra, though, in the interval, they have come from Egypt to Greece. Shakespeare uses the same technique as in *Macbeth* and implies that a heated dispute has already occurred. Cleopatra enters threatening vengeance upon Enobarbus because he has opposed her coming to the war, and Enobarbus tells her roundly that her presence will deprive Antony of heart and brain and time. Antony and Canidius enter talking of Caesar's speed. Antony announces that he will fight by sea, and Cleopatra chimes in, "By sea! what else?" (l. 29), in a way indicating that she had hoped the matter was settled. The forces for and against are now lined up in morality-play fashion: on the side of wisdom Enobarbus, Canidius, and later a soldier to speak for the army; on the side of lust and folly Cleopatra. Antony reaffirms his decision to fight by sea and the choice is made. Canidius is used, like Kent in *King Lear*, to make sure that no one misses the point:

> *Sold.* By Hercules, I think I am i' th' right.
> *Can.* Soldier, thou art; but his whole action grows
> Not in the power on't. So our leader's led,
> And we are women's men.
>
> (III.vii.68-71)

As they tell how first the Egyptians and then Antony fled from the battle, Enobarbus, Scarus, and Canidius keep reminding us, by imagery—"we have kiss'd away / Kingdoms" (III.x.7-8)—as well as by explicit statement, that Antony has lost because of his infatuation for Cleopatra. He is "The noble ruin of her magic": "Had our general / Been what he knew himself, it had gone well" (III.x.19, 26-27). When Cleopatra comes to him, Antony both confesses that he has been ruined by complete subjection to her and demonstrates, as he does so, the extent of his infatuation:

> Fall not a tear, I say; one of them rates
> All that is won and lost. Give me a kiss.
> Even this repays me.
>
> (III.xi.69-71)

It is these speeches that give to the choice and the resulting sea fight a moral dimension that justifies Shakespeare's technique, which here operates at its highest economy and poetic effectiveness and makes these scenes acceptable as a climax of the play. The choice to fight by sea has been one between the captain's heart and the gypsy's lust, and the gypsy has won.

But the reversal is merely in Antony's fortunes; it is not dependent upon, or even related to, an interior change such as that which gives real significance to Macbeth's agreement to murder Duncan or even Brutus' decision to kill Caesar. And the result for Shakespeare's portrayal of Antony is all-important. He is, in fact, a reversal from the Shakespearean to the normal Elizabethan tragic hero. A tragic flaw he has throughout the play. But there is no true *hamartia* or tragic error as opposed to a habit of error, and the play has not one reversal but several, all indecisive and on the surface, because Antony's fall is really determined from the first moment of the play. But, after all, critical theory required only that a hero fall from high fortune to disaster. Have we any right to expect that Shakespeare, having for a time transcended the contemporary notion of tragedy, should invariably continue to do so? I think not.

The remainder of Antony's story oscillates among moods of assumed courage, hope, and despair; and the second defection of the Egyptian navy is a distinct anticlimax. More interesting than the confused scenes of challenges and fighting and revelry, at least from the present point of view, is a fundamental ambiguity in Shakespeare's treatment of Antony. I am not concerned, of course, with interpreting the play but rather with suggesting why contradictory interpretations exist. For various devices are used to interpret Antony to the audience, and they seem to work at cross purposes. Enobarbus' role is consistent enough. He is used to say that Antony "would make his will / Lord of his reason" (III.xiii.3-4) and that Caesar has "subdu'd / His judgement too" (ll. 36-37). In the whipping of Thyreus this faulty judgment results in a flagrantly unjust act, and Enobarbus glosses:

> To be furious,
> Is to be frighted out of fear; and in that mood
> The dove will peck the estridge; and I see still,
> A diminution in our captain's brain
> Restores his heart. When valour preys on reason,
> It eats the sword it fights with. I will seek
> Some way to leave him.
>
> (III.xiii.195-201)

Though Maecenas repeats this verdict in the next scene (IV.i), it is Enobarbus who really confirms it by leaving Antony. But, as Shakespeare knew, and as anyone able to read him adequately knows, there is more to life than cold rationality. We seldom love the sinner because it is our duty in charity to do so even while we hate the sin; more often we respond to the human warmth and the willingness to take risks that may lead to sin but must also enter into human love or bravery. Mary Magdalene is the eternal symbol of this paradox. The Antony who could love Cleopatra enough to ignore Actium could love Enobarbus enough to forgive desertion. So he sent Enobarbus' treasure after him. To emphasize the human greatness of Antony, Shakespeare develops carefully, though rapidly, Enobarbus' lesser tragedy of conflict between head and heart, though we might well be spared, I think, the improbability of watching him die, apparently of a broken heart (IV.ix). The finality and the moral judgment of his resolve to "seek / Some ditch wherein to die" (IV. vi.37-38) are all that we need.

We are quite prepared, with Enobarbus, to rate the tragic hero Antony above the coldly efficient Octavius. But our reaction is badly confused by what follows. Cleopatra has seemed willing enough to bargain with Octavius (III.xiii.73-85). Antony, enraged by the second desertion of her fleet, resolves in anguish:

> The witch shall die.
> To the young Roman boy she hath sold me, and I fall
> Under this plot. She dies for't. Eros, ho!
>
> (IV.xii.47-49)

Cleopatra's reaction is to take refuge in the monument and send word to Antony that she has killed herself. He then resolves to die:

> I will o'ertake thee, Cleopatra, and
> Weep for my pardon.
>
> (IV.xiv.44-45)

But she is not dead, and Antony needs no pardon, except perhaps for suspecting her of double-dealing (Shakespeare is careful to tell us later that his suspicions were unfounded; see IV.xiv.122). In death as in life Antony is "a strumpet's fool," and one might expect the irony to be underscored by some comment (though, unless I have overlooked something, it is not). The circumstances therefore divest Antony's suicide of the full effect it might have in building him up as a tragic hero. The manner of his death is positively unheroic, and Shakespeare drives the point home. After a reverie on the erotic pleasure of the hereafter, Antony summons Eros and continues:

> Since Cleopatra died
> I have liv'd in such dishonour that the gods
> Detest my baseness. I, that with my sword

Quarter'd the world, and o'er green Neptune's back
With ships made cities, condemn myself to lack
The courage of a woman; less noble mind
Than she which by her death our Caesar tells,
"I am conqueror of myself."

(IV.xiv.55-62)

All this leads, however, not to Antony's using his sword to show that he does not lack the courage of a woman but to his ordering Eros to do the job for him. Eros is made of sterner stuff than his master and shows his loyalty and devotion by choosing rather to kill himself. Here there is no ambiguity whatever about Shakespeare's intentions:

> Thrice-nobler than myself!
> Thou teachest me, O valiant Eros, what
> I should, and thou couldst not. . . .
> Come, then; and, Eros,
> Thy master dies thy scholar: to do thus
> I learn'd of thee.

(ll. 95-103)

Even a speedy and dignified death is denied Antony. Granted that Shakespeare had to keep him alive for the big scene with Cleopatra, he need not have made him almost ludicrous and implied, for good measure, that he had not really learned the lesson from Eros: "How! not dead? not dead? / The guard, ho! O, dispatch me!" (ll. 103-104).

How to reconcile the deaths of Enobarbus and Eros as messages from the dramatist to the audience I do not know. If Enobarbus' death invests Antony with tragic sympathy, that of Eros surely divests him of tragic bravery. Yet it seems perfectly obvious that from Actium on Shakespeare is trying to arouse compassion for Antony and even, despite the loss of judgment, to give him tragic stature. His last words are those of a great man, as they are some of Shakespeare's finest dramatic poetry. I can only conjecture that once again the dramatist yielded to the chronicler and that Shakespeare, perhaps in haste, became so engrossed in the details that he lost the overall pattern—the death of Eros, for example, is in itself a touching display of devotion, and Antony's admission that he needs to learn is honest and generous. Perhaps we should be grateful for these impressions and not try to unify them into a tragic hero.

With the death of Antony, the play reverts in yet another respect to the characteristics of Elizabethan narrative tragedy. For Cleopatra changes from a confusing antagonist to a more confusing tragic heroine. The placing of her subsidiary tragedy after that of Antony, which dominated the first four acts, was necessary, of course, because of the historical account, which was too well known to be trifled with. But, as we shall see, Shakespeare pursued the story for its own sake, without really clarifying the relation of Cleopatra's death to Antony's or, in fact, providing it with a clear meaning of any kind. Like Jonson in his preface to *Sejanus*, he was content with "integrity in the *Story*." In concluding with the tragic death of the antagonist, *Antony and Cleopatra* is like Marlowe's *Edward II* (ca. 1592). But Mortimer's death is merely discussed; it is not given a whole act. In the attention devoted to Cleopatra, the play is reminiscent of a much lesser tragedy than Marlowe's, namely *Locrine* (ca. 1591), which concludes with the subordinate tragedy of Sabren. Lest we accuse Shakespeare of reverting to the ways of his apprentice days, Fletcher's *Bonduca* (ca. 1613) also concludes with a subsidiary tragedy, that of Hengo, and the surrender with honors of his uncle Caratach. Bonduca is very nearly forgotten by the end of the play.

There is, to be sure, no reason why Shakespeare could not have written a joint tragedy of Antony and Cleopatra. But this would have required relating Cleopatra's fortunes to Antony as clearly as his were determined by her, and preparing early in the play for her resolution to die with Antony. This Shakespeare did not do. He wrote instead what might aptly have been called "The lamentable dotage and death of Mark Antony, with the tragical fall of amorous Cleopatra." If the reader doubts this estimate of the situation, I suggest that he witness several performances of the play and then analyze his reactions carefully before he blames his disappointment on the production.

I do not propose to argue an interpretation of the last act reserved for Cleopatra. My impressions, for what they are worth, are that she is of a piece throughout the play and gains a new role rather than a new character as she takes over the action. She would add Octavius to her collection of scalps if she could. She will bargain for an acceptable arrangement as long as that seems possible. She will die rather than be led in triumph at Rome—and no doubt slaughtered when the triumph is over. But she will die as pleasantly as possible and make a good show out of it. While the stage is hers, as when it was Antony's, she is both strumpet and queen.

Shakespeare's purpose must certainly have been to round out the traditional story rather than to develop Cleopatra into a particular kind of tragic character. I have argued that the guideposts to Antony's story are numerous but inconsistent. They may indicate haste and fatigue, change of design, or excessive preoccupation with details or any combination of these factors. The last act, in contrast, simply lacks the directives to the audience that are obviously needed. We wonder how seriously Cleopatra is trying to make terms with Caesar; whether, after Antony's death, she will "die" (V.ii.69) as Enobarbus had "seen her die twenty times upon far poorer moment" (I.ii.145-147); whether she really means her resolution to commit suicide "after the high Roman fashion." An aside or two would help us make up our minds. It is a sound principle, of course, that any statement must be taken literally in the absence of a clear directive by Shakespeare to the contrary. Cleopatra, however, has been established as a consummate and habitual actress from the first scene of the play, and we need instructions if we are to suspend our usual skepticism of her heroics. Her first reaction to Antony's death contains, moreover, an all too appropriate though indecent double meaning of the kind that Shakespeare uses elsewhere to deflate the emotion of a potentially tragic situation.[4]

One interpretation, in particular, though it has been ingeniously argued,[5] seems to me to be untenable for want of an aside. The little scene in which Seleucus reveals to Octavius Caesar that Cleopatra has hidden half her treasure and is roundly upbraided by her for doing so (V.ii) might well be playacting to fool Caesar while she prepares means for death. Her anger is neither more nor less convincing than many of her earlier tantrums. But it would have been perfectly simple for Shakespeare to give either her or Seleucus an aside; or she had plenty of opportunities to bid Seleucus, like the asp, call Caesar "ass / Unpolicied." No tenable explanation—not even the most serious charges of carelessness that I or others have leveled at Shakespeare—

4See IV.xv.63-66. Cf. *Merchant of Venice* II.viii.12-24, as preparation for III.i.
5*Antony and Cleopatra*, ed. M. R. Ridley, Arden edn. (London, 1954), pp. xlv-xlvii.

will enable us to assume that he inserted so elaborate a stratagem into his play without labeling it. To protect herself, Cleopatra has just lied to Antony at the cost of his life. Why should we not assume that she is also lying to Octavius? Or rather—since we are talking about dramatic technique—Shakespeare must surely expect us so to assume.

It is all too obvious, I fear, that *Antony and Cleopatra* is not one of my favorite Shakespearean plays. I trust that I can respond to its brilliant scenes and its purple passages. I can appreciate even more deeply its simple or even commonplace remarks that derive an incredible poignancy from their context—

> Unarm, Eros; the long day's task is done,
> And we must sleep.
>
> (IV.xiv.35-36)

But the play's the thing. As a play, and especially as the art of a playwright, *Antony and Cleopatra* seems to me far inferior to *King Lear* and *Macbeth*, and I am not sure that its inferiority in quality may not be due, in part, to its trying to be like them in kind. Fewer signposts or expository scenes and more straightforward dramatizing of the story might have produced a greater play. For it is one of the world's great stories. As such, it has much of woe or wonder. But it lacks understanding of the fundamental sort which we have come to expect in Shakespearean tragedy.

Our best approach to *Coriolanus*, as to *Antony and Cleopatra*, is through the concluding speech. It is the flattest to be found in Shakespeare's tragedies, even if we include in the final summary, as I think we must, what the two Lords say:

> *1. Lord.*   Bear from hence his body;
> And mourn you for him. Let him be regarded
> As the most noble corse that ever herald
> Did follow to his urn.
> *2. Lord.*   His own impatience
> Takes from Aufidius a great part of blame.
> Let's make the best of it.
> *Auf.*   My rage is gone,
> And I am struck with sorrow. Take him up.
> Help, three o' th' chiefest soldiers; I'll be one.
> Beat thou the drum, that it speak mournfully.
> Trail your steel pikes. Though in this city he

Hath widow'd and unchilded many a one,
Which to this hour bewail the injury,
Yet he shall have a noble memory.
Assist.

(V.vi.143-156)

This amounts to saying that Coriolanus is noble, but that Aufidius cannot be blamed for killing him; that even his enemies will remember him as great. It is significant in two respects. Once again, as in *Antony and Cleopatra,* our attention is wholly centered upon the individual character. No larger context of meaning is even suggested. But even the implied judgment of Coriolanus is strangely limited. He will leave a noble memory, but we are not told why —except that he has been a notable killer. The tone of the speech is almost negative, as though Shakespeare himself could not find a simple formula by which to indicate his hero's claim to fame. Granted, moreover, that the summary statements by which we remember Othello or Hamlet are not in the final speeches, there are no memorable descriptions of Coriolanus during the final episode. This is, I think, symptomatic of the effect that the play makes upon us. In contrast to *Antony and Cleopatra,* it is far more carefully constructed. Shakespeare must have expended considerably more pains upon planning it. But, again in contrast to its predecessor, it does not arouse our imagination to the highest pitch, and we must doubt that it aroused Shakespeare's.

The dramatic exposition is a sound introduction to the play. It establishes six characters whose interrelationship furnishes the action, and it amply prepares for the crucial struggle over the consulship. As the play opens, two citizens stigmatize Coriolanus as proud. As for his prowess in war, "Though soft-conscienc'd men can be content to say it was for his country, he did it to please his mother, and to be partly proud; which he is, even to the altitude of his virtue" (I.i.37-41). We should normally expect Coriolanus to appear next and illustrate what has been said. Instead Menenius Agrippa tells his fable and becomes a voice of wisdom and a moral norm to be used in evaluating Coriolanus' subsequent actions. He is one of Shakespeare's better characterizations—done from the heart as well as the head. Then Coriolanus appears, and we judge his scorn for the people and his splenetic way of putting it not only in the light of their remarks, for they are doubtless prejudiced, but in contrast with Menenius Agrippa's wise and calm and highly successful approach. Then we hear briefly that Tribunes have been granted the people and war has begun. Finally the Tribunes appear. Shakespeare's technique of handling them is interesting. In destroying the hero by working upon the pride which is his chief character flaw, they correspond roughly to Iago. They are developed in the same fashion, except that the villain's soliloquy now becomes the villains' dialogue. Their first effort further characterizes Coriolanus and, on the principle that men ordinarily suspect others of their own vices, shows them to be politically astute schemers. All together, the first scene is a masterful job of exposition that achieves two effective variations upon Shakespeare's usual methods.

As usual, the second scene introduces a different plot element in the play. Tullus Aufidius is not only general of the Volscians but sworn, if ever they meet, to fight Coriolanus to the death. No real characterization of him is attempted here or elsewhere in the play.

In the third scene we learn how Coriolanus has become the man that he is. First his mother, Volumnia, expounds her ideals of blood and bravery. How violent and unfeminine they are, and the kind of rearing that her son must have had, we gather as Virgilia, his wife, recoils in anguish from all the talk of blood. Shakespeare's best touch, however, is Valeria's tale how "the father's son" worried a gilded butterfly and tore it to pieces in a rage (ll. 62-71). Volumnia comments sagely, "One on 's father's moods," and Valeria clucks approvingly, "Indeed, la, 'tis a noble child" (ll. 72-73). It will not be these ladies' fault if the boy is not as fierce and insensitive as his father. Virgilia is less approving: "A crack" (that is, a little imp), she comments (l. 74). The emphasis of the scene is not upon father and son, however, but upon Volumnia. It confirms what the citizen implied. Volumnia has made Coriolanus what he is, and her approval of his exploits is what matters most of all to him. We suspect the bond by which he is tied to her.

So far the exposition has been masterful, and the play has moved rapidly. But we now follow Coriolanus to war through six scenes of chronicle-history narrative at its least exciting. They explain why Rome owes Coriolanus much and how he earned his name. They include one of Shakespeare's best character touches—Coriolanus' inability to remember the name of his former host (I.ix.82-90). They show another aspect of Coriolanus' pride—his refusal to accept praise or to hear his achievements discussed. But, if I may judge by my own reactions, in performance they slow down the play intolerably, and it never regains the momentum that it loses during these scenes. A tenth scene, in which Tullus Aufidius vents his hatred of Coriolanus at length, still further retards the play.

The basic trouble with these scenes is that, except for the details noted, they are not subordinated to the design of the play as a whole, nor are they related to any larger meaning. To show that the child is father to the man, and that character is warped when the mother is father to the child, is to hold the mirror up to nature. We are interested. To narrate one battle scene after another in which the Romans beat Volscians of whom we have hardly heard outside of this play is not, in its effect at least, to revert to chronicle-history technique. It is rather to descend into irrelevance. The battles of *Henry VI* involved the ancestors of Shakespeare's audience and determined his own way of life, as well as ours. If the fighting was part of a larger pattern of conflict, as it was, it had meaning beyond itself. In contrast, we simply do not care who thwacked whom before Corioli. We should be quite willing to take on trust the information that Coriolanus was a great hero who had done much for Rome and deserved honor. Two lines would name him Coriolanus. Then we could get on to watching human character—our own included—in action. The contrast in dramatic artistry between the three opening scenes and these seven I cannot explain, except to assume that genius has its mysteries of failure as well as of achievement.

I suspect, moreover, that Shakespeare himself felt these scenes awkward. For the second act opens with a kind of second exposition that establishes the background for the real conflict of the play by taking us back, in effect, to the first scenes. The dialogue between Menenius and the Tribunes once again brands Coriolanus as proud and wonderfully enriches our acquaintance—one is tempted to say friendship—with Menenius Agrippa. It also stigmatizes the Tribunes for the villains that they are. The conversation between Menenius and the ladies might well have included all that really matters in the war scenes. It makes two points of importance. Menenius by implication adds his voice to those accusing Coriolanus of pride: "he has more cause to be proud" (ll. 161-162). As Volumnia gloats over every wound, she reveals that she has designed her son for the consulship: "There will be large cicatrices to show the people, when he shall stand for his place" (ll. 163-165). Later she speaks directly to Coriolanus:

> I have liv'd
> To see inherited my very wishes
> And the buildings of my fancy; only
> There's one thing wanting, which I doubt not but
> Our Rome will cast upon thee.
>
> (II.i.214-218)

To which he replies ominously:

> Know, good mother,
> I had rather be their servant in my way
> Than sway with them in theirs.
>
> (ll. 218-220)

This speech prepares for what is technically the most interesting part of the scene, a dialogue in which the Tribunes plan the destruction of Coriolanus. In fundamental method it is exactly like the soliloquies in which Cassius tells the audience how Brutus' "honourable metal may be wrought" (I.ii.311-326); or Iago, how Othello may "be led by th' nose" (I.iii.389-410); or Edmund, how he will practice on his brother's "foolish honesty" (I.ii.195-200); or Lady Macbeth, how she will chastise, with the valor of her tongue, her husband into killing Duncan (I.v.16-31). But there are important differences between this passage and the others. On the debit side it occurs later in the play than any of the parallels cited. On the credit, Shakespeare takes full advantage of dialogue as opposed to soliloquy. Instead of dramatic convention we have very skillful and realistic character portrayal as the Tribunes start by describing Coriolanus' popularity and speculating that he will be consul. Then they inch their way into a scheme to destroy him, as it were testing and stimulating each other. He will destroy their power, they agree; but he will surely alienate the common people when he becomes consul. His pride may even prevent him from campaigning effectively. It will probably destroy him. They must make sure that it does. The last exchange of speeches outlines their plan to thwart him by warning the people that he is dangerous and then arousing his "soaring insolence" (l. 270), and then the Tribunes are summoned to the Capitol and to action. They go, however, not as machiavel villains but as human politicians with a little more than their fair share of pride and envy. The reader may well have winced at several passages in which I referred to them as villains—and rightly so. As figures in a dramatic formula they occupy the slot labeled "villain." As participants in the action they are merely very human characters opposing the hero. This transformation is surely one of Shakespeare's major achievements in *Coriolanus*, but he paid a heavy price for it. Our hate for a villain inevitably becomes sympathy for his victim. The less villainous Shakespeare made his antagonists, the more appealing he had to make his hero, if our sympathy was to stay with him as he erred and fell. Shakespeare's success with the Tribunes is, I am sure, part of his failure with Coriolanus.

Lest we miss the point of the scenes during which Coriolanus wins and then loses the consulship, Shakespeare introduces, at the beginning of the next scene, still more direct exposition to the audience from the mouths of two protatic officers. They summarize the dilemma of the people: "he seeks their hate with greater devotion than they can render it him. . . . But he hath so planted his honours in their eyes and his actions in their hearts that for their tongues to be silent and not confess so much were a kind of ingrateful injury" (II.ii.20-35). They also isolate exactly the error into which Coriolanus' pride has driven him: "Now, to seem to affect the malice and displeasure of the people is as bad as that which he dislikes, to flatter them for their love" (ll. 23-25).

The following sequence of events is, on the whole, clear both in what happens and in the guidance that Shakespeare gives us as to how we should interpret it. Coriolanus refuses to hear his virtues recited and leaves. He is recalled to solicit the people's voices, and Shakespeare establishes showing his wounds as a symbol of his willingness to conform to custom and to behave reasonably. Menenius Agrippa makes clear to us that their request is reasonable:

> Pray you, go fit you to the custom and
> Take to you, as your predecessors have,
> Your honour with your form.

> (II.ii.146-148)

301

But Coriolanus persists in his refusal, and the Tribunes alone remain to conclude, quite reasonably, that his behavior shows "how he intends to use the people" (l. 159). When Coriolanus appears in the next scene, Menenius Agrippa is still trying to make him behave reasonably and criticizes his untactful words with increasing sharpness. Alone with the people, he grumbles to himself and insults them even as he goes through the motions of seeking votes. Nevertheless, he is acclaimed consul. On the crucial issue of showing his wounds he remains adamant; as the citizens later testify, no man saw them. The way is now clear for the Tribunes, who instruct the people to reverse themselves and refuse Coriolanus. The people head for the Capitol and so do the Tribunes, to take advantage of his anger.

In the next scene (III.i) Senators and Cominius join Menenius in urging Coriolanus to remain calm, as his natural indignation at the people's reversal grows into rage and leads to the most violent denunciations not only of the citizens but of the Patricians who have allowed them to gain power. But Menenius remains the center of the Patrician party during the meeting and after. He induces Coriolanus to go home and arranges for him to stand trial in the marketplace. He also pronounces an extended judgment upon Coriolanus:

> His nature is too noble for the world;
> He would not flatter Neptune for his trident,
> Or Jove for 's power to thunder. His heart's his mouth;
> What his breast forges, that his tongue must vent;
> And, being angry, does forget that ever
> He heard the name of death.
>
> (III.i.255-260)

All this is true, but it needs to be supplemented by the kind of insight that the First Officer showed. Its limitations are those of Menenius, the dramatic character, and they show that Shakespeare is as much concerned with characterization as with guiding the audience. Menenius is himself a man of sweet reasonableness and good humor, an expert at smoothing over differences. But his motives and his methods are those of expediency, and he does not really understand Coriolanus at all or he would not talk of calm and compromise. His behavior in this scene is, however, one of the best touches in the play. He parallels Coriolanus' violence with humorous annoyance, and he sounds like a man beside a boastful boy:

> *Cor.*   On fair ground
> I could beat forty of them.
> *Men.*   I could myself
> Take up a brace o' th' best of them; yea, the two tribunes.
>
> > (III.i.242-244)

He can see both sides:

> *A Patrician.*   I would they were a-bed!
> *Men.* I would they were in Tiber! What the vengeance!
> Could he not speak 'em fair?
>
> > (ll. 261-263)

He is, in fact, a much subtler and better realized character portrayal than Coriolanus—better not because he is more diversified but because we readily accept his role in the play.

Volumnia comes into her own in the following scene, as Menenius and the Senators try to prepare Coriolanus to face the people. She has a triple function. She has raised Coriolanus to be what he is, and he has been accustomed to her approval. Presumably Coriolanus understands her standards if anything! He therefore provides with his first words our best insight into his tragic blindness—his complete inability to understand compromise, or tact and moderation, even when his mother argues for them: "I muse my mother / Does not approve me further" (III.ii.7-8). If he cannot understand all her values, she fails as completely to grasp what she has made of him. The irony and the tragedy of the ensuing scene is that Coriolanus is being urged by his mother, of all people, to attempt a course of action that he is simply incapable by nature of following through, as he well knows. To grant her present request, he must destroy his real self just as surely as he must destroy himself if he yields to her later on when she pleads for Rome:

> Why did you wish me milder? Would you have me
> False to my nature? Rather say I play
> The man I am.
>
> > (III.ii.14-16)

But if he cannot be false to his own nature, neither can he stand without the force that has given him that nature. Volumnia does not overrule him by her entreaties or her arguments, good though they are;

she threatens to give him up as hopeless, turning from him as from a disobedient child,[6] and he yields at once:

> *Vol.*   ...Do as thou list.
> Thy valiantness was mine, thou suck'st it from me,
> But owe thy pride thyself.
>   *Cor.*   Pray, be content.
> Mother, I am going to the market-place;
> Chide me no more.
>
>   (III.ii.128-132)

When the test comes, Coriolanus is inevitably true to his nature rather than to his promise, and the outcome of the trial in the market-place is predetermined.

Coriolanus' last words to the people who have banished him are sincerely intended to reveal not only their error but his. They are wrong, as he asserts, to think that they can live without their defender. But he is equally wrong to think that he can live without roots in his native soil. Both parties need the security of a social structure, and a structure must have both bottom and top. There is a world elsewhere as he asserts, but it is not his.

In reviewing the sequence of events just discussed, we must arrive, I think, at several critical judgments. The basic pattern represents an interesting variation upon Shakespeare's formula of moral choice. The hero is apparently faced with a conflict between his pride and Roman custom. But later it appears that a more fundamental opposition exists between his very nature and what he must do if he is to be consul. The tension is exacerbated by a first success which is relatively easy but which proves also to be only temporary. Then Coriolanus, urged by his friends and unable to disobey his mother, chooses a course which he knows to be contrary to his own nature, though consistent with the rational morality represented by Menenius Agrippa. This is something new to Shakespeare and hard to establish dramatically. Macbeth's choice to kill Duncan is obviously wrong because it is contrary to all Nature; Coriolanus' assent is merely unwise because it is contrary to his nature. The morality-play lineup of good and bad which seemed to exist at the beginning turns out to be an illusion. Granted Coriolanus' nature, the good is bad for him,

[6]Cf. *The Tragedy of Coriolanus*, ed. John Dover Wilson (Cambridge, Eng., 1960), p. xxxii.

and he must face not only the plots of his enemies but the plans of his friends. The act which destroys him therefore results from his inability to carry out the line of conduct that he has chosen.

All this is subtler and potentially more interesting than the pattern of *Othello* or *Macbeth*. But there are several weaknesses in execution. First, the basic pattern rests on a short exchange between Coriolanus and his mother that may receive insufficient attention. We need, in particular, to be told several times and in several ways that Coriolanus knows he simply cannot do what he is being asked to promise. Second, we need more sympathy for Coriolanus than the play develops. In part, this is merely repeating, in different terms, that we need to understand him better. But we also need something to replace the props of which the action has been deprived. We all hate sin, just as we all hate a villain. Iago is labeled a villain by the first words he utters; therefore we are automatically on Othello's side. Lady Macbeth is not labeled, but the murder which she urges is undoubtedly sin, and the crown a temptation adequate to sway any man. Our sympathies operate accordingly. The Tribunes, as we noted, are like Lady Macbeth in that their motives are too human for them to be conventional stage villains automatically to be hissed, but Coriolanus is being asked only to accede to ancient and hallowed custom. His stubbornness has no motive which we can understand and share. I suspect that Shakespeare intended the battle scenes which I treated so harshly to establish the kind of man that Coriolanus is. If so, Volumnia argues all too convincingly that he need only transfer to politics the strategy and tactics of warfare. She destroys the effect of those scenes, even while she diminishes our respect and sympathy for Coriolanus. Shakespeare should have found some compelling reason for Coriolanus' unbending nature or some effective technique for making us share his horror of showing his wounds and begging votes of the people. Neither of these operates in the play, and we miss them badly. But all this must not prevent us from seeing that *Coriolanus* was, potentially at least, a more sophisticated study of human character revealed in action than its predecessors.

The last half of the play is curiously parallel in structure to the first half. While concentrating on Coriolanus, Shakespeare took care of an important detail. The Romans, we are told (III.i.1-8), made peace with the Volscians on terms that left the latter about as strong as before. Of this power Coriolanus now attempts to take advantage. Once more we have a series of short scenes that are a relapse in technique. We hear Volumnia scold the Tribunes. A disloyal Roman and a Volscian, both otherwise unknown to the play, meet most opportunely to let us know that Rome is in confusion and the Volscian army in readiness. Coriolanus arrives at Antium and has a considerable soliloquy obviously intended by Shakespeare to emphasize the unnaturalness of his conduct and to prepare for the final choice that he must make between his hate and his friends and family:

> O world, thy slippery turns! . . .
>   So with me;
> My birthplace hate I, and my love's upon
> This enemy town. I'll enter. If he slay me,
> He does fair justice; if he give me way,
> I'll do his country service.

> (IV.iv.12-26)

The longer scene that follows included much work for the clowns among the King's Men. To them Shakespeare allots praise of Coriolanus, apparently intended to establish his power of personality as well as his reputation among the Volscians, which is almost as artificial as the praise of Hal by his enemies in *1 Henry IV* and in *Henry V*. Primarily, however, the scene unites Coriolanus with Tullus Aufidius and prepares for the second great choice of the play. But first we have still another short scene so that a lieutenant can describe Coriolanus' success, and Tullus Aufidius, his overweening pride. Shakespeare resorts to couplets to emphasize the final point of Aufidius' speech:

> One fire drives out one fire; one nail, one nail;
> Rights by rights falter, strengths by strengths do fail.
> Come, let's away. When, Caius, Rome is thine,
> Thou art poor'st of all; then shortly art thou mine.

> (IV.vii.54-57)

These do more than foretell the outcome of the play. They abruptly convert Tullus Aufidius from noble enemy to villain of the rest of the play and prepare for his final act of treachery.

The first two scenes of Act V are primarily buildup for the great effect to come. Shakespeare knew when he had set up an effective dramatic situation, and he liked to milk from it all the drama that he could. We dislike the Tribunes; so we rejoice in seeing them supplicate Menenius to intercede. We interpret what happened to Cominius as precedent more accurately than Menenius does himself, and the scene between him and Coriolanus is one of tremendous pathos, not least in his final broken speech to the watchmen, which still has a touch of his old humor. Twice, though at the cost of increasing suffering and betrayal of his better nature, Coriolanus has stood firm. We are now ready for his final testing. The scene begins with irony piled on irony. Coriolanus is planning to besiege Rome and confidently bids Aufidius report how he has rejected appeals from his friends. But Menenius Agrippa was, he feels sure, their last refuge. He will hear no more suits. But just then he hears the shout which, instinctively, he knows betokens another embassy. From this point on, the scene parallels the earlier choice in a fashion that must be deliberate. Volumnia pleads magnificently without knowing what she is really asking her son to do. She talks eloquently of a reconciliation between the Romans and the Volscians after which all will live happily together. Coriolanus knows better, though his full statement of what he knows is placed after his yielding to give it maximum effect. Once again Volumnia wins not by her eloquence, which is great, but by threatening a final break with him: "I am hush'd until our city be a-fire" (V.iii.181). This final breach with his mother Coriolanus once again cannot face. He yields, knowing that his act may be "most mortal to him" (l. 189). And, like the villain he now is, Aufidius adds his aside that from the situation he will work his former fortune.

The irony of Volumnia's happiness over her victory is sufficiently pointed out when it occurs. The next scenes further exploit dramatic possibilities inherent in the situation. Menenius is sure that the ladies will fail. The Tribunes, we learn, will be torn limb from limb if they do. Then universal rejoicing breaks out as the ladies arrive at Rome; it also provides more irony as it prepares for the last episode in Coriolanus' tragedy, which is acted at Antium. But Coriolanus does not die without himself adding a final touch of irony: he has missed the point of his whole tragedy! Aufidius calls him "thou boy of tears" (V.vi.101), and the insult is more than he can bear.

Measureless liar, thou hast made my heart
Too great for what contains it. "Boy!" O slave!
Pardon me, lords, 'tis the first time that ever
I was forc'd to scold.

(V.vi.103-106)

His heart—like his spleen—is indeed too great for a man, but he has been scolding someone throughout the play. His tantrums have brought him to his death, but for him they have not existed. In trying too hard to be a man, he has acted like an immature boy. But he keeps returning to the word: "Boy! . . . Boy!" It is a fitting obituary.

As a play, *Coriolanus* is therefore uneven. Its two great episodes are brilliantly conceived, and the second, at least, could hardly be bettered in the writing. In the first the design is obscured because details are not fully clear to the audience and Coriolanus does not wholly come alive. The scenes involved are, however, superb theater. In economy and vigor the opening exposition and the death of Coriolanus illustrate playwriting at its best. But the less said about the strings of short, ineffective scenes, the better. And the fact remains that Coriolanus does not really move us. He is, in the last analysis, only a tough fighter who rages at mistreatment. He has no vision of himself as part of a larger world or of the patience which it requires of mankind; his world opposed is Corioli or Rome or Antium, nothing more. His halting perception that he cannot be false to his nature does not become a vision that every man must be true to his best nature. So he inspires in us pity but hardly fear or wonder. The limitations of Shakespeare's canvas have prevented its many excellent details from becoming a great picture of human life.

This vision of man's life as part of a larger order had given meaning to all Shakespeare's earlier tragedies. Even Titus had suffered partly because he failed to heed Tamora's plea for an order in which mercy transcended human vengeance. Richard's murders rose above mere horror into a divine plan of purging and reuniting England. By the time of *Julius Caesar* Shakespeare had developed a metaphysic adequate to his vision. It guided him in planning the great plays of his maturity and in developing a technique to hold their mirrors up to nature. In *Antony and Cleopatra* and *Coriolanus* that vision faded and the metaphysic apparently lost its fascination. Only the technique remained. It could still be used effectively and even developed in new directions. Without the controlling vision, however, it operated fitfully and even confusedly. The two plays are still great, though one is tempted to say that *Antony and Cleopatra* is a great but not a good play. But the greatness is not that of the Shakespeare who is unique in his age and all others.

Though Shakespeare continued to employ the technique of the great tragedies, he also reverted, as we have observed, to methods characteristic of his own earlier plays and to the tragical histories of his contemporaries. Paradoxically enough, however, this change looked to his future as well as to his past. If the last two tragedies become more episodic than even his earliest tragedies, they also indicate a renewed interest in telling a good story simply because it was a good story and perhaps, incidentally, a moral *exemplum*. *Antony and Cleopatra*, especially, looks forward to the romances as well as back to the chronicle histories.

Why Shakespeare's vision faded or his interest changed—call the process what you will—one can only speculate. His work must to some extent have reflected his experiences of life, but of these we know too little even for conjecture. There may be, however, a perfectly obvious and relatively simple explanation of what happened. If one regards the two key speeches in *Troilus and Cressida*—Ulysses' on order in the universe and Hector's on the psychology of human sin—as summarizing the interdependent halves of Shakespeare's tragic view of life, then *King Lear* and *Macbeth* are his supreme achievements in giving dramatic expression to these ideas. Those veins had been worked, and Shakespeare had to find new ones. In the last two tragedies he prospected once more, but the ore was only silver. So he moved on to other kinds of work. This seems to me no more than a guess, but it has some plausibility. More important for our understanding of Shakespeare is what the final tragedies undoubtedly show: that he remained to the end a man of his theater. When the special vision and the creative energy that had produced the great tragedies faded, he retreated from all time into his own age. There is no need to vindicate Shakespeare's unique greatness. That has been beyond question ever since Ben Jonson so vigorously and soundly asserted it. But, despite the achievements of modern scholarship, there is still some need to assert his kinship with

his fellow dramatists as against the uncritical adulation of his nineteenth-century admirers—and of some in the twentieth. There is far
more need to correct the popular image, which, as one would expect, lags behind scholarship. Correcting that image cannot harm
Shakespeare. And it may help restore his fellows to public consciousness and even to the theater. Others besides Jonson and occasionally
Marlowe and Webster deserve to be performed. Isolating what is
unique in Shakespeare by trying to understand how he came to be
unique has also involved arguing that much is not unique. That is
all to the good.

(Whenever possible, the title of the earliest published version of the play has been given. The edition consulted, if different, has been indicated in square brackets beneath the original title. Manuscript plays are listed under the titles by which they are commonly known.)

TRAGEDIES

Alabaster, William. *Roxana. Tragœdia olim Cantabrigiæ, acta in Col. Trin. Nunc primum in lucem edita, summaque cum diligentia ad castigatissimum exemplar comparata.* London: R. Badger for Andrew Crook, 1632.

[*Roxana Tragædia. A plagiarij unguibus vindicata, aucta, & agnita ab Authore Gvlielmo Alabastro.* London: Gulielmus Jones, 1632.]

Alexander, Sir William, Earl of Stirling. *The Alexandraean Tragedie*, in *The Monarchicke Tragedies; Croesus, Darius, The Alexandræan, Iulius Cæsar. Newly enlarged.* London: Valentine Simmes for Ed. Blovnt, 1607.

[*The Poetical Works of Sir William Alexander, Earl of Stirling*, ed. L. E. Kastner and H. B. Charlton (Manchester, 1921), I, 231-341.]

———. *The Tragedie of Croesus*, in *The Monarchicke Tragedies*.
[*Poetical Works*, I, 9-111.]

———. *The Tragedie of Darivs*. Edinburgh: Robert Walde-graue, 1603.
[*Poetical Works*, I, 113-230.]

———. *The Tragedie of Iulius Cæsar*, in *The Monarchicke Tragedies*.
[*Poetical Works*, I, 343-442.]

Anonymous. *The Lamentable and Trve Tragedie of M. Arden of Feversham in Kent. Who was most wickedlye murdered, by the meanes of his disloyall and wanton wyfe, who for the loue she bare to one Mosbie, hyred two desperat ruffins Blackwill and Shakbag, to kill him. Wherin is shewed the great mallice and discimulation of a wicked woman, the vnsatiable desire of filthie lust and the shamefull end of all murderers.* London: for Edward White, 1592.

[*The Shakespeare Apocrypha*, ed. C. F. Tucker Brooke (Oxford, 1908), pp. 1-35.]

———. *The Tragedie of Cæsar and Pompey Or Cæsars Reuenge*. London: G. E. for Iohn Wright, [1606].

[*The Tragedie of Caesar's Revenge*, Malone Soc. Reprints (London, 1911).]

———. *The Tragedie of Claudius Tiberius Nero, Romes greatest Tyrant. Truly represented out of the purest Records of those times*. London: for Francis Burton, 1607.

[*The Tragedy of Tiberius 1607*, Malone Soc. Reprints (1914).]

———. *The Lamentable Tragedie of Locrine, the eldest sonne of King Brutus, discoursing the warres of the Britaines, and Hunnes, with their discomfiture: The Britaines victorie with their Accidents, and the death of Albanact. No lesse pleasant then profitable. Newly set foorth, ouerseene and corrected, By W. S.* London: Thomas Creede, 1595. [*The Shakespeare Apocrypha*, pp. 37-65.]

———. *The True Tragedie of Richard the third: Wherein is showne the death of Edward the fourth, with the smothering of the two yoong Princes in the Tower: With a lamentable ende of Shores wife, an example for all wicked women. And lastly the coniunction and ioyning of the two noble Houses, Lancaster and Yorke. As it was playd by the Queenes Maiesties Players*. London: Thomas Creede, sold by William Barley, 1594.

[*The True Tragedy of Richard the Third 1594*, Malone Soc. Reprints (1929).]

———. "The Second Maiden's Tragedy." Brit. Mus. Lansdowne MS. 807. [*The Second Maiden's Tragedy 1611*, Malone Soc. Reprints (1909).]

———. *The First part of the Tragicall raigne of Selimus, sometime Emperour of the Turkes, and grandfather to him that now raigneth. Wherein is showne how hee most vnnaturally raised warres against his owne father Baiazet, and preuailing therein, in the end caused him to be poysoned: Also with the murthering of his two brethren, Corcut, and Acomat. As it was playd by the Queenes Maiesties Players*. London: Thomas Creede, 1594.

[*The Tragical Reign of Selimus 1594*, Malone Soc. Reprints (1908).]

———. "Solymannidæ, Tragedia . . . 1581 Martii 5⁰ [March 5, 1582]." Brit. Mus. Lansdowne MS. 723.

———. *A Warning for Faire Women. Containing, The most tragicall and lamentable murther of Master George Sanders of London Marchant, nigh Shooters hill. Consented vnto By his owne wife, acted by M. Browne, Mistris Drewry and Trusty Roger agents therin: with their seuerall ends. As it hath beene lately diuerse times acted by the right Honorable, the Lord Chamberlaine his Seruantes.* London: Valentine Sims for William Aspley, 1599.

[Old English Drama: Students' Facsimile Edition (Amersham, Eng., 1912).]

———. *The Warres of Cyrus King of Persia, against Antiochus King of Assyria, with the Tragicall ende of Panthæa. Played by the children of her Maiesties Chappell.* London: E. A. for William Blackwal, 1594.

[Old English Drama: Students' Facsimile Edition (1911).]

———. *A Yorkshire Tragedy. Not so New as Lamentable and true. Acted by his Maiesties Players at the Globe. Written by W. Shakspeare.* London: R. B. for Thomas Pauier, 1608.

[*The Shakespeare Apocrypha*, pp. 249-261.]

B., R. [R. Bower?]. *A new Tragicall Comedie of Apius and Virginia, Wherein is liuely expressed a rare example of the vertue of Chastitie, by Virginias constancy, in wishing rather to be slaine at her owne Fathers handes, then to be deflowred of the wicked Iudge Apius. By R. B.* London: William How for Richard Ihones, 1575.

[Old English Drama: Students' Facsimile Edition (1908).]

Barnes, Barnabe. *The Diuils Charter: A Tragædie Conteining the Life and Death of Pope Alexander the sixt. As it was plaide before the Kings Maiestie, vpon Candlemasse night last: by his Maiesties Seruants. But more exactly reuewed, corrected, and augmented since by the Author, for the more pleasure and profit of the Reader.* London: G. E. for Iohn Wright, 1607.

[Old English Drama: Students' Facsimile Edition (1913).]

Beaumont, Francis, and John Fletcher. *Cupids Revenge. As it hath beene diuers times Acted by the Children of her Maiesties Reuels. By Iohn Fletcher.* London: Thomas Creede for Iosias Harison, 1615.

[*The Works of Francis Beaumont and John Fletcher*, ed. A. R. Waller, Cambridge English Classics (Cambridge, Eng., 1905-12), IX, 220-289.]

———. *The Maides Tragedy. As it hath beene diuers times Acted at the Blacke-friers by the Kings Maiesties Seruants.* London: for Francis Constable, 1619.

[*The Works of Francis Beaumont and John Fletcher*, I, 1-74.]

Brandon, Samuel. *The Tragicomoedi of the vertuous Octauia. . . . 1598.* London: for William Ponsonbye, [1598].

[*The Virtuous Octavia 1598*, Malone Soc. Reprints (1909).]

Brewer, Anthony. *The Love-sick King, An English Tragical History: with The Life and Death of Cartesmunda, the fair Nun of Winchester.* London: for Rob. Pollard and John Sweeting, 1655.

[*Anthony Brewer's The Love-Sick King*, ed. A. E. H. Swaen, Materialien zur Kunde des älteren englischen Dramas, Bd. 18 (Louvain, 1907).]

Cary, Elizabeth, Viscountess Falkland. *The Tragedie of Mariam, the Faire Queene of Iewry. Written by that learned, vertuous, and truly noble Ladie, E. C.* London: Thomas Creede for Richard Hawkins, 1613.

[*The Tragedy of Mariam 1613*, Malone Soc. Reprints (1914).]

Chapman, George. *Bussy D'Ambois: A Tragedie: As it hath been often presented at Paules.* London: for William Aspley, 1607.

[*The Plays and Poems of George Chapman: The Tragedies*, ed. Thomas Marc Parrott (London, 1910), pp. 1-74.]

———. *The Tragedie of Chabot Admirall of France: As it was presented by her Majesties Servants, at the private House in Drury Lane. Written by George Chapman, and James Shirly.* London: Tho. Cotes for Andrew Crooke and William Cooke, 1639.

[*The Plays and Poems . . . : The Tragedies*, pp. 273-337.]

———. *The Conspiracie, And Tragedie Of Charles Duke of Byron, Marshall of France. Acted lately in two playes, at the Black-Friers.* [London]: G. Eld for Thomas Thorppe, 1608.

[*The Plays and Poems . . . : The Tragedies*, pp. 149-207, 209-271.]

———. *The Revenge of Bussy D'Ambois. A Tragedie. As it hath beene often presented at the priuate Play-house in the White-Fryers.* London: T. S., sold by Iohn Helme, 1613.

[*The Plays and Poems . . . : The Tragedies*, pp. 75-148.]

———. *The Warres of Pompey and Caesar. Out of whose euents is euicted this Proposition. Only a iust man is a freeman. By G. C.* London: Thomas Harper, sold by Godfrey Emondson and Thomas Alchorne, 1631. (A second issue in 1631 is titled *Caesar and Pompey: A Roman Tragedy, declaring their Warres.*)

[*The Plays and Poems . . . : The Tragedies*, pp. 339-400.]

Cheke, Henry. *A certayne Tragedie wrytten first in Italian, by F. N. B. entituled, Freewyl, and translated into Englishe, by Henry Cheeke.* [London: 1589.]

Chettle, Henry. *The Tragedy of Hoffman or A Reuenge for a Father. As it hath bin diuers times acted with great applause, at the Phenix in Druery-lane.* London: I. N. for Hugh Perry, 1631.

[*The Tragedy of Hoffman . . . 1631*, Malone Soc. Reprints (1950 [1951]).]

Daborne, Robert. *A Christian turn'd Turke: or, The Tragicall Liues and Deaths of the two Famous Pyrates, Ward and Dansiker. As it hath beene publickly Acted.* London: for William Barrenger, 1612.

Daniel, Samuel. *The Tragedie of Cleopatra*, in *Delia and Rosamond augmented. Cleopatra.* London: for Simon Waterson, 1594.

[*The Complete Works in Verse and Prose of Samuel Daniel*, ed. Alexander B. Grosart, Spenser Society (London, 1885), III, 21-94.]

———. *The Tragedie of Philotas*, in *Certaine Small Poems Lately Printed: with the Tragedie of Philotas.* London: G. Eld for Simon Waterson, 1605.

[*Complete Works*, III, 95-181.]

Day, John. *Lusts Dominion; or, The Lascivious Queen. A Tragedie. Written by Christopher Marloe, Gent.* London: for F. K., sold by Robert Pollard, 1657.

[*Lust's Dominion; or, The Lascivious Queen*, ed. J. Le Gay Brereton, Materials for the Study of the Old English Drama, Vol. V (Louvain, 1931).]

Fletcher, John. *The Tragedie of Bonduca*, in *Comedies and Tragedies Written by Francis Beaumont and John Fletcher, Gentlemen. Never printed before, and now published by the Authours Originall Copies.* London: for Humphrey Robinson and for Humphrey Moseley, 1647.

[*The Works of Francis Beaumont and John Fletcher*, VI, 79-159.]

———. *The Tragedie of Valentinian*, in *Comedies and Tragedies*, 1647.
[*The Works of Francis Beaumont and John Fletcher*, IV, 1-92.]

Gager, William. "Dido." Christ Church College, Oxford, Latin MS.

———. *Meleager. Tragœdia noua. Bis pvblice acta in Æde Christi Oxoniæ.* Oxford: Iosephvs Barnesivs, 1592.

———. *Vlysses Redvx. Tragoedia Nova. In Aede Christi Oxoniae Publice Academicis Recitata, Octavo Idvs Febrvarii. 1591.* Oxford: Iosephvs Barnesivs, 1592.

Gascoigne, George. *Iocasta: A Tragedie written in Greke by Euripides,*

315

translated and digested into Acte by George Gascoygne, and Francis
Kinwelmershe of Grayes Inne, and there by them presented. *1566*, in
A Hundreth sundrie Flowres bounde vp in one small Poesie. London:
for Richarde Smith, [1573].

[*The Posies*, in *The Complete Works of George Gascoigne*, ed. John
W. Cunliffe, Cambridge English Classics (Cambridge, Eng., 1907-10),
I, 244-326.]

Golding, Arthur. *A Tragedie of Abrahams Sacrifice, Written in french
by Theodore Beza, and translated into Inglish, by A. G.* London:
Thomas Vautrollier, 1577.

Goldingham, William. "Herodes Tragœdia." Cambridge Univ. Library
MS. Mm.I.24.

["Appendix. 'Herodes Tragoedia' von William Goldingham," in War-
ren E. Tomlinson, *Der Herodes-charakter im englischen Drama*, Palaestra, Bd. 195 (Leipzig, 1934), pp. 135-174.]

Greville, Fulke, Lord Brooke. *Alaham*, in *Certaine Learned and Elegant
Workes of the Right Honorable Fvlke Lord Brooke, Written in his
Youth, and familiar Exercise with Sir Philip Sidney*. London: E. P. for
Henry Seyle, 1633.

[*Poems and Dramas of Fulke Greville, First Lord Brooke*, ed. Geoffrey
Bullough (Edinburgh, [1939]), II, 138-213.]

———. *The Tragedy of Mvstapha*. London: for Nathaniel Butter, 1609.
[*Poems and Dramas*, II, 63-137.]

Gwinne, Matthew. *Nero Tragædia Nova. Matthæo Gwinne Med. Doct.
Collegij Diui Joannis Præcursoris apud Oxonienses Socio collecta è
Tacito, Suetonio, Dione, Seneca*. London: Ed. Blounte, 1603.

Heywood, Thomas. *The Rape of Lvcrece. A true Roman Tragedie.
With the severall Songes in their apt places, by Valerius, the merrie
Lord amongst the Roman Peeres. Acted by her Maiesties Seruants at
the Red Bull, neare Clarken-well*. London: for I. B., 1608.

[*The Dramatic Works of Thomas Heywood, Now First Collected
with Illustrative Notes and a Memoir of the Author in Six Volumes*
(London, 1874), V, 161-257.]

———. *A Woman Kilde with Kindnesse*. London: William Jaggard, sold
by Iohn Hodgets, 1607.
[*Dramatic Works*, II, 89-158.]

Hughes, Thomas. *The misfortunes of Arthur (Vther Pendragons Sonne)
reduced into Tragicall notes by Thomas Hughes one of the societie of*

Grayes-Inne, in *Certaine Devises and Shewes presented to Her Maiestie by the Gentlemen of Grayes-Inne at her Highnesse Court in Greenewich, the twenty eighth day of Februarie in the thirtieth yeare of her Maiesties most happy Raigne*. London: Robert Robinson, 1587.

[*Early English Classical Tragedies*, ed. John W. Cunliffe (Oxford, 1912), pp. 217-296.]

J., B. *The Tragical History, Admirable Atchievments and various events of Guy Earl of Warwick. A Tragedy Acted very Frequently with great Applause by his late Majesties Servants. Written by B. J.* London: for Thomas Vere and William Gilbertson, 1661.

Jonson, Ben. *Catiline his Conspiracy*. London: for Walter Burre, 1611.

[*Ben Jonson*, ed. C. H. Herford and Percy Simpson (Oxford, 1925-52), V, 409-550.]

———. *Seianvs His Fall*. London: G. Elld for Thomas Thorpe, 1605.

[*Ben Jonson*, IV, 327-486.]

Kyd, Thomas. *The Tragedye of Solyman and Perseda. Wherein is laide open, Loues constancy, Fortunes inconstancy, and Deaths Triumphs*. London: Edward Allde, for Edward White, [n.d.].

[*The Works of Thomas Kyd*, ed. Frederick S. Boas (Oxford, 1901), pp. 161-229.]

———. *The Spanish Tragedie, Containing the lamentable end of Don Horatio, and Bel-imperia: with the pittifull death of olde Hieronimo. Newly corrected and amended of such grosse faults as passed in the first impression*. London: Edward Allde for Edward White, [n.d.].

[*Works*, pp. 1-99.]

Legge, Thomas. "Richardus tertius Tragedia trivespera habita Collegii divi Johannis Evangeliste Comitii Bachelaureorum Anno Domini, 1579. Tragedia in tres actiones divisa." Cambridge Univ. Library MS. Mm.IV.40.

[*The True Tragedy of Richard the Third; to which is appended the Latin Play of Richardus Tertius by Dr. Thomas Legge*, ed. Barron Field, Shakespeare Soc. (London, 1844).]

Lodge, Thomas. *The Wovnds of Ciuill War. Liuely set forth in the true Tragedies of Marius and Scilla. As it hath beene publiquely plaide in London, by the Right Honourable the Lord high Admirall his Seruants*. London: Iohn Danter, 1594.

[*The Wounds of Civil War . . . 1594*, Malone Soc. Reprints (1910).]

Marlowe, Christopher. *The Tragedie of Dido Queene of Carthage: Played by the Children of her Maiesties Chappell. Written by Christopher Marlowe, and Thomas Nash. Gent.* London: Widdowe Orwin for Thomas Woodcocke, 1594.

[*The Life of Marlowe and The Tragedy of Dido, Queen of Carthage*, ed. C. F. Tucker Brooke (London, 1930).]

——. *The troublesome raigne and lamentable death of Edward the second, King of England: with the tragicall fall of proud Mortimer: As it was sundrie times publiquely acted in the honourable citie of London, by the right honourable the Earle of Pembrooke his seruants.* London: for William Iones, 1594.

[*Edward II*, ed. H. B. Charlton and R. D. Waller (London, 1933).]

——. *The tragicall History of D. Faustus. As it hath bene Acted by the Right Honorable the Earle of Nottingham his seruants.* London: V. S. for Thomas Bushell, 1604.

[*The Tragical History of Doctor Faustus*, ed. Frederick S. Boas, 2nd ed. (London, 1949).]

——. *The Famous Tragedy of the Rich Iew of Malta. As it was playd before the King and Qveene, in his Majesties Theatre at White-Hall, by Her Majesties Servants at the Cock-pit.* London: I. B. for Nicholas Vavasour, 1633.

[*The Jew of Malta and The Massacre at Paris*, ed. H. S. Bennett (London, 1931).]

——. *The Massacre at Paris: With the Death of the Duke of Guise. As it was plaide by the right honourable the Lord high Admirall his Seruants.* London: E. A. for Edward White, [1600?].

[*The Jew of Malta and The Massacre at Paris.*]

——. *Tamburlaine the Great. Who, from a Scythian Shephearde, by his rare and woonderfull Conquests, became a most puissant and mightye Monarque. And (for his tyranny, and terrour in Warre) was tearmed, The Scourge of God. Deuided into two Tragicall Discourses, as they were sundrie times shewed upon Stages in the Citie of London. By the right honorable the Lord Admyrall, his seruantes. Now first, and newlie published.* London: Richard Ihones, 1590.

[*Tamburlaine the Great: In Two Parts*, ed. U. M. Ellis-Fermor (London, 1930).]

Marston, John. *Antonios Reuenge. The second part. As it hath beene sundry times acted, by the children of Paules. Written by I. M.* London: for Thomas Fisher, 1602.

318

[*The Plays of John Marston*, ed. H. Harvey Wood (Edinburgh, 1934), I, 65-133.]

————. *The Insatiate Countesse. A Tragedie: Acted at White-Fryers.* London: T. S. for Thomas Archer, 1613.

[*Plays*, III, 1-82.]

————. *The Wonder of Women Or The Tragedie of Sophonisba, as it hath beene sundry times Acted at the Blacke Friers.* London: Iohn Windet, 1606.

[*Plays*, II, 3-64.]

Mason, John. *The Turke. A Worthie Tragedie. As it hath bene diuers times acted by the Children of his Maiesties Reuels.* London: E. A. for Iohn Busbie, 1610.

[*John Mason's The Turke*, ed. from the quartos of 1610 and 1632 by Joseph Q. Adams, Jr., Materialien zur Kunde des älteren englischen Dramas, Bd. 37 (Louvain, 1913).]

Munday, Anthony, and Henry Chettle. *The Death of Robert, Earle of Hvntington. Otherwise Called Robin Hood of merrie Sherwodde: with the lamentable Tragedie of chaste Matilda, his faire maid Marian, poysoned at Dunmowe by King Iohn. Acted by the Right Honourable, the Earle of Notingham, Lord high Admirall of England, his seruants.* London: for William Leake, 1601.

[Old English Drama: Students' Facsimile Edition (1913).]

Norton, Thomas, and Thomas Sackville. *The Tragedie of Gorbodvc, whereof three Actes were wrytten by Thomas Nortone, and the two laste by Thomas Sackuyle. Sett forthe as the same was shewed before the Qvenes most excellent Maiestie, in her highnes Court of White-hall, the .xviij. day of January, Anno Domini. 1561 [i.e., 1562]. By the Gentlemen of Thynner Temple in London.* London: William Griffith, 1565.

[*Early English Classical Tragedies*, pp. 1-64.]

Peele, George. *The Tragedy of Alphonsus Emperour of Germany. As it hath been very often Acted (with great applause) at the Privat house in Black-Friers by his late Maiesties servants. By George Chapman Gent.* London: for Humphrey Moseley, 1654.

[*The Plays and Poems of George Chapman: The Tragedies*, pp. 401-471.]

————. *The Love Of King David And Fair Bethsabe. With the Tragedie of Absalon. As it hath ben diuers times plaied on the stage.* London: Adam Islip, 1599.

[*The Works of George Peele*, ed. A. H. Bullen (London, 1888), II, 1-86.]

Percy, William. "A Country Tragædye in vacunium, or Cupids Sacrifice." Huntington Library MS. HM 4.

Pikeryng, John. *A Newe Enterlude of Vice Conteyninge, the Historye of Horestes with the cruell reuengment of his Fathers death, vpon his one naturtll Mother. . . . The names deuided for vi to play.* London: Wylliam Gryffith, 1567.
[Old English Drama: Students' Facsimile Edition (1910).]

Preston, Thomas. *A Lamentable Tragedie, mixed full of pleasant mirth, conteyning the life of Cambises king of Percia.* London: Iohn Allde, [1570].
[Old English Drama: Students' Facsimile Edition (1910).]

Salterne, George. "Tomumbeius, siue Sultanici in Ægypto imperii euersio, tragœdia noua. Auctore Georgio Salterno Bristoënsi." Bodleian Library MS. Rawlinson poet. 75.

Sansbury, John. "Periander," in "The Christmas Prince." St. John's College, Oxford, English MS play.
[*The Christmas Prince*, Malone Soc. Reprints (1922), pp. 229-285.]

———. "Philomela," in "The Christmas Prince." St. John's College, Oxford, Latin MS play.
[*The Christmas Prince*, pp. 58-101.]

Shakespeare, William. *The Tragedie of Anthonie, and Cleopatra*, in *Mr. William Shakespeares Comedies, Histories, & Tragedies. Published according to the True Originall Copies.* London: Isaac Iaggard and Ed. Blount, 1623 (hereafter cited as 1623 Folio).
[*The Complete Plays and Poems of William Shakespeare*, ed. William Allan Neilson and Charles Jarvis Hill (Boston, 1942), is the edition consulted throughout.]

———. *The Tragedy of Coriolanus*, in 1623 Folio.

———. *The Tragicall Historie of Hamlet Prince of Denmarke. . . . As it hath beene diuerse times acted by his Highnesse seruants in the Cittie of London: as also in the two Vniuersities of Cambridge and Oxford, and else-where.* London: for N. L. and Iohn Trundell, 1603.

———. *The Tragedie of Iulius Cæsar*, in 1623 Folio.

———. *M. William Shak-speare: His True Chronicle Historie of the life* and death of King Lear and his three Daughters. With the vnfortunate life of Edgar, sonne and heire to the Earle of Gloster, and his sullen and assumed humor of Tom of Bedlam: As it was played before the Kings Maiestie at Whitehall vpon S. Stephans night in Christmas Hollidayes. By his Maiesties seruants playing vsually at the Gloabe on the Bancke-side. London: for Nathaniel Butter, 1608.

———. The Tragedie of Macbeth, in 1623 Folio.

———. The Tragœdy of Othello, the Moore of Venice. As it hath beene diuerse times acted at the Globe, and at the Black-Friers, by his Maiesties Seruants. London: N. O. for Thomas Walkley, 1622.

———. The Tragedie of King Richard the second. As it hath beene publikely acted by the right Honourable the Lorde Chamberlaine his Seruants. London: Valentine Simmes for Androw Wise, 1597.

———. The Tragedy of King Richard the third. Containing, His treacherous Plots against his brother Clarence: the pittiefull murther of his innocent nephewes: his tyrannical vsurpation: with the whole course of his detested life, and most deserued death. As it hath beene lately Acted by the Right honourable the Lord Chamberlaine his seruants. London: Valentine Sims for Andrew Wise, 1597.

———. An Excellent conceited Tragedie of Romeo and Iuliet. As it hath been often (with great applause) plaid publiquely, by the right Honourable the L. of Hunsdon his Seruants. London: Iohn Danter, 1597.

———. The Life of Tymon of Athens, in 1623 Folio.

———. The most lamentable Romaine Tragedie of Titus Andronicus: As it was Plaide by the Right Honourable the Earle of Darbie, Earle of Pembrooke and Earl of Sussex their Seruants. London: Iohn Danter, sold by Edward White and Thomas Millington, 1594.

———. The Historie of Troylus and Cresseida. As it was acted by the Kings Maiesties seruants at the Globe. London: G. Eld for R. Bonian and H. Walley, 1609.

Stephens, John. Cinthias Revenge: or Mænanders Extasie. London: for Roger Barnes, 1613.

Tourneur, Cyril. The Atheist's Tragedie: Or The honest Man's Reuenge. As in diuers places it hath often beene Acted. London: for Iohn Stepneth and Richard Redmer, 1611.
[The Works of Cyril Tourneur, ed. Allardyce Nicoll (London, 1930), pp. 173-255.]

————. *The Revengers Tragædie. As it hath beene sundry times Acted, by the Kings Maiesties Seruants.* London: G. Eld, 1607.

[*Works*, pp. 77-154.]

Verney, Francis. "The Tragedye of Antipoe, with other poeticall-verses written by mee Nicolas Leath junior in Allicante in June 1622." Bodleian Library MS. Eng. poet. e.5.

W., T. *Thorny-Abbey, or The London-Maid. A Tragedy*, in *Gratiæ Theatrales, or A choice Ternary of English Plays, Composed upon especial occasions by several ingenious persons; viz. Thorny-Abbey, or The London-Maid; A Tragedy, by T. W. The Marriage-Broker, or The Pander; A Comedy, by M. W. M.A. Grim the Collier of Croydon, or The Devil and his Dame; with the Devil and St. Dunstan; a Comedy, by I. T. Never before published: but now printed at the request of sundry ingenious friends.* London: R. D., 1662.

Webster, John. *The White Divel, Or The Tragedy of Paolo Giordano Vrsini, Duke of Brachiano, With The Life and Death of Vittoria Corombona the famous Venetian Curtizan. Acted by the Queenes Maiesties Seruants.* London: N. O. for Thomas Archer, 1612.

[*The Complete Works of John Webster*, ed. F. L. Lucas (London, 1927), I, 103-288.]

Wilmot, Robert. *The Tragedie of Tancred and Gismund. Compiled by the Gentlemen of the Inner Temple, and by them presented before her Maiestie. Newly reuiued and polished according to the decorum of these daies. By R. W.* London: Thomas Scarlet, sold by R. Robinson, 1591.

[*The Tragedy of Tancred and Gismund 1591-2*, Malone Soc. Reprints (1914).]

Yarington, Robert. *Two Lamentable Tragedies. The one, of the murther of Maister Beech a Chaundler in Thames-streete, and his boye, done by Thomas Merry. The other of a young childe murthered in a Wood by two Ruffins, with the consent of his Vnckle.* London: for Mathew Lawe, 1601.

[Old English Drama: Students' Facsimile Edition (1913).]

CHRONICLE HISTORIES

A., R. *The Valiant Welshman, Or The Trve Chronicle History of the life and valiant deedes of Caradoc the Great, King of Cambria, now called Wales. As it hath beene sundry times Acted by the Prince of*

Wales his seruants. Written by R. A. Gent. London: George Purslowe for Robert Lownes, 1615.

[*The Valiant Welshman,* ed. Valentin Kreb, Münchener Beiträge zur romanischen und englischen Philologie, Hft. 23 (Erlangen & Leipzig, 1902), pp. 1-74.]

Anonymous. *The Famous Historye of the life and Death of Captaine Thomas Stukeley. With his marriage to Alderman Curteis Daughter, and valiant ending of his life at the Battaile of Alcazar. As it hath beene Acted.* London: for Thomas Pauyer, 1605.

[Old English Drama: Students' Facsimile Edition (1911).]

———. "Charlemagne or The Distracted Emperor." Brit. Mus. Egerton MS. 1994.

[*Charlemagne or The Distracted Emperor,* Malone Soc. Reprints (1937 [1938]).]

———. "Edmond Ironside, the English King." Brit. Mus. Egerton MS. 1994.

[*Edmond Ironside or War Hath Made All Friends,* Malone Soc. Reprints (1937).]

———. *The Famous Victories of Henry the fifth: Containing the Honourable Battell of Agin-court: As it was plaide by the Queenes Maiesties Players.* London: Thomas Creede, 1598.

[Old English Drama: Students' Facsimile Edition (1912).]

———. *The Life and Death of Iacke Straw, A notable Rebell in England: Who was kild in Smithfield by the Lord Maior of London.* London: Iohn Danter for William Barley, 1593.

[Old English Drama: Students' Facsimile Edition (1911).]

———. *The First Part of Ieronimo. With the Warres of Portugall, and the life and death of Don Andræa.* London: for Thomas Pauyer, 1605.

[*The Works of Thomas Kyd,* pp. 295-337.]

———. *The Raigne of King Edward the third: As it hath bin sundrie times plaied about the Citie of London.* London: for Cuthbert Burby, 1596.

[*The Shakespeare Apocrypha,* pp. 67-101.]

———. *The True Chronicle History of King Leir, and his three daughters, Gonorill, Ragan, and Cordella. As it hath bene diuers and sundry times lately acted.* London: Simon Stafford for Iohn Wright, 1605.

[*The History of King Leir 1605,* Malone Soc. Reprints (1907).]

———. *A Larum for London, or The Siedge of Antwerpe. With the ventrous actes and valorous deeds of the lame Soldier. As it hath been playde by the right Honorable the Lord Charberlaine his Seruants.* London: for William Ferbrand, 1602.

[*A Larum for London 1602*, Malone Soc. Reprints (1913).]

———. *The True Chronicle Historie of the whole life and death of Thomas Lord Cromwell. As it hath beene sundrie times publikely Acted by the Right Honorable the Lord Chamberlaine his Seruants. Written by W. S.* London: for William Iones, 1602.

[*The Shakespeare Apocrypha*, pp. 165-190.]

———. "A Tragedy on the History of Sr. Thomas More." Brit. Mus. Harleian MS. 7368.

[*The Shakespeare Apocrypha*, pp. 383-420.]

———. "King Richard the Second, a tragedy." Brit. Mus. Egerton MS. 1994.

[*The First Part of the Reign of King Richard the Second, or Thomas of Woodstock*, Malone Soc. Reprints (1929).]

———. *The Troublesome Raigne of Iohn King of England, with the discouerie of King Richard Cordelions Base sonne (vulgarly named, The Bastard Fawconbridge): also the death of King Iohn at Swinstead Abbey. As it was (sundry times) publikely acted by the Queenes Maiesties Players, in the honourable Citie of London.* London: for Sampson Clarke, 1591.

['*The Troublesome Reign of King John': Being the Original of Shakespeare's 'Life and Death of King John*', ed. F. J. Furnivall and John Munro, Shakespeare Classics (London, 1913).]

Day, John. *The Travailes Of The three English Brothers. Sir Thomas, Sir Anthony, Mr. Robert Shirley. As it is now play'd by her Maiesties Seruants.* London: for Iohn Wright, 1607.

(Epistle signed Iohn Day, William Rowley, George Wilkins.)

[*The Works of John Day*, ed. A. H. Bullen (London, 1881), Pt. V.]

Dekker, Thomas, and John Webster. *The Famovs History of Sir Thomas Wyat. With the Coronation of Queen Mary, and the coming in of King Philip. As it was plaied by the Queens Maiesties Seruants Written by Thomas Dickers, And Iohn Webster.* London: E. A. for Thomas Archer, 1607.

[*The Dramatic Works of Thomas Dekker*, ed. Fredson Bowers (Cambridge, Eng., 1953-61), I, 397-469.]

Drayton, Michael, with Richard Hathaway, Anthony Munday, and Robert Wilson. *The first part Of the true and honorable historie, of the life of Sir John Old-castle, the good Lord Cobham. As it hath been lately acted by the right honorable the Earle of Notingham Lord high Admirall of England his seruants.* London: V. S. for Thomas Pauier, 1600.

[Old English Drama: Students' Facsimile Edition (1911).]

Greene, Robert. *The Scottish Historie of Iames the fourth, slaine at Flodden. Entermixed with a pleasant Comedie, presented by Oboram King of Fayeries: As it hath bene sundrie times publikely Plaide.* London: Thomas Creede, 1598.

[*The Plays & Poems of Robert Greene*, ed. J. Churton Collins (Oxford, 1905), II, 79-158.]

Heywood, Thomas. *The First And Second partes of King Edward the Fourth. Containing His mery pastime with the Tanner of Tamworth, as also his loue to faire Mistrisse Shoare, her great promotion, fall and miserie, and lastly the lamentable death of both her and her husband. Likewise the besieging of London, by the Bastard Falconbridge, and the valiant defence of the same by the Lord Maier and the Citizens. As it hath diuers times beene publikely played by the Right Honorable the Earle of Derbie his seruants.* London: F. K. for Humphrey Lownes and Iohn Oxenbridge, 1600.

[*The Dramatic Works of Thomas Heywood*, I, 1-187.]

————. *If you know not me, You know no bodie: Or, The troubles of Queene Elizabeth.* London: for Nathaniel Butter, 1605.

[*Dramatic Works*, I, 189-247.]

————. *If you know not me, You know no body. The Second Part. With the building of the Royall Exchange. And The famous Victory of Queen Elizabeth: anno 1588.* London: for Nathanael Bvtter, 1623.

[*Dramatic Works*, I, 249-351.]

Munday, Anthony. *The Downfall of Robert, Earle of Huntington, Afterward Called Robin Hood of merrie Sherwodde: with his loue to chaste Matilda, the Lord Fitzwaters daughter, afterwardes his faire Maide Marian. Acted by the Right Honourable, the Earle of Notingham, Lord high Admirall of England, his seruants.* London: for William Leake, 1601.

[Old English Drama: Students' Facsimile Edition (1913).]

Peele, George. *The Battell of Alcazar, Fovght in Barbarie, betweene Sebastian king of Portugall, and Abdelmelec king of Marocco. With*

325

the death of Captaine Stukeley. As it was sundrie times plaid by the Lord high Admirall his seruants. London: Edward Allde for Richard Bankworth, 1594.

[*The Works of George Peele*, I, 219-296.]

——. *The Famous Chronicle of king Edward the first, sirnamed Edward Longshankes, with his returne from the holy land. Also The Life Of Llevellen rebell in Wales. Lastly, the sinking of Queene Elinor, who sunck at Charingcrosse, and rose againe at Pottershith, now named Queenehith.* London: Abell Ieffes, sold by William Barley, 1593.

[*Works*, I, 75-217.]

Rowley, Samuel. *When you see me, You know me. Or the famous Chronicle Historie of king Henry the eight, with the birth and vertuous life of Edward Prince of Wales. As it was playd by the high and mightie Prince of Wales his seruants.* London: for Nathaniell Butter, 1605.

[*When You See Me, You Know Me . . . 1605*, Malone Soc. Reprints (1952).]

Shakespeare, William. *The History Of Henrie The Fovrth; With the battell at Shrewsburie, betweene the King and Lord Henry Percy, surnamed Henrie Hotspur of the North. With the humorous conceits of Sir Iohn Falstalffe.* London: P. S. for Andrew Wise, 1598.

——. *The Second part of Henrie the fourth, continuing to his death, and coronation of Henrie the fift. With the humours of sir Iohn Falstaffe, and swaggering Pistoll. As it hath been sundrie times publikely acted by the right honourable, the Lord Chamberlaine his seruants.* London: V. S. for Andrew Wise and William Aspley, 1600.

——. *The Cronicle History of Henry the fift, With his battell fought at Agin Court in France. Togither with Auntient Pistoll. As it hath bene sundry times playd by the Right honorable the Lord Chamberlaine his seruants.* London: Thomas Creede for Tho. Millington and Iohn Busby, 1600.

——. *The first Part of Henry the Sixt*, in 1623 Folio.

——. *The Second Part of Henry the Sixt, with the death of the Good Duke Hvmfrey*, in 1623 Folio.

——. *The third Part of Henry the Sixt, with the death of the Duke of Yorke*, in 1623 Folio.

——. *The Famous History of the Life of King Henry the Eight*, in 1623 Folio.

——. *The life and death of King Iohn*, in 1623 Folio.

329

330

Date Due

FE 15'66	OC 22'80		
MR 27'66	DE 5'80		
MY 24'66	AP 13'83		
Pauley	HUMANITIES		
RESERVE	MY 03'96		
OC 16 67			
NO - 4 67			
NO 19 67			
MY 22'68			
OC 21'68			
DEC 5'68			
DEC 20'68			
OCT 9 '70			
OCT 9 '70			
OCT 24 70			
MY 1 -71			
MAY 16 73			